Unfulfilled Union

Canadian Federalism and National Unity

Third Edition

Garth Stevenson

Brock University

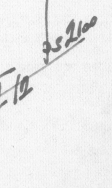

Canadian Cataloguing in Publication Data

Stevenson, Garth, 1943–
　　Unfulfilled union

3rd ed.
Includes bibliographical references and index.
ISBN 0–7715–5610–1

1. Federal government — Canada. 2. Federal-provincial relations — Canada.* I. Title.

JL27.S85　1988　　321.02′0971　　C88–093972–9

Cover Design/Susan Weiss
Text Designer/Jean Galt

ISBN 0–7715–**5610–1**

1 2 3 4 5　WC　92 91 90 89 88

Written, Printed, and Bound in Canada

Preface

The first edition of this book was written almost a decade ago, at a time when John Diefenbaker was still a member of Parliament, the Quebec referendum had not yet taken place, and rapid increases in oil prices had placed serious strains on Canadian federalism. Almost as soon as it appeared, the book was overtaken by a series of dramatic events, including the patriation of the constitution, which made it necessary to publish a second edition in 1982. In the preface to that edition I expressed the hope that revisions would not be required every three years, but a longer period of time has now elapsed and the additional developments that have occurred, as well as the continuing demand for the book, seem to justify yet another edition.

Although many "revised" editions of books on Canadian government have only cosmetic changes, or at best the addition of one new chapter, the reader should be forewarned that this edition is substantially different from its predecessor. Most of the chapters have been revised to varying degrees: the chapter on Quebec nationalism has been almost totally rewritten, and I have added new chapters on judicial review, economic policy, and the Canada–United States free trade agreement. On the other hand, the portions of the book dealing with the origins and early years of Confederation are essentially the same as before. I am currently in the midst of research for a book on federal-provincial relations in the nineteenth century, and it seems best not to anticipate the conclusions of that work by modifying the much briefer treatment of the same topic in the present volume.

Assorted persons and institutions have contributed in various ways to the completion of this edition. The Institute of Intergovernmental Relations at Queen's University, on whose advisory council I have served for the past six years, has given me the opportunity to meet at least annually with the other specialists in the field. The research generated by the Macdonald Royal Commission, in which I played a small part, has provided a wealth of valuable information for students of Canadian federalism. Norman Spector of the Federal-Provincial Relations Office supplied me with documentation on the Meech Lake Constitutional accord. R.A. McLarty of the Department of Finance sharpened my understanding of fiscal federalism by pointing out a number of errors and ambiguities in the second edition. The typing of the manuscript was begun by Leah Modin at the University of Alberta and completed by Barb Magee at Brock University. Lynne Feldman of Gage was a good-humoured and efficient editor. All of the above deserve my thanks but none of them, as the saying goes, is responsible for what follows.

Garth Stevenson
St. Catharines, Ontario
February 1988

Table of Contents

1 **The Meaning of Federalism**   1

Defining Federalism
Federalism on Other Continents
Explanations for Federalism
Evaluating Federalism

2 **Origins and Objectives of Canadian Confederation**   20

The Internal Difficulties of the Province of Canada
Strategic and Economic Motives
The Opponents of Confederation
The Terms of Union
The Inadequacies of the Constitution
Democracy and Confederation

3 **Judicial Interpretation of the Constitution**   43

Does Federalism Require Judicial Review?
The Judicial Committee and its Legacy
The Judicial Committee's Reputation
The Supreme Court After 1949
Should the Supreme Court be Reformed?

4 **The Political Economy of Decentralization**   72

The National Policy and its Opponents
The Impact of Depression and War
The Branch-Plant Economy
The Revival of Centripetal Forces

5 **A Province Unlike the Others**   94

The Legacy of Conquest
From Mercier to Duplessis
The Quiet Revolution and its Aftermath
The Parti Québécois in Office
Anglophones and Allophones

6 **Fiscal Federalism: The Search for Balance**   124

The First Seventy-Five Years
From Tax Rental to Tax Sharing
Equalization: Myth and Reality
The Future of Tax Sharing

7   Conditional Grants and Shared-Cost Programs   151

The Reasons for Conditional Grants
The Development of Conditional Grants
The Decline of Conditional Grants
Established Programs Financing

8   Federalism and Economic Policy   177

Stabilization
Regional and Industrial Development
Natural Resources and Energy Policy
Transportation
Canada as an Economic Union

9   Federal-Provincial Conflict and Its Resolution   210

Causes of Federal-Provincial Conflict
Disallowance and Reservation
Political Parties and Conflict Resolution
Judicial Conflict Resolution
Co-operative Federalism
Executive Federalism
Intrastate Federalism

10   Federalism and Constitutional Change   235

Early Constitutional Amendments
The Search for an Amending Formula: 1927–65
Constitutional Politics: 1965–79
The Patriation Initiative: 1980–82
Securing Quebec's Assent

**11   Epilogue: Continental Free Trade and
Canadian Federalism**   267

Appendices   275

    1. Constitution Act, 1867, Part VI
    2. Constitution Act, 1982
    3. 1987 Constitutional Accord

Index   313

1 The Meaning of Federalism

La France, la Russie, la Chine, les Etats-Unis ont dû passer par des révolutions sanglantes pour mettre fin au cancer des régionalismes égoistes, ces proliférations des cellules sociales qui détruisent l'équilibre de la nation et la tuent. Chacune de ces révolutions a mené à un gouvernement central plus fort. Les Canadiens sont-ils capables d'assez de sagesse et de lucidité pour protéger une formule politique, le fédéralisme sous une autorité centrale indiscutable qui protège les droits des provinces sans affaiblir son pouvoir, le fédéralisme qui, en 112 ans, a fait du Canada un grand pays? Sont-ils capables de faire cela avec intelligence, dans la paix?

ROGER LEMELIN[1]

During Canada's centennial celebrations in 1967, a national magazine invited its readers to participate in selecting the most typically Canadian joke. The winning entry proved to be a local version of the ancient elephant joke, which recounts how persons of various nationalities responded in different ways to the task of writing an essay on some aspect of the elephant. While the German wrote on the elephant as a military weapon, the Frenchman on the elephant's love life, and so forth, the Canadian essayist's title was "The elephant: Does it fall under federal or provincial jurisdiction?"

Not only the outcome but the occasion of this contest testifies to the pervasiveness of federalism in Canadian life. The centennial which we celebrated in 1967, after all, was not really the centennial of Canada, not even the centennial of the Canadian state (which was founded in 1841), but only the centennial of Canadian federalism. In geo-political terms it was also the centennial of the date at which New Brunswick and Nova Scotia became part of Canada, but that event was not the first, the last, nor even the most important step in Canada's territorial expansion, although it may have paved the way for the greater expansion that followed.

Federalism, clearly, is for most Canadians inseparable from their image of their country, and this has probably never been more true than it is at present. Except among separatists, belief in the desirability of some kind of federalism, however defined, seems to be virtually universal. Indeed even some separatists in western Canada favour a federation, although one that would be confined to the four western provinces. If political science students observed by the author over several years are in any way representative, it appears that Canadians are completely unable to imagine their country as being other than federal, or as having any existence apart from federalism. If pressed to consider alternatives, they invariably assume that this must mean the dissolution of the federal tie and independence for each of the ten provinces.

While unusual and perhaps even unique by world standards, this obsession with federalism is by no means misguided. Federalism is undoubtedly, for better or for worse, a fundamental attribute of the way in which Canada conducts its public business. Interest groups and political parties are structured along federal lines, corresponding with the structures of government itself, as are educational institutions, the professions, and even the private sector of the economy. Statistical data are collected and organized in such a way as to highlight the boundaries between the provinces. Intergovernmental conferences have become a basic part of the political process, arguably more important than Parliament or the provincial legislatures.

These facts are not in dispute, nor can they be explained away, even by those who agree with John Porter that the obsession with federalism is an obstacle to creative politics and who dismiss the reputed sociocultural differences between the various provinces as "hallowed nonsense."[2] Porter's point, however, is well taken when he argues that the attention given to federalism distracts attention from other issues, and may even be deliberately designed to do so. If politics is about who gets what, when, and how, Canadians are subtly but constantly encouraged to view these fundamental questions in jurisdictional or interprovincial terms. What does Quebec want? What does Alberta stand to lose? What is "Ottawa" taking from "the provinces" and what will they seek in return? Are we becoming more centralized or more decentralized?

A few lonely critics, like Porter, have argued that these are completely meaningless questions, designed only to mystify the masses. In contrast, politicians, the media, and an increasing number of academics often go to the other extreme and give the impression that these are the only significant questions in Canadian political life. The reality lies somewhere between the two extremes. Questions about federalism are real and important, even if they may sometimes be posed in mystifying language, but they are not the only questions in our political life. So pervasive is federalism to Canadians, however, that the more fundamental questions to which Porter and others have drawn attention cannot easily be considered or resolved outside of the federal context in which they occur.

DEFINING FEDERALISM

Despite their constant use by Canadians, and their frequent use in other countries, the word "federal" and its various derivatives are not lacking in ambiguity. Their history has been long and complex, and their polemical use is neither a recent nor a uniquely Canadian phenomenon. Even those who are professionally concerned with the study of federalism have failed to agree on what it means, what is included, and what should be excluded. As we shall see, almost any possible definition presents problems.

Certain words used in political discourse, like "legislature," "bureaucracy," or "election" are quite easily defined, for the fairly narrow and concrete phenomena to which they refer are easily recognized. Other words, such as "democracy," "liberalism," or "socialism" pose greater problems because they are broader in scope and too intimately associated with past and present ideological controversies to be defined in a manner that satisfies everyone. Some would go so far as to argue that these words are no more than ideological symbols, devoid of real content and substance. Certainly their repeated use as ideological symbols has left them vulnerable to such accusations.

Only a few political thinkers — Pierre Elliott Trudeau would probably be one of them — have endowed the concept of federalism with this heavy load of symbolic attributes. It has thus seemed plausible to treat federalism as a concrete, easily defined, and value-free concept. Yet somehow the effort to treat it thus never entirely succeeds. The concept of federalism seems to be a hybrid with some qualities from both categories of political concept.

In searching for definitions, the reader of the *Oxford English Dictionary* will find "federal" to mean "of or pertaining to a covenant, compact or treaty" but with the cautionary note that this definition is obsolete. Persevering, one finds a further definition: "of or pertaining to or of the nature of that form of government in which two or more states constitute a political unity while remaining more or less independent with regard to their internal affairs." Apart from the question-begging "more or less," which neatly evades the essence of the problem, this definition is notable chiefly for the fact that it establishes federalism as a form of *decentralized* government.

Even this apparent precision, however, vanishes when one seeks in the same dictionary the meaning of "federation," for this is said to mean "the formation of a political unity out of a number of separate states, provinces or colonies, so that each retains the management of its internal affairs." In this definition a new and different basis of distinction appears, for it is explicitly stated that the components of the federation, whether states, provinces, or colonies, previously enjoyed a separate existence.

Defining federalism in this way would seem to have the advantage that federal countries could be easily identified, but there are ambiguities here as well. The three Prairie provinces in Canada and a majority of the fifty states in the United States had no separate existence prior to the federal union; they were formed subsequently out of territories which the central government had acquired by purchase or conquest. Since it would be absurd to exclude Canada or the United States from any definition of federalism, the definition must be modified to specify that only *some* of the subnational units need to have enjoyed a previously separate existence.

So far we have been preoccupied mainly with distinguishing a federation from a non-federal or unitary state. However, a definition of federalism must also serve the purpose, which is even more essential in Canada's present circumstances, of distinguishing federalism from other forms of *decentralized* government. The European Community, for example, is not a federation because the powers of the Commission at Brussels and of the other community institutions are too insignificant in relation to the governments of the member countries. As was noted earlier, the use of the term "federal" with reference to a "covenant, compact or treaty" is now considered obsolete, although at one time the word was so used. The "sovereignty-association" proposed by the Parti Québécois, as well as other hypothetical arrangements that would drastically reduce the powers of the central government in Canada, must be excluded from any useful definition of federalism, not because they are undesirable (although the author happens to be of this opinion) but because to include them in a category that also includes the United States and the Federal Republic of Germany would make the category too heterogeneous to have any analytic usefulness.

This brings us to another problem of semantics, namely the distinction between a *federation* and a *confederation*. These closely related words were not at first clearly distinguished, and in Canada are still not, but in the rest of the world they have gradually acquired distinct meanings. Outside of Canada, "confederation" is a word used mainly by historians, most often in reference to various arrangements among sovereign states (usually for the purposes of mutual defence) that fall short of establishing a new state or a central government with meaningful power and authority. Perhaps the European Community, the North Atlantic Treaty Organization (NATO), and other such institutions are the closest contemporary equivalents of these early "confederations."

The earliest confederation in the English-speaking world was the New England Confederation, which lasted from 1643 to 1648, a period for much of which England was too distracted by its own bourgeois revolution to provide much protection for its North American colonies. Threatened by the Indian tribes and the nearby colonies of other European powers, the New Englanders formed an alliance and estab-

lished a commission of eight delegates, four from each colonial government, to decide collectively on questions of defence and external
relations. Since these delegates had no authority apart from that of the
colonial governments that appointed them, and since in practice it
soon appeared that any one government could veto a decision by the
commissioners, this confederation was more like a modern international organization than a modern federal state.[3]

In 1778, two years after the Declaration of Independence, the thirteen colonies formed a military alliance with rudimentary common
institutions somewhat similar to those of the earlier New England
Confederation. The agreement which brought this new arrangement
into force was known as the Articles of Confederation, an appellation
that would lead subsequent generations of Americans to associate the
word "confederation" with loose alliances of this type, while reserving the word "federal" for their present, more centralized constitution. However, the Americans of the eighteenth century had not yet
made this distinction. Instead, the word "federal" seems to have been
used in the sense in which the *Oxford English Dictionary* now regards
as obsolete, to refer to the Articles of Confederation themselves. At the
Philadelphia Convention of 1787, where the present constitution of
the United States was drafted, supporters of the Virginia Plan, on
which that constitution is based, used the term "federal" in that same
sense, and argued that a "merely federal" union, such as then existed,
was inadequate to secure the objectives of "common defence, security
of liberty, and general welfare." In its place they proposed to establish
what they called a "national" government, which would have authority to impose its will on the states.[4]

A delegate from New York, where opposition to the latter idea
seems to have been exceptionally strong, protested that the Virginia
Plan was unacceptable:

> He was decidedly of the opinion that the power of the Conven-
> tion was restrained to amendments of a Federal nature, and
> having for their basis the confederacy in being. . . . New York
> would never have concurred in sending Deputies to the Conven-
> tion, if she had supposed the deliberations were to turn on a
> consolidation of the states, and a National Government.[5]

In response to such sentiments, the nationalists who wanted "a
consolidation of the States" began to use the reassuring and familiar
word "federal" with reference to their own plans, although they did
not abandon its use with reference to the Articles of Confederation.

This deliberate attempt to blur what was in fact a fundamental
distinction can best be seen in the series of anonymous essays by
which Alexander Hamilton, John Jay, and James Madison attempted to
persuade the voters of New York to ratify the proposed new constitu-

tion. These essays, which still rank among the classics of political science, are themselves known as the Federalist Papers, although their purpose was to argue the inadequacy of "federalism" in its original sense. Once the union was achieved, the word "Federalist" was adopted as the name of the political party representing the mercantile and financial interests who wanted a strong central government and subordinate states. In fact Hamilton, the first leader of the Federalist Party, had presented at the Philadelphia Convention a plan for a constitution even more centralized than the one that was finally adopted.[6] Some of Hamilton's ideas, although rejected by his own countrymen, were later to be incorporated in the British North America Act of 1867.

As a result of these developments, the word "federal" and its derivatives became associated with a considerable degree of centralization, at least in the United States. The Swiss Confederation, which until 1848 was little more than a loose alliance of sovereign states, and the German Confederation, an even more nebulous organization established by the Congress of Vienna in 1815, helped to perpetuate the view that "confederation" referred to a compact that fell short of establishing a new central government. The Swiss, however, somewhat confused the issue by continuing to use the word "confederation" even after they had adopted a constitution that was "federal" in the new American sense.

As far as Canada is concerned, one constitutional historian has speculated that the use of the term "confederation" to describe the proposed union of the British North American colonies had exactly the same purpose as the adoption of the word "federal" by proponents of the Virginia Plan after 1787. In both cases, according to this view, a word normally associated with the absence of a strong central government was deliberately misused by those who in fact intended to create one in an effort to confuse those who might find such a project alarming.[7] John A. Macdonald was certainly using an idiosyncratic definition in 1861 when he stated that "the true principle of a Confederation" meant a system in which all the powers not specifically assigned to the provinces were given to the central government, unlike the American constitution whose tenth amendment, adopted in 1791, said precisely the reverse.[8] A.A. Dorion, the leading French Canadian opponent of Macdonald's "Confederation," was more correct, or at least more conventional, a few years later when he defined "a real confederation" as "giving the largest powers to the local governments and merely a delegated authority to the general government."[9] However, Macdonald won and Dorion lost, so that Macdonald's usage of the term has acquired semiofficial status in Canada, however bizarre it may seem to Americans. Dorion's definition may be historically justified but has become somewhat irrelevant, since none of the "confederations" that Dorion had in mind are still in existence, nor have any new ones under that name been established.

Both Canada and Switzerland, however, use the word "confederation" for what is actually a federal union in the modern American sense.

Although it is relatively easy to determine what federalism is not, the many writers on the subject have failed to agree on a satisfactory definition of what it is, even though almost every one of them has attempted to produce a definition. The most frequently used definitions, such as those used by K.C. Wheare, Daniel Elazar, W.H. Riker, and Geoffrey Sawer, emphasize institutional and legal criteria: two levels of government, each independent of the other; a written constitution specifying the jurisdiction of each; judicial review of legislation as a means of maintaining the jurisdictional boundaries; the requirement that each level of government have a direct relationship with the people; and so forth. Political scientists like Elazar and Riker tend to interpret these criteria rather broadly, while lawyers like Wheare and Sawer are most inclined to exclude doubtful cases. Wheare, although born in Australia and teaching in England, included as federal constitutions only those which closely resembled the constitution of the United States, with the result that only Australia and Switzerland passed the test. He admitted, however, that Canada was a federal state in practice, even though certain features of the British North America Act departed from the federal norm.[10].

Apart from the fact that they tell us little about how political systems really operate, these formal criteria are so restrictive that their applicability to even those considered the most federal of states can be questioned. Federal legislation in Switzerland is not subject to judicial review; provincial statutes in Canada can be disallowed; and the West German federal government is not completely independent of the *land* governments since the *länder* control the upper house of the federal parliament. One political scientist, Michael Reagan, has even questioned whether the United States qualifies as a federation by these criteria, since he considers that in practice there is no field reserved to the states in which Congress is unable to legislate.[11]

In reaction against the rigidity and formality of these traditional criteria, writers on federalism began in the 1950s to explore alternative approaches to its definition. W.S. Livingston abandoned institutional criteria almost entirely and developed the concept of a "federal society," which he defined as any society in which economic, religious, racial, or historical diversities are territorially grouped. A formally unitary state in which political practices and conventions protected such diversities, such as the United Kingdom, should be considered to have some federal characteristics. Rufus Davis went a step further, questioning whether any "federal principle" could really be developed to distinguish federal from non-federal states; the difference was merely one of degree. Carl Friedrich defined federalism not as a static situation but as a process, the process by which a number of separate political communities were gradually integrated.[12]

While political scientists shifted their attention from formal institutions to political processes and behaviour, economists took an entirely different approach to defining federalism. Wallace Oates, in his book entitled *Fiscal Federalism*, wrote that federalism existed in any state where the public sector was decentralized, so that some decisions about taxing and spending were made by smaller territorial subdivisions in response to demands originating within themselves.[13] From an economist's perspective it matters little whether such decentralization is protected by constitutional guarantees or whether it can be unilaterally revoked by the central government. At least in the short term, the economic consequences are the same in either case. While useful for its own purpose, this definition is so broad that hardly any state, at least in the industrialized world, could avoid being classified as federal.

It is probably rash to attempt yet another definition of federalism when so many authorities have failed to agree on one that is totally satisfactory. Possibly no single definition of so elusive and controversial a concept could be satisfactory for all purposes. Nonetheless, the following definition is offered in the belief that it meets three essential criteria for a definition of federalism: (1) the definition should not be unduly restrictive; (2) it should serve to distinguish a federal state both from a unitary state and from looser forms of association; and (3) it should emphasize the political aspects of federalism.

With these criteria in mind, federalism will be defined as follows. It is a political system in which most or all of the structural elements of the state (executive, legislative, bureaucratic, judiciary, army or police, and machinery for levying taxation) are duplicated at two levels, with both sets of structures exercising effective control over the same territory and population. Furthermore, neither set of structures (or level of government) should be able to abolish the other's jurisdiction over this territory or population. As a corollary of this, relations between the two levels of government will tend to be characterized by bargaining, since neither level can fully impose its will on the other.

The condition that neither level of government should be able to abolish the other's jurisdiction effectively distinguishes federalism both from a unitary state and from looser forms of association. In a unitary state there may be some decentralization for administrative and even legislative purposes, but the central government can take back the power it has delegated to the lower levels of government or can even abolish them, as the British Parliament abolished the Parliament of Northern Ireland. In an alliance, league, or common market, on the other hand, the member states can withdraw or secede, an action which clearly prevents the central institutions from exercising any jurisdiction over their territories or populations. If the definition is a valid one, it follows that in a true federation the provinces or states have no right to secede. If such a right existed before, they surrendered it when they entered the federal union.

A somewhat legalistic way of expressing these characteristics of federalism is to say that the provinces or states are not sovereign entities, but at the same time the central government does not possess full and complete sovereignty either, since it lacks the power to abolish the other level of government. These facts may be represented symbolically by a written constitution, judicial review, elaborate procedures for amendment, and statements to the effect that sovereignty resides in "the people" (as in the United States) or "the Crown" (as in Canada). These symbolic aspects of federalism are not unimportant, but their importance exists only because they metaphorically represent, and may provide ideological justification for, real facts concerning the distribution of political power.

As to which countries are federal by this (or any other) definition, opinions will vary. Any effort to classify a particular country should be based on observation of how its political institutions actually operate. In some countries military coups and other changes of regime have occurred so frequently that one cannot say what is their "normal" or usual pattern of political activity. Others have simply not been studied enough for reliable data to be available. There is no doubt, however, that the few countries which are invariably included on any list of federations — and Canada is unquestionably one of these — would qualify as federations under this definition. On the other hand, countries such as the United Kingdom, which may have characteristics in common with at least some of the federations, would not.

FEDERALISM ON OTHER CONTINENTS

The origins of American federalism have been discussed already, while those of Canadian federalism will be considered in more detail in the next chapter. It would be unduly parochial, however, not to make a few comments about the origins of Swiss and German federalism.

Although they differ in many respects, an important similarity is the fact that in both cases a looser, non-federal association between sovereign states was transformed into a true federation as a result of war. In Switzerland the conservative Catholic cantons launched the Sonderbund War of 1847 to protect themselves against the emerging threat of bourgeois liberalism. Their defeat enabled the more progressive cantons to impose a federal constitution following the American model and establish a modern liberal state in place of the outmoded "confederation." In the German case, the defeat of Austria by Prussia in the war of 1866 led to the dissolution of the loose "confederation" which had been established in 1815 as the successor to the old Holy

Roman Empire. With Austria now excluded from further involvement in German affairs, a Prussian-dominated federation was established in northern Germany in 1867. The southern states entered it voluntarily in 1870, at the end of which year it adopted the title of "German Empire."[14] Some form of German federalism has existed ever since, except during Hitler's dictatorship and for a few years after his defeat.

In the twentieth century federal unions have been formed in Australia (1901), the USSR (1924), Malaya (1948), Rhodesia and Nyasaland (1953), the West Indies (1958), and Cameroun (1961). In four of these six cases the federating units were colonies of the British Empire, although in the Australian case the initiative for federation was taken entirely by the Australians themselves. Soviet federalism permitted the new Russian republic to reunite with most of the outlying territories of the old empire, which had been temporarily detached from Russia during its civil war. The Federal Republic of Cameroun united two territories which had been held under United Nations trusteeship by Britain and France, respectively. In the early 1960s Malaya changed its name to Malaysia when it absorbed a number of other British colonies. The Rhodesia and Nyasaland and West Indian federations disintegrated at about the same time, with some of their components becoming independent and others remaining under British rule.

A number of other countries are frequently referred to as federations, although it cannot be said, at least without serious qualification, that they resulted from a union of previously separate entities. Argentina, Brazil, Mexico, and Venezuela all adopted "federal" constitutions in the nineteenth century, possibly in imitation of the United States. Most external observers, however, are sceptical about Latin American federalism, on the grounds that the component states do not retain any meaningful degree of autonomy.

Outside of North America and central Europe, federalism has had its greatest influence on the Indian sub-continent, where one-fifth of the world's population lives. The British ruled most of India, including the present Pakistan and Bangladesh, as a unitary colony from 1857 until 1935. In the latter year the Government of India Act established provincial legislatures, and thus a sort of quasi-federalism similar to what John A. Macdonald intended for Canada. In 1947 the British handed over their authority to two new states, India and Pakistan, which between them soon absorbed the various princely states that had never been under direct British rule. Both successor states have adopted constitutions that divide legislative powers between two levels of government, and the subnational governments, at least in India, enjoy considerable autonomy. However, the central government in India was able to "reorganize" the boundaries of the component states soon after independence, an event that would surely be unthinkable in such genuinely federal countries as Canada, Switzerland, or the United States. It is also interesting that the Supreme Court of India, in an important case upholding the central government's power to expropriate mineral resources belonging to the states, declared flatly that India was a decentralized unitary state rather than a federal one.[15]

The case of Nigeria is very similar. Although they had previously ruled it as a unitary state, the British endowed it with the dubious blessing of a federal constitution in 1954. It remained a federation after gaining its independence in 1960, but the federal constitution was suspended by the military regime during the ultimately successful civil war against the separatists in the southeastern province, who attempted with some foreign assistance to establish an independent "Biafra." Postwar Nigeria, however, has re-established subnational state governments, even though the boundaries of the new states bear no relation to the old.

Three European cases remain to be considered. Austria adopted a federal constitution in 1922, Yugoslavia in 1946, and Czechoslovakia in 1968. The Yugoslavian constitution of 1946 has since been replaced by a new one of almost unbelievable complexity, but its federal features have if anything been enhanced. All three countries are in a sense the successors of the Habsburg Empire which dissolved in 1918, and they share the common characteristic that their internal boundaries and component units have a longer history as distinct entities than have the countries themselves. On these grounds, and in terms of the real autonomy enjoyed by the subnational governments, Austria and Yugoslavia have at least as good a claim to be considered "federal" as India and Pakistan, even though they are not really unions of previously independent entities. The case of Czechoslovakia is more dubious.

EXPLANATIONS FOR FEDERALISM

An explanation for federalism which is particularly relevant to the central and eastern European experience was offered by Rudolf Schlesinger in a book published in 1945.[16] Schlesinger suggested that federalism arose in situations where national consciousness was focussed on a collectivity which did not coincide with the traditional boundaries of dynastic states. In Germany the national community included a number of dynastic states, while in the Austrian and Russian empires the dynastic state included a number of national communities. In either case federalism developed, with one level of government corresponding to the traditional social forces and boundaries while the other corresponded to the rising forces of nationalism, industrialism, and the bourgeoisie. In Western Europe, where the new communities and the old units tended to coincide, there was no need for federalism, and unitary states have been the general rule.

Many students of federalism, however, refuse to recognize as a federation any state that did not result from a union of previously separate entities which retained their identities after union. As a result, efforts to generalize about the reasons why federations come into existence tend to ignore the ambiguous cases or those in which the subnational governments were established by devolutions of power from the centre. K.C. Wheare lists the conditions leading to federal union as follows: the need for common defence, desire for independence from foreign powers, desire to gain economic benefits, some previous political association, similar political institutions, geographical closeness, similar social conditions, and the existence of political elites interested in unification.[17] No previous or subsequent writer on federalism has really added anything to this list.

Despite its completeness, or perhaps because of it, Wheare's list of conditions is not very informative. The first two conditions are almost indistinguishable, the last would seem to be present by definition, and several of the others are so vague as to be almost useless. Wheare does not present anything that can be called a theory of federal unification.

The most interesting theoretical question about the origins of federal unions is whether military insecurity or anticipated economic benefits is the more important motive, or whether in fact both must be present. It is also conceivable that a security motive might be more important in some cases and an economic motive in others.

The case for the pre-eminence of economic motives was made most memorably by Charles Beard in his classic study, *An Economic Interpretation of the Constitution of the United States*.[18] Beard suggested that the move of the Americans to adopt their present constitution was led by merchant capitalists and that the constitution itself was carefully drafted to protect their economic interests. For Beard, American politics after the Revolutionary War were dominated by the conflict between this class and the more numerous but less influential farmers who, in his view, mainly opposed the constitution. The merchants wanted a strong central government to repress further revolutionary outbreaks by agrarian radicals (such as Massachusetts had experienced in 1786–87), to prevent the repudiation of debts and the printing of paper money, and to protect their commerce on the high seas. The adoption of the constitution marked the swing of the revolutionary pendulum back to the right and the restoration of "order."

Not all economic interpretations of federalism emphasize class conflict, as Beard's does. The kind of economic motives that Wheare seems to have had in mind are those emphasized by more conventional American historians and their Canadian and Australian counterparts: larger markets, the removal of tariff barriers, penetration of the western hinterlands, and so forth. Marxist historians, of course, would view even these types of motives as reflecting the interests of ruling classes, and perhaps as leading to conflict with other classes that opposed them. Even where there was such opposition, however, the establishment of a federal state might not be necessary to achieve these objectives. Western European capitalists seem to be achieving quite similar objectives through the very limited integrative arrangements represented by the European Community, which falls far short of establishing federalism.

Security motives for federal union are emphasized by William H. Riker, who views federalism as a "bargain" by which political elites in the states or provinces agree to sacrifice some, but not all, of their autonomy in return for protection against an external threat or, more rarely, a share in the benefits of military expansion and conquest. The bargain is usually initiated by a relatively large and powerful entity (Virginia, the Province of Canada, or Bismarck's Prussia) and accepted by smaller states or provinces, which have both more to lose (because they will have relatively little influence within a larger union) and more to gain (because they could not hope to attain security, let alone expansion, by themselves).[19]

Obvious external threats to security were certainly present at the time of union in some federations, such as Switzerland, Bismarck's Germany, the USSR, and Pakistan. The importance of a security motive in the Canadian case will be discussed in the next chapter. Security motives are somewhat harder to discern, though not entirely absent, in other cases, such as those of Australia, postwar West Germany, and Cameroun.

It may be that no single factor can explain every instance of the formation of a federal union, and even in a particular case a variety of factors may contribute. The author of a recent book on federalism, R.D. Dikshit, adopts both of these assumptions. Dikshit's purpose is to explain not only why federal unions evolve, but also why they differ in the extent of the powers conferred on the central government, and why some federal unions are more durable and successful than others. Dikshit distinguishes factors leading to union from factors leading to the retention of some degree of regional autonomy. A preponderance of the first will lead to the formation of a unitary state, while a preponderance of the second will prevent any union from taking place. Only a balance between the two will lead to federalism, and only if the balance is maintained will federalism survive.[20]

Dikshit's factors leading to union are essentially the same as K.C. Wheare's, although he differs from Wheare in including a common language, culture, and religion as one of his conditions. His factors conducive to the maintenance of regional autonomy are essentially the reverse of the factors leading to union, for example, regionally grouped cultural diversity rather than cultural homogeneity, competitive economies with conflicting interests rather than the expectation of economic benefits from union, and so forth. Federal union does not demand that all of the factors in either category be present, for there are several possible combinations that will bring it about, although the precise nature of the new federal state will vary accordingly. West

Germany is a very centralized federation, according to Dikshit, because most of the factors leading to union were present in 1949, while the factors conducive to maintaining regional autonomy were virtually absent. Only the absence of a military threat (since the country was effectively protected by the United States) prevented a centralized unitary state from emerging instead of a federation. On the other hand, Pakistan at the time of its formation had practically all of the conditions which lead to the maintenance of regional autonomy, while the military threat from India was the only factor that contributed to union. The result was a weak federation that could not prevent the secession of its largest unit in the civil war of 1971.

EVALUATING FEDERALISM

For a Canadian audience it is perhaps necessary to explain that evaluating federalism means evaluating the consequences of having two distinct levels of government, rather than a national government only. Since most Canadians find it impossible to imagine Canada as a unitary state, few have considered it worthwhile to discuss and evaluate the relative merits of federal and unitary institutions. Some such discussion took place prior to 1867, but since then the vast majority of Canadians outside of Quebec have simply taken federalism for granted. In Quebec, admittedly, there has been controversy over federalism, but what is really being debated there is whether or not Quebec should be independent, not the advantages and disadvantages of federal institutions as such. No one in Quebec contemplates abolishing the provincial level of government.

In other parts of the world, by contrast, the respective merits of federal and unitary government have been lengthily, although inconclusively, debated. Among the more strikingly unfavourable assessments was that of former Nigerian Prime Minister Sir Abubaker Balewa, who at his last meeting with Harold Wilson said to him: "You are fortunate. One thing only I wish for you, that you never have to become Prime Minister of a federal and divided country."[21]

Since he was assassinated four days after making this remark, and since his death proved to be the opening of the Nigerian civil war, Balewa's pessimism was probably justified. Others have expressed, although in less memorable circumstances, his view that federations are characterized by disorder, conflict, and political bickering, which may be the less attractive side of the intergovernmental bargaining that is, by our definition, an almost inevitable aspect of federal politics. Defenders of federalism, on the other hand, would argue that regional and cultural conflicts are obviously not caused by federalism, since they exist in unitary states like Ethiopia, Spain, or the United Kingdom.

A classic argument against federalism was presented by A.V. Dicey, a late nineteenth-century writer on British constitutional law, who maintained that federalism produced weak and ineffective government, conservatism, and legalism.[22] Dicey's views, and especially his assertion that "federal government means weak government," may have some relevance for Canada today, almost a century after they were expressed. Federalism was weak, according to Dicey, because energy was wasted in conflicts between the two levels of government, because the central government had to respond to regional demands, or appear to do so, at the expense of efficiency and effectiveness, and because the power of either level to act was constrained by a rigid constitution. It was conservative because the existence of a rigid written constitution produced a "superstitious reverence" for existing principles and institutions. It was legalistic because lawyers and judges were inevitably called upon to interpret the constitution and define the respective powers of the two levels of government.

While much of Dicey's analysis is plausible, it is far from evident, with hindsight, that the unitary British system of government which he so admired avoided any of the defects which he associated with federalism. Nor is the untrammeled authority of the legislature invariably a blessing, as Dicey complacently assumed in the salad days of Victorian liberalism. Finally, the connection asserted between conservatism and legalism may be questioned. Particularly in the United States, the judiciary has often been more liberal and enlightened than either the executive or legislative branches of government.[23]

In Dicey's defence it may be argued that the United States, Canada, and Australia, all of which are federations, have lagged behind the unitary states of northern and western Europe in their provisions for social welfare, income security, full employment, and public ownership and control of the economy. Possibly the inefficacy of federalism, and the restrictions which it places on the power of the central government, are partly to blame.

The admirers of federalism have not lacked arguments of their own since the middle of the eighteenth century, when Montesquieu published his *De l'esprit des lois*. It is not entirely clear what Montesquieu meant by federalism, and no state that we would call federal existed in his lifetime, but his views greatly influenced the creators of the American constitution. As well as having originated the notion of "the separation of powers," Montesquieu argued that a federal republic was a means of combining the freedom possible in a small state with the security against external threats that was only possible in a large one.[24]

Since in the thermonuclear era it is doubtful whether any state can guarantee security, a modern variation on Montesquieu's view might be that federalism combines the economic advantages of large size with the possibilities for self-government that exist in a smaller political community. A non-federalist could argue that neither part of this proposition is fully supported by experience. The prosperity of Norway, Switzerland, Singapore, and Kuwait suggests that size is not a prerequisite to economic success. On the other hand, the reputed benefits of grass-roots democracy and freedom in a "small" subnational political system may really exist in the Swiss canton of Appenzell-Inner-Rhodes but bear no discernible relation to the facts of political life in Quebec, Ontario, New York, or California, all of which are larger than many nation-states.

Another argument sometimes heard in support of federalism is really the converse of Dicey's argument against it. According to this view, a "weak" state whose power is divided between two sets of authorities and restrained by legal restrictions is safer than a "strong" and vigorous state, because it is less likely to be oppressive. Dispersed and divided power is less dangerous than concentrated power, and the cumbersome decision-making procedures in a federal state make it less likely that unpredictable eruptions of popular sentiment will be reflected in public policy. Even if government at one level tries to be oppressive, government at the other level, as well as the judiciary, will prevent it from doing too much harm. This is essentially Madison's argument in the celebrated number ten of the Federalist Papers, and it recurs in several of the other papers as well. It was also a favourite argument of American conservatives during Franklin Roosevelt's New Deal and of Australian conservatives during the Labor Government of Gough Whitlam. When subjected to critical examination, this argument for federalism looks remarkably like an ideological facade for vested economic interests.

A somewhat different but related argument for federalism is that it protects minorities and enables cultural, linguistic, religious, and ideological diversity to flourish. A prominent supporter of this perspective is Pierre Elliott Trudeau, whose well-known but often misunderstood hostility to "nationalism" is really no more than the view that the state should not be intolerant of diversity and should not be identified with any ethnic or cultural group. In a federal state, he would argue, this is less likely to happen.

Several examples can be cited of diversities protected by federalism. Multilingualism in Switzerland provides an obvious example. West German states and Canadian provinces have adopted a variety of solutions to the difficult problem of the relationship between Roman Catholic and public education. Socialists in prewar Vienna and the CCF-NDP in Saskatchewan achieved important reforms that would not have been possible at the national level. The more progressive American and Australian states extended the vote to women and abolished capital punishment long before there was nation-wide support for these innovations.

Nonetheless, in certain respects this optimistic view of federalism is not fully supported by experience. Federalism may protect those minorities which happen to make up a majority within one of the provinces or states, but it protects them precisely by allowing them to act as majorities, which means that they in turn can oppress the sub-minorities under their jurisdiction. Federalism has ensured the survival of the French language in Canada, but it has been of no benefit to Chinese in British Columbia, Hutterites in Alberta, or Jehovah's Witnesses in Quebec. All of these groups were unpopular at various times, and the provincial governments were more responsive to the hostile sentiments directed against these minorities than was the more remote central government. Had Canada been a unitary state, these groups might have benefited. The history of blacks in the American South and of Australian aborigines in the state of Queensland supports a similar conclusion.

One is tempted to conclude that both the arguments against federalism and the arguments in its favour can be as easily refuted as supported. Franz Neumann, in his essay "On the Theory of the Federal State," concluded that federalism might be good, bad, or indifferent, depending on the circumstances, and that it was impossible to evaluate federalism in general.[25] W.H. Riker, in his book on federalism, stated that each particular case of federalism had to be examined separately to determine the balance sheet of costs and benefits. Attempting to perform this exercise himself, although in a rather superficial manner, he decided that federalism had benefited francophones in Canada, white racists in the United States, and business interests in Australia.[26] In a later essay, however, he concluded rather inconsistently that federalism really made no difference in terms of policy outcomes, a statement which he attempted to support by arguing that federal Australia was little different from unitary New Zealand.[27] From this he reached the further conclusion, which readers of this volume may be unhappy to hear, that the study of federalism was a waste of time! While it is hoped that Riker was incorrect in this conclusion, his earlier view that each case of federalism should be examined individually on its own merits is one with which the present writer would concur.

In succeeding chapters of this volume, attention will be focussed exclusively on Canadian federalism, beginning in the next chapter with an account of its origins and purposes, and of the constitutional document in which those purposes were expressed. Chapter 3 describes how that constitutional document has been interpreted by the judiciary, both before and after the abolition of appeals to the Judicial Committee of the Imperial Privy Council, and how those interpretations have replaced John A. Macdonald's version of federalism with something closer to the American model. Chapter 4 seeks to explain how federalism is affected by economic trends, and specifically how economic trends contributed to making the provincial governments much more powerful and important than Macdonald intended. Chapter 5 examines some distinctive characteristics of the province of Quebec that have affected the evolution of Canadian federalism, particularly, but not exclusively, since 1960. Chapter 6 considers the distribution of revenues between the two levels of government and Chapter 7 deals with conditional grants, shared-cost programs, and the spending power of Parliament. Chapter 8 shows how federalism has affected the making and implementation of economic policy by the Canadian state. Chapter 9 discusses various methods of resolving or avoiding conflicts between governments and between regions. Chapter 10 examines and evaluates the various changes to the formal constitution in the 1980s, as well as the ongoing process of constitutional change. The final chapter attempts to speculate about the future of Canadian federalism in a context of free trade between Canada and the United States.

NOTES

1. Roger Lemelin, "Pourquoi le Québec votera Trudeau," *La Presse*, 16 May 1979.
2. John Porter, *The Vertical Mosaic: An Analysis of Social Class and Power in Canada* (Toronto: University of Toronto Press, 1965) 382.
3. W.H. Bennett, *American Theories of Federalism* (University of Alabama Press, 1964) 179–95.
4. James Madison, *Journal of the Federal Convention*, (New York: Books for Libraries Press, 1970) 73–74.
5. Madison, 167–68.
6. Madison, 185–87.
7. W.P.M. Kennedy, *The Constitution of Canada* (London: Oxford University Press, 1922) 400–05.
8. Joseph Pope, *Correspondence of Sir John Macdonald* (Toronto: Oxford University Press, 1921) 11.
9. Canada, Legislature, *Parliamentary Debates on the Subject of the Confederation of the British North American Provinces* (Quebec, 1865) 250.
10. K.C. Wheare, *Federal Government*, 4th ed. (New York: Oxford University Press, 1964) 18–20.
11. Michael Reagan, *The New Federalism* (New York: Oxford University Press, 1972) 10–11.
12. W.S. Livingston, "A Note on the Nature of Federalism," and Rufus Davis, "The Federal Principle Reconsidered," both reprinted in *American Federalism in Perspective* ed. A. Wildavsky (Boston: Little Brown, 1967); Carl Friedrich, *Trends of Federalism in Theory and Practice* (New York: Praeger, 1968).
13. Wallace E. Oates, *Fiscal Federalism* (New York: Harcourt, Brace, Jovanovich, 1972) 17.
14. For a fuller account, see Burt Estes Howard, *The German Empire* (New York: Macmillan, 1913) 1–18.

15. Asok Chanda, *Federalism in India: A Study of Union-State Relations* (London: Allen and Unwin, 1965) 111–18.

16. Rudolf Schlesinger, *Federalism in Central and Eastern Europe* (London: Kegan Paul, 1945).

17. Wheare, *Federal Government*, 37.

18. Charles Beard, *An Economic Interpretation of the Constitution of the United States*, 3rd ed. (New York: Free Press, 1965). The book was first published in 1913.

19. W.H. Riker, *Federalism: Origin, Operation, Significance* (Boston: Little Brown, 1964) 12–13.

20. R.D. Dikshit, *The Political Geography of Federalism* (New Delhi: Macmillan, 1975) 226–33.

21. Harold Wilson, *The Labour Government, 1964–70* (Middlesex: Penguin Books, 1974) 256.

22. A.V. Dicey, *Introduction to the Study of the Law of the Constitution*, 10th ed. (London: Macmillan, 1961) 138–80.

23. On this point see Jennifer Nedelsky, "Law, Legitimacy, and the Transformation of the Liberal State," paper presented at the annual meeting of the Canadian Political Science Association, Halifax, May, 1981.

24. Montesquieu, *De l'esprit des lois* (Paris: Garnier, 1973) I, 141–44.

25. "On the Theory of the Federal State," in Franz Neumann, *The Democratic and the Authoritarian State* (Glencoe: Free Press, 1957).

26. Riker, *Federalism* 151–55.

27. W.H. Riker, "Six Books in search of a subject, or does federalism exist and does it matter?" *Comparative Politics* II (1968–69) 135–46.

2 Origins and Objectives of Canadian Confederation

The essential work of the Fathers of Confederation was to weld the scattered British possessions in North America into a unity within which Canadian capitalism could expand and consolidate its power, to provide for the capitalist entrepreneurs of Montreal and Toronto a half-continent in which they could realize their dreams and ambitions. The dynamic drive which brought Confederation about had its centre in Montreal among the railway and banking magnates who were dreaming of new fields to conquer. It was for this purpose, and not merely to illustrate the abstract beauties of brotherly love, that Macdonald and Cartier built up their Anglo-French entente; it was for this purpose that Galt and Head and Monck drafted their paper schemes of British-American union and carried on their obscure negotiations behind the scenes. Federalism was only an accident imposed by the circumstances of the time; union was the essential achievement.

FRANK H. UNDERHILL[1]

The unification of the British North American colonies in 1867 was part of a general pattern of events that saw the reconstruction of existing states and the establishment of new ones in many parts of the world. The unification of Italy had begun a few years earlier and was completed by the end of the decade. Bismarck's North German Confederation came into existence on the very same day as the new British Dominion, and in the same year that the Austrian Habsburg Empire was reorganized into the Austro-Hungarian Dual Monarchy. In the following year the Meiji restoration began the transformation of Japan into a modern industrial state.

While these events occurred overseas, the most important and the most painful of the decade's upheavals took place in immediate proximity to British North America, and had a direct impact upon it. The American Civil War established, at a cost of 700 000 lives, the domination of industrial capital in the United States. In the process it permanently resolved the ambiguity that had persisted in American federalism by indicating clearly that the states were not sovereign entities in a loose alliance but parts of a single nation. Although this view had been eloquently stated by the great Federalist John Marshall, who was Chief Justice of the United States from 1801 until 1835, it was only after the Civil War that it became universally accepted.

All of these events reflected the impact of the Industrial Revolution and of the enhanced international competition for markets and raw materials that it produced. Their effect was to stimulate further the forces of industrialization and economic growth by removing barriers to the flow of commodities and capital at the same time that they enhanced the ability of the various states to promote the accumulation of capital and to defend themselves against one another. In part the events took place simultaneously because similar circumstances were at work in each of the countries concerned, while in part they directly affected one another. Just as the reorganization of Austria was in part a response to that of Germany, so the reorganization of British North America was in part a response to that of the United States, while Japan was inspired to modernize itself largely by the growing threat which it faced from the major Western powers.

The event we call "Confederation" arose from a convergence of internal and external circumstances, and probably no single factor can explain it. Its complexity is enhanced by the fact that it simultaneously did three things, none of which would have been possible without the others. It reorganized the internal government of "Canada" in the pre-Confederation sense of Ontario and Quebec; it united this entity with New Brunswick and Nova Scotia; and it provided for the expansion of the federalized state westward to the Pacific. In the process of doing so it paved the way for economic development, and ended a potentially dangerous power vacuum in the northern part of North America.

THE INTERNAL DIFFICULTIES OF THE PROVINCE OF CANADA

On the recommendation of Lord Durham's report, the Province of Canada was established in 1841 by uniting the two colonies of Lower and Upper Canada. The distinction between the civil law of the lower province and the common law of the upper one was retained. Also, despite a brief attempt to impose unilingualism (one of Durham's recommendations), the status of the French language was eventually recognized. At about the same time, the principle was established that the government was dependent on the confidence and support of the elected lower house of the legislature.

In spite of these developments, the governing of both English-speaking and French-speaking Canadians within a unitary or at least a quasi-unitary state proved difficult, and discontent increased on both sides. From about 1849 onward a rather distinctive system of intercultural elite accommodation had developed. Cabinets were constructed to include representatives of both cultural communities, although there was never a requirement that the cabinet be supported by a "double majority" including majorities of the parliamentarians from each. Governments were headed by two party leaders — one from each section rather than a single prime minister — and there were separate attorneys general for the two sections in consequence of the different legal systems. Some of the legislation adopted by the provincial Parliament applied to only one of the sections, with parallel but distinct legislation applying to the other. Thus matters such as education and municipal affairs could be dealt with differently in the two halves of the province.

While this was an ingenious solution, it seems that it did not work particularly well. Each section of the province harboured the belief that it was being constrained and dictated to by the other. Since they were of roughly equal size and had equal representation in Parliament, such a belief was equally plausible on both sides. Once the western half became the more populous, its residents found the equal representation of the two sections to be an intolerable affront to liberal principles, although the injustice of it had somehow managed to escape their notice when they were a minority.

Ethnic and religious antagonisms were exacerbated by many of the issues which came before the legislature, and were reinforced by divergences of economic interest between the sections. Farmers and businessmen in the western part of the province, like their counterparts in the larger western hinterland of a later date, resented the commercial hegemony of Montreal and the measures that were taken with the aim of funnelling their commerce through that city.

For all of these reasons it became increasingly difficult to construct governments that could retain the confidence of the lower house. By about 1857 things were widely believed to be approaching an impasse, and a variety of changes in the existing constitution began to be proposed as possible solutions. These included the establishment of representation by population; the transformation of the unitary state into a federal union of the two sections; complete separation between the two, as had existed for half a century before 1841; and even a formal requirement that the government be supported by a double majority. Each of these solutions had a fatal flaw: "rep by pop" would leave the mainly French-speaking lower section at the mercy of the more populous upper one; a federation with only two parts would make each of the two provincial governments in practice more powerful than the central one; separation would destroy the economic and commercial unity of the St. Lawrence system; and the double majority requirement might make the formation of any government impossible.

Since neither the status quo nor any of these alternatives was widely acceptable, the territorial expansion of Canada began to be viewed as a possible means of escape from its difficulties, although this probably would not have been considered had not economic motives (which will be considered subsequently) pointed in the same direction. Expansion might be either eastward, to include the other British colonies on the Atlantic seaboard, or westward, to absorb the inland fur-trading empire of the Hudson's Bay Company, with each half of the Province of Canada tending to prefer the alternative that corresponded to its own point of the compass. Expansion in both directions at once might satisfy both sections, permit federalism (a separate government for each section with a central government over both) while avoiding the dangers of a double-headed monstrosity, and enable French-speaking Canadians to accept representation by population in the lower house at the same time as the more onerous conventions of the existing system could be safely eliminated.

In 1858 the Cartier-Macdonald ministry committed itself to seeking a federal union of British North America, and the Province of Canada, New Brunswick, and Nova Scotia sent delegations to London to discuss the project. This initiative failed because it came too soon. The internal problems of the province were already insoluble by any other means, and the various economic interests that led to Confederation were already becoming apparent. However, the external conditions outlined at the beginning of this chapter did not yet exist. The 1860s were to be the decade of state-building, in Canada as elsewhere.

STRATEGIC AND ECONOMIC MOTIVES

The change that took place in the new decade was the emergence of an external threat to the security of British North America. It will be recalled that W. H. Riker considered this a necessary condition for the formation of any federal union, and that other writers on federalism, such as Dikshit and Wheare, considered it important although not essential. In the Canadian case it probably was essential, both to secure the necessary amount of support for unification in the colonies themselves and, equally important if not more so, to win the support of the British government. Although internally self-governing, the colonies were exposed to direct Imperial influence through their governors, and this influence was now brought to bear in favour of a federal union. In addition, any change in the status of the colonies required legislation by the Parliament in Westminster.

The threat, of course, came from the United States. British relations with the government in Washington had deteriorated during the American Civil War, a situation for which the British were more to blame than the Americans (and for which the Canadians bore little if any responsibility), but which exposed Canada to the threat of an American invasion in the event of war. By 1864 it was apparent that the industrial North would win the war and incorporate the southern states back into the union, presenting the British Empire with a very powerful and unfriendly opponent. Another source of danger inherent in the outcome of the Civil War was the removal of the controversy over slavery from the agenda of American politics. Previously that controversy had prevented the United States from expanding northward, since to do so would have upset the delicate balance between slave states and free states. This obstacle to the annexation of Canada had now disappeared. Although the British government had discouraged efforts toward Confederation until 1864, it reversed itself in that year for reasons of military defence and security.[2] A united British North America, especially one tied together by railways, would be more defensible and could bear a larger share of the costs of its own defence. In particular, the port of Halifax with its British naval base could be used to send British troops to Canada even when the St. Lawrence was frozen, and without the necessity of crossing American soil.

The American threat also made the need for Confederation more apparent to the colonists themselves, or at least to those who were exposed to it. Not surprisingly, enthusiasm was minimal in Nova Scotia, which had no boundary with the United States and was defended by the Royal Navy. There was no enthusiasm at all in Newfoundland, which was hundreds of miles away from American territory. New Brunswick and Canada felt more exposed. The Confederation debates in the Canadian Parliament, which took place a few weeks before the end of the Civil War, contain many references to the American danger, particularly vehement on the part of the two members for Montreal, George Etienne Cartier and D'Arcy McGee.[3] John A. Macdonald and George Brown, who both had somewhat ambivalent attitudes toward the United States, were more restrained in their comments, but they also emphasized the defensive advantages of Confederation. Soon after the Civil War ended, the effect of such arguments was reinforced by the activities of the Fenians, Irish guerrillas who had learned their military skills while serving in the United States army.

All historians of Confederation have emphasized, and with good reason, the decisive role of capitalist entrepreneurs and their interests in bringing about Confederation. There were few countervailing interests at a time when the working class was largely disenfranchised, the salaried middle class hardly existed, and prominent politicians were directly involved in railways, banks, and insurance companies to an extent that would seem scandalous today. Confederation was no different from contemporaneous nation-building ventures elsewhere or from the formation of the United States a century before with respect to the decisive role played by the entrepreneurial class.

There has been some controversy among historians as to the character of this class in Canada during the Confederation period. The traditional view, while noting the preponderance of financial, commercial, and transportation enterprises among the activities of the dominant class, has not sharply distinguished these elements of British North American business from those involved in manufacturing or commodity production. A contrary view, which has gained wide popularity in recent years, is associated particularly with the economic historian R.T. Naylor.[4] According to Naylor and his followers, the dominant fraction of the Canadian bourgeoisie at Confederation and afterward were what Marx referred to as "merchant capitalists." According to Marx this kind of capitalism, characteristic of primitive colonial economies, serves primarily as an intermediary between the staple-producing colonial economy and the truly dominant economic interests of the metropolitan centre (the latter meaning the United Kingdom in the Canadian case). Thus it allegedly does not lead to the accumulation of much capital in the colony itself, and eliminates either the motive or the opportunity to create an independent industrial economy. Also, merchant capital is said to be politically reactionary, discouraging the progress of liberal democracy.

This interpretation of Canadian history appears plausible to many because it purports to explain why Canada industrialized less rapidly than the United States, a fact for which there are more obvious explanations. Interpreted from this perspective, Confederation ceased to be viewed as a creative exercise in nation-building, and was regarded instead as a somewhat shabby colonial manoeuvre, or even as a factor contributing to Canada's alleged backwardness. The Naylor interpretation thus contributed to the excessive enthusiasm for the provincial level of government, and the hostility toward the federal level, expressed by many Canadian intellectuals in the 1970s.

However, the merchant capital theory deserves to be treated with considerable scepticism. British colonialism had neither the means nor the desire to impede Canada's economic development after the middle of the nineteenth century. The British abandonment of mercantilism in favour of free trade had destroyed the old mercantile economy in Canada and forced Canada to pursue a different and more independent strategy of economic development. Responsible government, achieved at about the same time, passed political power from the old merchant cliques who had advised the colonial governors to a more progressive element of the bourgeoisie, and Canada became free to pursue independent economic policies, including protective tariffs against British manufacturers. H. Clare Pentland convincingly argues that at this time Canada developed an internal market and ceased to be a staple-producing colonial economy.[5]

Montreal had been the chief Canadian stronghold of merchant capital in the heyday of British mercantilism before 1849, and it was still the largest city and leading economic centre, as it remained for some time. The Bank of Montreal was the dominant financial institution and included the government of the Province of Canada among its customers. The Montreal bourgeoisie, and their political spokesmen, like Galt and Cartier, were particularly interested in uniting with the Maritimes and building the Intercolonial Railway, which would funnel more trade through their city.

Toronto, although then much smaller than Montreal, was rising rapidly as an economic centre. Its importance in the Confederation movement has been emphasized by J.M.S. Careless in his biography of George Brown.[6] A number of Toronto businessmen, including Brown, had recently organized the Bank of Commerce as a counterweight to the Bank of Montreal. Manufacturing was also developing in and around the city and the production of railway locomotives in Toronto had begun as early as 1853, long before it began in most European countries. Toronto businessmen had little interest in the Maritimes, but looked with increasing enthusiasm toward the West, which they viewed as potentially a vast extension of Toronto's agricultural hinterland in Upper Canada.

These different interests of capitalists in the two halves of the province corresponded with more widely held sentiments in their respective sections, in part, of course, because the dominant economic interests had the means to propagate their own viewpoints. In Canada West the farmers, partly because of George Brown and his *Globe*, supported westward expansion which would ease the pressure of a growing population on the limited supply of land, and end the necessity of migrating to the United States in search of new agricultural opportunities. In Canada East French-speaking Canadians, most of whom were farmers, feared the growing economic, demographic, and political power of Canada West and feared even more the consequences of annexing a western hinterland that would be merely an extension of it. Some French Canadians, George Cartier and his followers, later accepted westward expansion, but only as part of a package that included federalism, (a province of Quebec with its own legislature) and absorption of the Maritimes (as a counterweight to Ontario and the West).

This complex of interests was tied together by the Great Coalition of 1864. George Brown, the spokesman for Toronto business, joined forces with John A. Macdonald, whose political allies included Cartier and Galt, the spokesmen for Montreal business. Brown accepted expansion to the east, Cartier accepted expansion to the west, and Macdonald accepted federalism, despite serious reservations (even though he had been a long-time supporter of uniting the colonies). Macdonald's preference for a unitary state, which he called a "legislative union," was consistent with his relative detachment from specifically regional interests, part of the secret of his political success. However, a federal union was the only kind that could possibly be acceptable to French Canadians or Maritimers, and Brown shrewdly understood that a federal state would be "capable of gradual and efficient expansion in future years." [7] The United States had convincingly demonstrated that federalism was ideally suited to facilitate the westward course of empire.

Economic motives for Confederation were perhaps weaker in the Maritime colonies than in the Province of Canada, but they were by no means completely absent. The promised Intercolonial Railway would benefit the northern and eastern parts of New Brunswick and the central part of Nova Scotia and so predictably there was more support for Confederation in those areas than around the Bay of Fundy. Fishing interests hoped to gain more effective protection from American competition. The argument that Confederation would make it possible to negotiate a new reciprocal trade agreement with the United States was used to some effect. Nova Scotia's coal industry, in which Charles Tupper had a personal as well as political interest, hoped to gain access to Canadian markets. Generally speaking, the more modern sectors of the Maritime economy — coal, iron, railways, and manufacturing — supported Confederation, while the traditional sectors of wood, water, and sail opposed it.

An additional economic motive for Confederation, which the Maritimes shared with the Province of Canada, was provided by the expectation that the United States would terminate its reciprocal trade agreement with the colonies, as it actually did in 1866. This forced all the colonies to reorient their trade on an east-west rather than a north-south basis. It threatened to end the arrangements by which Canada had used American seaports for its trade with Britain during the winter months. It also meant that Maritime fishermen could no longer fish in American waters, and would need help to defend their own waters from American encroachments.

> The change in the Quebec resolutions at the London Conference in December 1866 which gave the federal government control over seacoast and inland fisheries reflected the importance of the new instrument of Confederation as a means of resisting New England. With the ending of reciprocity, Nova Scotia, New Brunswick and Quebec took refuge behind an organization more efficient for the checking of encroachments on British fishing grounds, the prevention of smuggling, and bargaining for a new treaty.[8]

THE OPPONENTS OF CONFEDERATION

The opponents of Confederation, like its supporters, represented diverse interests. Unlike the supporters, they had little contact across provincial boundaries, little support from the United Kingdom, and no agreement among themselves as to what alternative should be proposed. In Canada West (Ontario) most of the opponents were agrarian radicals or "Grits" who refused to follow George Brown into the coalition government. They were interested in westward expansion, but not in a link with the Maritimes, which they expected to reinforce the power of commercial interests, particularly in Montreal. Some wanted to break the link between the two halves of the Province of Canada, but on this issue they were not unanimous.

In Canada East (Quebec) a few anglophones looked forward with dismay to the revival of the political boundary between the two halves of the province, even under a federal union. Most of the opposition, however, came from francophone petit-bourgeois nationalists, the *Rouges*, who were less optimistic than Cartier about the chances of cultural survival in a multiprovince federation. Their preferred solution was a federal arrangement between the two halves of the Province of Canada, with the other colonies excluded and westward expansion indefinitely delayed.

In the Maritimes opposition came from business interests, both commercial and industrial, that feared Canadian competition. They were reinforced by other interests that desired closer contacts with the United States, especially in the area around the Bay of Fundy where ties with New England were traditionally close. Especially in Nova Scotia (and in Newfoundland, which resisted the lure of Confederation for more than eighty years) the anti-Confederationists were able to exploit a widespread popular feeling of attachment to their province as an autonomous community. Some supported Maritime union and others the status quo.

THE TERMS OF UNION

The terms of what became Canada's constitution reflected both the diversity of interests and motives behind Confederation and the ideological preferences of the colonial politicians who attended the conferences at Quebec in 1865 and London in 1866. Prominent among these motives were enthusiasm for "a Constitution similar in Principle to that of the United Kingdom," a phrase which appears in the preamble to the British North America Act, and a desire to avoid what were considered the undesirable aspects of the American constitution. John A. Macdonald in particular was obsessed with the belief, a somewhat superficial one for a man so shrewd in other respects, that the American Civil War might have been avoided if the American constitution had granted only limited and specified powers to the individual states, rather than leaving them with all powers not granted to the federal government.[9] He acknowledged that the political circumstances in 1787 had probably left the Americans with no alternative, but he was determined to avoid the same mistake himself.

Fortunately for Macdonald, circumstances were more propitious for him than they had been for Alexander Hamilton, whose views on federalism and on other political subjects had been very similar to his own. The forces of agrarian radicalism were much weaker in British North America than they had been in the thirteen colonies, and their political representatives, being on the opposition benches, were excluded from the conferences that drafted Canada's constitution. Canada also lacked any equivalent of the southern plantation owners, who had opposed the centralization desired by the Federalist merchants. In addition, there were no vested interests attached to provincial autonomy in what became Ontario and Quebec, since the governments of those provinces did not exist between 1841 and 1867. It was both easy and logical to give specifically defined powers to those governments which were to be established, while leaving the general, unspecified, or "residual" power with the government that already existed, that of Canada.

Only in the Maritimes did Macdonald have to deal with already existing governments that would have to be enticed into accepting a completely new level of government superior to themselves. Even there he was aided by discreet pressure from London and the fact that some of the Maritimers, like Charles Tupper, shared his preference for a centralized regime. The chief concerns of the Maritime delegates at the conferences were provincial revenues and representation in the Senate, rather than the division of legislative powers. The demands for provincial legislative powers came mainly from the French Canadians, for whom the establishment of a Quebec legislature was the major attraction of Confederation. The powers which they demanded for that legislature were mainly related to social institutions, education, the family, and the legal system. Even the celebrated provincial jurisdiction over "property and civil rights," expressly designed to protect Quebec's legal system by repeating a phrase first used in the Quebec Act of 1774, at first included the qualifying phrase "excepting portions thereof assigned to the General Parliament." These words were removed at the last moment by the British Colonial Office.[10]

The stated preference for "a Constitution similar in Principle to that of the United Kingdom" combined a widely shared sentiment with more pragmatic and mundane considerations. Access to British capital and markets was essential to the economic objectives of Confederation, and British assistance would be needed to defend Canada against the United States. A firm assertion of loyalty to British principles might encourage pro-Canadian sentiments in the United Kingdom, where they were not particularly strong. Many influential people in the United Kingdom believed that the colonies were economically worthless and a source of friction with the United States, and that they should be encouraged to sever their connection with Britain.

British principles also had certain implications for the constitution itself. Monarchy, which is based on the principle that political authority flows from the top downward, had never before been combined with federalism, and in a sense they were logically incompatible.

However, it suited the kind of union that Macdonald and most of his colleagues wanted to create. Ottawa would be subordinate to London and the provinces would be subordinate to Ottawa, with a British governor general in Ottawa and a federally appointed lieutenant-governor in each province, each of whom would have the power to "reserve" legislation for the final decision of the government that had appointed him. Both London and Ottawa could disallow the acts of the level of government immediately below them, even though such acts had received the assent of the governor general or lieutenant-governor. The judicial system revealed similar hierarchical notions. Ottawa would appoint the judges of the provincial courts, and it was understood, although not stated, that the final court of appeal would be the Judicial Committee of the (Imperial) Privy Council, which already exercised that function for all of the colonies.

These provisions of the BNA Act have offended constitutional purists, and led K.C. Wheare to deny that Canada really had a federal constitution, although he admitted that it functioned as a federal system in practice.[11] Their effect, however, should not be overstated. Reservation of acts by a lieutenant-governor soon became unusual, although the power was unexpectedly used in Saskatchewan as late as 1961. Disallowances of provincial legislation have been more frequent (although there has been none since 1943) but they could not prevent a determined provincial government from repeatedly adopting the same legislation, nor could the federal Parliament itself legislate in provincial areas of jurisdiction. Furthermore, an American authority stated in the 1920s that "virtually every provincial law which has been disallowed by the Dominion government during the past fifty years would probably have been declared unconstitutional if passed by an American state legislature."[12] The states in the prototype of modern federalism, at least after the Fourteenth Amendment in 1869, enjoyed no more real autonomy than the Canadian provinces.

Insofar as specification was required, the BNA Act established the framework of a central government closely resembling both its British prototype and its immediate predecessor, the government of the Province of Canada. Although the latter had experimented with the rather un-British innovation of an elected upper house, an appointed Senate was provided. The newly established (or re-established) provincial governments of Ontario and Quebec would be organized along similar lines, although Ontario was given a unicameral legislature, setting a precedent which all the other provinces eventually followed. All provinces were given the freedom to modify their own institutions, apart from the office of lieutenant-governor.

The heart of any federal constitution is the division of legislative powers. In the Quebec and London resolutions, and in the BNA Act (which followed their provisions quite closely), powers were allocated so that the central government could carry out the major objectives of

Confederation. For reasons already referred to, Parliament was given all legislative powers not specifically assigned to the provincial legislatures. The Quebec Resolutions described this as a power to make laws for "the peace, welfare, and good government of Canada," consciously or unconsciously recalling the "general welfare" clause of the United States constitution. Regrettably, the Colonial Office later changed this to "Peace, Order, and good Government," contributing to a lasting myth that the Fathers of Confederation were less "liberal," whatever that may mean, than their American counterparts.

The federal government was given unlimited power to tax and borrow, the latter being particularly important at a time when colonial governments depended on the London bond market. Tariff and commercial policy would also be under its control, as would the banking system and the currency, the postal service, weights and measures, and patents and copyrights. Jurisdiction over agriculture (and immigration) was shared with the provinces, while, at the London Conference, fisheries were placed under federal jurisdiction, for reasons already discussed. For the sake of uniformity the criminal law was placed under federal control, a departure from American practice that perhaps reflected Macdonald's experience as a defence counsel in criminal cases.

The provisions for transportation, an essential part of the economics of Confederation, were complex. The federal government was given jurisdiction over navigation and shipping, and was also required to begin building the Intercolonial Railway within six months of the union and to complete it as quickly as possible. Macdonald originally proposed to list all the means of interprovincial communication that were placed under federal authority, but roads and bridges were excluded at the suggestion of Leonard Tilley, the Premier of New Brunswick.[13] This still left the federal government with steamships, railways, canals, telegraphs, and other works and undertakings connecting two or more provinces, and with steamships connecting Canada with other countries. Parliament could also assume jurisdiction over "works" entirely within one province by declaring them to be for the general advantage of Canada. In the legislative debates on the Quebec Resolutions, Macdonald cited the Welland Canal between Lake Erie and Lake Ontario as an example of the "works" that would fall under this provision.[14]

The provinces were given responsibility for the administration of justice, apart from criminal procedure, and the organization of the courts. They would also be responsible for municipal institutions, which were well developed in the Province of Canada although not in the Maritimes. The enumerated provincial responsibilities included those matters which were then viewed as defining the distinctiveness of French Canada: education, the family, social institutions, and the law relating to "property and civil rights." The prospect of provincial control over such matters was welcomed by the French Canadian clergy, who undoubtedly foresaw that they would be able to exercise considerable influence over Quebec's provincial legislature. Religious minorities whose rights to separate educational systems were already assured "by law," would be protected from provincial interference with those rights. This provision protected the Protestant anglophones of Quebec and the Roman Catholics — mainly Irish at that time — of Ontario. Its applicability elsewhere was less clear; a few years after Confederation, New Brunswick succeeded in abolishing its Roman Catholic separate school system on the grounds that the latter existed only by custom, and not by law.[15]

The provincial governments were given certain powers over economic matters, which proved important later on. They shared jurisdiction over agriculture with the federal government, could borrow on their own credit, could incorporate companies "for provincial objects," and controlled roads, bridges, and whatever other "works" were not under federal jurisdiction.

The provinces were also given ownership of natural resources and the power to legislate concerning the public lands and the timber on those lands. With hindsight these provisions would appear to have been seriously mistaken, if the intention was to ensure the preponderance of the federal government. However, mineral resources, apart from Nova Scotia's coal, were then of little importance, and the timber trade, which had dominated British America for fifty years, was declining by the 1860s, the victim both of its own failure to conserve the resource on which it was based and of British and American actions that restricted its access to markets.[16]

The fact that provincial powers and revenues were, by design, so closely associated with this declining industry may explain Macdonald's confident belief that the provincial level of government would also decline in importance. The future apparently belonged to agriculture, commerce, manufacturing, and the opening of the West, all of which would be mainly or exclusively under federal jurisdiction.

At the Quebec Conference in 1864 a strangely prophetic discussion concerning the division of energy resource rents between the two levels of government took place. Tupper and McCully of Nova Scotia objected that the federal government might impose an export duty on coal, thus cutting into provincial royalty revenues. A.T. Galt, the Canadian Minister of Finance, replied that Ottawa would not want to impose export duties, but only to prevent the provinces from doing so. The Attorney General of Nova Scotia pointed out that Nova Scotia's royalty was not an export duty since it affected the price to all consumers, domestic and foreign.[17] The issues raised in this discussion have not yet been resolved.

Resource revenues, however, were a relatively minor aspect of public finance in 1867. All of the provinces had depended mainly on customs tariffs and excise taxes for their revenues prior to Confederation, and these sources of revenue were assigned exclusively to the federal government. The provincial power to impose direct taxes was of little immediate value, since such taxes would have been politically unacceptable. In fact the fear of direct taxation probably contributed significantly to anti-Confederation sentiment in the Maritimes. The only available solution was to make the provincial governments largely dependent on federal grants or subsidies. The Quebec Resolutions provided for grants of eighty cents per capita, based on 1861 levels of population. Since this formula did not satisfy the Maritimes, the London Conference modified it by providing that grants to New Brunswick and Nova Scotia would be based on their actual populations until each province reached a ceiling of 400 000 inhabitants. Additional grants were also provided to all provinces, ostensibly for the support of their legislatures.[18]

The terms of union clearly embodied a very centralist concept of federalism, which was perpetuated after 1867 when most of the politicians who had drafted the terms pursued their careers at the federal level, where they dominated Canadian politics for some time. The chief among them, of course, was John A. Macdonald, the principal author of the Quebec Resolutions and the BNA Act. As Prime Minister from 1867 until 1873, and again from 1878 until his death in 1891, Macdonald continued to expound the views that had inspired his constitutional draftsmanship, while at the same time he attempted to put them into practice. The Macdonaldian version of federalism, although it was increasingly challenged in the last years of Macdonald's life, thus enjoyed a more or less official status at the outset.

Macdonald was well aware, as was every other knowledgeable observer of Canadian life, that the new Dominion was a fragile and artificial creation whose impressive constitutional facade contrasted with a very limited degree of social and economic integration. He did not, however, consider the diversity of Canadian society and the persistence of local attachments to be an argument in favour of political decentralization. On the contrary, it was precisely these circumstances that made a strong central government essential. As a Hamiltonian conservative, Macdonald believed that the state could and should play an autonomous and creative role, rather than merely reflecting the social diversity that lay beneath it. A weakly integrated society needed a strong central government just as a broken leg needs a plaster cast to bind it together. With an optimism that now seems rather naive, Macdonald was convinced that the "gristle" of Confederation would "harden into bone" if the centralized constitution were given a chance to operate for several years. In a letter written in 1868 he expressed his confidence that the centripetal forces would prevail:

I fully concur with you as to the apprehension that a conflict may, ere long, arise between the Dominion and the "States' Rights" people. We must meet it, however, as best we may. By a firm yet patient course, I think the Dominion must win in the long run. The powers of the General Government are so much greater than those of the United States, in its relations with the local Governments, that the central power must win.[19]

Although the passage of time did not confirm the validity of this forecast, one can perhaps understand the confidence with which it was made in 1868. It must be remembered that Macdonald, Cartier, and other federal politicians had been members of a Canadian government before as well as after Confederation. The new Dominion had inherited from the old Province of Canada a sense of continuity and a functioning administrative machine, not to mention the recently completed buildings on Parliament Hill in Ottawa. It must have been easy to overlook how much had changed with the coming of federalism and the launching of the new provincial governments at Quebec City and Toronto. In the first few years those provincial governments were in any event almost subservient to the federal one, with which they were linked by personal and party ties. Cartier, through his personal followers and clients, practically ran the government at Quebec City, while Ontario's first premier actually occupied a seat on the government benches in Ottawa at the same time as he governed the province. Even if they had wanted to resist federal leadership, these governments would not have been able to do so since the provinces over which they presided were newly established entities with meagre administrative and political resources. Macdonald's use of the terms "General Government" and "local governments" rather than "federal" and "provincial" had some basis in fact.

These circumstances proved to be of short duration, and, in his second and longer period of office as Prime Minister, after 1878, Macdonald faced far more serious competition from the provincial governments. Yet he continued to believe that with enough persistence, the centripetal forces would triumph in the end. Inherent in his concept of federalism was the view that Canada was a nation, with national interests, whatever sources of disunity it contained. In 1865, during the parliamentary debates on the Quebec Resolutions, Macdonald had referred to "a new nationality" and had described the Maritimers as "people who are as much Canadians, I may say, as we are."[20] If there was a nation there must be national interests, and only a powerful "General Government" could express and represent them. These presumed national interests were expressed, after 1878, as the so-called "National Policy," whose three elements were a protective tariff to promote industrialization, immigration to populate the West, and a transcontinental railway.

In order to pursue what were defined as national interests, the federal government had been given extensive powers under the BNA Act, reinforced after 1869 by its control of the lands and resources in the vast territories acquired from the Hudson's Bay Company. The powers of provincial governments had been kept at a minimum in the hope that they would thus have little power to obstruct the pursuit of national interests. If they nonetheless attempted to do so, Macdonald's concept of federalism required that they be dealt with firmly. The powers of the lieutenant-governor, in his dual role as a federal officer and as the chief executive of the province, and the power of the federal government itself to disallow provincial legislation, could be used if necessary. The threat of their use might also persuade an uncooperative provincial government to mend its ways.

The existence of the western hinterlands provided a justification for the centripetal concept of federalism, as well as an opportunity for the central government to assert its authority. Although some of the economic interests that supported Confederation were deeply interested in westward expansion, the sense of urgency that led to the acquisition of the Hudson's Bay Company's empire in 1869 and the addition of British Columbia to the Dominion two years later was mainly inspired by the fear that these territories would otherwise be absorbed by the United States. British Columbia joined Confederation as a province, and Louis Riel forced a reluctant federal government to create another new province in Manitoba, but the central government and the economic interests behind it were not inclined to give the West more than a minimal degree of autonomy. It is not accidental that 77 percent of all provincial statutes disallowed by the federal government, the vast majority of them, before 1911, originated in the West.[21] The tight control over frontier settlement by the Mounted Police, and the retention of Prairie lands and resources by the federal government long after provincial governments had been organized, were part of the same pattern.

The fear that any relaxation of control would open the gates to American influence was at least partially responsible for the creation of these policies. Their legacy was an understandable resentment in the West itself, and a deeply rooted anti-western prejudice in central Canada, where many people were persuaded that westerners could not be trusted to resist American blandishments. Recent controversies over energy resources have revealed the persistence of both sets of attitudes.

Macdonald's concept of federalism recognized that in addition to national interests there were provincial, regional, and local interests. These were considered legitimate and genuine, although less important than the national interest, and to some extent the provincial governments represented them. However, they were not represented exclusively by the provincial governments. Instead, the task of representing them was shared by both levels of government. Macdonald expressed this view to the lieutenant-governor of Nova Scotia in 1886:

> *The representatives of Nova Scotia as to all questions respecting the relations between the Dominion and Province sit in the Dominion Parliament, and are the constitutional exponents of the wishes of the people with regard to such relations. The Provincial members have their powers restricted to the subjects mentioned in the BNA Act and can go no further.*[22]

In other words, Nova Scotian interests were represented through the House of Commons, the Senate, the cabinet, and other federal institutions, as well as through the provincial government. Nova Scotia's representatives in Ottawa were the proper persons to interpret its interests in regard to the matters placed under federal jurisdiction, or matters not specifically assigned to either level of government. Its representatives in Halifax only represented its interests in matters placed under provincial jurisdiction. In this particular instance, Macdonald was advising the lieutenant-governor not to grant a dissolution to Nova Scotia's Liberal government, which wanted to fight an election on the issue of secession. A provincial government, in Macdonald's view, had no authority to deal with such questions.

The implications of this theory should be obvious. The federal government represented the whole of the national interest, and a portion of provincial and local interests as well. Provincial governments could not represent the national interest at all, and represented only the portion of provincial and local interests that was not represented by the federal government. If all this was true, there could be little question of the two levels of government being equal in status.

THE INADEQUACIES OF THE CONSTITUTION

A careful reading of the British North America Act of 1867 suggests that the Fathers of Confederation had a good grasp of political economy as the subject was then understood, and that they produced a constitution well-suited to achieve the purposes for which it was designed. Railway-building and westward expansion did in fact take place. The cultural conflicts that had paralysed the Province of Canada were made more manageable. The United States was forced to accept, although not welcome, the existence of a neighbouring British Dominion, as it tacitly recognized by negotiating the Treaty of Washington in 1871. In all of these areas the British North America Act was a success.

It was less of a success, however, in serving the symbolic and ideological purposes of a constitution. "A Constitution similar in Principle to that of the United Kingdom" may have seemed an adequate statement of ideological purpose at the time, but it had little capacity to stir the masses, and as Imperial ties grew weaker it became simply unintelligible. The fact that the Act was an Imperial statute, while unavoidable, had the serious consequence, among others, that there was no official text in the French language. Thus it could hardly acquire any symbolic significance for between one-quarter and one-third of the new Dominion's population.

By the standards of today, the position accorded to French Canada in the Act was inadequate and, from the viewpoint of national unity, counterproductive. However, it reflected the economic and demographic realities of the time. There were few francophones outside of Quebec and little expectation, in an age of limited personal mobility, that there would ever be many more. Even in New Brunswick the Acadians made up only 15 percent of the population, as compared to more than one-third a century later; the ethnic composition of the province was only subsequently to be altered by the lower birth rate of the anglophones and their greater tendency to migrate to the United States. In the province of Quebec also, the anglophones constituted a higher proportion of the population than they do today. In several rural counties of Quebec they were a majority and in Montreal they comprised about half the population. Moreover, industry and commerce were almost entirely controlled by anglophones, in Quebec as elsewhere. Canadians of French ethnic origin were actually a smaller proportion of the population in every one of the original provinces than they are now, but they were a larger proportion than now of the total Canadian population, a paradox explained by the fact that the western provinces and Newfoundland, which have few French Canadians, are included in the total today.

For these reasons all French Canadian politicians took it for granted that Quebec would be bilingual, and none seems to have expressed any interest in extending bilingualism to the other provinces of the original Confederation. Institutional bilingualism at the federal level, corresponding to that which the anglophone minority enjoyed in Quebec, seemed a reasonable trade-off. A Quebec government and legislature, even with limited powers, was an improvement over the Act of Union. Moreover, Quebec was one province out of four, not one out of ten, and had approximately one-third of the seats in both houses of Parliament. Thus it was easy to be optimistic, as Cartier was, about French Canada's future under the BNA Act, and even easier to conclude that no better bargain was realistically available. Disillusionment would come later with the ungenerous response of other provinces to the growth of their francophone minorities, the development of the prairie after its annexation into an overwhelmingly anglophone region, and the slow but steady erosion of Quebec's influence in federal politics.

DEMOCRACY AND CONFEDERATION

Before leaving the subject of Confederation, it is appropriate to make some observations concerning the procedures by which the terms of the federal bargain were worked out and then brought into force. These procedures restricted effective participation to a very small number of persons, and even symbolic participation by the voters was virtually excluded. The effect was to deprive the constitution, and the federation itself, of democratic legitimacy, a problem that has become more, rather than less, acute over the years. Another unfortunate effect has been the reinforcement of an ideological notion that was very intimately associated with the denial of popular participation then and later: the so-called compact theory of Confederation.

The Fathers of Confederation, both Conservatives and Liberals, were not supporters of democracy. Universal suffrage had few supporters in the nineteenth century; John Stuart Mill, later to be considered a founder of modern liberal-democratic theory, was one of those who argued against it. Even the word "democracy" did not become respectable before the First World War, when it was adopted as a slogan of wartime propaganda, and it is arguable that the word was accepted then by political and economic elites only because it had been emptied of most of its content. One should not be surprised, therefore, that political elites in the 1860s saw no reason to consult the people about Confederation. Moreover, as Stanley Ryerson has argued, the series of difficult compromises which it involved could have made consultation hazardous:

> With all its intricately balanced commitments to the Grand Trunk directors, the Colonial office, and the governments of the Maritimes, it needed to be put through with an absolute minimum of popular involvement or debate.[23]

Ryerson was referring here to the plan for Confederation that emerged from the Quebec Conference, but the "intricately balanced commitments" had begun even earlier with the formation of the coalition government in the Province of Canada. It was in the unrecorded negotiations at that time that agreement was reached between the political representatives of what became "Quebec" and "Ontario," and that agreement was embodied in the proposals that the Canadian politicians made to their Maritime counterparts. At the Quebec Conference Canada functioned as a single province, although it had two votes in recognition of its duality. The Canadians unveiled a plan which the Maritimers were able to modify only slightly, and which became the Quebec Resolutions. Yet many important questions, particularly those pertaining to relations between the two linguistic communities in the Province of Canada, were hardly discussed at the Quebec Conference because they had been decided earlier, and because the Maritimers were not particularly interested in them. The rather placid proceedings of the Quebec Conference bore little resemblance to the Philadelphia Convention of 1787, which had had to confront both the issues that divided the thirteen colonies from one another and the issues that divided them internally.

The participants at Quebec were members of governments responsible to elected legislatures, but this did not mean that they were totally subject to those legislatures. Then as now, party discipline permitted governments to play the legislature off against the electorate, and vice versa. Charles Tupper's government in Nova Scotia, elected in 1863, did not have to face the electorate again until after Confederation had been achieved, and it also managed to avoid submitting the terms of the federal bargain to the Nova Scotia legislature, where to do so might have exposed fissures in the governing majority. Retribution came at the provincial election in 1867, when the supporters of Confederation were swept out of office, but this was too late to affect the outcome.

In New Brunswick the pro-Confederation government of Leonard Tilley had less control over the legislature, although Confederation itself was probably more popular in New Brunswick than in Nova Scotia. Unable either to risk submitting the Quebec Resolutions to the legislature or to control his caucus if he avoided doing so, Tilley requested a dissolution and was defeated at the polls. The anti-Confederation government, in turn, was forced to seek a dissolution and Tilley was returned to office in 1866, an event which suggests that the electorate had probably accepted Confederation. (The corruption and external interference in this election was about equally divided between government and opposition.) However, the legislature never had the opportunity to vote on the terms of Confederation in New Brunswick.

In the Province of Canada the Quebec Resolutions were submitted to the legislature, which debated them in the winter of 1865. They were approved by majorities in both houses and in both linguistic communities, although the latter was not of course a formal requirement for any kind of action by the legislature. In both houses agrarian radicals from Canada West, where American ideas of popular sovereignty had some support, moved that approval be deferred until the people had been given a chance to express their views, presumably in an election. Both motions were easily defeated by the government's supporters, as was a motion in the upper house that called for a referendum.[24] What the result of either an election or a referendum at that time would have been is a question that cannot now be answered; for both practical and ideological reasons the government was in no hurry to find out.

The government of the Province of Canada also refused to allow the legislature to amend the Quebec Resolutions, maintaining that they must either be accepted completely or rejected. To justify this position, Macdonald and other government spokesmen referred to "the implied obligation to deal with it as a treaty," by which they meant that to allow amendments would be to break faith with their counterparts in the Maritimes who had accepted the original terms, and would require a reopening of interprovincial negotiations.[25]

This was the origin of the celebrated "compact theory," or the view that Confederation was a contractual arrangement among provincial governments and can only be revised in any part by their unanimous consent. Ironically, this theory was later to be exploited by autonomy-minded provincial governments, some of which represented the very parties and interests that had opposed Confederation in the 1860s. Yet a deeper strain of consistency underlies the compact theory, in both its earlier and later versions. Its later adherents, like its originators, have wished to restrict popular participation in the making of important political decisions. In both cases a respectable justification for this objective has been sought by emphasizing the right of "provinces" (meaning provincial politicians) rather than the right of the people to be consulted. In thus distracting attention from the real issue, successive generations of politicians have hindered the development of a fully realized sense of political community from sea to sea. The ultimate effect in our own time has been to threaten the survival of the federal state so laboriously patched together between 1864 and 1867.

As described more fully in Chapter 10, the undemocratic procedures used to bring Confederation about not only undermined its legitimacy from the outset, but established a tradition of making fundamental constitutional changes with little or no involvement by the people. In 1982 that tradition, which the then premier of British Columbia described as "the Canadian way," was formally entrenched in our written constitution in the shape of a new explicit procedure for constitutional amendment. The British Parliament at that time renounced its own jurisdiction over Canada's constitution, but its power was surrendered to the Canadian federal and provincial governments, not to the Canadian people. The amending procedure or "formula" adopted at that time does not allow Canadians the opportunity to vote on constitutional amendments, a right enjoyed by citizens of the Swiss and Australian federations, or the possibility of electing special constitutional conventions to ratify amendments, a procedure that is available to citizens of the United States. Although Parliament and the provincial legislatures are technically involved in the Canadian amending process, the rigid party discipline that prevails at both levels of Canadian government makes the possibility that they would overturn an intergovernmental agreement exceedingly remote. There is thus no real similarity between the Canadian procedure and the process of constitutional amendment in the United States. In the latter country the separation of powers means that the disposition of constitutional amendments by Congress and the state legislatures cannot be determined or even greatly influenced by executive governments at either level. The openness of the American process is in startling contrast to the situation in Canada, where constitutional changes of the most fundamental importance are negotiated at semi-clandestine meetings among a handful of politicians, and the public are not even informed of the tradeoffs and concessions that were made to secure agreement. The agreement on the amending "formula" itself in November 1981, and the subsequent agreement on a package of further changes five and a half years later, are cases in point. The agreement of November 1981 also added significant qualifications to the Charter of Rights and Freedoms which most Canadians had assumed to be the principal item on the federal government's list of priorities. In the circumstances it is not surprising that the commitment of Canadians to Canada is so weak and that most of them appear to regard constitutional issues with a mixture of apathy, cynicism, and resentment.

NOTES

1. Frank H. Underhill, "The Conception of a National Interest," in his *In Search of Canadian Liberalism* (Toronto: Macmillan of Canada, 1961) 177.

2. Chester Martin, "British Policy in Canadian Confederation," *Canadian Historical Review*, XIII (1932) 3–19.

3. *Confederation Debates*, 53–62 and 125–46.

4. R.T. Naylor, "The rise and fall of the third commercial empire of the St. Lawrence," *Capitalism and the National Question in Canada*, ed. Gary Teeple (Toronto: University of Toronto Press, 1972) 1–42.

5. H. Clare Pentland, *Labour and Capital in Canada* (Toronto: James Lorimer, 1981) 130–31.

6. J.M.S. Careless, *Brown of the Globe*, 2 volumes (Toronto: Macmillan, 1959 and 1963).

7. *Confederation Debates*, 86.

8. Harold Innis, *The Cod Fisheries: The History of an International Economy* (New Haven: Yale University Press, 1940) 364.

9. Joseph Pope, ed., *Memoirs of Sir John A. Macdonald* (Toronto: Oxford University Press, 1930) 242–43.

10. W.R. Lederman, "Unity and Diversity in Canadian Federalism," *Canadian Bar Review LIII* (1975) 597–620.

11. K.C. Wheare, *Federal Government*, 4th ed. (New York: Oxford University Press, 1964) 18–20.

12. W.B. Munro, *American Influences on Canadian Government* (Toronto: Macmillan, 1929) 37.

13. Joseph Pope, *Confederation: Being a series of hitherto unpublished documents bearing on The British North America Act* (Toronto: Carswell, 1895) 22–30.

14. *Confederation Debates*, 40.
15. Peter M. Toner, "New Brunswick Schools and the rise of provincial rights," *Federalism in Canada and Australia: the early years*, ed. Bruce Hodgins (Waterloo: Wilfrid Laurier University Press, 1978) 125–35.
16. A.R.M. Lower, *Great Britain's Woodyard: British America and the Timber Trade* (Montreal: McGill-Queen's University Press, 1973).
17. Joseph Pope, *Confederation*, 79–80.
18. J.A. Maxwell, "Better Terms," *Queen's Quarterly*, XL (1933): 125–39.
19. Joseph Pope, ed., *Correspondence of Sir John Macdonald* (Toronto: Oxford University Press, 1921) 74–75.
20. Canada, Legislature, *Parliamentary Debates on the Subject of the Confederation of the British North American Provinces* (Quebec, 1865) 27–28.
21. Data compiled from G.V. Laforest, *Disallowance and Reservation of Provincial Legislation* (Ottawa: Queen's Printer, 1955).
22. Pope, ed., *Correspondence of Sir John Macdonald*, 379.
23. Stanley Ryerson, *Unequal Union: Confederation and the Roots of Conflict in the Canadas* (Toronto: Progress Books, 1968) 369.
24. *Confederation Debates*, 269–316, 327–33, 962–1020.
25. *Confederation Debates*, 31.

3 Judicial Interpretation of the Constitution

I do not think the United States would come to an end if we lost our power to declare an Act of Congress void. I do think the Union would be imperiled if we could not make that declaration as to the laws of the several states. For one in my place sees how often a local policy prevails with those who are not trained to national views and how often action is taken that embodies what the Commerce clause was meant to end.

OLIVER WENDELL HOLMES[1]

In Chapter 1 reference was made to A.V. Dicey's view that federalism contributed to "legalism," or to an exaggerated influence of judges and lawyers over public affairs. In the United Kingdom, at least prior to its membership in the European community, there were no legal limits on the power of Parliament and no higher authority which could strike down an act of Parliament, although Parliament itself could, of course, reverse its own decisions. This fact is the source of the familiar but somewhat misleading assertion that the United Kingdom has no written constitution. In a federation, on the other hand, legislative bodies at both the national and provincial level derive their authority from a written constitution which none of them can unilaterally amend, and which divides legislative powers between the two levels of government. The constitution is a higher form of law than any ordinary statute, and a statute may be considered "unconstitutional" if the legislating body is deemed to have exceeded the authority granted to it by the constitution. While Dicey conceded that this was at least theoretically possible under the written constitutions of certain unitary states, such as France and Belgium, he argued that in practice the courts hardly ever overruled the will of the national legislature in those countries. However, in the United States the Supreme Court struck down acts of Congress and of state legislatures quite frequently and its power to do so was "an essential property" of American federalism. Under the American system, according to Dicey, "the Bench of judges is not only the guardian but also at a given moment the master of the constitution."[2]

DOES FEDERALISM REQUIRE JUDICIAL REVIEW?

Dicey wrote at a time when the Supreme Court of the United States was unusually active in striking down legislative enactments, and he did not sufficiently emphasize, perhaps because he did not understand, the fact that its decisions were usually intended to protect the individual against government rather than to protect one level of government against the other. Since his time writers on federalism have frequently assumed that federalism implies judicial review, and vice versa. It is possible, however, that the connection between the two may be less direct and more the result of historical accident than is generally assumed. The power of the Supreme Court to overrule Congress was not specifically stated, although it may have been implied, in the United States constitution. The power was first asserted, and first used, by the Supreme Court in the celebrated case of *Marbury vs. Madison* (1803) which arose out of a trivial dispute over political patronage and had nothing to do with federalism as such. For a long time thereafter the power was used sparingly, and in fact there was only one other case of an act of Congress being struck down before the Civil War. Between 1865 and 1936 acts of Congress were declared unconstitutional about once a year, but since that time the power has again been used very sparingly. Acts of state legislatures have, of course, been struck down much more frequently, usually on the grounds that they interfere with individual rights and freedoms guaranteed by the Fourteenth Amendment.

As the quotation at the beginning of this chapter suggests, federalism may not, in fact, require that the courts have the power to strike down acts of the national legislative body. The voters are arguably the best judges of whether the central government is exercising powers that would be better left to the provinces or states. The provinces or states themselves have a variety of political and administrative means which they can use to frustrate the initiatives of the central government, and those means are typically more effective, reliable, and predictable in their outcomes than any recourse to the courts. Even Dicey had to admit that in Switzerland, an undeniably federal country, the courts cannot strike down the acts of the Federal Assembly. As he pointed out, such a power would be unnecessary there because the people themselves can strike down any statute through a referendum.[3] In other federations, such as Canada, this possibility does not exist, but elections provide opportunities to punish a central government that is believed to be encroaching on provincial jurisdiction. In Canadian federal politics the opposition parties frequently accuse the government of being insufficiently sensitive to the provinces, and these accusations probably contributed to the defeat of incumbent governments in 1896, 1957, and 1984.

There is a much stronger case, however, for the view that a viable federation requires judicial review, and at times judicial veto, of acts by the individual provinces or states. Provincial governments are not well-qualified, and are not expected, to consider the broader national interest, or the interests of persons living outside of the province's jurisdiction. Their efforts to serve the needs, or respond to the demands, of voters and business enterprises within their own boundaries may interfere with the welfare of those who reside or are located elsewhere in the country. The latter have no direct way of influencing the provincial government, even though their interests may be adversely affected by it. Apart from the inconvenience to individual groups and corporations, provinces might cause inconvenience and frustration to one another if they imposed conflicting regulations on activities that transcend their boundaries. In more technical language, provincial statutes and other decisions may create externalities against which there is no redress through the political process. Thus a judicial umpire may be needed, as Oliver Wendell Holmes observed, to identify transgressions and to enforce the rules that are needed to prevent such externalities and to enable different provinces to co-exist within a federal framework. Perhaps for this reason judicial review of provincial acts appears to exist in all federations.

Judicial decisions in constitutional cases, apart from their immediate purpose, have a secondary function of helping to define the prevailing political ideologies and values of a society. In Canada the scope for performing this function was perhaps limited by the absence of a constitutional charter or bill of rights (until 1982), and the almost exclusive preoccupation of our constitutional jurisprudence with federalism. This very fact, however, had important consequences for Canadian political ideas and ideologies. The humanities and social sciences were rather slow to develop in Canada, few intellectuals participated in politics, and the traditional parties were more interested in distributing patronage than in formulating new visions of state and society. All of this placed the burden of defining Canadian political ideas disproportionately on the judiciary, while the nature of the written constitution ensured that the ideas articulated by the judiciary would be concerned to a significant and perhaps excessive degree with federalism. Thus the Canadian preoccupation with federalism, expressed in the joke reported on the first page of this book, is not accidental or inexplicable. What is regrettable is that the function of defining the nation's political beliefs was so largely left, until 1949, in the hands of a tribunal located *outside* of the nation's boundaries.

THE JUDICIAL COMMITTEE AND ITS LEGACY

In contrast to the United States, Canada did not provide explicitly for a Supreme Court in its federal constitution, but Parliament was given the power to establish "a General Court of Appeal" and any other courts that might be needed. (The federal government, unlike its American counterpart, was also given the power to appoint the judges of the superior, district, and county courts in each province, placing most of the judicial patronage in federal hands.) After an unsuccessful effort by Macdonald, the Supreme Court of Canada was finally established by Alexander Mackenzie's Liberal government in 1875, eight years after Confederation.[4]

Two reasons explain the relative lack of urgency in establishing the Supreme Court. The first is that the powers of disallowance and reservation were available as a first line of defence against unconstitutional actions by the provincial legislatures. The second and more important is that "a General Court of Appeal" for the British overseas empire, including Canada, already existed in the shape of the Judicial Committee of the Privy Council.

Strictly speaking, the Judicial Committee, as its name suggests, was not really a court at all. Its origins lay in the prerogative power of the Crown to dispense justice, a power that was ended in the British Isles by the bourgeois revolution of the seventeenth century but that survived in the overseas empire, where the regular administration of justice was assumed to be less reliable and effective than in the metropolis. British subjects overseas, not having access to regular British courts, could appeal for justice "to the foot of the throne," and the practice developed of having a committee to advise the Crown on how to respond to such appeals. In 1834 the practice was given a statutory basis by the Imperial Parliament, and the Judicial Committee that was to play such a large role in Canadian history came into existence. Formally it remained a committee to advise the Crown rather than a court issuing definitive judgments, although in practice its recommendations were always incorporated without modification in the Crown's decision. Because it was supposed to offer advice, its recommendations were always, in theory, unanimous, and there were no dissents or minority opinions such as now occur frequently on the Supreme Courts of both Canada and the United States. Another important characteristic of the Judicial Committee was that a large number of persons were members of it at any particular time for a variety of reasons, while cases were heard by panels of no more than five members. Consequently, its judgments were less predictable, since their outcome might depend on who was selected to hear a particular case. For example, two similar Canadian cases, the *Radio reference* of 1932 and the *Labour Conventions reference* of 1937, were heard by completely different panels of judges despite the lapse of only five years, a circumstance that may explain the apparent lack of consistency between the two decisions. Furthermore, since the Judicial Committee was technically an advisory body rather than a court, it was not bound by the doctrine of *stare decisis*, which requires courts to make their decisions consistent with earlier decisions of courts at the same, or at a higher, level.

The Mackenzie government attempted to abolish appeals to the Judicial Committee when it established the Supreme Court, but the idea was shelved because of vigorous opposition from the Colonial Office in London. Ironically, the abolition of appeals was also opposed by John A. Macdonald, although the Judicial Committee's decisions were to play a decisive part in undermining his plans for a highly centralized federation. Appeals were not, in fact, abolished until 1949, with the result that for almost a century the most influential concepts of Canadian federalism were mainly defined by men who had no practical knowledge of Canada or of federalism, and who were not even required to live in that country. The Supreme Court of Canada demonstrated some independence in its early years, but as time went on it increasingly deferred to the doctrines laid down by the Judicial Committee. Even if if had not done so it would have had little effect, since any of its decisions could be overruled. Many cases involving the interpretation of the federal constitution were appealed directly from the superior courts of the provinces to the Judicial Committee, giving the Supreme Court no opportunity to rule on them at all.

Since Canada, until 1982, lacked any equivalent of the U.S. Bill of Rights or the Fourteenth Amendment, Canadian constitutional jurisprudence was only occasionally and almost accidentally concerned with the relationship between the individual and the state. Instead, its overwhelming preoccupation was with federalism, and particularly with defining the legislative powers of Parliament and the provincial legislatures. Cases that required the courts and the Judicial Committee to perform this task sometimes arose out of disputes between individuals or corporations, one of whom might claim to be acting in accordance with a statute while the other would respond that the statute was beyond the powers (*ultra vires*) of the legislative body that had adopted it. In other cases a government or its attorney general might be sued by an individual or corporation who was inconvenienced by a particular statute and who would claim that the statute was *ultra vires*. A third way in which constitutional issues can arise is through reference cases, a procedure whereby a government can request an opinion on the constitutionality of an actual, or even a hypothetical, statute without waiting for it to be challenged by private litigants.

In the United States, and even in Australia, the courts have refused to hear such cases, arguing that they violate the principle of judicial independence from the executive. In Canada, however, provisions in the Supreme Court Act and in various provincial statutes allowing for reference cases have never been challenged. Whether they originate at the federal or provincial level, reference cases can always be appealed to the highest tribunal, which until 1949 meant the Judicial Committee. Many important cases relating to the division of powers originated in this way.

The Fathers of Confederation, as noted in the preceding chapter, provided elaborate lists of both federal and provincial legislative powers, unlike their American counterparts who had not specified the powers of the state legislatures and had defined those of Congress in rather vague and general terms. No sensible reading of Sections 91 and 92 can avoid the conclusion that the intention was to give most powers to Parliament and only narrowly defined powers to the provincial legislatures. Nonetheless, some of the phrases used were ambiguous and the enumeration of provincial powers, although apparently intended to limit them, actually provided plausible arguments for limiting federal powers. Such arguments would not have been available if the American prototype had been followed more closely. This was particularly true of Section 92-13, Property and Civil Rights in the Province, which was open to a variety of interpretations. In theory this provision should have been more than counterbalanced by the preamble to Section 91, giving Parliament a general power to legislate "for the Peace, Order and Good Government of Canada, in relation to all Matters not coming within the Classes of Subjects by this Act assigned exclusively to the Legislatures of the Provinces." In practice, as will be shown, that provision was not always given the most generous interpretation.

The first important case regarding the distribution of powers was *Citizens' Insurance Company vs. Parsons*, decided in 1881.[5] The insurance company attempted to avoid payment of a claim by arguing that the Ontario statute regulating fire insurance policies was *ultra vires*, since only Parliament could regulate trade and commerce. The Judicial Committee ruled that the phrase "Regulation of Trade and Commerce" in Section 91 could not refer to the regulation of any specific industry (such as insurance) but only to regulations of a general character affecting the economy as a whole or affecting trade or commerce that crossed a provincial boundary. Insurance, unlike banking, was not specifically included among the federal powers and should be regarded as falling under the rubric of property and civil rights. Mr. Parsons was compensated for the fire in his warehouse, and Ontario's ability to manage its own economy, which meant the greater part of the Canadian economy, was off to an early start.

Three important cases in the latter part of the nineteenth century were concerned with the regulation of alcoholic beverages. Brewing and distilling, then as now, were among Canada's major industries, and taverns played an important part in the social and political life, such as it was, of the young Dominion. On the other hand, both levels of government were under pressure from temperance groups and the Protestant churches to restrict and regulate drinking, or to abolish it entirely. In the 1882 case of *Russell vs. the Queen*, the Judicial Committee upheld the Mackenzie government's Canada Temperance Act, which severely restricted the sale of intoxicating beverages, as a valid exercise of Parliament's power to legislate for the "Peace, Order and Good Government of Canada."[6] In doing so it maintained that the legislation was intended to regulate public order and safety, and thus could not be included within property and civil rights or any of the other enumerated provincial powers. It was therefore not necessary to say whether it pertained to the regulation of trade and commerce, as the Supreme Court had earlier declared, since any powers not specifically given to the legislatures could be exercised by Parliament under the "Peace, Order and Good Government" clause. However, in the case of *Hodge vs. the Queen* a year later, the Judicial Committee ruled that the provinces also had the power to regulate the liquor traffic within their boundaries, to impose penalties for violations of the law, and to delegate their powers to municipalities.[7] In 1885 it struck down, without giving reasons, a federal statute that would have given officials appointed by the federal government the power to issue liquor licences. Possibly the reasons for this decision were considered obvious since "Shop, Saloon, Tavern . . . and other Licenses" are assigned to provincial jurisdiction by Section 92.9.

In 1896 a reference case, originating with the government of Ontario, gave the Judicial Committee the opportunity to express further thoughts on the beverage industry, and also to do something which it had explicitly refused to do in the Hodge case, namely to lay down general rules for the interpretation of the BNA Act.[8] The task was assumed by Lord Watson, a Scottish Conservative, who was the dominant influence on the Judicial Committee in the last decade of the nineteenth century. Possibly because he belonged to a minority nation within a unitary state, Watson was very sympathetic to the Canadian provinces in their efforts to maximize their powers in relation to the federal government. The 1896 decision upheld an Ontario statute allowing for prohibition by local option and also ruled, more hypothetically, that the province could prohibit the sale or production of any alcohol within its borders. The decision was chiefly important, however, in the rules that it laid down for interpreting the peace, order and good government power, which it seemed to regard as little more than a supplement to Parliament's enumerated powers, and one which could not be used to "trench" on the enumerated powers of the legislatures. In support of this view, Watson produced a new interpretation of the concluding part of Section 91. It states that any matter coming within the enumerated federal powers "shall not be deemed to come within the Class of Matters of a merely local or private Nature" about which the provinces can legislate. Although on the face of it this sentence appears to be designed as a limitation on the scope of Section

92.16, Watson chose to interpret it as applying to all of the sub-sections of Section 92 and as a limitation on federal rather than on provincial power.

The practical effect of the 1896 decision was to place the federal and provincial levels of government on a basis of equality. In doing so it reinforced an earlier judgment delivered by Lord Watson which had not been concerned with the division of legislative powers at all but which provided a more explicit and memorable statement of his views on Canadian federalism. This was the *Maritime Bank* case, in which in 1892 the Judicial committee was called upon to determine whether the provincial government in New Brunswick possessed the Crown's traditional prerogative of priority over ordinary creditors in the collection of debts. In giving an affirmative answer to this seemingly technical question, it based its reasoning on the highly questionable assumption that the BNA Act had not altered the relationship between the Crown and the provincial governments, and that the latter were therefore equal in dignity and status with the federal government.

This view, which directly contradicted two earlier decisions of the Supreme Court of Canada, was clearly contrary to the intentions of Sir John A. Macdonald (who had died the previous year) and was given no visible support by the actual terms of the BNA Act of 1867. Section 91 of that document asserts that the Queen is part of the legislative process at the federal level, but she is not mentioned in Section 92, which outlines the legislative powers of the provinces. The lieutenant-governor of a province represents, and is appointed by, the federal government, not the Crown. None of this inhibited Lord Watson from asserting that:

> the object of the Act was neither to weld the provinces into one, nor to subordinate provincial governments to a central authority, but to create a federal government in which they should all be represented, entrusted with the exclusive administration of affairs in which they had a common interest, each province retaining its independence and autonomy.[9]

This decision, or more precisely the reasoning on which it was based, fundamentally altered the whole nature of Canada's federal constitution. It appeared to lend credence to the argument that the purpose of Confederation had been to protect and promote provincial interests rather than to create a new nation, and it did so just as the generation that had direct memories of the Confederation negotiations and debates was passing from the scene. Henceforth, the ideological weight of Imperial authority was placed on the side of those who espoused provincial autonomy, and the supporters of centripetal federalism were placed on the defensive.

When Lord Watson was on the bench the Judicial Committee,

despite its apparent enthusiasm for the provinces, never actually invalidated any federal legislation. That task was largely left to Watson's disciple, Viscount Haldane, who was the most influential member of the Judicial Committee from 1912 until 1928. Haldane's career illustrates the Shakespearian observation that "the evil that men do lives after them; the good is oft interred with their bones." His achievements as a philosophical scholar, and as the minister who reorganized the British Army in time for the First World War, are largely forgotten. His sometimes bizarre interpretations of the British North America Act, on the other hand, still influence the lives of millions who have never heard his name.

Various explanations, none of them conclusive, have been offered for Haldane's apparent antipathy to federal legislation, including his Scottish origin, his Hegelianism, his resentment at the anti-imperialist policies of the Laurier government, his admiration for Lord Watson, his paternalistic attitude toward the provinces, and the fact that he had been a successful counsel for the Province of Quebec at the very outset of his legal career.[10] J.R. Mallory has suggested that the Judicial Committee in the Haldane era was not so much opposed to federal legislation as it was opposed to interventionist government in general, and supportive of the unregulated private enterprise economy.[11] This view is given credence by the large number of provincial statutes that were also struck down, most frequently on the grounds that they imposed indirect taxation. It is also perhaps relevant that the United States Supreme Court struck down an unusually large number of regulatory statutes at roughly the same time, including acts of both Congress and the state legislatures. Thus it is at least arguable that business interests throughout North America were increasingly relying on the courts to protect them against growing populism and collectivism, with federalism providing merely a convenient excuse. In fairness to Haldane and the Judicial Committee, it should be pointed out that the Supreme Court of Canada followed the general trend.

In 1914 Haldane delivered the Judicial Committee's judgment in *John Deere Plow Company vs. Wharton*, which struck down British Columbia legislation affecting a company with a federal charter.[12] The chief importance of the opinion, however, was its assertion that the federal government's power to incorporate companies derived from the "Peace, Order and Good Government" clause, while its power to impose limitations on their activities was a part of the power to regulate trade and commerce. This rather subtle distinction would be used by Haldane in a later cause to support the assertion that the trade and commerce power might be used to supplement the federal government's general powers, but where the latter were not applicable, the trade and commerce power had little or no effect.

The so-called *Alberta Insurance Reference* of 1916 continued Haldane's assault on the trade and commerce power. (The case had nothing to do with Alberta, which merely happened to be first in alphabetical order of the five provinces that intervened as respondents.) The Insurance Act had been adopted by Parliament in 1910, but the Conservative government that took office a year later apparently had doubts about its validity and referred the question to the Supreme Court. The act required all insurance companies operating in Canada to obtain a federal licence. Four justices of the Supreme Court thought it was *ultra vires* but two, including the Chief Justice, thought otherwise. In a rather brief opinion, considering the importance of the case, Haldane reiterated the narrow interpretation of the trade and commerce power in *Citizen's Insurance Company vs. Parsons*. He rejected any analogy between the insurance industry and the liquor trade whose regulation had been upheld in *Russell vs. the Queen*, and declared the size and importance, or "dimensions" of the industry to be irrelevant.[13] The latter statement indicated that Haldane was even more rigid in restricting federal powers than his mentor, Lord Watson, who had suggested in the 1896 reference on liquor legislation that the "dimensions" of a problem might determine whether it fell under the "Peace, Order and Good Government" clause. The most Haldane would concede was that foreign insurance companies seeking to operate in Canada could be required to have a federal licence, but such companies controlled only a small part of the industry.

The even more celebrated *Board of Commerce* case in 1922 gave Haldane another opportunity to expound a narrow interpretation of the trade and commerce power.[14] It was also in this opinion that he invented the doctrine, which regrettably has survived to the present day; that the "Peace, Order and Good Government" clause refers to an "emergency" power that can only be used in exceptional circumstances. The case concerned two statutes, the Board of Commerce Act and the Combines and Fair Prices Act, which the coalition government had adopted in 1919 to control prices and prevent collusion among producers or merchants at a time of unprecedented inflation and growing popular unrest. The Supreme Court had been evenly divided on the validity of the legislation and thus issued no judgment. Haldane, on behalf of the Judicial Committee, declared that the legislation was primarily concerned with property and civil rights, and thus *ultra vires*. He further declared that it could not be considered legislation for the peace, order and good government of Canada except possibly in the event of "war and famine." (The First World War had ended a few months before the legislation was adopted.) Although the federal government's lawyers made the reasonable argument that the legislation was intended to regulate trade and commerce, Haldane rejected that argument by referring to his earlier opinion, in the *John Deere* case, that the power to regulate trade and commerce was virtually meaningless unless it could be said to supplement another federal power. He also said that the legislation could not be regarded as criminal law (although it provided for the imprisonment of offenders) since the subject matter did not "by its very nature" belong to the domain of criminal jurisprudence.

Worse was to come in the case of *Toronto Electric Commissioners vs. Snider* three years later. This decision overturned a federal statute enacted eighteen years previously, the Industrial Disputes Investigation Act, on the grounds that labour relations were a part of "property and civil rights" and therefore under provincial jurisdiction.[15] The stage was thus set for the union-bashing activities of Mitchell Hepburn, Maurice Duplessis, and a score of their imitators in provinces large and small. Since the assertion of a relatively robust federal legislative power in *Russell vs. the Queen* was becoming increasingly incongruous with the Judicial Committee's later opinions, Haldane chose to rationalize that embarrassing precedent by referring to the emergency doctrine which he had invented in the *Board of Commerce* case. It must have been the case, he solemnly asserted, that drunkenness in 1882 had been so widespread as to resemble "an epidemic of pestilence" and that federal legislation had been needed "to protect the nation from disaster." However, such mundane matters as inflation or unemployment apparently did not justify the same degree of concern.

The Haldane approach to the BNA Act did not end with his death in 1928, for a year later the Judicial Committee invoked the familiar spectre of "property and civil rights" to strike down a provision requiring fish processing plants to have a federal licence. This decision included the implausible assertion that "no reasonable construction" of the phrase "seacoast and inland fisheries" could include the processing plants within federal jurisdiction.[16] "Property and civil rights," on the other hand, could apparently include almost anything.

By 1931, however, the Judicial Committee seemed to have had a change of heart, possibly because the soon to be enacted Statute of Westminster, releasing Canada and the other "Dominions" from the constraints of the Colonial Laws Validity Act, would make the abolition of Canadian appeals to the Judicial Committee a practical possibility. At any rate, three decisions in the space of little more than a year somewhat restored the Judicial Committee's popularity with Canadian nationalists, and probably staved off the threat of abolition for another decade.

The first of these decisions, *Proprietary Articles Trade Association vs. Attorney General of Canada*, used the federal criminal law power to uphold the Combines Investigation Act, and thus discarded the narrow interpretation of that power which Haldane had favoured in the Board of Commerce case.[17] This was soon followed by the *Aeronautics Reference*, which restored the "Peace, Order and Good Government" clause to something of the vitality it had enjoyed in *Russell vs. the Queen*. The federal government had referred the question of jurisdiction over air transport to the Supreme Court after Quebec had challenged its claim to exclusive jurisdiction, and the Supreme Court had upheld the provincial jurisdiction. The Judicial Committee reversed this verdict, partly on the grounds that air transport was governed by a treaty which imposed obligations on the entire British Empire, and that Parliament had the power to implement such treaties under Section 132 of the BNA Act. However, the decision also stated that those aspects of air transport not governed by the treaty and not falling under subjects, such as postal service, explicitly assigned in the BNA Act were also under federal jurisdiction because they related to the peace, order and good government of Canada. Lord Sankey, who delivered the judgment, also said:

> . . . while the Courts should be jealous in upholding the charter of the Provinces as enacted in s. 92 it must no less be born in mind that the real object of the Act was to give the central Government those high functions and almost sovereign powers by which uniformity of legislation might be secured on all questions which were of common concern to all the Provinces as members of a constituent whole.[18]

The third case, the *Radio Reference*, was analogous in that it also involved regulatory jurisdiction over a technology that had not existed in 1867. A treaty was also involved, but with the significant difference that Canada had signed the treaty as a sovereign state, making the reference to imperial obligations in Section 132 inapplicable. However, as Viscount Dunedin put it in the Judicial Committee's judgment, "it comes to the same thing."[19] The power to implement treaties, now that Canada had achieved virtual independence, was implied by the general power to make laws for the peace, order and good government of Canada. In any event, broadcasting by its very nature extended beyond the limits of any province.

Any rejoicing which these three decisions may have caused in the centralist camp was shown to have been premature early in 1937, when the Judicial Committee delivered its opinions in what came to be called the "Bennett New Deal" cases. In 1930 the Conservative party led by R.B. Bennett had taken office just as the Canadian economy was collapsing under the impact of the Great Depression. By 1934 the economic situation had worsened and the government appeared to have little or no prospect of avoiding defeat in the next election. Nonetheless, in the last year of its mandate the government brought forward innovative legislation to alleviate the effects of the economic crisis. The business community was alarmed and the voters were apparently not impressed, since they returned Mackenzie King and the Liberals to office in October 1935. Within a few weeks the new government referred much of Bennett's legislation — dubbed the "New Deal" in imitation of President Franklin D. Roosevelt — to the Supreme Court, and six of the latter body's decisions were then appealed to the Judicial Committee. The federal case was argued by a team of lawyers including Louis St. Laurent, who had not yet entered politics but who would later succeed Mackenzie King as Liberal leader and Prime Minister. The provinces of British Columbia, New Brunswick, Ontario, and Quebec intervened in some or all of the six cases, mainly to argue that the legislation was *ultra vires*.

The Judicial Committee dealt with the cases in six simultaneous decisions, five of them delivered by Lord Atkin and one by Lord Thankerton. Three of the decisions actually upheld federal powers to prohibit discriminatory or predatory price-fixing, to regulate various other trade practices, and to assist financially destitute farmers in coming to terms with their creditors. Federal powers in relation to the criminal law, trade and commerce, and bankruptcy and insolvency were the bases of these decisions. However, the remaining three decisions, which declared five of the Bennett statutes to be *ultra vires*, attracted considerably more attention and controversy, then and later.

The first of these, usually referred to as the *Labour Conventions* case, struck down the Weekly Rest in Industrial Undertakings Act, the Minimum Wages Act, and the Limitation of Hours of Work Act.[20] Counsel for the federal government admitted that all three acts dealt with matters normally considered a part of property and civil rights. (It will be remembered that labour relations had been placed in this category by *Toronto Electric Commissioners vs. Snider*.) However, they argued, as R.B. Bennett had done earlier, that the three statutes really implemented Canada's obligations under three labour conventions, or international treaties, which Canada had ratified. The decision in the *Radio Reference* seemed to suggest that measures necessary to implement treaties were a federal responsibility, regardless of their impact on the various fields of provincial jurisdiction. (Parenthetically, it might be noted that the Supreme Court of the United States had reached a similar conclusion regarding that country's federal constitution in 1918, when it ruled that an international treaty protecting migratory birds took precedence over the game laws of the individual states.) British Columbia and New Brunswick argued against the federal statutes. Ontario also rejected the argument that a treaty could override provincial jurisdiction, but it expressed approval of the three statutes and hoped that they could be upheld on other grounds. The Judicial Committee, in a decision that some observers have considered to be inconsistent with its earlier decision in the *Radio Reference*, stated that the power to implement treaties was divided between the federal and provincial levels of government, depending on whether the subject matter of the treaty falls under federal or provincial jurisdiction. Lord Atkin described the situation in a memorable metaphor: "While the ship of state now sails on larger ventures and into foreign waters she still retains the watertight compartments which are an essential part of her original structure."[21] In other words, Canada's new international status did not alter the existing federal division of powers which had been devised for a federation within the British Empire. This was the most consequential of all the "New Deal" decisions, and one of the most important in the entire history of the Judicial Committee. A generation later it would provide the rationale for Quebec and other provinces to challenge the federal government's exclusive power to conduct foreign policy, on the grounds that since the implementing power was divided, the treaty-making power should be also. This line of reasoning had been foreshadowed in Ontario's argument before the Judicial Committee, although it was not endorsed by the Judicial Committee itself.

The second decision struck down the Employment and Social Insurance Act, which had attempted to establish a system of unemployment insurance. The federal government argued, reasonably enough in the circumstances, that the problem of unemployment had attained such dimensions as to be a national problem related to the peace, order and good government of Canada, and that the provinces could not deal with it individually because they could not control interprovincial migration. Ontario supported this position and New Brunswick was the only province to oppose it. However, the Judicial Committee ruled that the legislation dealt with property and civil rights, since it could force employees and employers to contribute to an insurance fund.[22]

Finally, the Judicial Committee struck down the Natural Products Marketing Act and a subsequent amendment, which together established a Dominion Marketing Board. The Act allowed the Board to assume control over the marketing of various agricultural commodities provided the producers of the commodity in question requested this and provided at least a portion of the produce was traded outside the province of origin.[23] British Columbia, whose own efforts to establish a marketing board had been ruled *ultra vires* a few years previously, supported the federal scheme but New Brunswick, Ontario, and Quebec argued against it. The Judicial Committee found that the legislation intruded into the area of property and civil rights within the provinces, since its terms implied the admission that some of the produce might *not* be traded outside the province of origin. In effect, this was the reverse of the argument that had been used to strike down British Columbia's legislation on the grounds that it interfered with the regulation of trade and commerce. Although the term "Catch 22" had not been invented in 1937, this was certainly a classic illustration of its meaning. Lord Atkin vaguely suggested that co-operation between the two levels of government might resolve the problem, but he was not very explicit as to how this might be accomplished.

Even though they largely confirmed the findings of the Supreme Court, these decisions in the midst of the worst economic crisis in Canadian history caused widespread consternation and indignation. The Judicial Committee appeared to have made a mockery of the phrase "Peace, Order and Good Government." The federal government responded with a Royal Commission on Dominion-Provincial Relations, a constitutional amendment to place unemployment insurance securely under federal jurisdiction, and the setting in motion of a process that culminated in the abolition of appeals to the Judicial Committee in 1949.

In its last years as Canada's final court of appeal, the Judicial Committee struck down only one more piece of federal legislation: a prohibition of margarine which it ruled to be an improper use of the criminal law power.[24] On the other hand, it reaffirmed that the Canada Temperance Act was legislation for the peace, order and good government of Canada, admitted that the Parliament of Canada now had the power to abolish appeals in constitutional cases, and significantly broadened federal jurisdiction over highway transport.[25] This more liberal trend, however, could not reverse the federal government's determination to abolish appeals to the Judicial Committee. The necessary amendment to the Supreme Court Act was adopted by Parliament soon after Louis St. Laurent became Prime Minister.

THE JUDICIAL COMMITTEE'S REPUTATION

Not surprisingly, the Judicial Committee's interpretations of the distribution of legislative powers were widely and severely criticized. One of the earliest and most persistent critics was F.R. Scott, professor and later dean of law at McGill University, who published the first of his many articles on the subject in 1930, and continued to express the same views long after appeals to the Judicial Committee had been abolished.[26] Scott argued that the Judicial Committee had distorted the centralist intentions of the Fathers of Confederation. As a social democrat and one of the founders of the CCF party, he also believed that a strong central government was even more necessary in the twentieth century — to redistribute income, provide social security, and constrain the power of big business — than it had been in the nineteenth. Finally, as a civil libertarian, he was unimpressed with the record of provincial governments and legislatures in relation to their religious, ethnic, and ideological minorities.

Another eloquent critic of the Judicial Committee was W.F. O'Connor, the legal and parliamentary counsel to the Senate at the time of the "New Deal" decisions. In response to those decisions, the Senate adopted a resolution directing O'Connor to investigate whether the distribution of powers in the BNA Act reflected the intentions of the

Fathers of Confederation, whether the Judicial Committee's interpretations had been faithful to those intentions and to the text of the Act,
and whether any formal amendments were necessary. O'Connor's
report, published in 1939, demonstrated that the text of the Act was
faithful to the intentions of the Fathers but that the Judicial Committee
had so completely distorted the meaning of the Act as to give Canada
virtually a new constitution.[27] He recommended not constitutional
amendment but a return to strict observance of the constitution with
which Canada had originally been provided.

Bora Laskin, who would later be Chief Justice of Canada from 1973
until 1984, was also critical of the Judicial Committee, and especially
of its narrow interpretations of the peace, order and good government
power. In an article published in 1947, Laskin concluded that Canada
had paid a heavy price for Lord Watson's determination to uphold
provincial autonomy, but that what had resulted had been not provincial autonomy in any positive sense but rather the inability of any
government to deal effectively with social and economic problems of
national significance.[28]

As memories of the Depression faded, and as provincialism became
more popular in academic circles after 1960, retrospective evaluations
of the Judicial Committee began to change as well. Critics had accused
it of ignoring both the socioeconomic realities of Canada and the
literal text of the BNA Act, but defenders of the Judicial Committee
denied one or the other, although rarely both, of these allegations.
Suggesting that the BNA Act had been too centralized for Canada's
needs, Pierre Elliott Trudeau told an academic audience in 1964 that if
the Judicial Committee had not leaned toward provincialism, "Quebec separatism might not be a threat today: it might be an accomplished fact."[29] Not long afterward, a book by G.P. Browne attempted to
refute the O'Connor report, arguing that the Judicial Committee's decisions had been logical, consistent, and faithful to the terms of the BNA
Act.[30] An influential article by Alan Cairns in 1971 provided a somewhat more qualified case for the defence.[31] Cairns admitted that the
Judicial Committee had its weaknesses, including its remoteness from
Canada, its frequent changes of personnel, and its failure to explain its
own motives, but he suggested that it had creatively adapted an over-
centralized constitution to a diversified country and that most of its
decisions, including those in the Bennett New Deal cases, were in
accordance with the wishes of most Canadians. Gil Remillard, before
he became Minister of Intergovernmental Affairs in the second
Bourassa government, praised Watson and Haldane for disregarding
the centralist bias of the BNA Act and thus allowing Quebec to flourish
within Canadian federalism.[32] By the time Remillard's book appeared
in 1980, the Supreme Court of Canada had in its turn become a focus of
controversy. Like the frogs in Aesop's fable who rejected both King Log
and King Stork, Canadians are sometimes difficult to satisfy.

THE SUPREME COURT AFTER 1949

With the abolition of appeals to the Judicial Committee in 1949, the Supreme Court of Canada became supreme in fact as well as in name. Simultaneously, the number of justices was increased from seven to nine, (and the representation from Quebec increased from two to three). The minimum number of justices required to hear a case remained at five.

For more than two decades after it became supreme, the Supreme Court of Canada attracted little criticism, but less praise. Unlike Americans, Canadians were not accustomed to regarding their Supreme Court as one of the three great branches of the state, and the Court itself seemed to shun publicity. Most of its time continued to be occupied with ordinary disputes that had no constitutional significance, or with criminal appeals. Provincial governments did not produce much controversial legislation in those years, and federal governments were generally cautious in exercising Parliament's legislative powers. "Co-operative federalism," as defined in Chapter 9 of this book, was at its height, and the federal-provincial agenda was dominated by tax-sharing and conditional grants, rather than by the competitive exercise of regulatory powers that had previously, and would again, often require judicial settlement.

Insofar as it was called upon to interpret the constitution, the Supreme Court, in those years, did interpret Parliament's legislative powers more generously than the Judicial Committee had done before 1949. In the quarter century that followed the abolition of appeals no federal statute was declared unconstitutional on the grounds that it trespassed on provincial jurisdiction. On the other hand, the Court was also relatively permissive in dealing with provincial legislation. In the years 1950 through 1970 more than two-thirds of the cases involving the constitutionality of provincial statutes resulted in the statute being upheld. The Judicial Committee had invalidated about half of all the provincial statutes upon which it had ruled.

The first important constitutional case to arise following the abolition of appeals was a rather peculiar one. The government of Nova Scotia drafted a bill allowing that province to delegate its power over labour relations to the Parliament of Canada, and also to accept powers delegated in the reverse direction. The bill was referred to the provincial Supreme Court and then on appeal to the Supreme Court of Canada. Both courts found that the delegation procedure was unconstitutional.[33] More significant in the long run was the case of *Prince Edward Island Potato Marketing Board vs. Willis* a year later, which distinguished between the delegation of rule-making powers to an administrative body, and the delegation of law-making powers from one legislature to another.[34] In this case the Court ruled that the federal government could legally delegate powers to regulate interprovincial trade to a provincial marketing board. This decision overcame the stalemate which the Judicial Committee had caused by ruling that provincial boards could only market produce consumed within the province of origin, while federal boards could only market produce consumed elsewhere.

In the same year that it decided the *Willis* case, the Supreme Court struck down an effort by a Manitoba municipality to regulate the location of an airport, and in doing so based the federal jurisdiction over aeronautics firmly on the peace, order and good government power rather than on the now obsolete provision regarding imperial treaties.[35] This case, *Johanneson vs. West St. Paul*, marked a return to the notion of a broad residual power as in *Russell vs. the Queen*. In the 1966 case of *Munro vs. National Capital Commission*, the Court used the peace, order and good government power to uphold a federal agency's right to expropriate farmland in the vicinity of Ottawa to create a greenbelt around the national capital.[36] No one argued the need to demonstrate that suburban sprawl resembled Haldane's "epidemic of pestilence." Clearly Parliament's general legislative power had come a long way from the nadir which it reached in 1925.

The power to regulate trade and commerce was also given a somewhat broader interpretation. In 1957 a reference case involving Ontario legislation on the familiar subject of agricultural marketing gave the court the opportunity to define the meaning of that power.[37] Although only one proposed amendment to the provincial act was struck down, and that only on the grounds that it would impose an indirect tax on producers, four of the justices provided broad and liberal interpretation of the trade and commerce power, rejecting Haldane's notion of it as an "ancillary" or supplementary power and recognizing the impracticality of a rigid distinction between interprovincial and intraprovincial trade. A year later in *Murphy vs. CPR*, this broad notion of the trade and commerce power was used to uphold the Canadian Wheat Board's monopoly over the grain trade, including grain consumed within its province of origin.[38] In *Caloil vs. Attorney General of Canada* (1971), the Supreme Court ruled that Parliament had the power to prohibit the shipment of a commodity from one province to another.[39]

Of the relatively few cases striking down provincial enactments in this period, the most celebrated concerned civil liberties in the province of Quebec under the right-wing government of Maurice Duplessis. Some of these cases involved administrative decisions or municipal by-laws, and not all of them raised constitutional issues. One that did was *Switzman vs. Elbling*, decided in 1957.[40] This struck down Duplessis' notorious "padlock law," adopted in 1937 with the support of most of the Liberal opposition, which had allowed the attorney general of the province to padlock premises v'hich he believed were used "for the propagation of communism." Switzman,

whose apartment had been padlocked by the police in 1949, was sued
for damages by his landlady. Elbling and his lawyers responded by
claiming that the law was unconstitutional since it intruded on the
federal jurisdiction over criminal law. F.R. Scott argued Switzman's
case before the Supreme Court of Canada, which accepted the argument. The sole dissenting vote was cast by Justice Taschereau, whose
father had been the Liberal premier of Quebec from 1920 until 1936.
Outside of Quebec the decision was generally applauded.

An important reference case decided in 1967 involved both the
ownership of and regulatory jurisdiction over mineral resources under
the Pacific Ocean in the vicinity of British Columbia. When the federal and provincial governments were unable to agree on this question, the former referred it to the Supreme Court. The Court ruled that
the territorial sea, immediately adjacent to the coast, had not been part
of the colony of British Columbia before Confederation and therefore
was a federal responsibility. The argument regarding the outer continental shelf, traditionally regarded as international territory, was
more interesting. An international treaty of 1958, drafted under the
auspices of the United Nations, had given Canada and other countries
certain rights over continental shelves adjacent to their territories. The
Supreme Court in a unanimous "joint opinion," ruled that these rights
should be exercised by the federal government for reasons that hinted
at a repudiation of the reasoning in the Labour Conventions case.

> *Canada is the sovereign State that will when it enacts legislation
> dealing with the shelf be recognized by international law as
> having the rights stated by the 1958 convention, and it is Canada
> that will have to answer the claims of other members of the
> international community for breach of the obligations and
> responsibilities imposed by the convention.*[41]

In the 1970s the Court began to develop a somewhat higher profile
than had been customary. Partly this resulted from a change in the
agenda of federal-provincial relations and of public policy: regulatory
issues became more prominent, and Prime Minister Trudeau was
determined to enlarge the Court's role by entrenching a Charter of
Rights in the constitution. Bora Laskin, a noted legal scholar who was
appointed to the Court in 1970 and became Chief Justice only three
years later, tried to increase the standing of the Court in the eyes of
Canadians, and his own prestige contributed to this objective. A minor
contributing factor may have been the modest celebration of the
Court's centennial in 1975. More important than the celebrations,
however, were amendments to the Supreme Court Act in that year
which gave the Court considerably more control over its own docket,
restricted the right of appeal, and allowed a larger proportion of its
time to be devoted to cases of constitutional significance.

It was ironic in view of Laskin's reputation as a centralist that the Court under his leadership became more restrictive in its interpretation of federal powers than at any time since 1949. Admittedly Laskin himself was often in the minority, interpreting federal powers more generously than most of his colleagues. In the year that Laskin became Chief Justice, by coincidence three generally pro-federal justices retired from the Supreme Court including Douglas Abbott, a former Minister of Finance. They were replaced by three justices who were more inclined to restrict federal powers and to broaden the powers of the provinces.

The new situation first became evident in 1976 with the Court's judgment in the Reference re. anti-inflation act.[42] This was technically a federal victory, since the mandatory wage and price controls enacted by Parliament in 1975 were upheld, but, the decision resurrected Haldane's interpretation of "Peace, Order and Good Government" as an emergency power rather than a residual power. Four justices, including the Chief Justice, said that since inflation had attained the status of an emergency the legislation was clearly constitutional, and there was no need to decide the hypothetical question of whether it would have been valid if no emergency existed. Three justices explicitly stated that the legislation was only valid because there was an emergency. Two justices, both from Quebec and both appointed in 1973, said that the legislation was ultra vires.

This was followed by a series of decisions holding federal statutes, or portions thereof, unconstitutional on the grounds that they interfered with provincial fields of jurisdiction. It is an ironic fact that the Supreme Court presided over by Bora Laskin produced more such decisions in eleven years than the Judicial Committee dominated by Viscount Haldane produced in sixteen. However, it must be conceded that the statutes struck down in the Laskin era were less important, and the legal arguments against them more credible, than had been true in the earlier period.

The first of these decisions, MacDonald vs. Vapor Canada Ltd., struck down a section of the Trade Marks Act which the Court said could not be justified under either trade and commerce or criminal law powers, and which therefore intruded on property and civil rights.[43] This marked a return to a narrow interpretation of federal powers, and a corresponding tendency to use "property and civil rights" as a catch-all category that was very characteristic of the Judicial Committee. The next two cases struck down portions of the Federal Court of Canada Act adopted by Parliament in 1975, on the grounds that Parliament could not give that Court jurisdiction to interpret either the civil code of Quebec or the common law of the other provinces.[44] The next case, resulting from an Ontario reference on the interminably complicated subject of agricultural marketing, resulted in a judgment that Parliament could not impose administrative charges on egg producers as part of a joint federal-provincial scheme to regulate the trade in eggs, since the scheme affected eggs that were produced and consumed in the same province.[45]

Two almost simultaneous decisions, *Dominion Stores vs. the Queen* and *Labbatt Breweries vs. Attorney General of Canada*, continued the practice of striking down federal regulatory statutes on the grounds that they interfered with property and civil rights. The first decision said that Parliament could not impose product standards on fruit sold in supermarkets, since retail sales were within a province and thus did not fall under the heading of "trade and commerce," even though the apples had originated in another province.[46] The second struck down portions of the Food and Drug Act defining and restricting the use of the term "light beer." [47] This decision repeated the old doctrine that the trade and commerce power could not be used to regulate a specific industry but only to make rules of general application. It also said that the peace, order and good government power was irrelevant since misleadingly named beer was neither an emergency nor a problem of national dimensions.

The decision in *Boggs vs. the Queen* defined the criminal law power restrictively by ruling that Parliament had acted beyond its powers in placing the offence of driving with a suspended licence in the criminal code.[48] The reason why this was not valid criminal law was because a licence could be suspended for a variety of administrative reasons and not only because the holder had committed a criminal offence. In *Reference re. exported natural gas tax*, the Court ruled that Parliament could not tax natural gas which still belonged to the province of Alberta at the time when the tax was imposed; a decision based on Section 125 which says that the property of a province (or of Canada) is not subject to taxation.[49] Finally, in *McEvoy vs. Attorney General of New Brunswick*, the Court decided that Parliament could not give a new provincial court jurisdiction over criminal offences because such offences had been tried before the Superior Court of the province at the time of Confederation.[50]

None of these decisions attracted much comment or controversy, and paradoxically, it was during this time that the Supreme Court was most frequently accused of bias against the provinces. The accusation was largely based on half a dozen decisions between 1977 and 1981 pertaining to the sensitive areas of communications, language policy, and natural resources. Unlike the federal government, provincial governments did not hesitate to denounce the Supreme Court publicly if they found its decisions inconvenient.

The first of these controversial decisions, *Dionne vs. Public Service Board of Quebec*, extended the federal jurisdiction over broadcasting to cable television, which it declared to be an integral part of a national system of communications rather than a local public utility as Quebec argued.[51] While the Lévesque government in Quebec took this decision quite calmly, the Blakeney government in Saskatchewan seems to have developed a lasting resentment against the Court. This was a result of the decision in *Canadian Industrial Gas and Oil vs. Saskatchewan*, which declared its system of petroleum royalties and taxes to constitute an indirect tax and also an intrusion on the regulation of trade and commerce.[52] There was greater indignation a year later when the decision in *Central Canada Potash vs. Saskatchewan* declared that the province could not regulate the production of potash as a means of fixing the export price.[53] Yet the province had little difficulty in devising a new system of taxation which overcame the objection in the first case. The potash regulating scheme, which in any event had ceased to operate long before the decision was rendered, could not have been permitted under any federal constitution worthy of the name.

Two important cases decided almost simultaneously were *A.G. Quebec vs. Blaikie* and *A.G. Manitoba vs. Forest*. The first struck down those portions of the Lévesque government's language charter which purported to make French the only official language of statutes, the legislature, and the courts.[54] The second decision determined that Manitoba was also required to be officially bilingual under the terms of the Manitoba Act, and belatedly struck down the enactments by which that province had attempted to make English its only official language.[55] The two provinces supported one another in their respective disputes, while the province of New Brunswick and the federal government intervened to argue against them. A further decision on the Blaikie case following a rehearing extended the application of Section 133 to government regulations made under statutory authority and to court rules of practice. It said, however, that the requirement of bilingualism in Quebec did not apply to municipal by-laws or to the regulations of school boards, since both municipalities and school boards had existed in Quebec prior to the establishment of the provincial legislature in 1867.[56] Later still, in 1985, the Court imposed a deadline on Manitoba to translate all of its provincial statutes into French.[57]

Less likely to stir popular emotions, but still significant in the evolution of Canadian federalism, were three decisions relating to the administration of justice which had broader implications for the scope of federal powers. In Canada the Criminal Code is a federal statute, but offences under it have always been prosecuted by the provinces, even though there is no explicit constitutional provision to this effect. In more recent times the federal government has taken unto itself the task of prosecuting the offences under various other statutes. In *the Queen vs. Hauser*, the section of the Narcotics Control Act providing for federal prosecutions was challenged but upheld by the Supreme Court.[58] A majority of the Court said that narcotics was a particular subject of concern like temperance, aeronautics, or broadcasting, and that the Narcotics Control Act was therefore based on the peace, order and good government power rather than the criminal law power. One justice said that it was based partly on the criminal law power and partly on the power to regulate trade and commerce, but the latter aspect was enough to justify federal prosecution of offences. A minority of two, including Justice Dickson who became Chief Justice of Canada in 1984, said that the Narcotics Control Act was simply a part of the criminal law and that prosecution should therefore be handled by the provinces.

A few years later the question of prosecutory power again arose in relation to two other federal statutes: the Combines Investigation Act and the Food and Drugs Act. The first case concerned an attempt to prosecute the trucking subsidiaries of the two transcontinental railways under the former act. The Court unanimously upheld federal power to prosecute, even though a majority of the participating justices admitted that the Combines Investigation Act was based solely on the criminal law power.[59] (It will be recalled that this had been the finding in the PATA case of 1931.) By doing so, the majority left the way open for the federal government to prosecute all criminal offences, since the majority opinion delivered by Chief Justice Laskin said that the practice of leaving this task to the provinces was not required by the constitution. The second case, *the Queen vs. Wetmore*, was almost identical in its conclusions. However, Justice Dickson, who had argued that the Combines Investigation Act could be based in part on the power to regulate trade and commerce, argued that the Food and Drug Act had to depend solely on the criminal law power.[60] He therefore upheld provincial power to prosecute in the Wetmore case as he had done in the Hauser case.

In 1979 and 1981 the Supreme Court produced two of the most significant decisions in its entire history, both relating to the power to amend Canada's constitution. The reasoning in both decisions has, of course, been rendered obsolete by the adoption of a new and explicit amending procedure which came into effect in 1982. However, the Supreme Court's two decisions, particularly the latter one, were important in their time and are discussed more fully in Chapter 10.

SHOULD THE SUPREME COURT BE REFORMED?

Although the controversies of the Laskin era thrust the Supreme Court into the political limelight for perhaps the first time in its history, the entrenchment of a Charter of Rights in the constitution in 1982 ensured that the Court's prominence would not be a temporary phenomenon. Like its American counterpart, the Supreme Court of Canada is now an institution that wields significant political power. While opinions may differ on the desirability of this development and on the ability of the Supreme Court to carry out its present responsibilities, there is no doubt that the coming of the Charter reinforced pressures to "reform" the Court that were already evident before 1982. Although federal governments have themselves made a number of proposals for change, it is fair to say that most of the impetus in this direction stems from the belief that the Supreme Court is, or at the very least might become, biased in favour of the central government and against the provinces. Those who express this point of view, however, seldom offer much convincing evidence to support it.

The allegation that the Supreme Court is biased against the provinces has been convincingly refuted by Peter Hogg in an article whose main conclusions can be summarized as follows. In the first place, there is no evidence that federal governments deliberately "pack" the Court with sympathetic appointees (apart from Chief Justice Bora Laskin, no recent appointee had a previous reputation as an enthusiast for broad definitions of Parliament's powers). Admittedly, provincial statutes are struck down more frequently than federal ones, but this is largely because there are more of them, and this was also true in the days when the Judicial Committee was still Canada's highest court of appeal. Also, federal governments since 1949 have usually been more cautious than those of certain provinces in testing the limits of their powers, and thus have naturally faced fewer legal challenges. Moreover, it is true in all modern federations, not just in Canada, that the Courts have had to deal harshly with provincial legislation that is in conflict with existing federal legislation or that affects the interests of people outside the province concerned.[61] Hogg's conclusion that the Supreme Court has not really been biased received confirmation from an unexpected source: a study commissioned and published by the provincial government of Quebec. In that study Gilbert l'Ecuyer concluded that the Court had merely adhered to the terms of the BNA Act, which he admitted was more than could be said for the Judicial Committee:

> Sauf en de tres rares occasions, les decisions de la Cour Supreme rendues depuis 1949 semblent bien fondees en droit et fideles au texte des articles 91 et 92 du B.N.A. Act de 1867 ainsi qu'aux intentions des Peres de la Confederation.[62]

Of course, if one would prefer decisions that were neither firmly based on the law nor faithful to the intentions of the Father of Confederation, one's desire to "reform" the Supreme court might be strengthened by this conclusion.

One constitutional remedy that has become much less fashionable in recent years is the creation of a specialized constitutional court that would hear only constitutional cases. Such an institution exists in the Federal Republic of Germany. The idea has received a certain amount of support in Quebec and was proposed in a discussion paper by the government of Alberta as recently as 1978. However, the predominant view in Canada is that it would be very difficult to distinguish between cases that are "constitutional" in nature and those that are not. The force of the argument for a specialized tribunal was further weakened by the amendments to the Supreme Court Act in 1975 which restricted the right of appeal and removed from the Court much of its non-constitutional caseload. On the other hand, the scope of the expression "constitutional law" has been greatly broadened by the Charter. Many appeals in criminal cases, for example, are likely to be on constitutional grounds, and it is obvious that the Supreme Court will have to deal with them as well as with the traditional issues related to federalism. A specialized court to deal only with the latter would be a backward step and would serve no useful purpose.

Two proposals that have enjoyed broader support, however, are the entrenchment of the Supreme Court in Canada's constitution and, more controversially, the involvement of the provincial governments in the process of appointment. The argument for entrenchment is essentially symbolic; an explicit reference to the Supreme Court in the constitution would emphasize its importance as a major national institution, and would avoid any impression that it is subordinate to Parliament. Such an impression is bound to persist as long as the Court's existence is dependent on an Act of Parliament. The argument for involving the provinces in appointments is ostensibly based on a more substantive concern: the belief that the Court is, or might be, biased toward the central government in its decisions. The desire of provincial governments to share in judicial patronage is probably an equally important consideration, although provincial governments are understandably reticent to say so.

Entrenchment was partially achieved by the Constitution Act of 1982, but in a rather anomalous way that did not really achieve the symbolic benefits attributed to the concept. The Supreme Court Act was not listed among the documents that were said to comprise Canada's constitution, but Section 41 included "the composition of the Supreme Court of Canada" as one of five matters that could only be changed with the unanimous consent of all provinces. ("Composition" was presumably meant to mean the requirement that three justices be from Quebec, and six from the common-law provinces.) Section 42 also provided that other constitutional amendments related to the Supreme Court required the consent of at least two-thirds of the provinces comprising at least half of the population.

The Meech Lake accord of 1987, between the federal government and the ten provinces, provided for a more explicit form of entrenchment by specifying that the existing Supreme Court would be "continued as the general court of appeal for Canada." It also specified the number of justices, the minimal qualifications required for appointment, and the requirement that at least three justices be members of the Quebec bar. The accord also provided for provincial participation in appointments, an idea that had been intermittently on the constitutional agenda for nearly twenty years.

As early as 1971, in the so-called "Victoria Charter," the federal government proposed an elaborate scheme for involving the provincial governments in appointments. This would have required the Minister of Justice to consult with the attorney general of "the appropriate province" before making an appointment. It also provided complicated procedures for resolving the dispute if the Minister of Justice and the provincial attorney general were unable to agree.[63]

In 1986 the Quebec government (ironically headed by the same premier, Robert Bourassa, who had rejected the Victoria Charter in 1971) included participation in appointments to the Supreme Court among the five conditions that must be met if Quebec were to accept the legitimacy of the constitutional changes that had been imposed without its consent in 1982. The Meech Lake accord, which the eleven heads of government were able to agree upon about a year later, embodies a procedure for appointments somewhat different from that envisaged by the Victoria Charter. Nominations would be made in the first instance by the provincial governments, but would require the approval of the federal government, which would actually make the appointment. No procedure is provided for resolving disputes that might arise if a provincial nominee were unacceptable to the federal government. This means that the government of Quebec can virtually impose its own choice if a Quebec appointment is required to fill the minimum quota of three seats on the bench allocated to that province. The governments of the common-law provinces, however, gain considerably less from this arrangement, since if the federal government finds the nominee of one provincial government unacceptable, it can ask any of the other provincial governments to nominate an alternative. The provision noted earlier, to the effect that "at least" three judges must be from Quebec, gives the federal government ten possible choices to fill any vacancy, apart from a vacancy in one of the three seats reserved for Quebec judges.

Although these provisions are unlikely to improve the quality of the Court, they are probably more workable than the procedures envisaged in the Victoria Charter, and they are not an excessive price to pay for Quebec's acceptance of the constitution. The common-law provinces will have an incentive to nominate persons acceptable to the central government so as to ensure that the appointment does not go to another province, so the judges appointed from those provinces are unlikely to be much different from those that would have been appointed in any event. It is possible that more Quebec nationalists will be appointed to the Supreme Court as a result of the accord, but this will probably not have a decisive effect on the Court's decisions. Even when appointed unilaterally by the federal government, the civil law judges have tended over the years to be somewhat more "provincialist" in interpreting the divison of legislative powers than their common-law colleagues. Furthermore, now that the Charter of Rights and Freedoms is entrenched in our constitution, constitutional jurisprudence is no longer as exclusively concerned with federalism as it was previously; the relationship between the individual and the state, rather than the relationship between the two levels of government, is becoming the primary consideration. It is possible that the Supreme Court and the constitution will serve to unite Canadians, or at least to divide them along non-geographical lines, rather than to reinforce their traditional obsession with federal-provincial relations.

NOTES

1. Oliver Wendell Holmes, *Collected Legal Papers* (New York, Harcourt, Brace, and Horne, 1920) 291.
2. A.V. Dicey, *Introduction to the Study of the Law of the Constitution* 10th ed. (London: Macmillan, 1961) 175.
3. Dicey, 170.
4. James G. Snell and Frederick Vaughan, *The Supreme Court of Canada: History of the Institution* (Toronto: University of Toronto Press, 1985) 1–27.
5. Richard A. Olmsted, *Decisions of the Judicial Committee of the Privy Council relating to the British North America Act, 1867 and the Canadian Constitution 1867-1954*, (Ottawa: Queen's Printer, 1954) 94–124. This collection includes the full text of all the opinions and a summary of the arguments of counsel. As it is more easily accessible to Canadian students than the original British law reports, all notes citing Judicial Committee cases in this book refer to the Olmsted collection. Published with permission of the Minister of Supply and Services Canada.
6. Olmsted, I, 145–59.
7. Olmsted, I, 184–202.
8. *A.G. Ontario vs. A.G. Canada*, Olmsted, I, 343–66.
9. *Liquidators of the Maritime Bank vs. Receiver-General of New Brunswick*, Olmsted, I, 263–71.
10. See Jonathan Robinson, "Lord Haldane and the British North America Act," *University of Toronto Law Journal* XX (1970) 55–69, and Stephen Wexler, "The Urge to Idealize: Viscount Haldane and the Constitution of Canada," *McGill Law Journal* XXIX (1984) 609–50.
11. J.R. Mallory, *Social Credit and the Federal Power in Canada* (Toronto: University of Toronto Press, 1976) 47–56.
12. Olmsted, I, 717–31.
13. Olmsted, II, 1–10.
14. *In re The Board of Commerce Act, 1919, and the Combines and Fair Prices Act, 1919*, Olmsted, II, 245–54.
15. Olmsted, II, 394–412.
16. *A.G. Canada vs. A.G. British Columbia*, Olmsted, II, 617–29.

17. Olmsted, II, 668–84.
18. Olmsted, II, 709–31.
19. Olmsted, III, 18–30.
20. A.G. Canada vs. A.G. Ontario, Olmsted, III, 180–206.
21. Olmsted, III, 206.
22. Olmsted, III, 207–18.
23. Olmsted, III, 228–39.
24. Canadian Federation of Agriculture vs. A.G. Quebec, Olmsted, III, 665–90.
25. A.G. Ontario vs. Canada Temperance Foundation, Olmsted, III, 424–40; A.G. Ontario vs. A.G. Canada, Olmsted, III, 508–38; A.G. Ontario vs. Winner, Olmsted, III, 775–820.
26. Frank R. Scott, Essays on the Constitution: Aspects of Canadian Law and Politics (Toronto: University of Toronto Press, 1977). This collection includes papers published between 1928 and 1971.
27. Canada, Senate, session of 1939, Report by the Parliamentary Counsel Relating to the Enactment of the British North America Act, 1867, any lack of consonance between its terms and judicial construction of them and cognate matters.
28. Bora Laskin, "Peace, Order and Good Government Re-examined," Canadian Bar Review XXV (1947) 1054–87.
29. Pierre Elliott Trudeau, Federalism and the French Canadians (Toronto: Macmillan, 1968) 198.
30. G.P. Browne, The Judicial Committee and the British North America Act (Toronto: University of Toronto Press, 1967).
31. Alan C. Cairns, "The Judicial Committee and its Critics," Canadian Journal of Political Science IV (1971) 301–45.
32. Gil Remillard, Le federalisme canadien, (Montreal: Editions Quebec/Amerique, 1980), I, 163–66, 189–93.
33. A.G. Nova Scotia vs. A.G. Canada (Ottawa: Supreme Court Reports, 1951) 31.
34. 2 S.C.R. (1952) 392.
35. 1 S.C.R. (1952) 292.
36. S.C.R. (1966) 663.
37. Reference re the farm products marketing act (Ontario) (1957) S.C.R. 198.
38. S.C.R. (1958) 626.
39. S.C.R. (1971) 543.
40. S.C.R. (1957) 285.
41. S.C.R. (1967) 792.
42. 2 S.C.R. (1976) 373.
43. 2 S.C.R. (1977) 134.
44. McNamara Construction vs. the Queen (1977) 2 S.C.R. 655; Quebec North Shore Ltd. vs. C.P. Ltd. (1977) 2 S.C.R. 1054.
45. Re Agricultural Products Marketing Act (1978) 2 S.C.R. 1198.
46. 1 S.C.R. (1980) 844.

47.   1 S.C.R. (1980) 914.

48.   1 S.C.R. (1981) 49.

49.   1 S.C.R. (1982) 1004.

50.   1 S.C.R. (1983) 704.

51.   2 S.C.R. (1978) 191.

52.   2 S.C.R. (1978) 545.

53.   1 S.C.R. (1979) 42.

54.   2 S.C.R. (1979) 1016.

55.   2 S.C.R. (1979) 1032.

56.   1 S.C.R. (1981) 312.

57.   1 S.C.R. (1985) 721; 2 S.C.R. (1985) 347.

58.   1 S.C.R. (1979) 984.

59.   2 S.C.R. (1983) 206.

60.   2 S.C.R. (1983) 284.

61.   P.W. Hogg, "Is the Supreme Court of Canada biased in constitutional Cases?" *Canadian Bar Review* LVII (1979) 721–39.

62.   Gilbert l'Ecuyer, *La cour supreme du Canada et le partage des compe-tences, 1949–1978* (Quebec: Ministere des affaires intergouvernemen-tales, 1978) 387.

63.   The full text of the so-called Victoria Charter is printed in Canada, Parliament, Fourth Session, Twenty-Eighth Parliament, *Report of the Special Joint Committee on the Constitution* (Ottawa: Queen's Printer, 1972) 106–10. Articles 26–33 outline the proposed procedure for appointments to the Supreme Court.

4 The Political Economy of Decentralization

Provincialism has paralleled the new industrialism . . . Confederation as an instrument of steam power has been compelled to face the implications of hydro-electric power and petroleum.

HAROLD INNIS[1]

. . . among the more or less centralized federations of the modern world, most writers would agree that Canada is about as decentralized as one can get.

W.H. RIKER[2]

The preceding chapter described how the judiciary have interpreted Canada's federal constitution, and how the processes of judicial interpretation transformed Macdonald's centralized quasi-federal constitution — by which he hoped to avoid some of the perils of American federalism — into a federal constitution not greatly different from that of the United States. As noted in that chapter, the Judicial Committee in particular has been blamed by Canadian nationalists for weakening the central government's ability to deal with national problems. While the criticism is largely deserved, the judiciary cannot bear the entire responsibility. If underlying economic and social trends had been conducive to centralization in Canada, as they largely were in the United States after the Civil War, the judiciary would not have been able, and would perhaps not have been willing, to resist them indefinitely. If centripetal forces had really been strong, the effects of the Judicial Committee's interpretations could have been largely overcome through constitutional amendments or various devices of constitutional adaptation. (This actually happened to some extent during the Second World War and its immediate aftermath.)

In any event, experience since 1949 does not suggest a very strong relationship between judicial interpretation and the evolution of the federal state. During this period, the Supreme Court of Canada has largely reversed the Watson-Haldane tradition in its interpretation of the BNA Act. Yet, through most of the same period, power has flowed to the provincial governments at the expense of the central government, at times with the latter's approval or acquiescence, and in apparent disregard of what the Supreme Court was doing. One must seek other factors to explain why the judicial abandonment of the centrifugal concept was not followed by centralization in practice. The fact that it was not distinguishes Canada sharply from the United States, where this did in fact happen from 1937 onward.

Norman Rogers, in a pioneering article, emphasized "changes in political consciousness and sentiment" as the source of centrifugal and centripetal trends in Canadian federalism.[3] Although this theory is impossible to support on the evidence, it seems to be widely popular, perhaps because of its reassuring implication that Canadians always get the kind of federalism they want, and will presumably continue to do so. Rogers also contended, as have a multitude of subsequent writers, that the provincial governments could not be kept in a subordinate position because there was no widespread sense of attachment to Canada as a nation. J.M.S. Careless, following in this tradition, perceived a relationship between the various "limited identities" of Canadians, identities which are ethnic and religious as well as provincial and regional.[4]

Yet there is reason for considerable scepticism about cultural explanations for the strength of Canadian provincialism. Apart from the concentration of francophones in Quebec, ethnic and religious divisions tend to cut across, rather than to reinforce, provincial boundaries. The cultural differences between the predominantly anglophone provinces are certainly no greater than those between Texas and Massachusetts, for example, and are actually diminishing under the impact of urbanization and the mass media.[5]

Other possible explanations that have been offered seem equally fruitless. The greater competence of provincial bureaucracies in recent years, for example, is an important fact, but it would seem more likely to be a consequence than a cause of the fact that provincial governments have gained in power and importance. For similar reasons one cannot explain very much by asserting that the subjects enumerated in Section 92 of the BNA Act proved to be unexpectedly more important than those enumerated in Section 91. Many of the tasks performed by the modern state are not explicitly enumerated in either section, and no conceivable reading of the BNA Act would support the illogical distribution of tasks, functions, and powers between the two levels of government that has actually emerged. The important question to answer is why so many matters have, in practice, been regarded as falling under provincial jurisdiction, in whole or in part, and why the central government has had to share its power with the provincial governments, or to defend it against provincial pressures, to an extent that has few if any parallels elsewhere.

The answer to this problem seems to lie in certain characteristics of the political economy of Canada, which both produced conflicts between different classes and class fractions and at the same time caused these contending forces to identify their interests with different levels of government, and vice versa.

To understand how and why this happened it is important to point out, as Lord Durham did in his report almost a century and a half ago, that the primary function of the state in Canada has been to assist in economic growth, rather than to guarantee internal and external security, as was the case with European states. Expressed in Marxist language, this is what the American political economist James O'Connor called the "accumulation" function, meaning that the state directly contributes to the accumulation of profit.[6] Often in Canada it has done this by providing various guarantees and incentives to private enterprise or by intervening directly to supply services such as electric power or transportation without which private profit-making would be impossible. In other words, some of the risks or costs of private enterprise are assumed by the state and paid for by the taxpayer. Laissez-faire never existed in Canada. The state has always been a fundamental and essential part of the economic process, and its support has always been of crucial importance to business interests.[7]

Confederation, as we have seen, was largely although by no means exclusively the result of economic motives. Its effect was both to expand the geographical jurisdiction of the Canadian state and to overhaul its machinery so that economic functions both old and new could be performed more effectively. The terms of Confederation, most of which related to economic matters, represented the common denominator of agreement among a variety of economic interests and objectives in the different colonies. Confederation did not, however, end the diversity and conflict among those interests, which soon found expression through a feature of the post-Confederation state which itself was partly the result of that diversity and conflict, namely the existence of two distinct levels of government. In addition, conflict between the dominant class and other classes, particularly the farmers, also had an impact on the dynamics of Canadian federalism.

Under a federal regime, conflicting economic interests could theoretically find expression in either or both of two ways: through accommodation and compromise at the level of the central government, assuming that all were represented there to some degree; or through different governments, federal and provincial. Class fractions that perceive the central government as more sympathetic to opposing interests than to their own will tend to seek redress by strengthening the provincial level of government, This occurs, particularly if they are geographically distributed in such a way that one provincial government represents a geographical area within which one of the frustrated class fractions is particularly important and influential. In such circumstances the provincial government in question will speak for the class fraction concerned, and will carry out on its behalf the Canadian state's traditional function as the ally and supporter of private enterprise. Efforts will be made to curtail and undermine the power and authority of the unsympathetic and potentially hostile central government, usually by ideological appeals to the virtues of local autonomy, decentralization, and the cultural values allegedly embodied in the province. Any increase in the taxing, spending, and regulatory powers of the provincial level of government will be welcomed, since it will enable that level of government to perform the accumulation function more effectively on behalf of the locally dominant class fraction.

The central government, on the other hand, will be supported by those class fractions which have the most access to it and influence over it, and which can rely upon it to act in support of their economic objectives. Another reason for preferring this level of government may be the fear that overly powerful provincial governments will "balkanize" the country by pursuing policies that restrict the free flow of commodities across provincial boundaries. In addition, classes and class fractions within a province that find the provincial government hostile or unresponsive to their needs will support the strengthening of the central government as a counterweight and may call upon the central government to intervene on their behalf against the provincial government.

Considerations of this kind can lead to fairly long-term alliances between particular class fractions and different levels of government, but changing circumstances may lead to a temporary or even permanent transference of allegiance to the other level. A class fraction which enjoys some influence at both levels of government can also use each one to prevent the other from straying too far out of line, an important consideration in view of the degree of autonomy possessed by modern state apparatuses and the limited but real responsiveness of politicians to subordinate class demands expressed through the electoral process. What Lord Palmerston once said about British foreign policy could be applied to the politics of business in a federal state: its alliances are determined by its interests, not the other way around.

THE NATIONAL POLICY AND ITS OPPONENTS

To some degree the extent to which class fractions will rely on the provincial level of government to act on their behalf (and thereby strengthen that level of government in relation to the federal level) depends on how successful the federal level is in accommodating and satisfying all the various fractional interests. Immediately after Confederation a high degree of success in doing this seemed possible. The economies of the different provinces were somewhat similar in character, and severe conflicts of interest among them did not seem likely. Careful efforts were made to represent diverse provincial interests in the cabinet, the Senate, the civil service, and other federal institutions. The most apparently important conflict within the dominant class was the traditional and fierce rivalry between the business interests of Montreal and Toronto. The long delay and indecision over awarding the Pacific Railway contract, as well as the Mackenzie government's policy of having the government itself construct the line, were both the result of not wishing to favour either city at the expense of the other. After 1878, however, this was replaced by Macdonald's National Policy, under which Montreal received the railway contract although Toronto in the long run reaped greater benefits from the National Policy's other element, the protective tariff.

For the moment, however, Montreal appeared to be ascendant, and under the skilful leadership of Oliver Mowat the government of Ontario became a rallying point for those who opposed the National Policy: farmers and lumbermen who disliked high tariffs and wanted freer trade with the United States as well as relief from the financial burden of railway subsidies and incentives. Since Ontario was the largest and richest province and since farming and lumbering were still the major industries of central Canada, this was a powerful coalition, as suggested both by Mowat's long tenure in office and by the razor-thin majorities of the federal Conservatives.

Ontario's wealth, power, and size, as well as the contribution of the lumber industry to its provincial treasury, made the government of that province a virtual state within a state; certainly a far cry from the meek and subordinate quasi-municipality that the Fathers of Confederation (including Mowat himself) had expected it to be in 1865. Province-building, as well as nation-building, had begun, with Ontario taking the lead.[8] Provincial powers to manage the public lands and resources, to incorporate companies, and to regulate the vast and nebulous area of "property and civil rights" were used for the benefit of those economic interests that rallied under the provincial banner.

By the turn of the century, Ontario had made considerable progress in this direction. At the same time the difficulty of accommodating all economic interests at the federal level had been greatly increased by the growing size and diversity of the Canadian economy and the class and regional conflicts had been exacerbated by the uneven impact of the National Policy itself. Regardless of the BNA Act, the provincial governments were becoming as important and powerful as the federal one. Disallowance of their legislation virtually ceased, except in the case of British Columbia, which was small and remote enough to be insulted with impunity. Even the British Columbia government might have escaped having its legislation disallowed, had not its obsessive dislike of Orientals both embarrassed the British Foreign Office and interfered with the supply of cheap labour for railway-building.

Canada's economic development progressed rapidly in the early part of the twentieth century, but the development was unevenly distributed across the country, producing the phenomenon that would come to be known as regional disparity. The increasing concentration of ownership in the industrial and financial sectors of the economy increased the economic power of Toronto and Montreal to the detriment of smaller centres like Halifax, Saint John, and Quebec City which were gradually reduced to subordinate positions. Secondary manufacturing became concentrated in southern Ontario and the Montreal region, not because of the tariff as is often alleged, but because these locations were close to markets and raw materials. Average levels of wealth and personal income began to vary noticeably from one province to another, with the Maritime provinces, and to some extent Quebec, deteriorating in relation to Ontario and the West.

These developments affected the federal system in two ways. Maritime businessmen, never unanimously convinced that Confederation had been to their benefit, were increasingly inclined to blame federal transportation and tariff policies for the deterioration of their regional economy, and attempted to use the provincial level of government as an instrument to retain as large as possible a share of the national income. In Ontario, paradoxically, good fortune had a similar if not greater impact. The Ontario government, because of Ontario's wealth and prosperity, had the financial means to pursue economic policies that contributed to the further accumulation of wealth within the province. Ontario's vast size, as well as its wealth, equipped the Ontario government to perform an economic role that was unusual, if not unique, for a subnational state within a federation, and thus to gain the support of Ontario businessmen. Simultaneously, Ontario businessmen tended to view the federal level of government as an instrument for redistributing Ontario's wealth to the benefit of the voters in other provinces. Thus uneven development made the federal government a target for resentment in both rich and poor provinces, while causing the accumulation functions of the provincial level of government to be emphasized.

Related to uneven development, and also a consequence of the National Policy, was the emergence of three distinct sectors of the Canadian economy, each with divergent economic interests and class relationships.[9] Of particular importance to the development of federalism was the fact that the three sectors were concentrated in different provinces and regions. Thus each provincial government tended to become the representative for a distinct set of interests, rather than a microcosm of the country as a whole.

Secondary manufacturing was one of the three sectors and, as already mentioned, it was heavily concentrated in Ontario. Confederation exposed Maritime manufacturing to Ontario competition, while the National Policy protected Ontario manufacturing from foreign competition and greatly stimulated new industrialization to substitute indigenous products for imports.

The seemingly interminable reign of the Ontario provincial Liberals ended in 1905, suggesting that their traces of agrarian populism and their free trade philosophy were no longer in tune with the character of the province. The new Conservative government was based on an alliance between industrial workers and industrial capitalists, whose mutual solidarity was cemented by the commitment to further industrialization and the need to resist agrarian and anti-tariff interests whose main strength now lay outside of Ontario. Herein lay the source both of the political conservatism of the Ontario working class and of the paradox that the richest and most satisfied province, which also happened to contain the federal capital, remained until very recent times the most militant in resisting the federal government and waving the banner of provincial rights. Even if Ottawa, as viewed from the outlying provinces, seemed partial to the interests of industrial Ontario, the Ontario government was still a far more trustworthy instrument of industrial interests than the federal government. This was shown when Laurier unexpectedly and anachronistically espoused the cause of free trade with the United States and called an election on the issue in 1911. The provincial government of Ontario played a major role in bringing about his defeat.

The second major sector of the economy was export-oriented agriculture. Ontario had originally dominated this sector as well, but after the completion of the CPR main line in 1885 the major growth of this sector occurred in the "Northwest," or the area now occupied by the provinces of Manitoba, Saskatchewan, and Alberta. Prairie wheat became Canada's major export staple and the whole east-west economy was increasingly oriented around it.

Agricultural commodities for export were produced by independent farmers who owned their land and equipment, in contrast to the wage earners who produced manufactured goods. The antagonism of the farmers was directed against the banks, the mortgage companies, the railways, and the grain merchants. The protective tariff was also a source of resentment, since it increased the farmer's expenses while offering no benefit in return. Thus the farmer's economic interests were contrary to those of the manufacturing sector.

An important feature of the agricultural economy was the geographical separation between the farmer and the objects of his antagonism. While the latter were located in Ontario, in Montreal, and to some extent in Winnipeg, the farmers were concentrated on the western Prairies: in Saskatchewan, where they and their families comprised an actual majority of the population; in Alberta, where they were by far the largest occupational group; and in the western part of Manitoba. As a consequence, the conflict between the farmers and their class opponents appeared superficially to be a "regional" rather than a class conflict. A related consequence was that the governments of Saskatchewan and Alberta (Manitoba was a more ambiguous case, at least after the turn of the century) represented and spoke for agricul-

tural interests, just as the Ontario government represented and spoke
for industrial interests. On the other hand, the farmers viewed the
federal government, quite accurately, as the representative of their
opponents. Class conflict became federal-provincial conflict.

The third sector of the economy consisted of the export-oriented
resource industries: lumbering, mining and smelting, pulp and
paper. These industries resembled the agricultural sector in their
dependence on foreign rather than domestic markets, but they
resembled the manufacturing sector in that they were based on large-
scale enterprises employing wage labour rather than independent
commodity production. Class conflict was pronounced, partly
because of working conditions and partly because there was no issue
that united employees and employers, as the tariff united them in the
manufacturing sector. Foreign direct investment, largely American,
was important from the outset in this sector. The mining industry was
insignificant until about thirty years after Confederation, but grew
rapidly thereafter. Forestry had been important since long before Confederation. Pulp and paper expanded rapidly after the United States
removed its tariff on newsprint in 1913.

The resource sector was less geographically concentrated than the
other two sectors, and was important in every province apart from
Alberta, Saskatchewan, and Prince Edward Island. (Alberta already
produced coal and oil by 1914, but for domestic consumption only.)
However, British Columbia was the only province where the resource
sector predominated, producing a distinctive political culture that in
many respects makes it more like an Australian state than a Canadian
province. Resource-oriented areas in other provinces, such as northern Ontario, Cape Breton Island, and the Abitibi region of Quebec,
developed a sense of distinctiveness and an antagonism toward other
parts of their provinces, occasionally expressed in secessionist movements but more frequently in votes for provincial opposition parties.

Only in British Columbia would it be accurate to say that resource
capital had virtually exclusive influence over the provincial government, which acted as its representative in the same way that the
Ontario government represented the manufacturers and the Saskatchewan government the farmers. In all provinces where it existed,
including British Columbia, the resource sector tended to divide the
province internally, along class lines and in some cases along regional
lines. The antagonism between north and south, for example, is an
enduring theme of Ontario politics. However, the resource sector, like
the others, reinforced the centrifugal pressures in Canadian federalism. More than either of the other sectors, it was intimately associated
with provincial government, because the provinces owned most of the
lands and resources. This gave resource capital a weight in provincial
politics that was disproportionate to its real importance in provinces
like Ontario and Quebec. On the other hand, resource capital was

relatively indifferent to the federal level of government, since it required neither protective tariffs nor the elaborate financial and transportation infrastructure of the wheat economy. Thus the rise of the resource sector contributed to the growing importance of provincial governments and the declining relevance of the federal level to the accumulation function of the state. This was particularly true in British Columbia, Quebec, and Ontario.

Another consequence of resource development was the revival and strengthening of the alliance between the provincial governments of Quebec and Ontario, which had tentatively begun in the time of Mowat and Mercier. Originally based on the common characteristics of large size and political opposition to John A. Macdonald, the alliance was more firmly based in the twentieth century on a common interest in the resources of the Laurentian Shield and a desire to minimize the federal government's influence over their development.

These patterns of economic development produced, in the early twentieth century, a federal system very different from that which the Fathers of Confederation had intended. Manufacturing capital in Ontario (and to some extent in Quebec), resource capital in British Columbia (and to some extent in Ontario and Quebec), farmers in Alberta and Saskatchewan (and to some extent in Manitoba), could all rely on provincial governments to represent their interests and assist in their economic activities. The manufacturers were fortunate enough to exercise influence at two levels of government, sharing power and access with resource capital at the provincial level and with the banks and railways at the federal level. Resource capital and the farmers were weaker at the federal level but contrasted sharply in the extent to which federal policies were relevant to them. Farmer-controlled provincial governments had very limited ability to protect the farmers against federal policies injurious to their interests, while resource capital was less likely to be affected by federal policies, and, in addition, could usually rely on the two largest and strongest provincial governments as allies. The manufacturers had influence in the federal government but were not entirely dependent on it. The farmers resented it but could not be indifferent to it. The resource exploiters had little need of it and could largely ignore it. Only the banks, the life insurance companies, the steamship lines, and the transcontinental railways were almost exclusively oriented toward the central government and dedicated to strengthening its authority in relation to the provinces.[10] The wage-earning class had little influence anywhere and thus no clear preference for either level of government, although the federal government and those of Ontario and British Columbia made occasional and sporadic responses to its demands.

The behaviour of the various provincial governments followed fairly consistent patterns throughout the early twentieth century regardless of which parties were in office. British Columbia was almost constantly in conflict with the federal government, a pattern of behaviour that was partly a genuine reflection of the economic interests it represented and partly a tactic to distract attention from its internal class conflicts. The agricultural provinces of Alberta and Saskatchewan were also prone to intergovernmental conflict, moderated in the case of Saskatchewan by the fact that it enjoyed great influence in federal politics after 1921. Ontario was truculent when the federal government either flirted with lower tariffs or presented obstacles to Ontario's self-centred strategy of industrialization; in practice this happened when the federal Liberals were in office. Quebec, reflecting the predominant power of railways and finance in Montreal, was relatively passive but sometimes made common cause with Ontario on resource issues. Manitoba ceased to be farmer-dominated by about 1900, and behaved similarly to Quebec, since Winnipeg was a commercial metropolis like Montreal. The Maritime provinces were discontented with their economic circumstances, a fact reflected in occasional outbursts of truculence, but their increasing dependence on the federal government limited their opportunities for disruptive behaviour. The decline of independent economic entrepreneurship in the region and the dominant economic role of the federal state, which operated most of the region's railways as well as its harbours and coastal shipping, produced clientelistic relationships of a kind found in other underdeveloped areas, such as southern Italy. Close ties between federal and provincial parties and governments, as well as the large numbers of cabinet posts and senatorial seats assigned to the region relative to its population, were used to secure economic benefits from Ottawa. Public disagreements between the two levels of government were not conducive to this process, and tended to be avoided.

THE IMPACT OF DEPRESSION AND WAR

The Depression of the 1930s produced some changes in the political economy of federalism. The agricultural sector declined catastrophically, weakening the three Prairie provinces but also weakening the federally oriented banks, railways, grain merchants, and financial institutions. The resource sector also suffered (although to a lesser extent), apart, that is, from gold mining, which was the only industry that actually expanded during this period. Manufacturing suffered least, largely because the Ottawa Agreements of 1932 increased its share of British Empire markets at the expense of its competitors in the United States. The overall effect was to strengthen Ontario and Quebec, where both gold mining and manufacturing were concentrated, and to weaken the peripheries of the country, especially the Prairie West, where the fiscal structure of provincial and local government collapsed completely. The federal level of government was called upon to rescue the peripheries, but faced increasingly determined and

successful obstruction by the governments of the two central provinces.[11]

The transcontinental wheat economy, like the British Empire of
which it was part, failed to recover its importance after the Second
World War. As it declined, the dominant economic interests that had
sustained the federal government in its nation-building role declined
with it. The old commercial centres of Montreal and Winnipeg, both
of which had been severely battered by the Depression, lost their
traditional importance. Toronto replaced Montreal as the major Canadian metropolis; Vancouver and later Calgary surpassed Winnipeg as
subordinate metropolitan centres in the West. Saskatchewan, the
major wheat-producing province, suffered a decline of 100 000 in its
population between 1936 and 1951.

The decline of the wheat economy weakened the political and
economic unity that had grown up around it, symbolized by the network of transcontinental railways and the terminal grain elevators at
Port Arthur, Fort William, and Montreal. At the same time it redistributed wealth, power, and influence among the provinces. The natural
resource sector of the economy, traditionally associated with strong
provincial governments and closely tied to the United States,
expanded rapidly, particularly in Alberta, British Columbia, and the
new province of Newfoundland. Manufacturing grew, although less
rapidly, and became more Americanized, more concentrated in southern Ontario, and less dependent on the protective tariff. All of these
changes had consequences for federal-provincial relations.

Manufacturing was greatly stimulated by the war: enough to
produce a false and comforting belief (until Germany and Japan recovered) that Canada had become a major industrial power. Many new
industries were established under the auspices and in some cases the
direct ownership of the federal state. Yet at the end of the war they were
mainly sold or given away to American corporations. Canada's strong
position in relation to new technologies like jet aircraft, atomic energy,
and synthetic rubber was largely frittered away or sacrificed to cold
war politics and a growing American-inspired prejudice against state
enterprise. The British Empire's preferential trading system was virtually demolished at American insistence. Canadian industry produced
American-style consumer goods for Canadian markets or else was
integrated into American markets by special arrangements like the
Defence Production Sharing Agreement of 1958 (a formalization and
extension of the earlier Hyde Park Agreement) and the Auto Pact of
1965. To an increasing extent Canadian industry was American-
owned, American-oriented, and concentrated in southern Ontario,
which grew increasingly integrated with and eventually indistinguishable from the neighbouring states of New York and Michigan.
The uneven development of Canada was thereby exacerbated and the
Ontario government's role as the instrument of manufacturing capital

was reinforced, with the difference that the manufacturing capital was now predominantly American. The gradual dismantling of tariff barriers in what was oddly termed "the free world" made the federal level of government increasingly irrelevant to manufacturing interests.

The greatest expansion occurred in the resource sector of the Canadian economy, mainly in response to the depletion of American raw material supplies during the war and the preference of the United States for seeking new supplies in a country that was politically reliable and geographically proximate. Uranium in the Algoma district of Ontario, nickel in northern Manitoba, oil in Alberta and Saskatchewan, natural gas in Alberta and British Columbia, iron ore in northern Quebec and the newly annexed coast of Labrador, were all discovered and brought into production in the postwar years. Except for uranium, the development of all these resources was dominated by American-controlled corporations. All of them, including uranium, were oriented toward American markets insofar as they were not consumed within Canada itself. Hydro-electricity, another provincial resource, was used in Quebec and British Columbia to make aluminium for the American market. After 1964 electricity was also exported directly to the United States from British Columbia, Manitoba, Quebec, and Labrador. Ironically it was the postwar government of Louis St. Laurent, the convinced centripetal federalist, that did the most to orient the Canadian economy in this direction, thereby contributing to the increasing irrelevance of the central government and the increasing power and importance of the provincial governments.

The effect of developments in both the manufacturing and resource sectors was to integrate the Canadian economy into that of the United States. From Confederation until 1946, the United States had never taken more than 50 percent of Canadian exports. By 1950 it took 65 percent, a proportion that was maintained thereafter. With continental integration, the government of the United States in a sense became the central government for the whole of North America. Whatever interests the regional fractions of the Canadian ruling class had in common were interests that to a large degree they shared with their American counterparts. More and more, however, they relied on their provincial governments to develop their northern frontiers, to build roads and supply electricity, and to represent their divergent interests in federal-provincial bargaining and even in a variety of quasi-diplomatic external activities. None of this was really apparent until the 1960s, but the seeds had been sown.

THE BRANCH-PLANT ECONOMY

Closely associated as both cause and consequence with the reorientation of Canada's trade was the increasing importance of American direct investment, particularly in the manufacturing and resource sectors of the economy. By 1960, American interests controlled 44 percent of the capital invested in Canadian manufacturing, 64 percent in petroleum, 53 percent in mining and smelting, while the percentage of capital under Canadian control in these three sectors of the economy had fallen to 41, 27, and 39 percent, respectively.[12] In some sectors of manufacturing, such as rubber products, chemicals, and the automobile and aircraft industries, Canadian-controlled capital had for all practical purposes disappeared. Canadian capital remained dominant, by contrast, in banking, transportation, communications, life insurance, and retail trade, as well as in many of the less technologically advanced sectors of manufacturing.

As a result of these developments, the control of the Canadian economy was fragmented in a peculiar fashion. The indigenous "big bourgeoisie" controlled the banks, insurance companies, department stores, and other such enterprises extending across the country, but were poorly represented in manufacturing and the natural resource industries. A comprador fraction, in Wallace Clement's words, managed the American branch plants that predominated in the industrial sectors of the economy.[13] A third fraction, large in numbers and political influence if not in economic power, controlled the small-scale enterprises in the service industries and those sectors of manufacturing where Canadian capital still predominated.

Of these fractions only the first still identified its interests predominantly with the federal level of government, with which many of its activities had been closely associated since Confederation. The power of this fraction, while extensive, was too narrowly based to enable it to carry out the movement toward centralization of state power that other advanced countries were then experiencing. For the comprador fraction, the Canadian federal government was in a sense the least important among three levels of government: the continental, national, and provincial. Viewing Canada as part of a North American economy (and many multinationals are organized to reflect this assumption, with the Canadian and American operations organizationally separated from those overseas), they were naturally more oriented to Washington than to Ottawa. On the other hand, the provincial level of government was significant to them because the activities of a manufacturing or resource firm were typically concentrated in a single province and because provincial government controlled their terms of access to the two major inputs of natural resources and labour. The third fraction, with essentially localized operations, was also provincially oriented, although less so in the case of manufacturing enterprises, which relied on the protective tariff, than in the case of service industries.

The Canada of Diefenbaker and Pearson was thus as drastically different from that of Laurier and Borden as the latter had been different from the Canada of Macdonald and Mackenzie. Once again, the result was a massive shift in power from the federal government to the provincial governments; the ground which the latter had lost during the war had been recaptured by 1960, and provincial powers, revenues, and activities then expanded even more rapidly. Although the federal government was more involved than previously in health, welfare, and cultural activities, the provincial governments were increasingly managing and regulating the economy, a circumstance that contributed to its fragmentation.

As in the past, economic differences between the provinces contributed to different patterns of federal-provincial relations. The Atlantic provinces made strenuous efforts to attract American direct investment, often with scant regard for either economic rationality or the national interest, but poverty and a tradition of clientelism made them relatively passive in their dealings with the federal government. Newfoundland was to deviate from this pattern after 1972, when the promise of resource wealth coincided with the political emergence of the local (and anti-Confederationist) bourgeoisie that had been excluded from direct political power by the populist Premier J. R. Smallwood.

In Quebec, as will be shown in the next chapter, matters were greatly complicated by internal ethnic divisions and conflicts, as well as the complex nature of the provincial economy. In part because of these peculiarities, the provincial assault on federal power was backed by a uniquely strong and broadly based alliance of class forces after 1960. Although Montreal had been the traditional stronghold of the centralist fraction of the Canadian bourgeoisie, that fraction had become too weak provincially and nationally to prevent the provincial state from being used to undermine its position.

Ontario remained the principal centre of secondary manufacturing, with the difference that its manufacturing was now predominantly controlled by American capital and increasingly indifferent to the tariff protection provided by the federal level of government. Counterbalancing this to some extent were the relatively declining importance of the province's natural resource sector and the gradual migration of the federally oriented financial sector from Montreal to Toronto. Nonetheless, Ontario continued for three decades after the Second World War to pursue an aggressively provincialist course, usually in collaboration with the government of Quebec. The Americanization of the Ontario economy was evident during the 1960s in the opposition of Premier John Robarts to any controls on foreign direct investment, and in the provincial government's increasing penchant for continentalism and freer trade. Robarts strengthened the traditional alliance with Quebec against the hard-pressed federal government, and thereby inexplicably acquired a reputation as an architect of national unity. In 1967 his government named Ontario's principal limited access highway after Macdonald and Cartier in what was apparently intended as a symbolic gesture. The names of Mowat and Mercier would have been far more appropriate to the circumstances.

Manitoba and Saskatchewan suffered from the collapse of the wheat economy during the Depression and were slow to recover thereafter, although natural resources stimulated a certain amount of economic growth in the postwar period. Nationalization of much of the grain trade, the rise of Calgary and Edmonton, and the increasing tendency to export grain through Vancouver rather than the Great Lakes deprived Winnipeg of its traditional role as the economic centre of western Canada, and Manitoba lapsed into a state of dependence and stagnation almost comparable to that of the Maritime provinces. The rather passive approach to federal-provincial relations that had begun in the interwar period under Premier John Bracken continued as a result.

In Saskatchewan the continuing predominance of agriculture made the economy vulnerable to rapid fluctuations of income and dependent on various kinds of assistance and support from the federal government. It also produced an unusual class structure in which the farmers have remained the predominant indigenous class. The unusually extensive role played by provincial state enterprises in the economy has lessened the opportunities for both indigenous business and American direct investment, and seems designed to perpetuate agrarian class predominance. Yet it has also produced a large salaried middle class in the public sector which used rising resource revenues from about 1973 onward to adopt an increasingly truculent posture in federal-provincial relations. Nonetheless, Saskatchewan remains more moderate in this regard than several of the other provinces.

Alberta changed more dramatically in the postwar years than any other province, with the possible exception of Quebec, although opinions differ as to the character and significance of the changes. As late as 1946, Alberta's population was still slightly smaller than Saskatchewan's, but thirty years later it was twice as large. The reason, of course, was the massive development of oil beginning in 1947 and of natural gas for American and central Canadian markets a few years later. Both commodities had been produced in small quantities before the war, and the Alberta economy had always been less dependent on grain than had Saskatchewan's, but 1947 marked a fundamental change nonetheless. American capital flowed into the province, exploiting Alberta's traditional hostility toward Montreal and Toronto finance to strengthen the province's ties with Texas and California. Alberta soon had a greater proportion of American ownership in its non-agricultural economy and also a greater reliance on mineral resources than any other province.

Although never renowned for cordiality toward the central government, Alberta became increasingly hostile as world oil prices began to rise in the 1970s, sharpening the conflict between the interests of producers and consumers. Larry Pratt and John Richards have argued that the rise of a new bourgeoisie, represented by Premier Peter Lougheed's Progressive Conservatives, led to this exacerbation of federal-provincial conflict. However, the present writer has suggested elsewhere that there was little real change in Alberta's class structure and that international circumstances simply increased the province's wealth and its bargaining power as a producing region.[14] On whose behalf it bargained is not entirely clear. Pratt and Richards perceive a conflict between the American oil companies and the social forces allegedly represented by Lougheed's government, but it was the federal government that moved decisively to curb American influence in the petroleum industry through the National Energy Program of 1980, and the Alberta government that protested. The social base of Alberta Progressive Conservatism consists of small business people who live by selling goods and services to the large oil and gas companies, and who thus view any restriction on foreign direct investment as a threat to their own welfare.

British Columbia was the most rapidly growing province until it was overtaken by Alberta in the 1970s, but its growth did not bring any fundamental change in its character. It remained a resource frontier, although Vancouver increased in importance as a commercial and transportation centre. The behaviour of the provincial government adhered quite closely to the prewar pattern, which is to say that it remained a thorn in the side of the federal government. British Columbia still has relatively few ties with the rest of the country, and its chief concerns are to resist any redistribution of wealth at its expense or any federal intrusion into what it regards as its own affairs.

This brief sketch of the political economy of postwar Canada may suggest why the Canadian bourgeoisie was neither willing nor able to promote the centralization of state power that has occurred over the last fifty years in most other industrialized countries, including the United States. Admittedly, there has been some change in the last few years, in Ontario if not elsewhere, for reasons that will be explored below. Yet the extent of the change should not be overstated. In 1980 *The Financial Post* surveyed the chief executives, of what it described as a representative sample of large and small business enterprises, to discover their views on the federal-provincial division of powers. Even though the wording of the question made it clear that this was an exclusively federal power at present, 63 percent believed that the power to regulate trade and commerce should be shared with the provinces; 48 percent thought that the provinces should retain jurisdiction over securities markets; 27 percent thought the power should be shared; and only 25 percent thought it should be exclusively federal, as it is in the United States. The majority of respondents believed that provinces should be allowed to give preference to local firms in making government purchases, and almost half thought that provinces should be allowed to discourage the takeover of local firms by firms located in other provinces.[15] These views, however, are moderate compared to those of the Edmonton Chamber of Commerce, which recommended in 1980 that the federal powers over trade and commerce, census and statistics, navigation and shipping, interest, and bankruptcy should be transferred to the provinces.[16] Times had apparently changed since 1938 when the same chamber of commerce petitioned the federal government to disallow the Social Credit legislation of Premier William Aberhart.

In some federal countries, notably Australia, the working class, unions, and the political left have tended to counteract centrifugal forces arising from the structure of the economy. In Canada, this tendency has been much less significant, and the weakness of the left, at least up to the time of writing, has been more a symptom than a fundamental cause of the difficulties involved. Certain economic issues, such as the protective tariff and, more recently, energy policy have divided the Canadian working class along sectoral and regional lines just as they have divided the Canadian bourgeoisie. In addition, Canada's linguistic duality has been a much more significant barrier to the solidarity of the working class than to that of the bourgeoisie, in part because the francophone component of the working class is relatively much more important. At least until recently, the francophone working class in Quebec has shown very little interest in the NDP, which has appeared culturally alien and irrelevant to its concerns. In the 1970s, as described in the next chapter, the separatist Parti Québecois was able to mobilize the majority of Quebec's francophone working class, in part because of the conflict between anglophone capital and francophone labour that has traditionally characterized the private sector of Quebec's economy. It should also be noted that Canadian federalism itself has contributed to the political fragmentation of the working class. Since health, education, industrial relations, urban affairs, public welfare, and the administration of justice all fall under provincial jurisdiction, many of the issues most obviously related to the distinctive interests of the working class have been removed from the agenda of national (i.e., federal) politics. That agenda has thus been apparently dominated by non-class issues or issues whose relevance to the working class is less obvious, and federal politicians have been able to argue with some plausibility that the working class as such has no interests distinct from the common "national interest." Since so much of federal politics appears to be about issues that divide Canadians along regional or cultural lines rather than along lines of class, the regional and cultural diversities are made to appear more fundamental than they really are. On the other hand, provincial politicians, who have jurisdiction over those aspects of public policy most obviously related to class, can argue that class solidarity rather than class conflict is needed within the province to present a united front to adversaries in other parts of Canada. Maurice Duplessis in Quebec, and later Peter Lougheed in Alberta, made particularly effective use of this argument. Federalism has thus facilitated the mystification by which politicians at both levels of government seek to impede the progress of the political left. As Gad Horowitz argued more than twenty years ago, the sublimation or suppression of "class politics" has been detrimental to Canadian unity as well as to working class interests:

> . . . a nation like Canada, which is in danger of falling apart on regional-ethnic lines, may be held together by a politics which unites the people of various regions and ethnic groups around the two poles of left and right. . . . Class politics would translate popular discontent into demands for change in national social and economic policy. Non-class politics translates popular discontent into provincialism or separatism. Non-class politics perpetuates the power of established elites and endangers the existence of the nation.[17]

THE REVIVAL OF CENTRIPETAL FORCES

By the early 1970s, it appeared to some observers that the fragmentation of the Canadian economy and the absence of any strong sense of national identity had reached the point at which the survival of Canada as a united federal state could not be taken for granted. Indeed the federal government itself, faced with increasingly rambunctious provincial governments, appeared to lack either the will or the ability to resist their numerous demands, or to formulate and implement coherent policies of its own. While this impression was not entirely unwarranted, there were some countervailing forces at work whose importance would only become fully apparent in the 1980s.

The earliest indication of these forces was the change in the behaviour of the Ontario government toward its federal counterpart after William Davis became Premier of Ontario in 1971. Davis abandoned the traditional Ontario strategy of making common cause with the government of Quebec against the federal government in favour of a more decentralized federal system. Instead, and despite their different party labels, he quite consistently supported Prime Minister Trudeau on such issues as energy policy, wage and price controls, regulation of foreign direct investment, federal-provincial fiscal relations, and the amendment of the constitution. Although the western provinces and even Newfoundland increasingly joined Quebec in demanding a transfer of powers from the federal to the provincial level of government, Ontario began encouraging the federal government to resist these demands.

With the support of the Ontario government, the federal government undertook a number of important initiatives in economic policy in the 1970s, including an export tax on crude oil, imposition of a "made in Canada" price for both oil and gas, establishment of Petro-Canada and the Foreign Investment Review Agency, and a brief experiment with mandatory wage and price controls. Toward the end of the decade, the federal government also attempted unsuccessfully to bring *caisses populaires* (credit unions) under the jurisdiction of the Bank Act. Most of these initiatives involved forays into the jurisdictional "no man's land" between federal and provincial legislative powers, and most faced some provincial opposition, notably from Alberta and Saskatchewan in the case of the energy-related initiatives, and from Quebec in the case of the *caisses populaires*. The support of the Ontario government facilitated these initiatives, particularly as it made it more difficult for the Progressive Conservative opposition to resist them.

In 1980, when the federal Liberals returned to office after an interlude of less than a year, they began more consciously to pursue centralizing policies, again with the support of Ontario. The most dramatic and important of these policies were the National Energy Program, described in Chapter 8, and the patriation of the constitution with an entrenched Charter of Rights and Freedoms, described in Chapter 10. The latter initiative was opposed by every provincial government apart from Ontario and New Brunswick. Another indication of federal willingness to defy the provinces was the Canada Health Act of 1983, described in Chapter 7, which even the Davis government opposed. A less successful initiative at about the same time was the federal government's Bill S–31, which would have prevented provincial governments or their agencies from owning shares in interprovincial transportation companies. This bill was apparently introduced at the behest of Canadian Pacific Limited, and had the specific purpose of protecting that enterprise from the threat of a takeover by Quebec's *caisse de dépôt et de placement*, which had acquired about 10 percent of the shares and was seeking representation on the board of directors.[18] Throughout this period, and until the Liberals were defeated in 1984, the federal government expressed considerable concern about the effects on the Canadian economy of provincially-imposed barriers to the interprovincial movement of labour, capital, and commodities. The appointment in 1982 of the Royal Commission on the Economic Union and Development Prospects for Canada, headed by former Finance Minister Donald S. Macdonald, was in part the result of this concern.

The most credible explanation for all of these developments is that elements of the central Canadian bourgeoisie were becoming apprehensive about the consequences of aggressive resource-based provincialism in Alberta and Saskatchewan and of rising nationalism in Quebec. Western provincialism began to appear threatening in 1973 when the international price of oil, and thus the potential value of the energy resources owned by Alberta and Saskatchewan, quadrupled within a few months. Significantly, both the Alberta and Saskatchewan governments soon abandoned their traditional indifference to constitutional discussions and began to demand that the constitution be revised to reflect their new economic power. Quebec nationalism, as described in the next chapter, had been on the rise since 1960, but the election of a Parti Québécois government headed by René Lévesque in November 1976 appeared to make the secession of that province from the Canadian federation a distinct possibility. Despite the assurances of the Parti Québécois that independence would be accompanied by economic association with the rest of Canada, the business community (including the business community in Quebec itself) did not find this concept either credible or reassuring.

Ontario, in particular, felt threatened on two fronts. At a time of increasingly strong international competition, the secondary manufacturing industries that were the basis of its economy faced the threat of much higher prices for fuel, energy, and transportation, as well as the possible fragmentation of the Canadian market by an independent Quebec and increasingly interventionist and protectionist policies of other provincial governments. The Ontario government naturally reacted sooner to these grim possibilities than the federal government, which responded to a much broader range of interests and which for political reasons had to be cautious in dealing with Quebec, at least prior to that province's referendum on sovereignty-association. Both the Ontario government and its business allies, however, realized that only a strong federal government, responding to the large bloc of votes which Ontario represented but capable of imposing its will on the other provinces, could protect Ontario's economy against the dangers which it faced. The Ontario government thus abandoned its traditional provincialism in favour of a more pro-federal approach to intergovernmental relations. The federal government responded only gradually, but the return of the Liberals with an increased majority in 1980, and the rejection of sovereignty-association by the voters of Quebec in a referendum three months later, helped to dissolve its inhibitions. As a result, the years from 1980 to 1984 were marked by unusually acute federal-provincial conflict, with Ontario and the federal government forming an alliance against most of the other provinces with Quebec and Alberta leading the opposition.[19]

Prime Minister Trudeau retired in 1984 and Premier Davis in 1985, and their respective parties were both defeated in the federal and provincial elections that followed soon afterward. Simultaneously the apparent eclipse of Quebec nationalism and the rapid decline in the price of oil, which undermined the economic base of western provincialism, reduced the need for the Ontario-federal alliance which Trudeau and Davis had represented. Canadian federalism thus seemed to have attained a temporary equilibrium between its centrifugal and centripetal forces in the latter part of the decade. Federal-provincial relations, which tend to be bitter and conflictual when the balance of power is shifting rapidly from one level of government to the other, were more placid and harmonious after 1984, when Brian Mulroney headed a Progressive Conservative federal government. Whatever the future may hold, however, future trends in the Canadian economy are likely to have a decisive impact on Canadian federalism. Some of the possibilities are considered in the concluding chapter of this book.

NOTES

1.   Harold Innis, "Decentralization and Democracy," in *Essays in Canadian Economic History* (Toronto: University of Toronto Press, 1956) 368.
2.   W.H. Riker, "Federalism," in F.L. Greenstein and N.W. Polsby, *Handbook of Political Science* (Mass.: Addison-Wesley, 1975), Vol. 5, 132–33.
3.   Norman Rogers, "The Genesis of Provincial Rights," *Canadian Historical Review* XIV (1933) 9–23.
4.   J.M.S. Careless, "Limited Identities in Canada,"*Canadian Historical Review*, L (1969) 1–10.
5.   The decline of regional distinctiveness is discussed in Roger Gibbins, *Prairie Politics and Society* (Toronto: Butterworth, 1980).
6.   James O'Connor, *The Fiscal Crisis of the State* (New York: Oxford University Press, 1973).
7.   H.G.J. Aitken, "Defensive Expansionism: the State and Economic Growth in Canada," *The State and Economic Growth*, ed. H.G.J. Aitken (New York: Social Science Research Council, 1959).
8.   The term "province-building" is taken from E.R. Black and A.C. Cairns, "A Different Perspective on Canadian Federalism," *Canadian Public Administration* IX (1966) 27–45.
9.   Andrew Jackson, "Divided Dominion: Class and the Structure of Canadian Federalism from the National Policy to the Great Depression," Paper presented at the annual meeting of the Canadian Political Science Association, London (Ontario), 1978.
10. A partial exception was the Canadian Northern Railway, whose construction was heavily subsidized by the four western provinces in an effort to break the monopoly of the CPR. See T.D. Regehr, *The Canadian Northern Railway* (Toronto: Macmillan, 1977).
11. Richard Alway, "Hepburn, King, and the Rowell-Sirois Commission," *Canadian Historical Review* XLVIII (1967) 113–41.
12. *Foreign Direct Investment in Canada* ("The Gray Report") (Ottawa: Information Canada, 1972) 20.
13. Wallace Clement, *The Canadian Corporate Elite* (Toronto: McClelland and Stewart, 1975). The term "comprador" referred originally to Chinese merchants in the heyday of Portuguese colonialism. It is used by Marxist scholars to describe those capitalists in a dependent country

who profit from their country's relationship with an imperialist power.

14. Larry Pratt and John Richards, *Prairie Capitalism: Power and Influence in the New West* (Toronto: McClelland and Stewart, 1979). The review by Garth Stevenson appears in *This Magazine* 14, no. 4 (July–August, 1980) 33–37.

15. Robert Catherwood, "Business speaks out on the Constitution," *The Financial Post* 6 September 1980: 9.

16. Submission by the Edmonton Chamber of Commerce on Constitutional Amendment, Second Report (Edmonton, August 1980) 2.

17. Gad Horowitz, "Toward the Democratic Class Struggle," in *Agenda 1970: Proposals for a Creative Politics*, Lloyd and McLeod, (Toronto: University of Toronto Press, 1968).

18. Allan Tupper, *Bill S-31 and the Federalism of State Capitalism* (Institute of Intergovernmental Relations, Queen's University, Kingston, 1983).

19. A useful account of federal-provincial relations after 1980 is David Milne, *Tug of War: Ottawa and the Provinces under Trudeau and Mulroney* (Toronto: Lorimer, 1986).

5 A Province Unlike the Others

If French Canadians are able to claim equal partnership with English Canadians, and if their culture is established on a coast-to-coast basis, it is mainly because of the balance of linguistic forces within the country. Historical origins are less important than people generally think, the proof being that neither Eskimo nor Indian dialects have any kind of privileged position. On the other hand, if there were six million people living in Canada whose mother tongue was Ukrainian, it is likely that this language would establish itself as forcefully as French. In terms of realpolitik, French and English are equal in Canada because each of these linguistic groups has the power to break the country.

PIERRE ELLIOTT TRUDEAU[1]

Prime Minister Louis St. Laurent's now-celebrated remark that Quebec was "une province comme les autres" was greeted with indignation at the time and subsequently with derision, but it raises questions that cannot be avoided in the study of Canadian federalism. How differently would Canadian federalism have evolved if Quebec did not exist as a mainly francophone enclave within a mainly anglophone Canada? To what extent has Quebec in its relations with the federal government acted differently from other provinces? Is conflict between the Quebec government and the federal government comparable to that which involves other provincial governments, or are its causes fundamentally different? More generally, what is the relationship between Canada's cultural duality and its federal institutions and how, if at all, do the latter need to be adapted to the former?

For obvious reasons few subjects have inspired a more voluminous output of literature in both official languages, and it is neither possible nor desirable in a book on Canadian federalism to explore all of its ramifications. Quebec is a complex and interesting society, and it cannot be studied solely on the basis of its relations with the rest of Canada, important as those are for Canada and for Quebec itself. This chapter will suggest some aspects of Quebec's internal dynamics which have affected Canadian federalism, but it does not pretend to be a comprehensive treatment of Quebec society and politics.

THE LEGACY OF CONQUEST

French Canadians have never fallen prey to the illusion, common among anglophones, that 1867 was the actual beginning of Canadian history. In a society whose preoccupation with history appears greater than most, as suggested by the provincial motto "Je me souviens," Confederation is viewed in the context of what preceded it. The late Premier Daniel Johnson described the BNA Act as the fifth constitution, which sought to regulate the relations between anglophones and francophones in Canada, the others being the Royal Proclamation of 1763, the Quebec Act of 1774, the Constitution Act of 1791, and the Union Act of 1840.[2]

The first three of these documents, following one another in rapid succession during what was arguably the most decisive period of Canadian history, testify to the uncertainty and confusion of British policy, which faced the almost unprecedented problem of incorporating a viable community of European settlers into the British Empire at the same time as the foundations of British rule were collapsing in the thirteen colonies immediately to the south. The Royal Proclamation, intending to impose British laws and institutions, was reversed by the Quebec Act, which gave a quasi-official status to the Roman Catholic religion and re-established the French civil law regarding "property and civil rights," an expression of which Canadians would hear more subsequently. The Constitution Act separated the area effectively occupied by French Canadians from the future Ontario and provided both with representative institutions. A half-century later Lord Durham, in his celebrated report, was to describe this event as follows:

> Not only, however, did the Government adopt the unwise course of dividing Canada, and forming in one of its divisions a French community, speaking the French language, and retaining French institutions, but it did not even carry this consistently into effect, for at the same time provision was made for encouraging the emigration of English into the very Province which was said to be assigned to the French.[3]

In fact the anglophone minority in the predominantly francophone province already existed, at least in embryonic form. Its nucleus consisted of the merchants who arrived in the footsteps of the British army that conquered the colony between 1759 and 1763, and who rapidly took control of the colonial economy. By 1791 their numbers had been supplemented by demobilized soldiers and Loyalist refugees from the United States. By the time Lord Durham arrived on the scene, the anglophones comprised 28 percent of Quebec's population, and were a majority in Montreal, the Ottawa Valley, and the so-called eastern townships which lie between the St. Lawrence River and the American border.[4] Control of the economy was firmly in anglophone hands although, then as now, the vast majority of Quebec anglophones were not of the dominant class and enjoyed little or no economic power.

In the early decades of the nineteenth century, the politics of Lower Canada were marked by increasing conflict between British governors and the francophone-dominated Assembly. After 1784 the governor at Quebec was officially styled the governor general and was supposed to be responsible for defending what remained of British North America against any dangers from the United States. Most incumbents of the office were soldiers, and the War of 1812 reinforced their prejudices against North American democracy. Disregarding the Assembly as much as possible, they tended to take advice from the anglophone mercantile bourgeoisie with whom they interacted socially. The Assembly retaliated by refusing to appropriate funds for the canals and other public works desired by the merchants. Lacking opportunities in business, educated francophones who did not pursue a religious vocation became doctors, lawyers, and notaries, but the limited demand for their professional services gave many of them the time and the motivation to devote themselves to oppositional politics. A prolonged agricultural crisis, and the growing attractiveness of American ideas during the radical administrations of Presidents Andrew Jackson and Martin Van Buren, helped to undermine the legitimacy of Quebec's colonial regime. In 1837 and 1838 the *patriotes* resorted to an armed rebellion that was brutally but effectively suppressed by British troops.

These tragic events were the occasion for Lord Durham's celebrated mission to the colony and his still more celebrated report. Although some prominent *patriotes* had been anglophones, Durham chose to interpret the rebellion as an ethnic conflict, or, as he put it, "two nations warring in the bosom of a single state." His solution was to assimilate the French Canadians. To this end he proposed that the two Canadas should be reunited under a single legislature, that British immigration should be encouraged, that English common law should be imposed, and that English should be the only official language. The Union Act of 1840 was the first step in implementing this program. It also fulfilled a long-cherished aspiration of the Montreal merchants, who regarded the Ottawa River boundary as economically irrational and rejoiced at the disappearance of a francophone-dominated legislature.

Durham had underestimated the French Canadians, and his plan for their destruction was not to be realized. The Union Act enabled them to form an alliance with Upper Canadian reformers whose goal was responsible government. Louis-Hippolyte Lafontaine perfected this strategy despite the scepticism of both the extreme right and the anti-clerical left.[5] The governors who followed Lord Durham did not seriously pursue Durham's policies of imposing the common law and prohibiting the use of French in the legislature. By 1849 responsible government had been achieved and Governor General Lord Elgin indicated his understanding of Canadian realities by reading the speech from the throne in French. He also signed the Rebellion Losses Bill, which compensated *patriotes* whose property had been destroyed by British troops in 1837-38. Anglophone Tories responded by pelting the governor general's carriage with refuse, burning down the legislative building, and threatening to join the United States.

In the 1850s French Canada consolidated its gains. Although the Union Act remained in force until 1867, the distinct character of "Canada East" and "Canada West," the future Quebec and Ontario, was tacitly recognized in a number of ways. In Canada East the educational system was modernized (although the Church retained predominant influence), seigneurial tenure was abolished, and a new civil code, similar to that of Napoleon Bonaparte, replaced the archaic private and commercial law that dated from before the Conquest. Despite this progress, the control of the economy remained in anglophone hands while francophone society was dominated by and francophone politics heavily influenced by the clergy. Protestant merchants and Catholic bishops formed a tacit alliance based on an ethnic division of labour. Confederation, supported by both merchants and bishops albeit for different reasons, provided guarantees for both in the terms of the BNA Act, as outlined in Chapter 2 of this book.

What developed in Quebec was neither a homogeneous nor a pluralistic society, but two tenuously related and distinct societies coexisting on the same territory. The BNA Act reinforced their distinctiveness and their separation by giving the Quebec legislature jurisdiction over the matters that were of greatest concern to the clergy at the same time as it protected the language, the Protestant educational system, and the political representation of the anglophone minority. Even the economic activities of the two communities were largely distinct. The anglophone bourgeoisie, centred in Montreal and mainly interested in finance, industry, railways, and shipping, had its activities placed under federal jurisdiction. The francophone bourgeoisie, centred in Quebec City and mainly interested in land and forest resources, had its activities placed under provincial jurisdiction.

Quebec was thus divided within itself, not only culturally, but economically as well. Although the economic division did not correspond precisely with the cultural and linguistic one, there was a rough approximation between their boundaries. In the decades after Confederation, the Montreal-based and predominantly anglophone bourgeoisie dominated not only the Quebec economy but the entire Canadian economy. It was strong enough to survive and indeed to benefit from the tendency toward concentration, centralization, and monopoly that characterized the Canadian economy in the early decades of the twentieth century.

That fraction of the bourgeoisie, predominantly francophone, whose activities were on a smaller scale and confined within the province, was less fortunate. Like its counterparts in Nova Scotia and New Brunswick, it began to decline in importance after Confederation and continued to do so in the early twentieth century.[6] Despite limited financial resources, the Quebec government did its best to promote the interests of the francophone bourgeoisie by subsidizing and building railways into the northern and eastern hinterlands of the province and encouraging the development of forest resources by local capital.[7] But by the turn of the century, this strategy of economic development had run its course. The francophone bourgeoisie lacked the capital to develop the new resource industries of mining, hydro-electricity, and pulp and paper. The economic policies of the provincial state began to place heavy emphasis on attracting American direct investment, a strategy that would continue through numerous changes of government after 1936.[8]

With the influx of American direct investment, French Canadians were reduced to an even more marginal economic position in the province where they comprised four-fifths of the population. As in other parts of Canada, the bourgeoisie was divided into the three distinct fractions described in Chapter 4, but the difference in Quebec was that the two most important fractions, and a part of the third, spoke a language different from that of the majority of the population. Anglophone Canadian capital predominated in finance, utilities, and transportation, including Montreal-based enterprises whose operations extended from coast to coast. American capital was dominant in the resource industries and the more advanced sectors of manufacturing. The francophone bourgeoisie were dominant only in the service industries, retail trade, construction, and two of the most backward sectors of manufacturing: leather and wood products. As of 1961, enterprises controlled by francophones accounted for only 21.8 percent of manufacturing employment in Quebec and for only 15.4 percent of value added in manufacturing. Control of the remainder of Quebec manufacturing was about evenly divided between anglophone Canadian capital and foreign capital.[9]

French Canadians participated in the anglophone-controlled sectors of the economy, but they did so as workers, not as owners or managers. In the nineteenth century most French Canadians had been farmers, and the wage-earning class in Quebec had had a very large anglophone (particularly Irish) component. In the twentieth century, although the anglophone working class in Quebec did not disappear, it was mainly the surplus French Canadian rural population that met the greatly increased demand for wage labour. This fact, combined with the relative decline of the francophone bourgeoisie, meant that in the twentieth century contacts between anglophones and francophones in Quebec largely took the form of contacts between management and labour. In 1961 professional, technical, and managerial categories accounted for 30.4 percent of the British Isles origin labour force in Quebec, but only 14.2 percent of employed persons of French origin fell into these categories.[10] Not surprisingly under the circumstances, the average employment income of male workers in the same year was $5824 for English or Scottish origin, $5374 for Irish, and $3879 for French.[11] Anglophones in Quebec enjoyed, on the average, an Ontario standard of living, while francophones subsisted at a standard comparable to that of the Maritime provinces.

These facts appeared to lend credence to two widely shared myths, both politically influential, and still present. The first was the view that the French Canadians were in some way culturally unfit for economic achievement, possibly as a consequence of their Roman Catholic religion.[12] Evidence often cited in support of this argument was the fact that the French Canadian educational system was not only elitist but dedicated to producing lawyers and priests, rather than engineers and businessmen. No doubt it was, but the fact must be interpreted in the light of two centuries of anglophone domination of the economy and restriction of opportunities that resulted. As for the excessive influence of organized religion in French Canadian society, it must be noted that the Quebec Act, the defeat of the *patriotes*, and the terms of Confederation all tended to reinforce that influence, for better or for worse.

The second myth was the view that in Quebec ethnic and class lines essentially coincided, with the French Canadians constituting a subordinate "ethnic class," while the anglophones and the bourgeoisie were synonymous. Within the French Canadian society there were alleged to be no class distinctions of any significance. The typical result of this sentiment, of course, was a highly uncritical sympathy for Quebec nationalism and separatism.[13]

Although it was already an urban and industrial society, Quebec in the 1950s presented a picture of social and political backwardness that gave credence to Goldwin Smith's description of it long before as "a relic of the historical past preserved by isolation."[14] There was no minister or department of education. High school students had to pay for their tuition. Public libraries were almost unknown. Hospitals were run by religious orders. A divorce required a special act of the federal Parliament. Censorship was so rigorous that a film was actually banned because it sympathetically portrayed the life of Martin Luther. Drive-in theatres, margarine, and Bermuda shorts were all prohibited. Presumed "radicals," including Pierre Elliott Trudeau, were denied appointments at the francophone universities. Jehovah's Witnesses were harassed and persecuted. Priests, although by no means all of them, denounced liberalism and democracy from the pulpit. A third of the Montreal City Council was appointed by interest groups, like the "corporatist" assemblies of the Iberian dictatorships. When a badly constructed bridge collapsed in his constituency, Premier Maurice Duplessis blamed it on Communist sabotage. Elections were conducted amid widespread corruption and even violence, much of which was tolerated or encouraged by the provincial police. Little criticism of these phenomena appeared in the *Montreal Gazette*, a fact perhaps made more explicable by the odd circumstance that its Quebec City correspondent was on the premier's payroll.[15]

Writing at mid-century about a region that has some intriguing parallels with Quebec, the American political scientist V.O. Key argued that "southern politics is no comic opera. It is deadly serious business that is sometimes carried on behind a droll facade."[16] How true that was in the case of Quebec was soon to be made clear.

FROM MERCIER TO DUPLESSIS

For twenty years after Confederation, Quebec politics were dominated by the Conservative party, which in turn was dominated by its counterpart in Ottawa. Quebec thus played a passive role in federal-provincial relations, and politics consisted largely of factional disputes within the dominant party. The *rouges* (Liberals) who had opposed Confederation, were decisively handicapped by the antipathy of the Church and could thus have little influence on public opinion.

This period, nonetheless, saw the invention in Quebec of what came to be called the compact theory of Confederation. As noted in Chapter 2, the theory could, in a sense, be traced back to some remarks by John A. Macdonald during the Confederation Debates in 1865. It also had obvious similarities with interpretations of American federalism that were common before the Civil War, particularly in the South. However, its real originator was Judge T.J.J. Loranger, a conservative Quebec nationalist. Loranger's writings on Confederation first appeared in a series of newspaper articles, and were then published as a book in 1884. He argued that antagonism between English and French Canadians was inevitable and that the concentration of power in the federal government was therefore a threat to the survival of Quebec. On the basis of some rather questionable interpretations of the BNA Act, Loranger argued that Quebec had the right to resist any centralizing tendencies because:

> The central government is the creation of the several governments that have given it the form and the totality of powers which they deemed suitable, and no more.[17]

The main substantive conclusion drawn from this premise was that no change in any aspect of the relations between the two levels of government, and certainly no increase in the federal government's powers and responsibilities, could be allowed to take place without the unanimous consent of all the provinces, and that consent could only be given by the provincial governments. Implicit in this line of reasoning was the view that only the provincial government represented Quebec's interests, while the federal government was an alien institution. Loranger's ideas were soon espoused by politicians in other provinces, and survive to the present day, notably in Alberta, but Quebec was where they first saw the light of day and where their influence was deeper and more lasting than anywhere else.

The suppression of the Northwest Rebellion in 1885 and the execution of its leader, Louis Riel, soon contributed significantly to the popularity in Quebec of Loranger's views on Confederation. The refusal of Macdonald's government to exercise the prerogative of mercy in Riel's case led to turmoil in the Quebec Conservative party, and some of its more nationalist elements were enticed by Honoré Mercier, leader of the provincial Liberals, into a new alliance called the Parti National. Mercier, a devout Catholic of conservative inclinations who had only joined the Liberals because of his opposition to Confederation, was able to persuade many right-wing nationalists and most of the clergy that the traditional rouge anti-clericalism would not influence his party. At the same time he catered to anti-federal sentiments exacerbated by the Riel affair, which he portrayed as evidence of English Canada's contempt for the rights of a francophone minority. Mercier became Premier in January 1887 and for nearly five years, until he was unseated in a railway scandal, waged a series of battles against the federal Tories. In some of those battles he made common cause with Ontario's Liberal Premier, Oliver Mowat, creating an alliance against the federal government that was to be revived by many subsequent premiers of the two central provinces.

Mercier's most dramatic initiative was to convene an interprovincial conference in 1887, the first since Confederation. Although only five out of seven premiers attended (the four original provinces, plus Manitoba), the occasion suggested that opposition to Macdonald's brand of federalism was widespread. The conference adopted twenty-two resolutions calling for amendments to the BNA Act of 1867. In an explicit endorsement of the compact theory, Mercier argued that provincial governments were the appropriate representatives of the people in such matters and that his conference was really the successor and counterpart to the Charlottetown, Quebec, and London conferences before 1867. This parallel ignored the rather fundamental difference between the two situations: in 1887 a federal level of government also existed, which was not represented at the conference.

Although most of Mercier's successors were less rambunctious than he was, he established an enduring pattern for Quebec's relations with the federal government: a pattern based on the assumption that "Ottawa," in the last analysis, was the government of the anglophone majority. The Quebec government, on the other hand, deemed itself to represent the interests of French Canada including, in an indirect way, the francophone minorities outside of Quebec. In 1890 the French language lost its official status in Manitoba, and a few years later the Catholic schools of that province were denied public funding. In 1905 the new provinces of Saskatchewan and Alberta were created without any guarantees for the French language, and in 1912 the Ontario government prohibited the use of French as a language of instruction in both public and separate schools. In 1917 a government with practically no representation from Quebec imposed military conscription despite, or perhaps because of, Quebec's lack of enthusiasm for the war. Such events naturally fuelled the flames of Quebec nationalism.

In response, Quebec governments continued and perfected the approach to federal-provincial relations which Mercier had pioneered. Confederation was interpreted as a "compact" or treaty which had enabled Quebec to preserve its religion, language, legal system, and way of life by giving the provincial government exclusive jurisdiction over such matters. The federal government must not intrude into cultural or social affairs (which were very broadly defined) and in return Quebec would not interfere with its anglophone minority or with the railways, banks, and other anglophone enterprises that had their headquarters in the province. New federal activities or initiatives were routinely denounced as violations of the compact. Fundamental changes to the federal system, including formal amendments to the constitution, were deemed to require Quebec's consent. Alliances with other provincial governments, particularly with Ontario, might be formed to counter federal initiatives, but Quebec reserved the right to criticize those same provinces for their treatment of francophone minorities.

From 1897 to 1936 Quebec was governed continuously by the Liberal party, and for most of those years the Liberals also controlled the federal government. As the federal Liberals depended heavily on Quebec votes, the Quebec wing of the party was influential, and its influence was used to inhibit, prevent, or water down any initiatives on the part of the federal government that might be viewed as trespassing on provincial jurisdiction. The federal government did virtually nothing about health, education, welfare, or urban affairs, and even its economic policies were extremely cautious and conservative. Quebec's preference for limited government was thus imposed on the rest of the country. Those Canadians, including many businessmen, who believed that an industrial country required a more activist style of government thus had to turn to their provincial governments, since the federal government could not assist them. This stimulated the growth of provincial government, particularly in the economically advanced provinces of Ontario and British Columbia, reinforcing regional disparities and causing Quebec to fall further behind the rest of the country. Furthermore, the federal Liberals used their support in Quebec to counteract the pressure for reform from industrial workers and Prairie farmers.

In 1935 Maurice Duplessis, the leader of the Conservative party in Quebec, combined his party with a dissident Liberal faction to form the Union Nationale. Assorted scandals and the hardships of the Depression had weakened the entrenched Liberal dynasty, enabling Duplessis to win an election and take office in 1936. Except for a brief wartime interlude, he remained premier until his death in 1959, making himself the most durable premier in Quebec's history. Duplessis was a colourful character who inspired extremes of both hatred and devotion. No one, at least in Quebec, was neutral about him. In fact, his policies differed little if at all from those of the Liberals, whom he had supplanted in 1936. It was his government's failure to change, rather than anything original in its performance, that explained its declining popularity with Quebec intellectuals during its last decade, and its subsequent notoriety. For most of his career, Duplessis' combination of social conservatism, economic laissez-faire, and extreme provincialism, garnished with large doses of graft, patronage, and electoral corruption, worked extremely well, whatever its long-term consequences. Duplessis understood Quebec politics to be the art of pleasing the voters, the bishops, and the anglophone bourgeoisie, not necessarily in that order, while making "Ottawa" the scapegoat for all real or imagined evils. He played the game superbly.[18]

Like Mercier, Duplessis had created a new nationalist party by combining the weaker of the two traditional parties with a dissident faction of the stronger. This fact enabled both men to denounce "Ottawa" with somewhat fewer inhibitions than other premiers whose parties were organizationally linked with federal counterparts. Both also benefited from the fact that their provincial opponents bore the same party label as the federal government, and could thus be tarred with the same brush. Duplessis, however, lost this advantage two years before his death, when the federal Liberals were defeated. Partly for this reason, he in turn might have been defeated at the polls in 1960, had he lived that long.

Mercier's most unusual initiative in federal-provincial relations was the conference of 1887. Duplessis' was the Royal Commission of Inquiry into Constitutional Problems, better known as the Tremblay Commission, which was appointed in 1953 and reported three years later.[19] The Commission was Quebec's response to the centralizing tendencies of the wartime and postwar Liberal governments in Ottawa, particularly their involvement, such as it was, in the previously sacrosanct domains of social security, education, and culture. Its report is worth reading, both as an eloquent statement of Quebec's traditional values — soon to be replaced by new values — and as a rationale for Quebec's policies on federalism, from Mercier to Duplessis. The Tremblay report argued that Quebec differed from the other provinces because its culture was based on Catholicism, rather than on Protestant individualism and materialism. Federalism was acceptable only insofar as it respected these differences by leaving everything even remotely connected with culture under provincial jurisdiction. The federal government was accused of violating the original "compact" by pursuing interventionist economic, social, and cultural policies from 1940 onward. The report recommended that provincial governments take over all direct taxation, all responsibility for social security, and partial responsibility for macroeconomic policy. Even in the fields of policy remaining to it, the federal government should be required to consult with the provinces. These demands — and more besides — were to be repeated by other Quebec governments after the death of Duplessis. Ironically, they would grow more strident as their original justification — Quebec's distinctively Catholic values and way of life — was overtaken by social, political, and ideological change.

THE QUIET REVOLUTION AND ITS AFTERMATH

In 1959, the same year that the St. Lawrence Seaway opened and the Montreal streetcar system closed, Premier Maurice Duplessis died while on a visit to the iron ore mining town of Schefferville. The following year a new Liberal government was elected and began a vigorous program of reform. By 1963 the phrase "Quiet Revolution," apparently first used by *The Globe and Mail*, was becoming a cliché in both official languages, terrorist bombs were exploding, and separatist organizations were proliferating.

Like most major events in Quebec history, the "Quiet Revolution" is still surrounded by controversy as to what it meant, what it accomplished, and why it happened. All would agree that it involved a massive increase in the activities of the state at the provincial level, a simultaneous decline in the influence of the Roman Catholic Church, and an intensification of political debate and controversy. To some extent it could be interpreted as an effort to catch up with other provinces, particularly Ontario, and to some extent it was parallelled by simultaneous developments in other previously backward provinces, such as Louis Robichaud's New Brunswick and Robert Stanfield's Nova Scotia. At the same time, some of its causes were unique to Quebec, and the developments there were certainly more dramatic and far-reaching than those occurring elsewhere.

Marxists have attributed the Quiet Revolution to various fractions of the Quebec (or sometimes the Canadian) bourgeoisie. Liberals have

given the credit to a rather vaguely defined "new middle class." Icono-
clasts, like Daniel Latouche, have questioned whether it ever took
place at all.[20] While the term is most often used to describe the period
from 1960 to 1966, when Jean Lesage was Premier of the province, its
chronological boundaries are sometimes extended back into the 1940s
and forward into the 1970s. It thus requires some temerity to present,
in a few paragraphs, a summary of what it was all about. Yet, because
of its importance for Canadian federalism, the task cannot be avoided
in a book of this kind.[21]

The 1960 election, in which the Liberals under Jean Lesage defeated
the Union Nationale, was the culmination of several tendencies that
had been developing for at least a decade. In the first place, Quebec
intellectuals were beginning to challenge the hegemony of the Church
and the highly conservative values which, at least in Quebec, were
associated with the Church at that time. The Liberal government of
Adélard Godbout, which held office for most of the Second World War,
had challenged that conservatism, to some extent, by making school
attendance compulsory, giving women the vote, and nationalizing the
company that supplied electric power to Montreal and its environs.
After the war, new ideas continued to simmer under the surface of the
Duplessis regime, as evidenced by the artistic manifesto *Refus global*
in 1948, the asbestos strike in 1949, and the founding of the left-liberal
magazine *Cite Libre* in 1950. Television, which came to Quebec in
1952, had a tremendous impact in conveying new ideas to a mass
audience. René Lévesque gained fame and popularity as a television
commentator before he entered politics in 1960.

The second important development was that the Church itself faced
increasing difficulties as a provider of education and social services to
a rapidly growing and industrializing province. To maintain its
"bureaucratic empires," as the sociologist Hubert Guindon described
the network of church-related institutions, it needed more financial
aid from the state, but Duplessis' insistence on a balanced budget and
his refusal to allow the acceptance of federal funds made this impossible. Relations between the Church and the Union Nationale thus deteriorated. Some clerics began to criticize the corrupt electoral practices
of the government and its hostility toward organized labour.[22]

Finally, francophone businessmen in Quebec were becoming disil-
lusioned with the laissez-faire economic policies of the Duplessis
government. Like many of their counterparts in the Maritimes and the
West, they demanded more interventionist policies from a more activist provincial government to counteract the economic power of
Ontario. (As noted in the last chapter, Ontario itself had pioneered
such policies long before, and they seemed to have contributed to its
success.)

The decline of the old transcontinental economy based on wheat,
railways, and high tariffs, and the growing economic integration

between Canada and the United States, had had even more profound effects on Quebec than on the other parts of Canada. Montreal had been the centre of the old economy, and the transition was associated with a shift of economic power and activity from Montreal to Toronto. Instead of being the centre of a national economy, Quebec became a peripheral region in a continental economy, with little choice but to join a competitive scramble for trade and investment against other provinces and states. This seemed to require a stronger and more active provincial government.

The change in Montreal's economic role also altered the balance of forces within Quebec by undermining the power and importance of the anglophone bourgeoisie that had flourished when Montreal was the centre of a transcontinental economy. In retrospect, it can be seen that their decline had commenced at least thirty years prior to the Quiet Revolution, although it was not evident at the time.

This decline in the importance of the anglophones created a vacuum which was filled only in part by the growing role of American capital in the Quebec economy. One objective of the "Quiet Revolution" was to ensure that it would be filled by francophones as much as possible, although whether this would be done by encouraging francophone entrepreneurs, by expanding the entrepreneurial role of the state, or by a combination of both was a matter of some dispute within the coalition of forces that supported the Lesage government.

By any standard the achievements of the Lesage government in its six years of office were considerable. It re-established the Ministry of Education, which had been abolished under clerical pressure shortly after Confederation, and established a Ministry of Cultural Affairs. Municipal institutions were reformed, and hospital insurance, youth allowances, student loans, and a contributory pension plan were instituted. *La societé générale de financement* was set up as a holding company to make capital available to francophone-controlled enterprises. The privately owned hydro-electric utilities were expropriated and turned over to Hydro-Quebec. *La caisse de dépôt et de placement* was created to invest the holdings of the pension plan and other large pools of state capital. Other state enterprises were set up for specific purposes such as mineral exploration and the establishment of a steel industry.

The "new middle class," often identified as the source of the Quiet Revolution, was really more the consequence than the cause of these developments.[23] In 1960 the "new middle class" hardly existed. However, public and parapublic bureaucracies expanded over the next decade and beyond as the provincial government became more active and interventionist. Persons of secular mentality rapidly replaced clerics, lay brothers, and nuns as the providers of education and social services. State enterprises such as Hydro-Quebec, operating entirely in French, replaced anglophone private enterprises in some parts of the economy, or performed functions that had previously not been performed at all. Persons employed in all of these bureaucracies, especially those at the managerial level, had a vested interest in the expansion of the provincial level of government which for most of them had been the means of rising into the middle class. They viewed the federal government as either a competitor, an irrelevancy, or a nuisance. Although the Quiet Revolution had not been strongly nationalistic at the outset, and although Lesage himself had been a federal minister from 1953 to 1957, the Lesage government catered to this growing element of its constituency by becoming even more anti-federal than Duplessis', and to much greater effect. The compact theory, with its implicit assumption that the terms of the existing constitution were adequate for Quebec, was discarded. Instead Quebec politicians, officials, and academics increasingly argued that the Quebec "nation" required new powers and "special status" to develop its potential.

A significant minority carried this view to its logical conclusion: the belief that Quebec should separate from Canada and become an independent sovereign state. This was not a completely new idea, but it had seemed beyond the realm of practical possibility in the heyday of the National Policy, when Montreal had been the major citadel of anglo-Canadian capitalism and one of the principal seaports of the British Empire. There were two other reasons why independence was rarely espoused before 1960: traditional Catholic nationalists were at best ambivalent in their attitudes toward the state, and their definition of "French Canada" included the minorities in other provinces as well as Quebec itself.

By the time of the Quiet Revolution, these conditions no longer existed. The developments outlined in Chapter 4 suggested that the Canadian federal state could not and would not offer serious resistance to a declaration of independence, the Montreal anglophones no longer dominated the Canadian economy, and neo-nationalists were philosophically committed to a strong state that would defend the interests of the Quebec nation. They also assumed that francophone minorities in other provinces, having no possibility of controlling a state, were doomed to assimilation regardless of what Quebec decided to do. Furthermore, separatism was associated with an iconoclastic mentality, which was in many ways beneficial and which grew out of the Quiet Revolution. Since the British North America Act had explicitly safeguarded the position of both the anglophone minority and the Roman Catholic Church, and since the power and influence of both were declining in the 1960s, there was a perhaps understandable tendency to regard the federal state as a relic of the old order, and even as an obstacle to the emergence of the new.

In any event, separatism began to be openly discussed very soon after the victory of Jean Lesage and his Liberals in 1960. Books were published extolling the idea, and a variety of separatist groups and organizations emerged, most of them ephemeral, ranging on the political spectrum from extreme left to extreme right. In 1966 a public opinion poll showed 8 percent of Quebec residents in favour of independence. The percentage in favour increased gradually, reaching 16 percent in 1970, 21 percent in 1973, and 24 percent in 1976. In each of those years, support for political parties committed to independence exceeded support for the idea itself.[24]

Two parties committed to independence ran candidates in the Quebec election of 1966. The Rassemblement pour l'Indépendance Nationale (RIN) espoused a socialist program and was mainly based in Montreal. The Ralliement National, a right-wing populist organization, found most of its strength in the northern hinterlands. Between them they received almost 10 percent of the popular vote. In the same election, the Union Nationale won a narrow majority of seats (although the Liberals received more votes) and unexpectedly returned to office under Daniel Johnson, a veteran of the Duplessis government. Johnson had opposed most of the Lesage government's major reforms while in opposition but did not attempt to reverse them while in office. He favoured a new constitution that would leave a semi-sovereign Quebec loosely associated with the rest of Canada.

The federal Liberal government of Lester Pearson, after assuming office in 1963, had pursued a course of conciliation and compromise with Lesage. It saw no reason to do so with Johnson, whom it regarded as a political opponent. Relations between the Quebec and federal governments deteriorated sharply and were made worse by Johnson's efforts to conduct an independent foreign policy, even though initiatives in this direction had begun under Lesage. Johnson was flattered and entertained like a visiting head of state by President de Gaulle of France, who made a triumphant tour of Quebec in 1967, and shouted the separatist slogan "Vive le Quebec libre" from the balcony of the Montreal city hall. After being rebuked by Prime Minister Pearson, the President cancelled a planned visit to Ottawa, returned home, and explicitly endorsed the cause of Quebec independence at one of his press conferences.

The decade that followed was the most tumultuous in Quebec's history since Lord Durham. In the fall of 1967, the more nationalist and reformist wing of the Quebec Liberal Party seceded from the party to form the Mouvement Souveraineté-Association, led by René Lévesque. A year later the MSA merged with the Ralliement National to create the Parti Québécois, whose goal was an independent Quebec economically associated with the rest of Canada. Almost simultaneously, Daniel Johnson died, to be replaced by the politically inept and colourless Jean-Jacques Bertrand. Bertrand's only notable achievement while in office was to abolish the appointed upper house of the legislature. Simultaneously, the elected Legislative Assembly was renamed the National Assembly, but such symbolic gestures were a poor substitute for the reforms introduced by the Lesage government. As the euphoria of the Quiet Revolution evaporated, a series of demonstrations erupted in Montreal: against the government, against federalism, against Italian immigrants, against anglophone McGill University, and even against the firm, owned by an anglophone Jew, that held the taxi monopoly at the airport. The city adopted a by-law, later upheld by the Supreme Court, allowing it to prohibit any demonstration. Terrorist bombings and other incidents, which had occurred sporadically since the spring of 1963, increased sharply after the death of Johnson.[25] In the 1970 election, the Union Nationale received only 20 percent of the vote and the Liberals returned to office under a youthful economist, Robert Bourassa, who had briefly flirted with René Lévesque's MSA. Bourassa's majority was large on paper, but fragile in fact. Almost half of the francophone voters in Montreal had supported the Parti Québécois.

Meanwhile the leadership of the federal Liberal party, and hence of the federal government, had been taken over in April 1968 by Pierre Elliott Trudeau, a co-founder of the anti-Duplessis magazine *Cite Libre* and a convinced opponent of Quebec nationalism, which he branded as obscurantist, illiberal, and counter-revolutionary. Trudeau had little more respect for provincial Liberals than he had for separatists, and his relations with Bourassa, whom he reportedly called "an eater of hot dogs," were strained despite their common party label.

In October 1970, terrorist groups in Montreal kidnapped the British consul, James Cross, and the Quebec Minister of Labour, Pierre Laporte. Trudeau assumed control of the crisis, refused to negotiate, sent troops to Ottawa and Montreal, and finally proclaimed the War Measures Act, a statute dating from 1914, which allows the federal cabinet to assume special powers in time of war or "apprehended insurrection." (Contrary to a belief that has attained epidemic proportions, the Progressive Conservative opposition, and even a few New Democrats, supported the proclamation.) The authorities arrested 450 people, mainly in Montreal, but none was charged with any offence. Laporte was killed but Cross was finally rescued in December. Trudeau's popularity soared to new, albeit temporary, heights in both Quebec and other parts of Canada.

These events ended nationalist terrorism in Quebec and thus indirectly benefited the peaceful and democratic nationalists of the Parti Québécois, who, of course, could hardly acknowledge their gratitude to the federal authorities. The "October crisis," as it came to be known, also discredited Bourassa, who had appeared indecisive and subservient to the federal government. Subsequently an assortment of scandals, demonstrations, and conflicts with organized labour further undermined his popularity. Bourassa nonetheless won re-election in 1973 by absorbing the right-wing clientele of the moribund Union Nationale. He then alienated his most reliable supporters, the non-francophones, by restricting access to English schools and making French the only official language. In 1976 he called an early election to forestall the revival of the Union Nationale, which threatened to split the federalist vote, and perhaps even relegate the Liberals to third place. The Liberals were decisively defeated by the Parti Québécois, and René Lévesque became Premier.

THE PARTI QUÉBÉCOIS IN OFFICE

Like the Lesage government of 1960-66, but to an even greater extent, the Lévesque government of 1976-85 has been analysed by social scientists endeavouring to determine what combination of classes and class fractions it represented. No consensus has emerged, and the various conclusions perhaps reveal more about the political biases of the scholars than about the Parti Québécois itself. The "new middle class" interpretation, particularly popular among anglophone scholars, is certainly more plausible when applied to the Lévesque government than it is in relation to the Quiet Revolution of the 1960s, but it is not without its problems. Québécois scholars, who have naturally contributed a disproportionate share of the literature on the subject, have attached to the Lévesque government a variety of labels: including bourgeois, petit-bourgeois, and social democratic.

It should be remembered that democratically elected governments and political parties are rarely, if ever, the exclusive representatives of a particular class, even when they have a class-related label such as "Labour" or "United Farmers." In the more usual case when the label is deliberately ambiguous one must be even more cautious. Insofar as one can determine who or what a governing party represents, this may mean any one of three things: who votes for the party, who are the active political elites of the party (particularly the persons elected to office under its banner), and whose interests are actually served by its policies. As regards the last question, which is perhaps the most important, interpretations of the same facts may differ. It is frequently difficult to distinguish the effects of the party from those of the state, which has a certain continuity regardless of who is in office.

The voting profile of the Parti Québécois, although it evolved over time, can be succinctly described. Language was the most significant variable, with those whose mother tongue was not French giving little support to the party. Age was also a highly significant variable: those who had come of age during and after the Quiet Revolution were much more likely to support the party than older voters. More educated voters were more likely to be party supporters than the less educated, and less religious voters were more inclined to support the Parti Québécois than those who attended church regularly. In 1970 and 1973 the party had far more support in Montreal than elsewhere, but this difference was less pronounced in 1976 and disappeared entirely in subsequent elections. In terms of occupation, the party's strongest support was among "professionals and semi-professionals," and it is significant that the term "semi-professional" is virtually synonymous with the celebrated "new middle class." Business people and farmers were the least likely to support the party, at least before it became the government, while "white collar" employees and the working class both gave it approximately 50 percent of their votes (excluding non-francophones) in 1976. Only about half of those who voted for the party in 1976 were actually in favour of Quebec becoming a sovereign state.[26]

The occupational background of candidates, elected members, and ministers in the Parti Québécois differed from that of their Liberal and Union Nationale counterparts and tended to confirm the "new middle class" stereotype. Parti Québécois politicians were much less likely than their opponents to be either business proprietors or business managers, and much more likely to be semi-professionals. There were very few working class candidates in any of the parties. Among Parti Québécois candidates the most frequent occupational designation was "professeur," which includes secondary as well as postsecondary instructors. In 1981 almost one-third of the party's candidates so described themselves.[27] By the time it lost office in 1985, however, the Parti Québécois had become more similar to previous governing parties in its clientele, its personnel, and its policies.

Who benefited from the policies of the Parti Québécois is, of course, the most controversial question and the most difficult to answer. The objective that was the party's *raison d'être*, namely sovereignty-association, was not achieved, and whether it would have benefited anyone is, to say the least, very questionable. Federalists argued, at the time, that it would benefit only a small nationalist elite (the new middle class again) while radicals who supported unconditional independence argued that "association" was designed to reassure the business community, and thus demonstrated the fundamentally "bourgeois" character of the Parti Québécois.

Apart from sovereignty-association and language policy (both considered below), the policies and programs of the Lévesque government had some affinities with those of NDP governments in western Canada and thus deserved the label social-democratic. Policies in this category included anti-scab legislation, no-fault automobile insurance, partial nationalization of asbestos mining, measures to prevent the conversion of good agricultural land to other uses, and the prohibition of contributions by corporations to political parties. On the other hand, the "favourable bias" toward labour, which the Parti Québécois proclaimed at the outset, became less conspicuous the longer it continued in office (a recurring syndrome with Quebec governments) and in 1982 and 1983 the government rolled back wage increases in the public sector and legislated striking teachers back to work. Premier

Lévesque's memoirs, published in 1986, display remarkable bitterness toward the public sector unions.[28] The government's economic policies, like those of most other Canadian provincial governments, relied mainly on the private sector and provided many kinds of direct and indirect aid to enterprises based in the province. However, its friendliness toward business was not really reciprocated either before or after the referendum on sovereignty-association. Most of the business community tolerated the Parti Québécois, but most appeared to welcome the return of the Liberals in 1985.

The idea of "sovereignty-association" was Réne Lévesque's distinctive contribution to the politics of separatism, although it had affinities with older notions such as the "associate states" proposal of the Societé St. Jean Baptiste in the mid-sixties. Lévesque first unveiled the idea in 1967 and managed, not without some difficulty, to secure its acceptance by the more militant separatists who rallied under his banner the following year. The concept remained unchanged in essence when the party took office in 1976.

The basic purpose of the sovereignty-association concept was to reassure those who were sympathetic to independence in principle but apprehensive about its economic consequences. That the apprehension was fairly widespread is not surprising, since Quebec's manufacturing industries depend heavily on markets in other parts of Canada, particularly Ontario. Public opinion polls suggested that support for sovereignty-association in the 1970s ranged between about 30 and 40 percent, or about twice as high as the support for independence alone.[29]

The proposal for sovereignty-association envisaged Quebec as a fully sovereign state linked with Canada by a treaty of association. The two states would have a common external tariff but no tariff on goods moving between them, although there might be some restrictions on the free movement of agricultural produce. The proposal also envisaged a common currency for the two states, although this feature caused controversy within the Parti Québécois. There would be four common institutions to co-ordinate the interests of the two states: a monetary authority, a commission of experts, a community council, and a court. All except the monetary authority would be based on the principle of equal representation of the two partners, despite their disparity in size. Adherents of the Parti Québécois often used the analogy of the European Community in defending their concept, and the proposed institutions were based on that model.[30]

Even adding "association" to "sovereignty," however, did not make it acceptable to the majority. The 1970 election left the Parti Québécois as the third largest group in the legislature, although it had actually won more votes than the Union Nationale. In the 1973 election campaign, the party attempted to win the support of non-separatist voters by stating that independence would not follow immediately or inevitably from its victory at the polls. Instead it promised to begin negotiations for withdrawal from Canada but to submit the question to the people of Quebec in a referendum not more than two years after taking office. Separation would not actually take place before the referendum. Even this reassurance did not bring success, and in the 1976 election campaign, which finally brought it to power, the party promised that the referendum would take place before negotiations with the rest of Canada even commenced. Moreover, the referendum might take place as many as four years, instead of two, after the party took office.

Once electoral victory had been achieved, the Parti Québécois government proved remarkably reluctant to reveal either the date of the referendum or the wording of the question. Although the government was generally popular, this was so in spite of, rather than because of, its commitment to independence. Support for sovereignty-association was not apparently increasing, and cynics began to doubt whether there would be a referendum at all.

Finally, in December 1979 it was announced that the referendum would take place the following May and would not, strictly speaking, require a decision on sovereignty-association. That question would be decided by a second referendum, to be held after negotiations with the federal government. The first referendum would only ask for a mandate to begin the negotiations. The precise text of the question on the ballot was as follows:

> The Government of Quebec has made public its proposal to negotiate a new agreement with the rest of Canada based on the equality of nations.
>
> This agreement would enable Quebec to acquire the exclusive power to make its laws, levy its taxes, and establish relations abroad, in other words sovereignty, and at the same time to maintain with Canada an economic association including a common currency.
>
> No change in political status resulting from these negotiations will be effected without approval by the people through another referendum. On these terms do you agree to give the Government of Quebec the mandate to negotiate the proposed agreement between Quebec and Canada?[31]

The long delay in scheduling the referendum was based on a serious, although understandable, miscalculation. As had been generally anticipated, the Trudeau government lost the federal election of May 1979. The new Progressive Conservative government had minimal representation from Quebec and was headed by Joe Clark, a westerner highly sympathetic to provincial demands for more autonomy. These circumstances, had they continued, would probably have ensured a victory for sovereignty-association in the referendum, since the Clark government would have abstained from direct participation in the campaign and federalists would not have been able to argue that "French power" was alive and well in Ottawa. Unfortunately for the Parti Québécois, the Clark government lost a crucial vote in the House of Commons just six days before the date of the referendum was announced, and in March 1980 Trudeau returned to office with a fresh mandate. Trudeau and his government assumed the de facto leadership of the federalist forces in the referendum campaign, promising "renewed federalism" and ridiculing the "separatists" in terms reminiscent of Trudeau's editorials in the 1960s. On 20 May 1980 the voters rejected sovereignty-association by a margin of 60 to 40, larger than most federalists had hoped for, and too large to be attributed solely to the votes of non-francophones, who comprised only 18 percent of the population. Even in the east end of Montreal, once considered the major stronghold of separatism, sovereignty-association was rejected. Votes in favour predominated, however, in the mining, aluminium, and pulp and paper towns of northern Quebec, which export their products to the United States and have few economic ties with the rest of Canada. In southern Quebec only seven constituencies, most of them held by prominent members of the provincial cabinet, voted to give the government the mandate which it sought.

The defeat of the Quebec government in its own referendum set the stage for the realization of Trudeau's long-cherished project, the "patriation" of Canada's constitution with an entrenched charter of rights. The process by which this occurred, and the response of the Quebec government, are described in Chapter 10. In the midst of the constitutional debates, and to the surprise of many observers, the Parti Québécois was re-elected in April 1981. The Liberals, who had replaced Bourasssa with Claude Ryan, the former editor and publisher of *Le Devoir*, gained seats and votes but did not achieve the victory they had expected. The Union Nationale, which had elected eleven members in 1976, was again eliminated from the National Assembly.

Quebec's exclusion from the constitutional settlement of November 1981, to which all other provincial governments consented, exposed latent tensions in the Parti Québécois. Premier Lévesque and the liberal mainstream of the party had always co-existed uneasily with the radical separatists who had entered the party after the dissolution of the RIN in 1969. At the Parti Québécois convention of December 1981, the latter element turned out in force and persuaded a majority of delegates, who were presumably reacting against the constitutional fiasco, to delete "association" with the rest of Canada from the party program. They also horrified the Premier by giving a standing ovation to one of the convicted kidnappers of his old colleague Pierre Laporte. The moderates responded to the endorsement of unqualified separatism by organizing a vote of the party's entire membership, which reaffirmed its support for sovereignty-association in February 1982.

Unity was temporarily restored, but a fundamental question remained. How could a party united only by its commitment to sovereignty survive when that option had been rejected, perhaps irreversibly, by the voters?

When Brian Mulroney became Prime Minister of Canada in September 1984, Premier Lévesque ended Quebec's boycott of federal-provincial conferences which had been in effect since the constitutional settlement of November 1981. The Premier and other senior members of the Parti Québécois now argued publicly that the party should fight the next election without mentioning sovereignty. This was too much for many of Lévesque's colleagues, and during the last weeks of 1984 almost half the cabinet resigned, with several of them also leaving the Parti Québécois to sit as independents in the National Assembly. In January 1985 a special party convention endorsed Lévesque's "revisionist" position, in effect making the Parti Québécois a moderately nationalist party like the old Union Nationale. The resemblance appeared to grow later in the year, when Lévesque retired as party leader and Premier, to be replaced by Pierre-Marc Johnson, a son of former Premier Daniel Johnson. Johnson was popular, effective, and moderate, but it was too late to salvage the government. The Liberals, again led by Robert Bourassa, returned to power with a decisive majority in December 1985.

Bourassa was the fifth Quebec Premier to regain the office after an interval in opposition, and he will probably not be the last, although the feat has never been performed in any other Canadian province. His return was the culmination of a decline in Quebec nationalism that had been apparent since the referendum. As Dominique Clift argued, declining interest in the state and the nation seemed to be associated with a growing commitment to possessive individualism and the private sector of the economy, similar to the neo-conservativism in the United States.[32] A tax incentive scheme introduced by the Lévesque government dramatically increased the number of Quebec residents who participate in the stock market, francophone Quebec students now typically look forward to careers in business rather than in the public sector, and Bourassa appointed a minister in charge of privatizing Quebec's assortment of state enterprises. It would be wrong to assume, however, that the decline of Quebec nationalism is necessarily permanent and irreversible, for temporary declines in the past have been followed by periods of revival. Speaking a language that sets it apart from the rest of North America, Quebec will always be a distinct society in a way that no other Canadian province can be one, and it will always feel threatened, to some extent, by the overwhelming anglophone majority on the North American continent. For these reasons it will not easily become "a province like the others."

ANGLOPHONES AND ALLOPHONES

Quebec's anglophones occupy a position that is unique in Canada, and possibly in the world. They are a linguistic minority within a province that is itself a linguistic minority within a federal state, but they are a part of the linguistic majority in Canada and North America. They are also a privileged minority, although less so since the 1970s than before. Quebec nationalists often point out that Quebec anglophones enjoy far more rights and privileges than francophones in other provinces, even if the gap has closed somewhat in recent years. While this is in fact the case, it can only partially be attributed to the goodwill of Quebec francophones. More significant reasons for it have been the demographic balance in Canada and North America as a whole, and the fact that Quebec anglophones controlled the commanding heights of the Quebec (and Canadian) economy from the Conquest until quite recent times.

As shown in Table 5.1, anglophones have gradually declined as a proportion of Quebec's population, largely because they are far more likely than francophones to leave the province in search of economic opportunities. This tendency has been accelerated by recent political developments but, in fact, has existed for many generations. The anglophone community has also become more heterogeneous. From the middle of the nineteenth century it was divided between Catholics (mainly Irish) and Protestants, while in the twentieth century it included a significant number of Jews. These divisions were particularly significant since institutions in Quebec were traditionally structured on the basis of religion rather than language or ethnicity. More

Table 5.1
Population of Quebec by Mother Tongue (percent)

	French	English	Other
1871*	78.1	20.3	1.6
1931	79.7	15.0	5.3
1941	81.6	14.1	4.3
1951	82.5	13.8	3.7
1961	81.2	13.3	5.5
1971	80.7	13.1	6.2
1976	81.2	12.8	6.0
1981	82.5	11.0	6.5
1986**	81.4	8.9	6.0

* For 1871 only, mother tongue is assumed to correspond with ethnic origin, since data on mother tongues were not collected in that year.

** In 1986, respondents were allowed to reply that they had multiple mother tongues, and 3.7 percent replied in this manner.

recently Quebec's population has been supplemented by a great variety of immigrants from all over the world, who, to varying degrees, have entered the anglophone community, entered the francophone community, or remained largely separate from both. This development coincided with the post–1960 shift from religion to language as the basis of institutional segmentation in the province, except insofar as the federal constitution required otherwise. Finally, it should be noted that Quebec anglophones have lost their privileged economic status since the Quiet Revolution, as a consequence of developments both within and outside the province. The changing dynamics of anglophone-francophone relations within Quebec have significantly affected, although they have also been affected by, Quebec's relations with the rest of Canada.

At least until the Quiet Revolution, relations between anglophones and francophones in Quebec corresponded closely to the consociational model of elite accommodation which Arend Lijphart developed to explain the stability of certain culturally segmented European nations.[33] Most anglophones could not speak French and took little interest in provincial politics. In effect they delegated the power to act on their behalf to the powerful anglophone business community and to a small elite of professional politicians, most of whom were fluent in French. From Confederation until 1976, every Quebec cabinet contained anglophone ministers, and until 1944 an anglophone was almost always the provincial treasurer. On the other hand, no anglophone was ever Minister of Justice, the other senior portfolio, until Herbert Marx was appointed in 1985. These ethnic stereotypes were also found at the federal level, where Justice was the traditional portfolio for the francophone "Quebec lieutenant" while Finance was reserved for persons of British ancestry until 1977.

Quebec anglophones used their influence in provincial politics to oppose Quebec nationalism, usually voting massively for the less nationalistic of the two major parties, and to protect the autonomy of their own social and cultural institutions from any interference by the provincial government. The latter task was facilitated by the francophone majority's preference for having its own social and cultural institutions controlled by the Church rather than the state. The government's virtual abdication of any responsibility for education, health, and welfare suited the interests of both the Catholic clergy and the non-Catholic minorities, allowing the former to dominate the social and cultural life of the majority and the latter to develop their own parallel networks of institutions. Catholics who were not francophones perhaps gained the least from these arrangements, but nonetheless there were anglophone Catholic schools, hospitals, and colleges.

The Quiet Revolution placed these arrangements at risk with its intensification of nationalism, transfer of responsibilities from

Church to state, and efforts to increase francophone participation in
the economy. The provincial bureaucracy, from which anglophones
had always been virtually excluded, began for the first time to intrude
seriously on the autonomy of their civil society.[34] Anglophones, nonetheless, admired Jean Lesage and they continued to vote overwhelmingly for the provincial Liberals, as they had done since 1939.

By 1967 the Quiet Revolution was losing momentum, and appeared
to have raised more hopes than it had been able to satisfy. Frustrated
francophones, particularly in Montreal where the anglophones were
numerous and conspicuous, became increasingly hostile to the privileged minority in their midst. Like the aristocracy before the French
Revolution, the anglophones now seemed to possess inherited privileges out of proportion to their real power and importance, a circumstance that made them tempting targets. The declining francophone
birthrate also caused anxiety, sincere on the part of some francophones, and deliberately fostered for political purposes by others,
that Montreal might become a predominantly anglophone city, even
though the trend since Confederation had in fact been the opposite
direction. The traditional tendency of immigrants in the city to choose
English as their new language, a tendency tolerated and even
encouraged by francophones in the past, now seemed to add insult to
injury. In 1968 violence erupted over a dispute between francophones
and Italians on the Catholic school board in the working class suburb
of St. Leonard. The Italians wanted to continue English instruction for
their children while the francophones, influenced by nationalist
groups like the RIN, wanted to phase it out.

Business people, regardless of ethnic background, tended to agree
with the Italians, since English schools encouraged immigrants to
choose Montreal instead of its rival Toronto and since bilingualism
facilitated the integration of Quebec into the North American economy. Under pressure from the business community, the Bertrand government adopted Bill 63, guaranteeing the right of parents to choose
whether their children would be educated in French or in English.
This corresponded to the views of the Roman Catholic Church, which
believes that the state should not interfere with the family, but was
anathema to nationalists, who turned out in thousands to demonstrate
against the government. As a minor concession to the nationalists, the
government appointed a Royal Commission, headed by Jean-Denis
Gendron, to investigate the position of the French language in Quebec.

The Gendron Commission reported in December 1972, almost three
years after the fall of the Union Nationale government. It concluded
that the fears of the nationalists were exaggerated, and recommended
against any legislation that would force immigrants into French
schools. Instead it suggested that the highest priority should be measures to increase the use of French in the private sector of the economy,

since it was the economic importance of English that motivated immigrants to choose that language for their children.[35]

The Bourassa government secured a fresh electoral mandate and then, in 1974, introduced Bill 22, the Official Language Act. This declared French to be the only official language of Quebec, but did not challenge the use of English in the legislature and the courts, as guaranteed by the federal constitution. Following Gendron's recommendations, the act introduced token measures to encourage the use of French in private business, and required professionals such as doctors and nurses to pass a test in the French language. It disregarded the Royal Commission's advice by providing that children whose mother tongue was neither English nor French (known in Quebec jargon as allophones) could only be admitted to English schools if they demonstrated facility in the English language. This legislation was, in fact, a reasonable compromise between increasingly polarized viewpoints, but it offended most allophones and anglophones while failing to satisfy the nationalists.

Tougher language legislation was a high priority for the Parti Québécois, and as soon as they took office they introduced Bill 1, later replaced by the only slightly less draconian Bill 101, the Charter of the French Language. This statute, adopted in 1977, declared that only the French-language text of statutes and legal judgments was official, imposed rigid standards of "francization" on all business enterprises with fifty or more employees, required all commercial signs and billboards to be in French only, and established elaborate bureaucratic machinery to implement and enforce its provisions. Access to English schools was restricted to children whose parents had received an English education in Quebec, children already enrolled in English schools in Quebec or the siblings of such children, or children whose parents had received an English education outside of Quebec but had been living in the province at the time the statute came into effect.

Although Bill 101 in many ways resembled its predecessor, Bill 22, the two bills revealed somewhat contrasting attitudes toward Quebec's anglophone minority. The provincial Liberals envisaged a Quebec in which French would be the dominant and only official language, but in which English would be a privileged second language, as French is in Ontario. René Lévesque personally inclined to this view, but most of his followers viewed English as merely one of several minority languages, and one that should have no privileged status not enjoyed by Italian, Greek, or Chinese. In other words, they wished English to have the same status in Quebec that French has in Alberta or British Columbia.[36]

The election of the Parti Québécois and the adoption of Bill 101 caused a massive anglophone exodus from the province. Sun Life, whose impressive office building was a symbol of corporate capitalism in Montreal, moved its head office to Toronto, as did many less prominent enterprises. By 1981 there were 100 000 fewer anglophones in Quebec than there had been in 1976, with Montreal Island absorbing practically all the losses. Real estate values collapsed, and many middle class francophones purchased houses in previously anglophone neighbourhoods at bargain prices.

Since middle-class anglophones were more likely to leave than working class anglophones, and since "francization" opened many managerial positions in the private sector for francophones, Bill 101 accelerated a process that had begun a decade earlier: the gap between the living standards and incomes of anglophones and francophones in Quebec narrowed, and by 1981 had virtually disappeared. Other factors contributing to this trend were the encouragement of francophone business enterprises by both federal and provincial governments since the Quiet Revolution, and generous wage settlements in the almost exclusively francophone public sector. Those anglophones who remained in Quebec in the 1980s were thus less resented than they had been in earlier decades. Most accepted the necessity of learning French and participating more fully in the life of the province. They reacted to the breakdown of consociational elite accommodation by developing more populist forms of political involvement, such as the anglophone pressure group Alliance Quebec, founded in 1982 and claiming soon afterward to have 40 000 individual members. Anglophone morale was also improved by the outcome of the referendum on sovereignty-association and by the subsequent entrenchment of minority language educational rights in the Canadian constitution, which caused the Supreme Court to strike down the restrictive educational provisions of Bill 101.

Despite these advances, the anglophone community in Quebec has not regained the power and importance that it had enjoyed before the Quiet Revolution. The Quebec economy now operates mainly in French and a new francophone bourgeoisie has relegated the old anglophone bourgeoisie to the sidelines. Toronto, rather than Montreal, is now the undisputed centre of anglo-Canadian business. Both major provincial political parties in Quebec are committed to the view that allophone children must be educated in French, a policy which the Canadian Charter of Rights and Freedoms implicitly endorses, and Quebec anglophones can thus no longer reinforce their numbers by assimilating immigrants. Young Quebec anglophones, like their counterparts in Atlantic Canada, tend to seek economic opportunities in Ontario. Probably the anglophone community of Quebec will survive indefinitely in some form, just as viable francophone minorities survive in several other provinces, but it will never again be the linchpin of Canadian unity as it was for almost a century after Confederation.

NOTES

1. Pierre Elliott Trudeau, *Federalism and the French Canadians* (Toronto: Macmillan, 1968) 31.
2. Daniel Johnson, *Egalite ou Independance*, 2nd ed. (Montreal: Les editions de l'homme, 1968) 25–35.
3. *The Report of the Earl of Durham, Her Majesty's High Commissioner and Governor-General of British North America*, 4th ed. (London: Methuen, 1930) 47.
4. Richard Joy, *Languages in Conflict* (Toronto: McClelland and Stewart, 1972) 85–86.
5. Jacques Monet, *The Last Cannon Shot* (Toronto: University of Toronto Press, 1969) is an excellent account of this period.
6. Jorge Niosi, "The New French Canada Bourgeoisie," *Studies in Political Economy*, No. 1 (Spring 1979) 113–62.
7. P.A. Linteau, R. Durocher, and J.C. Robert, *Histoire du Québec contemporain, de la Confederation a la crise* (Montreal: Boreal Express, 1979) 112–13, 159–60, 423–24.
8. Linteau, et al., 448–49.
9. *Report of the Royal Commission on Bilingualism and Biculturalism*, 3 (Ottawa: Queen's Printer, 1969) 54, 56.
10. Royal Commission on Bilingualism, 43.
11. Raymond Breton, Jeffrey G. Reitz, and Victor Valentine, *Cultural Boundaries and the Cohesion of Canada* (Montreal: Institute for Research on Public Policy, 1980) 149.
12. This view, although not its application to Canada, can ultimately be traced back to Max Weber, *The Protestant Ethic and the Spirit of Capitalism* (New York: Scribner's, 1958).
13. For a readable, and in some ways informative, example of writing from this perspective see Malcolm Reid, *The Shouting Signpainters* (Toronto: McClelland and Stewart, 1972).
14. Quoted in Robert M. Hamilton, ed., *Canadian Quotations and Phrases* (Toronto: McClelland and Stewart, 1952) 85.
15. Conrad Black, *Duplessis* (Toronto: McClelland and Stewart, 1977) 643–44.
16. V.O. Key, *Southern Politics* (New York: Knopf, 1949) 4.
17. T.J.J. Loranger, *Letters upon the interpretation of the federal constitution known as the B.N.A. Act* (Quebec: Morning Chronicle, 1984) 3.
18. A useful account of the Duplessis regime is Herbert F. Quinn, *The Union Nationale* 2nd ed., (Toronto: University of Toronto Press, 1979). A more analytical treatment from a Marxist perspective is Gerard Boismenu, *Le Duplessisme* (Montreal: Les presses de l'Universite de Montreal, 1981).
19. The full report was published simultaneously in French and English by the Quebec Government Printer. For a useful abridgment, see David Kwavnick, ed., *The Tremblay Report: Report of the Royal Commission*

of Inquiry on Constitutional Problems (Toronto: McClelland and Stewart, 1973).

20. Daniel Latouche, *Canada and Quebec, Past and Future: An Essay* (Toronto: University of Toronto Press, 1986).

21. The best single volume on the Quiet Revolution is William Coleman, *The Independence Movement in Quebec 1945-1980* (Toronto: University of Toronto Press, 1984) which also includes a summary and critique of the different interpretations. Various aspects of the Quiet Revolution are discussed in Gerard Bergeron and Rejean Pelletier eds., *L'etat du Québec en devenir* (Montreal, Boreal Express, 1980). See also Dale C. Thomson, *Jean Lesage and the Quiet Revolution* (Toronto: Macmillan, 1984).

22. Hubert Guindon, "The Social Evolution of Quebec Reconsidered," *Canadian Journal of Economics and Political Science* XXVI (1960) 533-51.

23. The "new middle class" interpretation first appeared in Hubert Guindon, "Social Unrest, Social Class, and Quebec's Bureaucratic Revolution," *Queen's Quarterly* LXXI (1964) 150-62.

24. Maurice Pinard and Richard Hamilton, "The Parti Québécois Comes to Power: An Analysis of the 1976 Quebec Election," *Canadian Journal of Political Science* XI (1978) 739-76.

25. A chronological list of such incidents appears in Gerard Pelletier, *The October Crisis* (Toronto: McClelland and Stewart, 1971) 197-205.

26. Pinard and Hamilton 739-76.

27. Andre Bernard and Bernard Descoteaux, *Quebec: elections 1981* (Montreal: Hurtubise, 1981) 215-20.

28. René Lévesque, *Attendez que je me rappelle* (Montreal: Editions Quebec/Amerique, 1986), 250-51, 349-51.

29. Breton, Reitz and Valentine, 184.

30. *Quebec-Canada: A New Deal* (Quebec: Editeur officiel, 1979) is the white paper outlining the details of the proposal as determined at the party's convention in June of that year.

31. R.B. Byers, ed., *Canadian Annual Review of Politics and Public Affairs 1979* (Toronto: University of Toronto Press, 1981) 306. Reprinted by permission of Les Publications du Quebec.

32. Dominique Clift, *Le declin du nationalisme au Québec* (Montreal: Editions Libre Expression, 1981).

33. Arend Lijphart, *The Politics of Accommodation: Pluralism and Democracy in the Netherlands* (Berkeley and Los Angeles: University of California Press, 1968). This analytical framework has been applied to Quebec in Christopher C. Cooper, "French-English Subcultural Segmentation: An Analysis of Consociational Politics in Quebec" M.A. thesis, University of Alberta, 1987.

34. Sheila McLeod Arnopoulos and Dominique Clift, *The English Fact in Quebec*, 2nd ed. (Montreal and Kingston: McGill-Queen's University Press, 1984) 95-108. The entire book is an excellent study of Quebec's anglophone community.

35. Government of Quebec, *Report of the Commission of Inquiry on the Position of the French Language and on Language Rights in Quebec*, 3 volumes (Quebec, 1972).

36. Lévesque, 270–71 and 389 for his views on minority language rights.

6 Fiscal Federalism: The Search for Balance

The federal government was caught in the middle. It was supposed to compensate the provinces on the one hand for lack of taxable capacity and on the other hand for its possession. That, however, may be the price of nationhood.

R. M. BURNS[1]

The financial aspects of federalism have held an enduring fascination for students of the subject, in Canada and elsewhere. Economists who specialize in public finance have had more reason than most other people to be interested in federalism, and have made important contributions to the writing on the subject. Moreover, those who approach federalism from other perspectives cannot ignore the financial aspect, and have rarely done so. Intergovernmental disputes and controversies over financial matters have been a persistent feature of Canadian federalism throughout its history. Changes in financial arrangements have been constantly resorted to as a means of adapting the federal system to new circumstances, although rarely with enough success to avoid the necessity of further modifications a few years later. The management of intergovernmental fiscal relations, especially in recent years, has employed armies of officials and has led to scores of intergovernmental conferences. Thus it would be possible, although somewhat misleading, to write the history of Canadian federalism merely as the history of intergovernmental finance.

The fiscal side of federalism has also attracted interest because it seems to offer a convenient way of measuring the degree of "centralization" in a federal system and the changing distribution of power and importance between the two levels of government. Even for those political scientists who are not quantitatively inclined, the numbers and percentages associated with fiscal federalism provide a reassuring illusion of concreteness and clarity in a field of study whose other aspects seem so often to be obscured by ambiguity, mystification, and the absence of universally shared assumptions.

The precision of fiscal federalism, however, is in some respects more apparent than real. Government revenues need not correspond with government expenditures, and neither revenues nor expenditures form a homogeneous category. Revenue from taxation is only a part of total revenue, and even definitions of taxation may vary, with natural resource revenues and liquor profits, to take only two examples, being sometimes classified as taxation and sometimes not. Revenues of provincial governments include substantial transfers from the federal government, both conditional and unconditional. When these funds are spent they become part of provincial expenditure, even though they have already been counted as part of federal expenditure. How they are classified, of course, determines how "centralized" the system appears to be. National accounts statistics treat all intergovernmental grants as expenditures of the recipient government, while public finance statistics distinguish conditional from unconditional grants, including the former with the expenditures of the government that makes them. These two alternative procedures, although the most widely used, by no means exhaust the list of possibilities.[2]

Expenditure, like revenue, has its ambiguities quite apart from the question of intergovernmental grants. The amount which a government spends may be related to its economic impact, its political power, or its need for increasing revenues, but all types of expenditure do not necessarily bear the same relationship to all three of these other variables. Expenditures may be at the discretion of the government concerned; they may be fixed; they may even be dictated by another government (as in the case of matching funds required by some conditional grants). Expenditures on goods and services have a totally different economic significance from transfer payments. The entirely different distinction between expenditure on the economic and on the social functions of government (in Marxist terms, accumulation and legitimization) should also be borne in mind. Unfortunately, none of these distinctions is often made in the regrettably abundant polemical statements about government spending. Sometimes these statements display a total absence of consistency, as when provincial politicians deplore the massive expenditures of the federal government as evidence of its general profligacy, but cite their own increasing expenditures to support the proposition that their "responsibilities" require a larger share of the income tax.

Comparisons of the expenditures or revenues of the two levels of government at various times are often used to support statements about centralization or decentralization. Subject to the reservations mentioned, they may have a certain utility for this purpose, but not for the reason that often seems to be assumed. Governments do not necessarily derive "power" from the fact that they have increased their expenditures, and they may exercise power without either raising or spending much money, as they do by permitting, regulating, or prohibiting various kinds of individual or corporate activities. The significance of financial data for the study of how power is distributed between governments is better seen by treating power as the independent variable. The more power a government gains, the better able it is to increase its revenues, and therefore its expenditures, at the expense of the taxpayer and (in a federal state) at the expense of the other level of government. Thus the easily quantifiable shifts in the fiscal balance of Canadian federalism followed the real shifts in the distribution of power between federal and provincial governments that took place for the reasons discussed in Chapter 4. The often-recounted history of federal-provincial fiscal negotiations and of the imposition of new taxes at one or the other level is significant as an indication of how governments used the power which circumstances had given them, not of how they acquired it. Politically strong governments can get the revenue they want. Politically weak governments (the provincial governments during the Second World War, the federal government more recently) cannot, just as politically weak groups of taxpayers cannot prevent increases in their taxes.

Public finance economists sometimes refer to the goal of maintaining a "vertical balance" in fiscal federalism, by which is meant an appropriate division of sources of revenue between the two levels of government.[3] Politicians often refer to the desirability of giving each level of government enough revenue to match its responsibilities. What "balance" is considered appropriate depends mainly on how "responsibilities" are assigned. While in theory this may be determined by the constitution, in practice it is determined politically by a process that reflects the kinds of circumstance described in preceding chapters.

Existing state functions may be shifted, in whole or in part, from one level to the other. New ones, when the demand for them arises, will tend to be assumed by the politically stronger level at the time, which can usually, if need be, find a constitutional interpretation to support its position. Even if there is no change in the allocation of functions, the expenses connected with different functions will increase at varying rates, but functions are not often reallocated for this reason. Thus the search for "vertical balance" in a federal state is never-ending, and constant adjustments must be made to bring the fiscal regime in line with the realities of political power.

Moreover, the problem is complicated if an effort is simultaneously made to maintain what the public finance economist calls "horizontal balance." This is a situation in which all of the provincial governments are equally well provided with the financial means to perform their functions, assuming that all have roughly comparable rates of taxation. If the same types of taxation are available to all provincial governments, and if all are responsible for the same functions (which is usually the case), the governments of rich provinces may have enough revenue but the governments of poor provinces will not. Either they have to levy higher taxes, or perform their functions less adequately, or both. If this is considered undesirable, horizontal balance could in theory be secured by one of two methods. Either the governments of poorer provinces could hand over some of their functions to the federal government, or else they could receive subsidies to bring their revenues closer to the level enjoyed by the governments of richer provinces. In practice horizontal balance, like vertical balance, is more often sought by adjusting the revenue side of the equation than by adjusting the allocation of functions. Thus in Canada over the last three decades, equalization payments have been the main instrument used to bring about horizontal balance.

The history of federal-provincial finance in Canada is one of continual efforts to bring the vertical balance of revenues into line with the constantly changing allocation of functions between the two levels, efforts that have been complicated by a somewhat more sporadic preoccupation with the horizontal balance. At times the system seemed to be largely self-regulating, while at other times more conscious manipulation was required, but at no time could federal-provincial finance be independent of the underlying realities of the Canadian political economy.

THE FIRST SEVENTY-FIVE YEARS

At the same time when the BNA Act was drafted, the main source of revenue for all the provincial governments was the customs tariff, which by necessity had become an exclusively federal tax, given the goal of creating a common market. The main business of government was the construction of railways, canals, and other public works. This task was mainly assigned to the federal level of government both prospectively and, in a sense, retroactively, since it assumed responsibility for most of the debts which the provinces had accumulated in the course of their efforts to perform this function before 1867. Each province was assigned an "allowance" for what was considered a normal level of debt. The Maritime provinces, with actual debts below this level, were rewarded by receiving interest on the difference, while Quebec and Ontario were supposed to pay, (although they never actually did) for the higher-than-average debts which the federal government assumed on their behalf.

Since all provincial governments were deprived of the important sources of taxation, their main source of revenue after Confederation was subsidies from the federal government. There were two kinds of subsidies: one was fixed at eighty cents per capita (based on 1861 census returns for Quebec and Ontario, but increasing for the other two provinces until they each reached a population of 400 000); while the other was a fixed sum for each province, ostensibly for the support of the provincial government and legislature. New Brunswick got an additional subsidy for ten years and was explicitly guaranteed the right to continue imposing its lumber dues, which would otherwise have been *ultra vires* as an indirect tax.

These arrangements left the provincial government with very limited financial resources, even by the standards of the time, and were declared with more optimism than good judgment to be "in full Settlement of all future Demands on Canada." That was not quite how it ultimately worked out. Less than two years after Confederation, Nova Scotia received "better terms" (a larger debt allowance and a temporary subsidy similar to New Brunswick's) by threatening to secede. The other provincial governments protested that this was unconstitutional, but soon adopted the more fruitful approach of seeking their own "better terms" whenever the opportunity arose. In the words of one writer, the concession to Nova Scotia "made a breach in the constitution not yet repaired." Surveying the record of more than sixty years, he concluded: "It is not mere coincidence that, of the twenty-six concessions made since 1867 to individual provinces, only five have gone to governments definitely of the opposite political faith. Moreover, all the important concessions have been made immediately before or immediately after a federal election."[4]

Newly admitted or established provinces received terms broadly similar to those of the original ones, sometimes made more generous by highly optimistic estimates of their populations. In 1907, with nine provinces now in existence, the BNA Act was amended to increase the subsidies for the support of legislatures and to raise the population ceiling for per capita grants to two and a half million, slightly more than Ontario's population at the time. Even above that level, a grant of sixty (instead of eighty) cents would be made for each additional person. Special concessions were made to Prince Edward Island and British Columbia, although the latter was still so dissatisfied with the outcome that it petitioned the British Parliament not to make the amendments.

These concessions to the provinces reflected their increasing power and importance, a much greater consequence of which, however, was their increasing ability to extract taxes from their populations and revenues from their natural resources. This ability was unevenly distributed, with the result that some provinces became largely self-supporting while others continued to rely more heavily on federal subsidies. None, however, was as totally reliant on the subsidies as had originally been expected. The reputed unwillingness of British North Americans to tolerate direct taxation — the only kind which the provincial governments could impose — seemed to evaporate as provincial governments demonstrated their usefulness to local economic interests. British Columbia and Prince Edward Island imposed taxes on land not long after Confederation. Quebec pioneered the use of a corporation tax in 1882, an innovation which the Judicial Committee of the Privy Council declared to be acceptable a few years later. Ontario established succession duties in 1892, and was soon followed by all of the other provinces. Even an income tax appeared in British Columbia as early as 1876.

One effect of these innovations was to establish, in some people's minds, the entirely unconstitutional doctrine, which Quebec's Tremblay Commission recited as late as 1956, that the field of direct taxation belonged exclusively to the provincial governments. Even after the First World War began, Ottawa hesitated for years before imposing an income tax (Britain had done so during the war against Napoleon a century earlier), and only took the plunge after a coalition government was formed in 1917.

Direct taxes were supplemented by natural resource revenues, especially in British Columbia and Ontario.[5] (The Prairie provinces of course had none until they received their lands and resources in 1930.) During the golden years between the Klondike gold rush and the First World War, provincial expenditures increased somewhat faster than federal, despite an almost incredible rate of railway building which occurred largely at the federal taxpayer's expense. Even after the federal subsidies to the provinces were increased in 1907, Ontario relied on them for less than one-quarter of its revenue.

As some provinces collected more from taxation than others, neither the statutory subsidies nor the various additional grants to dissatisfied provinces could prevent a horizontal imbalance from emerging. Since wealthy capitalists and corporations were concentrated in Toronto and Montreal, succession duties and corporation taxes were mainly collected by the two central provinces, permitting them in effect to tax the wealth that was accumulated by exploiting the eastern and western hinterlands. The hinterland provinces, particularly in the West, had nonetheless to meet many of the expenses associated with rapid economic development, and were forced to supplement their revenues with extensive borrowing.

Increasing provincial power continued to bear fruit in the 1920s, despite the temporary interruption caused by the war. Mackenzie King's government abolished some of the special taxes imposed in wartime and reduced the federal income and corporation taxes to very low levels. There was apparently little demand for an active or expensive government at the federal level. The provincial governments, on the other hand, were busy assisting the development of mines and forests, building highways, extending public utilities, and opening their northern frontiers. They were also beginning, although with much less enthusiasm, to spend more on health, education, and welfare. The sources of taxation developed before the war were supplemented by automobile licence fees, gasoline taxes, and profits from a newly invented institution that was to become a ubiquitous feature of Canadian life: the provincial liquor control board. By 1929 federal grants accounted for only one-tenth of provincial revenue. About two-fifths of all revenues went to the federal government, one-fifth to the provincial governments, and two-fifths to the local governments.[6]

The Canadian system of public finance had not been designed to deal with the Depression that followed the collapse of share prices on the New York Stock Exchange in 1929. Relief and welfare costs, ostensibly a municipal responsibility, increased so rapidly that in practice the federal government had to assume about two-fifths of them. The Prairie provinces, which were hit by dry weather as well as by disappearing markets, had difficulty even paying the interest on their debts. Municipal property taxes were raised to pay for welfare (producing a decline in property values) and were supplemented by municipal sales taxes in Montreal and Quebec City. Provincial governments tried to make ends meet by increasing their own taxes or inventing new ones (such as sales taxes in Alberta and Saskatchewan and a payroll tax in Manitoba). Federal taxes were also increased, adding to the misery of taxpayers whose incomes were declining. Special federal grants were made to Manitoba, Saskatchewan, and British Columbia, and the special grants to the Maritime provinces, which had begun in 1925, were increased. In 1936 all ten governments agreed to a constitutional amendment that would have opened the field of indirect taxation to the provinces, but it was rejected by the Senate.

In response to this situation, the federal government appointed, in 1937, the Royal Commission on Dominion-Provincial Relations, usually known as the Rowell–Sirois Commission.[7] The Commission conducted an impressive examination of Canadian federalism and presented its report in 1940. It recommended that the federal government again assume responsibility for all provincial debts, and for a portion of municipal debts in Quebec. Also, it advised that the federal government should take full financial responsibility for emergency relief to agriculture and to the employable unemployed. It should be given power to establish a social security plan, as the United States had recently done, and to implement the conventions of the International Labour Organization. The provincial governments should surrender their right to impose income, corporation, and succession taxes, receiving some compensation for the contribution of their natural resources to corporate profits. An independent commission (modelled after Australia's) should be established to remove political partisanship from the process of allocating federal grants to the provinces. "Adjustment grants" should be made to provinces insofar as this was necessary for them to provide an "average Canadian standard of government services." It was anticipated that all provinces except Ontario, British Columbia, and (surprisingly) Alberta would require them.

Predictably, the three provincial governments that had been declared ineligible for Adjustment Grants rejected the report, with Alberta's Aberhart denouncing it as a plot by international finance, and Ontario's Hepburn professing to find some arcane significance in the fact that Ontario was unrepresented on the Commission. (N.W. Rowell was from Ontario, but he had played little part in the Commission's work because of illness.) Thus the Commission, by correctly anticipating that these provinces would be the centres of growth in the post–depression economy, provoked them into recognizing their common interest in fiscal decentralization.

In the meantime, the problems of another war had replaced those of the Depression. The report was filed away and replaced by a federal pledge in the 1941 budget speech to raise income and corporation taxes to the maximum level that would be reasonable, on the assumption that the provinces levied no such taxes at all. Provinces that agreed not to tax incomes or corporations would be compensated either by an annual payment equal to their actual revenues from such taxes in 1940, or by a formula based on subtracting their succession duty revenues from the interest on their debts. Provinces that refused to agree would expose their residents to prohibitive taxation for no apparent purpose.

All agreed, with Saskatchewan and the Maritimes choosing the formula based on debts while the more prosperous provinces opted for straight compensation (Alberta switched to the debt option in 1945). The system was effective for financing the war but grossly inequitable: British Columbia received about fifteen dollars per capita each year, Ontario and the Prairie provinces about eight dollars, Quebec and the Maritimes about six dollars. However, the impact of this fact was softened by retaining largely unchanged the somewhat chaotic accumulation of "special" and "emergency" grants to individual provinces. In 1945, as the first ministers assembled for a major conference on postwar reconstruction, the major question at hand was whether the wartime fiscal system, the prewar system, the system recommended by the Rowell–Sirois Commission, or some fourth alternative would be adopted in the postwar period.

FROM TAX RENTAL TO TAX SHARING

At the conclusion of the Second World War, the federal government appeared to stand at the height of its power and prestige in relation to the provincial governments. Canada had operated in wartime practically as a unitary state, and the provincial governments had been reduced to insignificance. Popular sentiment appeared to expect a predominant federal role in planning the economy and in extending social legislation after the war, and the greatly expanded federal bureaucracy seemed well-equipped for the task.

The temporary and illusory nature of this federal predominance, however, was soon to be revealed. As the underlying logic of the postwar political economy asserted itself, the federal government proved unable to impose its will on the provincial governments, particularly those of the two central provinces. Pressure from these two forced a gradual but inexorable retreat from the postwar design of fiscal centralization and the surrender of an increasingly larger share of the direct tax fields to the provincial governments. At the same time direct taxes, especially the personal income tax, were gaining in importance relative to other forms of taxation. Thus the way in which the proceeds of this tax were divided was increasingly important for both levels of government. The fact that the provincial governments were so largely victorious in a conflict where so much was at stake indicated how illusory had been their apparent weakness at the end of the war.

Another interesting feature of the postwar period was the procedure by which federal-provincial negotiations over fiscal matters were carried on. It came to be accepted as a fact of life that the federal government could not, in practice, impose direct taxation without taking into account the views of the provincial governments, or at least of those in Toronto and Quebec City. This was certainly a very different situation from that which prevailed in the United States or Australia. In addition, power was shifting so rapidly toward the provincial level of government that it became necessary to revise the federal-provincial fiscal regime at least every five years, and in practice somewhat more frequently. The result of these facts has been a new and highly distinctive pattern of policy-making. New arrangements for federal and provincial division of direct taxes and related matters are established every five years, subject to occasional adjustments in the interim. Each five-year period is preceded by a series of intergovernmental conferences, involving officials, finance ministers, and first ministers.

In 1945 the federal government proposed that a fiscal regime somewhat similar to the wartime model should be continued in peacetime. Provinces would "rent" to the federal government, for periods of five years at a time, their constitutional right to impose income, corporation, and succession taxes. In return they would receive uniform per capita payments, escalating automatically with the growth in the GNP. Assuming a GNP at the 1941 level the initial payment would be twelve dollars per capita, but the actual GNP was already at about one and a half times this level, so that the proposed arrangement was more generous than the wartime one even for British Columbia.

The Prairie and Maritime provinces were quite content with this proposal, but British Columbia resented losing its privileged position under the earlier arrangement, and the two central provinces also raised strenuous objections. Premier George Drew of Ontario unveiled a detailed proposal of his own which included the sharing of income tax between the two levels of government (with the federal government acting as the collector), complete provincial control of succession duties, a formula to allocate the provincial share of corporation tax in proportion to sales (rather than by the location of the head office), and a "National Adjustment Fund" to redistribute some direct tax revenue from the rich to the poor provinces. None of this was achieved immediately, but Drew lived long enough to learn that he had been a much better prophet than his federal counterparts.

The failure to secure unanimous approval for the federal plan was followed by a more generous federal counter-offer which satisfied British Columbia but not Ontario or Quebec. In 1946 the federal government announced that it would make tax rental agreements with those provinces that desired them without waiting for unanimous consent. Provinces that did not agree would receive no tax rental payments, but they could levy their own taxes which would be partially credited against the federal taxes. The maximum credits would be 50 percent of the federal tax for succession duty, 5 percent of the federal tax for personal income tax, and 5 percent of taxable income for corporation tax. After some additional modification of the tax rental formula, in January 1947 all provinces except Ontario and Quebec signed tax rental agreements. Ontario and Quebec imposed their own corporation taxes and succession duties, receiving the federal credits, but neither imposed a personal income tax although they retained the right to do so. Newfoundland signed a tax rental agreement when it became a Canadian province in 1949.

This tax rental arrangement was due to expire in 1952. Efforts to entice the central provinces into a new one, and to prevent any defections, began in 1950 with the offer of a modified formula for computing the tax rental payments. The new formula continued the trend, which had begun with the federal government's final offer in 1947, toward a more direct relationship between the size of the payment and the value of the taxes rented. Provinces would also be permitted to rent only one or two of the direct tax fields rather than all three. As a result of these changes, Ontario agreed in 1952 to rent the corporation and income tax fields, although it retained its succession duty. The federal government also revived the notion of a constitutional amendment to open the field of indirect taxation to the provincial governments, but decided not to proceed with it when Quebec withheld its approval. Presumably Premier Duplessis calculated that the amendment would reduce the likelihood of other provinces supporting Quebec's rigid position on direct taxation.

The Quebec government appeared more isolated than at any time in the past, but it was soon to win a victory of the greatest importance. No province, including Quebec, had imposed a personal income tax since 1941, but in 1954 Quebec adopted legislation which imposed a personal income tax equal to 15 percent of the federal tax (although with slightly more generous exemptions), despite the fact that the federal tax credit available to it as a non-renting province was still only 5 percent. The preamble to the act declared somewhat provocatively (and inaccurately) that the provincial governments had priority in the

field of direct taxation under the BNA Act. The Liberal opposition in
the provincial legislature denounced the Union Nationale government for imposing "double taxation."

It appeared as though Duplessis had miscalculated, but he was
unexpectedly saved by Prime Minister St. Laurent, who met Duplessis
privately at Montreal's Windsor Hotel in October 1954. Several letters
and a telephone conversation followed, and in January St. Laurent
agreed to raise the federal income tax credit immediately to 10 percent.[8] He thus betrayed the Quebec provincial Liberals, who had been
privately assured by the federal finance minister that the 5 percent
credit was not negotiable.[9] St. Laurent's action was also unfair to the
other provincial governments, which had signed rental agreements in
good faith and now saw the only province that had failed to do so
rewarded for its intransigence.

The agreement with Duplessis was symptomatic of the fact that the
federal government was losing interest in the tax rental agreements. In
a letter explaining the compromise to the other premiers, St. Laurent
stated that his government was "not wedded to the principle of tax
rental agreements."[10] A few months later the federal government proposed terms for the forthcoming (1957-62) set of fiscal arrangements
that virtually abandoned any distinction between agreeing and non-
agreeing provinces. Provinces that signed an agreement would be
given not a fixed rental payment but a percentage of the actual yield
from federal taxation of their residents. Provinces that did not sign an
agreement would receive exactly the same in the form of tax credits,
the only difference being that they would have to handle their own
collection and could impose higher taxes if they wished. The provincial share of income tax would be 10 percent (the same as the credit
which Quebec already received), their share of succession duties
would be 50 percent, and their share of corporation tax would amount
to 9 percent of taxable income (or about one-fifth of the total tax yield).
In effect this was the tax sharing which George Drew had proposed a
decade earlier, although the term "tax rental" continued to be used.
Since tax sharing naturally meant a very uneven distribution of benefits among the provinces (depending on the incomes of their residents) it would be supplemented by equalization payments to all
provinces except Ontario, whether or not they signed an agreement.

Shortly after these arrangements came into force, the new Diefenbaker government was elected and proceeded promptly to increase the
provincial share of the personal income tax from 10 to 13 percent. In
1959, shortly after Duplessis died, it also increased Quebec's corporation tax credit in return for a promise that the increased proceeds
would be used for grants to universities. (Duplessis had prohibited
Quebec universities from accepting federal grants, although all universities outside of Quebec received them.)

The demolition of the tax rental system was completed in 1960. The governments of the two central provinces, like sharks that grow bolder at the smell of blood, escalated their demands at the July conference. Quebec's new Liberal Premier, Jean Lesage, demanded 25 percent of personal income tax, 25 percent of corporation tax, and complete control of succession duties. Ontario's Leslie Frost asked for 50 percent of both personal income tax and corporation income tax, unless the BNA Act could be amended to give provincial governments access to indirect taxation.

Further meetings followed in October 1960 and February 1961, at which the federal government announced its intention to end the tax rental system. In effect all provinces would be given a deal similar to but more generous than that which Quebec, as a non-renting province, enjoyed under the existing arrangements. As an added concession, the federal government would continue, if provincial governments so desired, to collect direct taxes on their behalf, even though the rates of taxation would no longer be subject to its control. Since equalization would continue, and since it would not even be necessary to establish tax collection machinery, the Atlantic provinces and Manitoba had no objection to this proposition. The only protest came from Premier Tommy Douglas of Saskatchewan, who had witnessed the ultimate consequences of fiscal decentralization while ministering to a prairie Baptist church in the 1930s.[11]

With the transition from tax rental to tax sharing completed in form as well as in fact, federal–provincial fiscal relations became largely a process of bargaining over the federal and provincial shares of the three major direct taxes. The process became an almost continuous one, with provincial demands constantly increasing at the expense of the federal government. The 1962–67 fiscal arrangements provided for the provincial share of the personal income tax to begin at 16 percent in the first year, increasing by one percentage point in each year of the agreement. The new government headed by Lester Pearson agreed in 1964 to accelerate the timetable of federal tax reductions or "abatements" so that the provincial share actually reached 24 percent (instead of 20 percent) in the last year of the agreement, and this quite apart from the effect of the higher-than-standard rates that already existed in certain provinces. The same government had earlier agreed to reduce the federal share of death taxes (estate or succession) from one-half to one-quarter.

Another innovation at this time was the so-called "opting out" procedure, by which provinces indicating their desire to assume full responsibility for certain shared-cost programs would be compensated by larger-than-normal abatements. This measure came in response to Quebec's complaints about conditional grants in areas which it alleged were under provincial jurisdiction, and was probably suggested by the precedent of the agreement concerning university grants in 1959. Although all provincial governments were offered the chance to "opt out," Quebec was the only one that accepted.

The Ontario and Quebec governments continued to insist that their "responsibilities" required larger shares of direct taxation, despite the fact that the total yield from such taxation was increasing rapidly as the prosperity of the 1960s pushed more taxpayers into higher income brackets. At Ontario's suggestion a Tax Structure Committee representing all eleven governments was established but failed to achieve any consensus. At the 1966 conference of treasurers and finance ministers the federal minister, Mitchell Sharp, indicated that the provinces could not expect an endless series of concessions. The provinces, however, showed no inclination to moderate their demands.[12] Ontario again demanded 50 percent of the personal income tax and was joined by normally docile Manitoba, whose Premier Duff Roblin was already an unannounced candidate for the federal Conservative leadership. Quebec's Daniel Johnson, presumably with tongue in cheek, demanded a complete federal withdrawal from direct taxation in his province. Sharp's position was that since provincial politicians were always talking about their "responsibilities," further abatements would be given to them only if they actually assumed additional responsibilities. He offered them a second opportunity to "opt out" of certain shared-cost programs, as Quebec had already done, but again the other provinces expressed no interest. This offer was followed within weeks by an entirely unexpected announcement that federal grants to universities would be terminated and replaced either by an additional abatement (4 percent of personal income tax and 1 percent of corporation income) or by a per capita grant of fourteen dollars (later raised to fifteen) that would increase in proportion to GNP. The abatement, unlike previous ones, would be "equalized" so as to be equally beneficial to all provinces. This proved to be the only abatement that was forthcoming, and it was, in effect, closer to being a conditional grant than a genuine abatement.

There was thus little, if any, net gain for the provinces in the 1967–72 fiscal arrangements, and Ontario, in particular, was extremely unhappy with the outcome. To make matters worse, the federal government in 1968 imposed a temporary "social development tax" to pay for its share of medicare. This was actually an increase in the personal income tax, but was considered as a separate tax so that it would not have to be shared with the provinces. The provincial governments were mollified only slightly, if at all, by the reconvening of the Tax Structure Committee in 1969.

The fiscal arrangements for 1972–77 involved a number of changes. Federal tax reforms that took effect in 1972, the culmination of a process dating back almost a decade, were accompanied by a revenue guarantee to protect the provincial governments against any shortfalls in their income tax and corporation tax revenues that might result. The guarantee was expected to last only for five years, presumably long enough for the provinces to adapt to the new tax regime. As part of the same package of tax reforms, the federal government abolished its estate tax, in compensation for the fact that capital gains were now subject to personal income tax. (The same rationale led most provinces to abandon their succession duties over the next few years.) The Social Development Tax mentioned in the preceding paragraph and the Old Age Security Tax (discussed in Chapter 7) were also absorbed into the personal income tax, leaving only two kinds of direct tax at the federal level. An additional change was that henceforth provincial personal income tax would be calculated as a percentage of the federal tax, rather than as a percentage of a theoretical "100 percent" which included both the federal and provincial taxes. The theoretical 100 percent had in fact been meaningless since 1962, given the freedom of the provinces to set their own rates of taxation, but the change had the symbolic effect of reminding the provinces that if they required more income tax revenue they would have to get it at the expense of the taxpayers and not at the expense of the federal government. In other words, there would be no more abatements, except possibly in return for the provinces assuming additional responsibilities for spending on health, education, and welfare. Federal income tax continued to be lower in Quebec than elsewhere, because that province paid the full cost of hospital insurance and the various other programs from which it had "opted out" in 1965.

The most contentious and important federal–provincial fiscal issues of the 1970s involved not the traditional income and corporation taxes, but an assortment of new federal taxes on crude oil, natural gas, and motor fuel. The provinces had long regarded revenue from natural resources as a sacrosanct area of provincial jurisdiction, even though the revenues that most of them derived from this source were exceedingly modest. In the 1970s the international prices of most mineral resources increased significantly, to the potential benefit of provincial treasuries. The increases were particularly pronounced in the case of oil because the African and Middle Eastern countries that exported it to the industrialized capitalist nations were able to form a successful cartel, known as OPEC (Organization of Petroleum Exporting Countries). This led to what came to be called the "energy crisis" and, in Canada, to a three-cornered struggle between the federal government, the western provincial governments, and the oil companies to capture the financial benefits.[13]

At the provincial level there were significant increases in the "royalties" which Alberta, Saskatchewan, and British Columbia charged for the privilege of removing their oil and natural gas from the ground. Royalties on other minerals such as nickel and copper were also increased in some provinces, although the financial gains from these commodities were considerably more modest. The federal government responded in May 1974 by announcing that corporations would no longer be able to deduct the cost of provincial resource taxes and royalties from their taxable income. This decision did not directly affect provincial revenues, but it tended to limit the level of royalties that provincial governments could impose without causing a flight of capital from the province concerned. The provincial governments were, if anything, more unhappy than the mining and petroleum companies themselves.

The high price and presumed scarcity of oil and natural gas inspired a variety of federal policy initiatives, which are discussed in Chapter 8. For present purposes, only those which affected the fiscal balance between the two levels of government need be mentioned. These included an export tax on crude oil and gasoline, imposed in September 1973, and a special excise tax on all gasoline, including that which was used within Canada, imposed in June 1975. The budget of October 1980, part of what was termed the National Energy Program, imposed a new tax on all natural gas and a special corporation tax of 16 percent on net revenues from oil and gas production. It also imposed an incremental oil revenue tax to capture the benefits of anticipated price increases for the federal treasury, but this tax was soon discontinued when the increases failed to take place.

These measures contributed to an unusually high level of conflict and animosity between the federal government and the three western-most provinces from 1973 onward. On the other hand, Ontario, which had often been at loggerheads with the federal government regarding fiscal issues prior to 1973, was not directly affected by the various energy taxes, and indeed tended to support them. In any event, the "energy crisis" proved to be a temporary phenomenon, and most of the controversial taxes had been removed by 1986.

These dramatic developments somewhat overshadowed the traditional agenda of fiscal federalism, but the negotiation of fiscal arrangements for 1977–82 and for 1982–87 was not without controversy. Since the main issue in both cases was the financing of health insurance and postsecondary education, these arrangements are discussed in Chapter 7. As will be recalled from the preceding discussion, the linkages between tax sharing, health insurance, and postsecondary education funding had emerged as early as the 1960s, with opting out and the abandonment of federal grants to universities. What happened in 1977 was, in effect, the federal government unloading onto all the provinces the responsibilities that, at least initially, only Quebec had been interested in assuming. In the same year, however, it retreated from its own earlier resolve that there would be no more unconditional abatements. In place of the revenue guarantee which had been intended to compensate the provinces for the effects of tax reform in 1972, and which was now scheduled to expire, the provinces were given an additional tax point from 1977 onward. By the early 1980s, provincial revenues from the personal income tax (by far the largest source of revenue for both levels of government) were about two-thirds as large as those of the federal government; a far cry indeed from the situation a generation earlier.

In earlier decades, as we have seen, the provinces had frequently argued that the distribution of revenues between them and the federal government left the provinces with inadequate means to perform their responsibilities under the constitution or, in other words, that they were the victims of a vertical fiscal imbalance. By the 1980s, the shoe appeared to be on the other foot, since the central government was chronically unable to cover its expenditures through its tax revenues and was thus forced to borrow the rest. In turn the continuous increase in the national debt increased the annual burden of interest payments and thus itself contributed to the gap between revenues and expenditures.

The problem of the federal deficit thus loomed large in the politics of the 1980s. Although most of the provinces had annual deficits as well, the combined deficits of all provinces were considerably less than the federal deficit, and the provinces individually and collectively were able to cover a much larger percentage of their expenditures without borrowing than was the central government. Furthermore, payments to the provinces accounted for a large share of federal expenditure.

It would certainly be an oversimplification to conclude from these facts that the provinces are the cause of the federal deficit. David Wolfe has argued persuasively that the most significant cause of the deficit is the shortfall of revenue resulting from the many tax concessions and exemptions conferred on individual and corporate taxpayers. In effect, it seems to be politically easier (although financially more costly) for the state to borrow from the upper and middle classes than to tax them at the level they could afford to bear. The political realities underlying this fact have nothing to do with federalism and would exist even if Canada were a unitary state. Canadian federalism in its present form, however, does have the consequence that the burden of the state's fiscal crisis is borne disproportionately by one level of government, namely the central government. It is understandable that the central government should view its grants to the provinces as one potential target of its efforts to reduce the deficit. It is also absurd for the provinces to argue that federal–provincial grants should be totally exempt from any efforts to reduce federal expenditures. Payments made to provinces are no more sacrosanct than transfer payments to individuals or payments to the suppliers of goods and services, including the federal government's own employees. At the same time it should be remembered that payments made to (or through) provincial governments do not only benefit those governments, but may benefit a variety of individuals, groups, and institutions. These issues are explored further in the section of this chapter that deals with equalization payments, and also in Chapter 7.

EQUALIZATION: MYTH AND REALITY

Equalization payments have since 1982 been accorded the status of a commitment entrenched in the constitution and have also been hailed as a consequence of our indigenous "redistribution culture."[15] Less romantically, they can be viewed as a more modern and sophisticated equivalent of the "better terms" traditionally bestowed on discontented provincial governments, and also as a response to a particular situation that faced the St. Laurent government in 1955. There is certainly no evidence that anyone at that time foresaw either the concrete fiscal implications or the symbolic status that they acquired subsequently.

"Better terms," as was noted earlier, are a tradition as old as Confederation itself, and somewhat more systematic efforts to resolve the problem of interprovincial differences in taxing capacity go back at least to 1927, when special federal subsidies to the Maritime provincial governments were commenced following the recommendation of a royal commission. The subsidies were substantially increased during the 1930s, and special subsidies were also given in those years to the western provinces (apart from Alberta which was punished for repudiating its debts under the Social Credit administration). Newfoundland also received special subsidies after it became a Canadian province, although the other special subsidies had by this time been eliminated.

Equalization payments in the strict sense, however, have been paid to the provinces only since 1957, and were part of the process of transition from tax rental to tax sharing that was described earlier in this chapter. It will be recalled that the fiscal arrangements commencing in that year established a direct relationship between the payments to each province in lieu of rented taxes and the actual yield of such taxes within the province. Equalization payments were established to make this feature, as well as the further fiscal decentralization in response to Ontario's demands that soon followed, acceptable to the Atlantic and Prairie provinces. At the same time, the decision to pay equalization to a province whether or not it signed a tax rental agreement avoided the so-called "discrimination" about which Quebec had complained during the lifetime of the earlier agreement.[16]

Unless corrective action is taken, the problem of horizontal imbalance naturally becomes worse as provincial autonomy increases. If most functions are performed and most taxes collected at the federal level, interprovincial variations in taxing capacity or in ability to perform the functions are irrelevant. For this reason, equalization payments were unnecessary in Canada under the tax rental system in its original form. Uniform per capita grants to the provincial governments, regardless of what proportion of federal revenue actually originated in each province, had the automatic effect of redistributing income from rich provinces to poor ones (apart, that is, from Quebec, which had made the deliberate choice to deny its residents the benefits of this redistribution).

The basic principle of equalization is that the actual ability of a province to raise revenue from a particular form of taxation is compared with a hypothetical standard. Initially the hypothetical standard was an "average" comprised of the two richest provinces (at that time Ontario and British Columbia). From 1962 until 1964, and again from 1967 until 1982, this average included all of the provinces, and was thus somewhat lower than the two-province average. Since 1982, for reasons explained below, only five provinces have been taken into account in calculating the hypothetical average. Since the total tax revenue in the provinces comprising the average is compared with the total tax base, or source of revenue, large provinces have more of an influence on the average than do the small provinces. This is important since the largest province (Ontario) has usually ranked first in revenue-raising capacity while the four poorest (Atlantic) provinces are also the four smallest.

When equalization began in 1957, the only types of revenue taken into account in calculating whether a province was eligible for equalization payments were revenues from the three shared taxes: personal income tax, corporation tax, and succession duty. Since Ontario ranked first in the ability to raise revenue from each of these sources, and since the hypothetical standard of comparison was based on only two provinces, every province other than Ontario was eligible for equalization. Beginning in 1962 a portion of revenue from natural resources was also taken into account in determining eligibility for equalization, with the result that British Columbia and Alberta soon ceased to be eligible. The Alberta government, at the time, argued that this was inappropriate, since Alberta's resource revenues were derived from the sale of depleting assets and could not be expected to continue indefinitely.

Subsequently it was decided that a province's eligibility for equalization should be determined on the basis of all its revenues, or very nearly so. The equalization formula introduced in 1967 was based on sixteen different types of revenue, a number that was gradually increased either by adding completely new categories or dividing existing categories. By the 1980s no less than thirty-eight different kinds of revenue were taken into account, including eight different kinds of revenue from crude oil or natural gas, and six different kinds of revenue from other minerals. For each of the thirty-eight categories a province's per capita capacity to raise that particuar type of revenue is compared with the hypothetical standard. If the province falls below the standard, it is said to have a positive entitlement to equalization, and if it falls above the standard, it is said to have a negative entitlement. Each province's positives and negatives are then added together to determine whether its overall entitlement is negative or positive. If the overall entitlement is positive the province will receive an equalization payment. However, and this must be emphasized since it appears to be widely misunderstood, a province with a negative entitlement does not have to contribute to equalization. The full cost of equalization is paid by the federal government.[17]

The numerical values of the positive and negative entitlements are based on the size of the province's population, the total revenue from that type of tax raised by provinces included in the hypothetical standard, and the amount of revenue that the particular province would raise if its rate of taxation was equal to the weighted average rate prevailing in those provinces. Thus a province does not get less equalization because its tax rates (and therefore revenues) are high, nor does it get more because its rates are low or non-existent.

Although its cost to the federal treasury gradually increased as more kinds of revenue were included in the calculation, and as provincial shares of income and corporation tax revenue became larger, equalization worked well for about twenty years after it was established. By 1977–78, however, the high price of crude oil had so increased Alberta's revenue base, and therefore the national average revenue base, that Ontario became eligible for equalization. Not only did this appear absurd, but it threatened to make the cost of equalization unbearable for the federal government if the price of oil continued to rise. Entitlements to equalization were based on provincial revenues, which included oil and gas royalties, but the funds available for equalization came out of federal revenues, which did not. This was an ironic result of the questionable decision to include oil revenues in the equalization formula fifteen years earlier; a decision that had originally been intended to reduce the number of recipient provinces. The logical response might have been to reverse that decision, but this would have substantially reduced the equalization payments to all of the recipient provinces, apart from Saskatchewan. Instead the federal government imposed an arbitrary rule that Ontario could not, under any circumstances, receive equalization, and began to consider how the equalization formula could be modified to reduce the impact of petroleum-related revenues, but without damage to the revenues and credit ratings of the poorer provinces.

As the 1977–82 fiscal arrangements drew to an end, both the Ontario and federal governments suggested the possibility of so-called two-tier equalization, in which responsibility for equalizing resource-related revenues would be shifted from the federal treasury to the treasuries of the resource-rich provinces. The response of Alberta, which at least initially would bear almost the entire burden of this proposal, can be as readily imagined as described, and the rest of the provinces were scarcely more enthusiastic. While perhaps justifiable in theory, the idea was never within the realm of practical politics.

In his 1981 budget speech, Minister of Finance Alan MacEachen proposed using Ontario's revenue bases, rather than the national average, as the basis for equalization. Since Ontario lacks oil and gas revenues, this would have eliminated those items from the calculation as well as ensuring that Ontario itself would never be eligible for equalization. On the other hand, the proposal was not ungenerous, since Ontario's revenue bases from most sources are well above the national average. For reasons not entirely clear, the Quebec government objected vociferously to the proposal, and the federal government eventually abandoned it. The solution finally adopted was an average based on only five provinces, rather than on all ten, as in the case of the 1977 formula. Resource-rich Alberta was excluded from the average, but to compensate for this the four Atlantic provinces, whose total population is about equal to Alberta's, were excluded also. Saskatchewan's revenues from oil, and British Columbia's from natural gas, thus continued to have some impact on the amount of equalization paid by the federal government. Saskatchewan lost its entitlement to equalization for the time being, although a decline in the price of oil placed it back on the list of recipients a few years later. The commencement of the 1982–87 fiscal arrangements coincided almost precisely with the entrenchment of equalization in the constitution, a development that might reduce the federal government's freedom of manoeuvre on future occasions. However, the principle of equalization had become so generally accepted by this time that the implications of its entrenchment attracted little comment.

In the 1987–92 fiscal arrangements the equalization formula, including the five-province standard, remained unchanged. Changes were made, however, in the procedure for calculating the tax base. These changes had the affect of making equalization somewhat more generous and were agreed upon by the Minister of Finance and his provincial counterparts late in 1986. Soon afterward, the Minister of Finance, concerned over the level of the federal deficit, announced that the changes would be gradually introduced over a two-year period rather than being implemented fully in 1987–88. The recipient provinces, now seven in number again because of the decline in Saskatchewan's resource revenues, protested, but to no avail.

Who benefits from equalization? In the three decades of its existence the program has not visibly affected personal incomes in the recipient provinces, apart from the incomes of provincial employees who would presumably have to be paid less if equalization were not available to augment the provincial revenues from which they are paid. Equalization has also not made rates of taxation uniform across the country. Residents of Quebec and the Atlantic provinces pay sales tax and personal income tax at higher rates than residents of Ontario, Alberta, and British Columbia, and there is no discernible tendency for rates to converge.

There is some logic in the opinion of the late Premier W.A.C. Bennett of British Columbia, who once said that if the federal government wanted to reduce economic disparities between provinces it should make payments to individuals rather than to provincial governments. As Keith Banting has pointed out, however, the two strategies are not mutually exclusive, and the federal government actually spends considerably more on pensions, family allowances, and other payments to individuals than it spends on equalization.[18]

Equalization presumably means that residents of recipient provinces (about 44 percent of Canada's population) can enjoy higher standards of public goods, such as education, highways, and environmental protection, than they would otherwise enjoy, and can do so without leaving their native province to live in Toronto, Calgary, or Vancouver. The benefits to provincial politicans and provincial employees in the recipient provinces are fairly obvious. Perhaps less obvious, but politically important, are the benefits to the professionals and small business proprietors in those provinces, whose livelihoods would be threatened by either an exodus of population (such as might result from higher taxes or deteriorating public services) or a reduction in the purchasing power of the provincial government. Equalization may also strengthen national unity by reinforcing positive sentiments toward the Canadian state, as Pierre Trudeau and other Quebec federalists frequently argued, but this is difficult to demonstrate conclusively. Another assertion that has been made is that equalization really benefits Ontario because it increases the ability of Canadians elsewhere to buy the products of Ontario's secondary industry. While attractive to those who are predisposed to see an insidious Ontario plot behind every action of the central government, this argument is not very persuasive. Provincial governments do not buy very much from Ontario, apart from English-language school textbooks. Individuals in recipient provinces buy the durable goods that Ontario exports to other parts of Canada, but they would still buy them, and would probably buy more of them, if the lack of equalization gave them an incentive to move to a richer province. Equalization as such does not increase their purchasing power.

Given the now universal support for the principle of equalization, it is ironic that the main argument used to justify the ending of the tax rental system was that the government that spent money should also have the responsibility for raising it, rather than depending on another government for financial support. This allegedly sacrosanct principle of parliamentary democracy would, of course, rule out any kind of equalization, but the principle was conveniently forgotten once it had served its ideological purpose. In all four Atlantic provinces, almost half of gross general revenue now consists of transfers from the federal government, a category which does not include the proceeds of provincial direct taxes for which the federal government merely acts as a collector. Equalization payments alone provide almost as much revenue as the total for all kinds of provincial taxes in Prince Edward Island. Even in Quebec and Manitoba, equalization contributes more to provincial revenues than the general sales tax. If responsible government has managed to survive in these circumstances, why could it not have survived in the other provinces under a tax rental system?

THE FUTURE OF TAX SHARING

A significant move away from integrated fiscal arrangements occurred in 1981. Alberta decided to follow the example of Ontario and Quebec by collecting its own corporation tax independently of the federal government. British Columbia was rumoured at the time to be contemplating a similar course of action but did not actually follow Alberta's example. Furthermore, in 1982 the Treasurer of Ontario asked the Ontario Economic Council to explore the possibility of Ontario collecting its own personal income tax, as Quebec does. A year later the Council recommended, in a lengthy monograph, that Ontario should not do so "at this time."[19] Nonetheless, the possibility was implicitly left open for the future.

Alberta's decision probably reflected in part the anti-federal sentiment generated by the struggles over energy policy. A related and more practical motivation was to facilitate tax incentives that would encourage oil and gas companies to continue exploration within the province. It was felt that this might be necessary to countervail the incentives contained in the National Energy Program, one of whose objectives was to encourage more exploration on the federally-administered continental shelf, rather than in Alberta. Alberta also followed the example of Ontario, and soon was imitated by Quebec, in reducing corporation taxes for firms engaged in manufacturing and processing. Subsequently Alberta instituted tax credits for corporations making contributions to political parties at the provincial level, a provision that clearly benefited the governing Progressive Conservatives. None of these initiatives would be possible if the federal government collected the tax on behalf of the provinces concerned. It might be noted that Alberta is the only Canadian jurisdiction whose tax legislation actively encourages corporate contributions to political parties; in Quebec, as in the United States, such contributions are not permitted.

Provincial corporation taxes are thus completely separate from the federal tax in the three provinces that account for the largest shares of the gross national product. In all three cases this aspect of provincial autonomy has been used more to provide business with incentives than to raise additional revenue. Alberta's corporation tax is, in fact, so riddled with exemptions that its net contribution to the treasury is negligible, and for all Canadian governments, including the federal government, corporation tax as a proportion of all tax revenue has declined over the last generation. Whatever the constitution may say on the subject, it would probably be desirable for the corporation tax to be an exclusively federal tax, as the Rowell-Sirois Commission recommended almost half a century ago. Provinces would then no longer be able to compete for investment by lowering corporation tax rates, a practice that in the long run benefits only the corporations themselves. The very uneven distribution of corporate activity among the provinces, the possibility that taxes imposed in one province can be passed on to consumers in another, and the potential that provincial corporation tax regimes could create obstacles to the free movement of capital across the country, all provide additional arguments in favour of making this tax exclusively federal. It hardly needs to be said, however, that the prospects of this happening are very remote.

While the governments of the larger provinces do not seem totally committed to the principles of tax sharing and fiscal integration, this is not a new development; their lack of enthusiasm was as conspicuous in the 1940s as it was in the 1980s. In the 1940s, the tax rental system was nonetheless established, and in 1987 the federal government proposed that the principles of tax sharing and fiscal integration be extended to include sales taxes as well as personal and corporation income taxes.

The federal government has imposed, since 1925, what is called a manufacturers' sales tax, accounting in recent years for about 12 percent of budgetary revenue at the federal level. It is an indirect tax, being imposed on producers or importers of goods and passed on by them to the consumers. This tax does not resemble that of any other industrialized nation and it has recently been criticized on several grounds: there are a variety of exemptions and special rates for particular goods ranging from bricks to bicycles, the procedure by which imports are valued in effect discriminates against Canadian-produced goods, and virtually the entire service sector of the economy escapes the tax.

At the provincial level, every province except Alberta imposes a general retail sales tax, at rates ranging from 12 percent in Newfoundland to 5 percent in Saskatchewan. This tax is considered direct since it is visible to the consumer; the courts have accepted the argument that the retail merchant does not pay the tax, but merely collects it on behalf of the provincial government. In every province except Saskatchewan there are also special sales taxes on motor fuel.

In 1978 the federal government attempted to stimulate the economy by offering financial compensation to provinces that would reduce their retail sales taxes. According to Jean Chrétien, the federal Minister of Finance at the time, all of the provincial treasurers had agreed in principle to this idea before it was announced to the public.[20] Subsequently, however, Quebec decided to retain the existing rate of tax on most goods while eliminating the tax entirely on household furniture, clothing, textiles, and footwear. Since Quebec produces most of Canada's output of these types of goods, the intent was obviously to concentrate the benefits of the additional demand created within the province. Quebec, nonetheless, claimed that it should receive the same federal compensation as it would have received for an across-the-board tax reduction, a claim that the federal government rejected.

Nine years later another Minister of Finance, Michael Wilson, unveiled a massive white paper on taxation.[21] This announced a number of changes in personal and corporation income tax, to take effect in 1988. More tentatively, it also proposed a second stage of tax reform that would eliminate the manufacturers' sales tax, replacing it with one of three alternatives. The first and preferred alternative was what was described in the White Paper as a National Sales Tax. This would be shared with the provinces, much as the personal income tax is at present, and would replace their retail sales taxes as well as the existing federal sales tax. The federal portion of the tax would be at a uniform rate across the country. The provinces would impose their portion of the tax on top of the federal tax at rates of their own choice, just as they now vary their rates of personal income tax, but they would have to agree with the federal government's categorization of goods and services that would be taxed. Like the value-added taxes used in most European countries, the tax would be imposed at each stage in the process of production, and also at the retail level, with the taxes already paid at preceding stages credited against the tax payable at each stage. Goods or services exported from one province to another would pay the tax at the rate applicable in the province of destination rather than that of the province of origin.

As the White Paper admitted, this scheme would require the agreement of the provincial governments before it could be implemented. It is possible that something less than unanimous agreement would suffice. One or two provinces might maintain their own, completely separate, sales tax just as Quebec retains its own, completely separate, personal income tax. However, if either Quebec or Ontario failed to participate in the National Sales Tax, most of the anticipated benefits might be lost. Difficulties in achieving consensus among the eleven governments could be anticipated, since the exemptions from retail sales tax vary from province to province. Services, which the White Paper proposes to tax, comprise most of the output of what is sometimes fondly referred to as "small business," a sector of the community that tends to be closely attached to the provincial level of government. Probably for this reason, most services escape the retail sales tax in most provinces, and Quebec's tax exempts all services, apart from telecommunications. The White Paper also proposed, with perhaps more courage than sagacity, to tax food. Apart from restaurant meals, food is not taxed in any province, although it is in some American states, and it is difficult to imagine the provinces agreeing to this proposal. Preliminary consultations with the provinces on these matters began almost simultaneously with the tabling of the White Paper, but few observers expected any rapid progress toward consensus.

One conclusion that can be drawn from the history of federal-provincial finance is that its evolution is almost entirely independent of the written constitution. Apart from the increase in statutory grants and subsidies in 1907 (which in retrospect is clearly a far less dramatic and significant change than many that have happened since), the entire process has been conducted without any formal changes in the rules by which it ostensibly is governed. Yet there have been not one but several changes of an almost revolutionary character.

The assumption that changes have been made in an effort to adjust the revenues of governments to their responsibilities is somewhat more plausible than the assumption that they have been dictated by the constitution, but it begs the question of how "responsibilities" are assigned, for in practice this too is largely independent of the constitution. There is nothing in the BNA Act about air transport or television or manpower training or public housing or industrial relations or hydro-electricity, nothing to suggest that the government of the larger provinces would conduct quasi-diplomatic activities in foreign countries or that both levels of government would be extensively involved in cultural activities. The provincial jurisdiction over health and welfare as it is presently understood could only be deduced from the BNA Act with the aid of a singularly fertile imagination. Even the courts have had little to do with the way in which most of these "responsibilities" are, in practice, assigned.

It appears that governments have, in practice, selected the "responsibilities" they wanted whenever those private groups and interests with a direct stake in the outcome of the activity concerned found it convenient for them to do so, and have then scrambled for the revenues needed to carry out the task. Governments whose expansion serves the interests of influential classes and class fractions have tended to expand, and to find both the forceful leadership and the revenues required to do so. Constitutional justifications are invented only after the fact.

NOTES

1. R.M. Burns, *The Acceptable Mean: The Tax Rental Agreements, 1941–1962* (Toronto: Canadian Tax Foundation, 1980) 133.

2. Richard M. Bird, *The Growth of Government Spending in Canada* (Toronto: Canadian Tax Foundation, 1970) 33–38.

3. The concepts of vertical and horizontal balance are discussed in R.L. Mathews, ed., *Intergovernmental Relations in Australia* (Sydney: Angus and Robertson, 1974) Chapters 9 and 10.

4. J.A. Maxwell, "Better Terms," *Queen's Quarterly* XL (1933) 136.

5. See the table of estimated resource revenues, by province and year, in Anthony Scott, ed., *Natural Resource Revenues: A Test of Federalism* (Vancouver: University of British Columbia Press, 1976) 42–43.

6. Canadian Tax Foundation, *The National Finances, 1985–86* (Toronto, 1986) 42.

7. The report of the commission was published in three volumes by the King's Printer in 1940. A one-volume edition was published in 1954.

8. Conrad Black, *Duplessis* (Toronto: McClelland and Stewart, 1977) 432–46 gives a fuller account.

9. Georges-Emile Lapalme, *Memoires*, Vol. II, *Le vent de l'oubli* (Montreal: Leméac, 1970) 170–80.

10. Quoted in Burns, *The Acceptable Mean: The Tax Rental Agreements, 1941–1962* 111.

11. Peter C. Newman, *Renegade in Power: The Diefenbaker Years* (Toronto: McClelland and Stewart, 1963) 126.

12. For a useful account of these negotiations see Richard Simeon, *Federal-Provincial Diplomacy: The Making of Recent Policy in Canada* (Toronto: University of Toronto Press, 1972) 66–87.

13. John Richards and Larry Pratt, *Prairie Capitalism* (Toronto: McClelland and Stewart, 1979) is probably the best book on the background to these events. The federal-provincial conflicts of the early 1980s are discussed in David Milne, *Tug of War: Ottawa and the Provinces under Trudeau and Mulroney* (Toronto: Lorimer, 1986) 69–116.

14. David A. Wolfe, "The Politics of the Deficit" in *The Politics of Economic Policy* ed. G.B. Doern, (Toronto: University of Toronto Press, 1985) 111–62.

15. For the notion of the "redistribution culture" as a part of the elusive Canadian identity, see Herschel Hardin, *A Nation Unaware: The Canadian Economic Culture* (North Vancouver: J.J. Douglas, 1974) 300–50.

16. Burns, *The Acceptable Mean*, 124–27, places particular emphasis on the desire to accommodate Quebec.

17. Thomas J. Courchene and David A. Beavis, "Federal-Provincial Tax Equalization: An Evaluation," *Canadian Journal of Economics* VI (1973) 483–502 is a more detailed description and analysis of equalization.

18. Keith G. Banting, *The Welfare State and Canadian Federalism* (Montreal and Kingston: McGill–Queen's University Press, 1982) 175.

19. *A Separate Personal Income tax for Ontario* (Toronto: Ontario Economic Council, 1983) Thomas J. Courchene, one of Canada's leading economists, was at that time the Chairman of the Council. The Council was abolished by Ontario's new Liberal government in 1985.

20. Jean Chrétien, *Straight From the Heart* (Toronto: Key Porter Books, 1985) 103–05.
21. The White Paper was published in several volumes. The volume entitled *Sales Tax Reform* (Ottawa: Department of Finance, 1987) discusses the federal-provincial implications on pp. 47–58.

7 Conditional Grants and Shared-Cost Programs

In a federal system the extent and nature of conditional grants are a useful indicator of the relative strength and vigour of the central and regional governments. When currents towards country-wide integration are running strongly we can expect grant-aided activities to proliferate and the federal authorities to be willing and able to enforce their own standards of appropriateness on the state or provincial administration. Conversely, when influences towards regional autonomy are strong we see resistance by these jurisdictions to the restrictions on their autonomy inherent in such procedures.

DONALD V. SMILEY[1]

An aspect of federal-provincial finance that was only briefly referred to in Chapter 6 is the whole area of conditional grants and shared-cost programs. The omission was an important one, not only because conditional grants and shared-cost programs have been an important feature of Canadian federalism at least since the Second World War, but also because their fate has become increasingly inseparable from the question, discussed in the preceding chapter, of how revenue sources are distributed between the two levels of government.

Like so many other aspects of federalism, conditional grants originated in the United States, where their history can be traced well back into the nineteenth century. The United States constitution contains no explicit provision for "grants-in-aid" (the term customarily used in that country), but their constitutional basis is often said to reside in Article 1, Section 8, which enumerates the powers of Congress, including the power "to lay and collect taxes, duties, imposts and excises, to pay the debts and provide for the common defense and general welfare of the United States." The first conditional grants actually involved the distribution of public lands rather than of the proceeds of taxation, but cash grants were not long in following.

In the twentieth century the American practice of making conditional grants has been extensively imitated in both Canada and Australia, although less so in other federations. In Australia they are usually known as special-purpose grants, and the Australian constitution makes explicit provision for them in Section 96:

During a period of ten years after the establishment of the Commonwealth and thereafter until the Parliament otherwise provides, the Parliament may grant financial assistance to any State on such terms and conditions as Parliament sees fit.

The Canadian and Australian expressions both suggest the basic characteristics of such grants, which distinguishes them from unconditional or general-purpose grants such as the statutory subsidies and equalization payments discussed in the preceding chapter. A conditional grant is earmarked for a particular program or activity, and is offered only insofar as the recipient government agrees to undertake the program or activity in a way that falls within the guidelines set by the donor government. Usually this means that the recipient government must spend some of its own funds, over and above what it receives in the grant. Activities financed in this way are sometimes known as shared-cost programs.

In Canada, however, it is not always easy to draw a clear distinction between conditional and unconditional grants. The "conditions" have characteristically been less rigid, even on paper, than those that prevail in the United States and, as J.A. Corry pointed out almost half a century ago, it has never been politically feasible to "punish" a province for failing to carry them out by terminating its grant.[2] Both of these facts tend to dissolve the distinction between conditional and unconditional grants.

Additional ambiguities have been added to the picture through the development of postwar fiscal arrangements. The tax rental payments were, in effect, conditional grants, although they were not earmarked for any specific purpose. On the other hand, the federal payments to the provinces for postsecondary education from 1967 onward were ostensibly designated for a specific purpose but are practically never considered to be conditional grants. Federal payments for "medicare," at least up to 1977, approximated much more closely the characteristics of a conditional grant, but Donald Smiley nonetheless described them as "an alternative to conditional grants" because they were simple to implement, involved no problems of defining shareable costs, and allowed for broad variations in the character of provincial programs.[3] Postsecondary education is a shared-cost program, even if it does not involve conditional grants. On the other hand, a conditional grant can exist without cost-sharing, although examples are fairly rare in Canada. In such a case the federal government pays the entire cost of the program to the provincial government and no provincial funds are required. Provincial governments are only involved because it is easier or cheaper for the federal government to purchase a service from them than to perform the task itself. An example would be the enforcement of the Canadian Labour (Safety) Code by provincial inspectors.

In Canada, as in the United States, the constitution makes no explicit provision for conditional grants, but the freedom of Parliament to dispose of its own consolidated revenue as it sees fit would seem to be an inevitable conclusion from its jurisdiction over "The Public Debt and Property" and "The Raising of Money by any Mode or System of Taxation." In fact, one could reasonably conclude on similar grounds that Section 96 of the Australian constitution is an unnecessary statement of the obvious. The so-called "spending power" of Parliament, however, is not entirely unrestricted by judicial enactment. The Judicial Committee of the Privy Council stated in 1937 that legislation disposing of Dominion property would still be *ultra vires* if it invaded fields of provincial jurisdiction.[4] Since the legislation overturned by this opinion was not a conditional grant to the provincial governments but rather the establishment of an unemployment insurance fund, the relevance of the opinion to conditional grants is not clear. It is probably significant that no provincial government has ever sought directly to challenge their legality. A provincial government that objects to them on principle can protect its autonomy by refusing to accept them, as Quebec did on more than one occasion.

Few of the voluminous arguments for and against conditional grants in Canada have been based primarily on legal criteria. Opponents of conditional grants often state that it is improper for the federal government to seek to influence the decision-making priorities of the provincial governments. This view cannot be derived from the constitution even if it may be justified on other grounds. Perhaps its real basis lies in another argument which both J.A. Corry and Donald Smiley have used against conditional grants, which is that they destroy the accountability of government to their electorates.[5] Since every Canadian citizen entitled to vote in a provincial election can also vote in a federal election, and vice versa, this argument does not seem exceptionally persuasive. A better one, strongly emphasized by Corry in his work for the Rowell-Sirois Commission, is that the "divided jurisdiction" inherent in shared-cost programs prevents bureaucracy from operating in the rational and orderly manner prescribed by Max Weber, since there is no single hierarchical chain of command when more than one government is involved. On the other hand, some recent studies of bureaucracy suggest that the Weberian model may, in any event, have little resemblance to reality since different departments and agencies of the same government enjoy considerable autonomy in practice, even though they may be formally subject to one centre of authority.

Smiley, in his monograph for the Canadian Tax Foundation, has enumerated a number of other arguments against conditional grants: no objective criteria of "national interest" can be discovered; the provinces are in practice just as competent to determine their spending priorities as the federal government; the effort to impose conditions and standards is usually futile; provinces that have already established a program qualifying for grants are given an unfair advantage over other provinces; poorer provinces must reduce their spending in other fields of activity so as to match the federal grants; provincial programs will gradually tend to become more uniform even without federal pressure; and "national standards" of public-sector activity can more effectively be achieved by unconditional equalization.

Supporters of conditional grants argue that some degree of uniformity in provincial government programs and activities is desirable on grounds both of equity and convenience, and that under a rigid constitution it can only in practice be achieved through conditional grants. The first argument, like its opposing argument about the impropriety of intruding on provincial priorities, must have, a priori, a moral justification if it has any at all. The argument about constitutional rigidity must be seriously qualified, for in practice rigidities in the sense of obstacles to federal action seem to be much more political and economic than legal. Whatever their source, conditional grants are not necessarily immune to them, as events from the time of Maurice Duplessis to the present have suggested.

A more sophisticated argument used in favour of conditional grants is based on the economic concept of spillovers or externalities.[6] Certain things that provincial governments do, or fail to do, have consequences outside the territorial boundaries of the province. For example, if Ontario fails to build and maintain an adequate highway across its northern hinterland, communication between Quebec and Manitoba may suffer. The scarcity of votes in northern Ontario and the southern orientation of the provincial government provide little incentive for action, while the adversely affected residents of Quebec and Manitoba have no way of influencing the provincial government at all. Thus it may be appropriate for the federal government, over which Quebec and Manitoba residents do have some influence, to use financial incentives in an effort to do so. This example, of course, is not hypothetical; it was precisely the justification for one of the most important and successful of shared-cost programs, the Trans-Canada Highway. The fact that the largest and wealthiest province was not crossed by a paved road until well into the second half of the twentieth century, and then only as a result of a federal initiative, provides grounds for great scepticism as to the widely reputed virtues of untrammelled provincial autonomy.

A somewhat more complex example of the external impact of provincial policy is provided by the field of education. The incentive for provincial governments to spend in this area may be reduced by the mobility of the population, to the extent that overall spending on education in Canada will be prevented from reaching an optimum level. A province with a net outflow of population, such as New Brunswick, may be reluctant to invest in the education of residents who are likely to move elsewhere as soon as they join the labour force.

On the other hand, a province with a net inflow of population, such as Ontario, may consider that it will attract so many educated people from elsewhere that it need not worry about educating its own residents.

This state of affairs would seem to provide a justification for federal action to ensure that spending on education is maintained at a high enough level to meet national needs. In fact the federal governments of both the United States and Australia have become increasingly involved in all levels of education for this very reason, mainly by means of conditional grants and, in Australia, by assuming total responsibility for financial support of the universities. In Canada, unfortunately, Quebec nationalism has succeeded in virtually preventing any federal activity in the educational field. Even Pierre Elliott Trudeau expressed vigorous opposition when the federal government offered grants to universities in the 1950s, and the practice was eventually abandoned in favour of channelling the funds through provincial governments as a virtually unconditional abatement.[7] Apart from the subsidies which it provides for teaching English in Quebec and French elsewhere, the federal government's role in elementary and secondary education is confined to the education of native peoples and the dependents of military personnel stationed in Europe.

This example suggests the validity of the point made earlier, that even conditional grants are not an infallible cure for the "rigidities" of federalism. Yet the economists with their externalities and spillovers do provide not only a valid argument in favour of conditional grants, but also some clues to explain why conditional grants and shared-cost programs have been developed so extensively, particularly in the three federations that have the most geographically mobile populations.

THE REASONS FOR CONDITIONAL GRANTS

Conditional grants are basically a device to stimulate public expenditure that would not otherwise take place. It is thus no accident that they proliferated in the quarter century after 1945, years of prosperity and optimism when faith in the efficacy of reform was at its peak. It is likewise no accident that they have become unpopular in recent years, at a time of well-orchestrated hostility to public expenditure and "big government."

An analysis along these lines, however, is misleading unless it takes into account the direction as well as the volume of public expenditure. Both the history of Canadian conditional grants and contemporary controversies over them must be seen in the context of the tendency of governments, especially provincial ones, to prefer some kinds of expenditure over others. As discussed in an earlier chapter, Canadian governments have traditionally preferred the types of expenditure that contribute directly to capital accumulation, a tendency first noticed by Lord Durham when he visited the country in 1839. Although Confederation ostensibly conferred most of the responsibility for stimulating capital accumulation on the federal level of government, the provincial governments, as we have seen, quickly found ways to become involved and, predictably, found such activities far more congenial than the social and "cultural" matters which had been entrusted to them by the BNA Act.

There were and are strong reasons for emphasizing expenditures on accumulation over other types of expenditure. Such an emphasis accorded with traditional British North American expectations and assumptions that long pre-dated Confederation. Accumulation expenditures directly benefited the influential classes in the provinces — businessmen, and in some cases farmers — persuading them that they received good value in return for their taxes and thus increasing the legitimacy and authority of the provincial level of government. Another advantage, directly relevant to the present discussion, was that the benefits of accumulation expenditures (public works, resource development, subsidies to business, and so forth) largely remained within the province; in other words there were few spillovers.

On the other hand, the provinces showed little disposition to spend heavily on legitimization, by which is meant such areas as health, welfare, social insurance, pensions, protection of the environment, or support of the arts, letters, and sciences. These activities did not directly, and in the short run, benefit the dominant classes; taxes levied to support them would be viewed as a burden disproportionate to the benefits received. Those residents of the province who would benefit directly were politically weak and poorly organized, usually without even a political party that reliably represented their interests. Ideology and tradition provided no impetus toward such expenditure. In addition, the mobility of the population ensured that the direct benefits of expenditure on legitimization might be largely reaped outside the province. The result of all these factors was a tendency of provincial governments to neglect their responsibilities for social policy even after twentieth-century urbanization and industrialization began to produce a pressing need for greater social expenditure. Faced with a choice between a dam and a hospital, between a railway and a university, between industrial subsidies and pensions, provincial governments in each case chose the first alternative. By the 1920s it was painfully evident that Canada lagged far behind the United Kingdom, Australia, New Zealand, and other advanced countries in developing what would later be known as the "welfare state."

Conditional grants were developed in Canada primarily as a means to overcome this situation by stimulating the provinces to spend more on legitimization than they otherwise would have been inclined to spend. A closely related motive was to ensure that the federal level of government would reap some of the benefits of legitimization. Louis St. Laurent, then Minister of Justice and Mackenzie King's "Quebec lieutenant," considered it particularly important in 1945 that the benefits of health and welfare programs be associated in people's minds with the central government, which was already engaged in a public relations contest with Duplessis' Union Nationale.[8]

There have, admittedly, been a number of shared-cost programs related to economic development, but in such cases the grant is frequently requested by the provincial government itself, and can hardly be regarded as conditional. One of the first specific purpose grants, for agricultural education, was made at the request of Ontario's Conservative government in 1912. Not surprisingly, the federal government that agreed to the proposal was of the same party and had recently been elected with decisive support from Ontario. A simultaneous proposal to assist the provinces in building highways was twice rejected by the Liberal-dominated Senate.[9] Even today there are a large number of specific-purpose grants administered by such departments as Fisheries and Oceans, Agriculture, or Energy, Mines and Resources, but most of these are tailored to the needs of particular provinces.[10] Significantly, they are almost totally exempt from the kinds of criticism that provincial governments direct against conditional grants in general. The Trans-Canada Highway was another major exception to the general rule that conditional grants are related to legitimization rather than accumulation, but the specific motivation for it has already been described. In only a very few special cases, of which this was one, do provincial governments need any federal encouragement to spend money on economic development.

Generally speaking, however, conditional grants have been mainly devoted to legitimization, precisely because the provinces cannot be relied upon to spend enough on this field of policy without substantial incentives, and in some cases actual coercion. The history of grant-aided programs in Canada shows this clearly, as does the functional distribution of conditional grant funds at any given time. In 1969–70, a time when the structure of ongoing grant-aided programs was virtually complete, and before the Trudeau government had begun its efforts to escape from responsibility for the programs, health and welfare accounted for about 88 percent of the funds disbursed in conditional grants to the provinces.[11] Of course, this fact also explains the close connection between hostility to conditional grants and the familiar North American rhetoric about the evils of government spending. When businessmen and right-wing politicians complain about government spending they are really, of course, referring to spending on health, education, and welfare. Spending on transportation, resource development, industrial subsidies, and so forth is never singled out for criticism, and the same persons who complain most loudly about "spending" in general frequently advocate more spending, rather than less, on the military forces, the police, and penitentiaries. Expressing opposition to spending in general, rather than admitting frankly what kind of spending is resented, is a deliberate strategy of mystification to attract the support of the very people who would suffer most from the demolition of the welfare state.

This interpretation of the impact of conditional grants does not explain why the federal government would be more likely to take an interest in legitimization than the provincial governments. Actually the similarity between the two levels in this regard has been more apparent than the contrast; federal governments, like provincial governments, have traditionally given more emphasis to economic than to social policy, and still do, as will be apparent even from a cursory reading of *Hansard*. Nonetheless, there are reasons why the motivation to spend on legitimization, weak as it is, is slightly stronger at the federal level. Usually the federal government has had more funds at its disposal than the provincial governments, and its control over the currency means that it can spend more than it receives in taxes and other revenue without having to worry about the state of the bond market. Thus it can afford to devote some attention even to secondary priorities like health and welfare. The federal government also has less need to worry about spillovers, because the persons who benefit directly from spending on health and welfare are not likely to leave the country permanently, however likely they may be to move from one province to another. Although Canada does compete against foreign countries, particularly the United States, for capital investment, the international competition is less intense than the interprovincial, so there is less need to spend every available dollar of public funds on activities that contribute directly to capital accumulation.

It would be wrong, however, to overestimate the federal enthusiasm for spending on legitimization. Major health and welfare programs have usually been conceded grudgingly, often at times when "minor" parties of social reform enjoyed unusual influence in Parliament or unusual support among the electorate. Moreover, the very fact that such programs are so often financed by conditional grants to the provinces, rather than being fully supported by federal revenues, suggests a certain lack of enthusiasm for them. By accepting only partial financial responsibility and leaving the provinces to assume the rest, the federal government purchases the political benefits (or avoids the political cost) of inaction, at minimum expense to its treasury. If some provincial governments refuse to accept the conditional grants, a risk that is always present, it will simply be unfortunate for the potential beneficiaries of the program. They can always be encouraged to blame the provincial level of government for their troubles.

THE DEVELOPMENT OF CONDITIONAL GRANTS

These generalizations can be illustrated by reference to the first major shared-cost program (there had been minor ones as far back as 1912), which was the Old Age Pensions Act of 1927. Contrary to a persistent myth, there was no legal reason why the federal government could not have assumed full responsibility for this program from the outset, as it was urged to do at the time by J.S. Woodsworth and his colleagues. Even Viscount Haldane could not possibly have invented a constitutional obstacle to the granting of pensions directly by the federal government. No provincial government would have objected either, apart from Quebec, which adhered to the ideological principle that the family rather than the state was responsible for supporting elderly persons. Since Quebec considered the financing of pensions by conditional grants to be just as objectionable as a strictly federal program, if not more so, provincial sentiments were certainly not the reason why a shared-cost program rather than an exclusively federal one was adopted. In fact the governments of British Columbia, Alberta, and Saskatchewan all urged the federal government to proceed with an exclusively federal program.[12]

The argument that a conditional grant had to be used because pensions fell under "provincial jurisdiction," a belief now deeply embedded in Canadian mythology, was a justification invented after the event. The original text of the BNA Act contained no reference to pensions. For that matter, the supposed constitutional obstacle did not prevent Mackenzie King, who was Prime Minister in 1927, from adopting an exclusively federal program of family allowances several years later, when the surging popularity of the CCF made it politically too hazardous to waste time waiting for the agreement of the provinces. The real reason why an exclusively federal pension plan was not adopted in 1927 is suggested by the response of the Deputy Minister of Justice in 1925 to a parliamentary committee's request for a statement of the constitutional position. While stating that "the subject matter of pensions has been entrusted to the provincial legislatures," he continued more significantly as follows:

"I do not mean to suggest that Parliament has not the power to legislate upon the subject so as to assist the provinces or to establish an independent voluntary scheme, provided that in either case the legislation does not trench upon the subject of property and civil rights in the provinces, as for example by obligating any person or province to contribute to the scheme. The enactment of such legislation would, however, involve the assumption by the Dominion of obligations involving heavy expenditures with regard to a matter which does not fall specifically within the Dominion field of legislation."[13]

"Heavy expenditures" were the last thing Mackenzie King wanted, so the persistent pressure from Woodsworth and other progressive members of Parliament was met with the half-measure of a shared-cost program dependent on provincial consent for its implementation. The western provinces and Ontario were fairly prompt in joining the program, but the provinces east of Ottawa, where the need for pensions was presumably even greater, were not. Nova Scotia and Prince Edward Island waited until 1933, New Brunswick until 1935, and Quebec until 1936, almost a decade after Parliament had adopted the legislation.

The Depression painfully underlined the inadequacies of the Canadian welfare state but did not produce a major expansion of shared-cost programs or other innovations in social policy. The so-called "Bennett New Deal," which was invalidated by the Judicial Committee of the Privy Council in a series of reference cases after Mackenzie King returned to office, did not rely on the cost-sharing mechanism. Presumably, the rapidly approaching end of Parliament's term made it politically essential for Bennett to act quickly and unilaterally, rather than waiting for provincial collaboration, particularly since all the provincial governments except New Brunswick and Prince Edward Island were politically hostile by the beginning of 1935. Both the Bennett and King governments assisted the provinces in carrying the burden of emergency relief expenses, but the only major ongoing shared-cost program established in the 1930s was allowances for the blind, which began in 1937. Although even the United States finally embraced the welfare state with Roosevelt's Social Security legislation, Canada lagged far behind.

The Rowell-Sirois Commission was naturally aware of the problem, but it disapproved of conditional grants for reasons already discussed. The argument of J.A. Corry's monograph, *Difficulties of Divided Jurisdiction*, was reflected in the conclusions of the Commission's report, which recommended a transfer of both legislative and taxing powers from the provincial to the federal level of government, federal assumption of provincial debts, and unconditional subsidies to the poorer provinces. These recommendations were ignored, however, and the years that followed the Second World War saw a massive proliferation of conditional grants and shared-cost programs. Predictably, they were heavily concentrated in the fields of health and welfare. In most other areas the provinces needed no urging to expand the scope of their activities.

The first major step, in 1948, was a National Health Program consisting of nine separate conditional grants: health survey, hospital construction, professional training, crippled children, mental health, tuberculosis control, health research, cancer control, and general public health. This was followed by a major revision of pension legislation in 1951, including a probably superfluous constitutional amendment which stated pensions to be a concurrent field of jurisdiction with provincial paramountcy. In place of the means-tested, shared-cost pensions of the 1927 legislation there were now two separate programs known respectively as Old Age Security and Old Age Assistance. The former established universal pensions for persons over seventy and was exclusively financed by the federal government. The latter provided additional support for persons over sixty-five who were in need, and was administered by the provinces with the aid of conditional grants.

In 1954 a new shared-cost program provided allowances for the disabled similar to the allowances for the blind that had commenced in 1937. In the following year another shared-cost program provided unemployment assistance to those who were not eligible for benefits under the contributory scheme of unemployment insurance. This institutionalized the recognition of the fact, which had become obvious two decades earlier, that responsibility for "relief" could no longer safely be left to the provinces and municipalities. In 1966, following three years of federal-provincial negotiation, all three of these welfare programs, as well as Old Age Assistance, were combined into a new shared-cost program known as the Canada Assistance Plan (CAP). The CAP also included provision for federal cost-sharing of child welfare, mothers' allowances, medical expenses of welfare recipients, rehabilitation and preventive welfare services, and certain special programs for native peoples. These increased federal responsibilities were largely undertaken in response to the demands of Ontario and British Columbia, which at that time were the only provinces with a sizable net inflow of population. Both had complained loudly and persistently about the burden of welfare costs, despite their prosperity and rapid rates of economic growth.[14]

In the meantime, health had eclipsed welfare as the major area of expenditure on conditional grants. The Liberal Party had proclaimed a vague commitment to the principle of health insurance as early as 1919, which was not a particularly startling move inasmuch as a Liberal government in the United Kingdom had actually implemented a form of health insurance several years earlier. The subject was raised again as part of the "Green Book" of federal proposals to the provinces in 1945. Legislation to provide for cost-sharing of hospital insurance was finally adopted in the last months of the long postwar Liberal regime, although it did not come into effect until after John Diefenbaker had formed his first government. Saskatchewan under the CCF had established its own plan long before the federal grants became available, and the remaining provinces joined promptly (with the exception of Quebec, which waited until the end of 1960 and, as will be seen, chose to opt out at the first opportunity).

Hospital insurance was soon followed by medical insurance. Prime Minister Diefenbaker's appointment of the Royal Commission on

Health Services, headed by Justice Emmett Hall, was interpreted by
some observers as a delaying tactic. If so, it was not a particularly
successful one, for the Commission recommended, in 1964, a shared-
cost program of medical insurance even more comprehensive than the
one that had recently been adopted in Saskatchewan at the cost of a
doctors' strike that helped to overturn the long-established CCF government. The following year Prime Minister Pearson placed "health services" near the top of the agenda at the federal-provincial conference of
first ministers and offered in his opening statement "to co-operate
with the provinces in making medicare financially possible for all
Canadians." Somewhat confusingly, he assured his audience that he
was "not proposing a new shared-cost program," given the fact that the
mechanics of such programs were currently under review by the Tax
Structure Committee.[15] His proposal did differ from existing shared-
cost programs in the extreme flexibility and permissiveness of the
terms and conditions on which federal aid would be offered. There
were only four requirements for a plan to be eligible, and two of these
were subsequently watered down or eliminated. No federal auditing
or supervision of provincial plans would be required or expected.

Although the premiers were not enthusiastic in their response to
this proposal, it was embodied in legislation in 1966 and adopted by
Parliament with only the western remnants of Social Credit dissenting. However, its proclamation was delayed by the right wing of the
Liberal party, including Minister of Finance Mitchell Sharp, who
argued that it would contribute to inflation. It did not actually come
into effect until 1 July 1968, at which time Pierre Elliott Trudeau was
Prime Minister. Only Saskatchewan and British Columbia were immediately eligible for grants. Ontario, which had opposed the whole
idea, soon produced a plan which violated at least one of Pearson's
four conditions, since it was initially administered on the government's behalf by private insurance companies, but which was none the
less declared eligible. The remaining provinces had all launched their
plans by the beginning of 1971, so that medicare became the second
largest shared-cost program, hospital insurance being the first.

It seemed likely, however, that medicare would be the last major
shared-cost program to be established, for reasons that must now be
discussed.

THE DECLINE OF CONDITIONAL GRANTS

During the two decades that followed the end of the Second World
War, a period characterized by the rapid proliferation of conditional
grants and shared-cost programs, the provincial governments presented little opposition to the trend. It appears that a rapid increase in
spending on health and welfare was considered acceptable and inevi-

table, so that under the circumstances the federal government's willingness to bear a large share of the expense was welcomed. The very expansion of grant-aided health and welfare programs produced a large number of provincial officials who benefited directly from the federal largesse and who had a vested interest in maintaining and expanding it.

The exception to this general rule was the province of Quebec, where the Liberal government of L.A. Taschereau, as noted above, had delayed for almost a decade the provision of shared-cost pensions to the province's residents. A similar policy was pursued in the postwar years by the Union Nationale government of Maurice Duplessis, whose political and social philosophy was basically similar to that of Taschereau. Provincial expenditures were relatively low and heavily oriented toward activities that directly assisted the accumulation of capital, a major reason for the cordial relations that Duplessis enjoyed with both Canadian and American corporations. The legitimization function of the provincial state remained unusually underdeveloped, even by Canadian standards. Admittedly, however, there was a partial justification for this in the fact that many of the responsibilities of providing for education, health, and welfare were assumed by the Roman Catholic Church, whose multitudes of largely unpaid personnel could perform the task of legitimization cheaply and fairly effectively.

Conditional grants were thus deeply resented because they would tend to distract attention from the goal of economic development, undermine the traditional division of labour between Church and state, and introduce the alien doctrine that the public authorities were directly responsible for social welfare. Moreover, they would tend, as in the other provinces, to create a group of officials with a vested interest in federal-provincial collaboration. Despite these reservations, most of the federal grants were reluctantly accepted by the Duplessis government, although two of the largest ones — those pertaining to hospital insurance and to the Trans-Canada Highway — were not. The Quebec universities, both anglophone and francophone, were also forbidden to accept federal subsidies.

To justify this policy, an ideological view of federalism was invented and expounded at great length in the 1956 report of the Tremblay Commission. This report asserted that the entire field of legitimization fell exclusively under provincial jurisdiction, and that this was appropriate because the provinces were distinct societies with their own "cultures" and values. Each provincial government must therefore be given complete freedom to perform the function of legitimization in its own way, or not to perform it at all. Moreover, it was asserted that the federal Parliament had no right to spend in areas outside of its legislative jurisdiction, which was defined as narrowly as possible. If in fact it had the funds with which to do so, this was treated as proof that it was taxing too heavily and should withdraw from direct taxation in favour of the provinces.

The Liberal government headed by Jean Lesage, who took office in June 1960, deviated only partially from this philosophy. At his first federal-provincial conference the following month, Lesage described shared-cost programs as undesirable, although he failed to present any convincing justification for such a view. He proposed that the federal government should withdraw completely from the funding of existing programs and should compensate the provinces for the additional expenditures they would have to assume by giving them tax abatements and unconditional subsidies. Meanwhile, he announced, Quebec would participate in the programs to which Duplessis had refused assent, such as hospital insurance and the Trans-Canada Highway. It would be unjust to do otherwise since Quebec residents were already "participating" through the payment of federal taxes which supported these programs in the other provinces.[16]

Despite Lesage's assertion that his decision to participate was only a temporary expedient, the Diefenbaker government did not respond to his suggestion that the federal government should replace the conditional grants already in force with abatements and unconditional subsidies. In 1964, however, the Pearson government introduced legislation that would allow any province, within a stated time, to opt out of a number of shared-cost programs, including hospital insurance, vocational training, old age assistance, allowances for the blind and the disabled, unemployment assistance, health grants, and several minor agricultural and resource programs. If a province opted out of any program, the federal government would terminate the relevant conditional grant to that province, but would pay compensation in the form of a tax abatement (for the larger programs) or a cash payment (for the smaller). Several provinces informally expressed some interest in this idea, if the terms were sufficiently generous. When the legislation came into effect in 1965, Quebec opted out of all the major programs, receiving 20 percentage points of the personal income tax, and out of some of the minor ones as well for which cash compensation was offered. No other province followed its example.

Even before this, Quebec had benefited from a special deal with respect to two new programs, youth allowances and student loans, both of which represented the fulfilment of campaign promises made by the federal Liberals in 1963. Neither was a shared-cost program, but Quebec already had comparable programs of its own and Lesage argued that it should therefore receive fiscal compensation. The Pearson government agreed to this demand in both cases.

In 1966 the provincial governments were offered a second chance to opt out of hospital insurance and certain health grants, as well as the Canada Assistance Plan which had just replaced several of the welfare programs from which Quebec had opted out earlier. Once again the other nine provinces expressed no interest.

The introduction of medicare, however, brought about a drastic change in provincial attitudes toward shared-cost programs. Only British Columbia and Saskatchewan were pleased by Pearson's announcement of the proposal in 1965, and the distress of the other eight provincial governments was increased by the federal government's uncharacteristically firm position on tax-sharing in the fiscal negotiations a year later. Minister of Finance Mitchell Sharp, the architect of the new position on tax-sharing, was himself not noted as an enthusiast for medicare; whether by accident or design his rigidity served to enlist the provinces as allies in his efforts to delay the implementation of the program.

Faced with the prospect of at least a temporary halt to the escalation of federal tax abatements, the provincial governments decided that the rate of growth of public expenditure on health and welfare must be reduced. Medicare, a new and major program of unpredictable expense, was certain to make this impossible. Ontario and Manitoba argued that the objectives of the Hall Commission could be achieved by providing public health insurance only for those unable to afford private insurance, but the federal government insisted that only plans which were universal, or nearly so, could qualify for federal assistance. Most of the provinces established medicare very reluctantly, and only after the Trudeau government had practically forced them to do so by imposing on their residents a special medicare tax, known as the Social Development Tax. The Ontario government in particular was bitterly resentful, as suggested by Premier Robarts' celebrated outburst at the televised constitutional conference in 1969, when he called medicare a "Machiavellian fraud."[17]

Resentment against medicare, and against what the provinces viewed as federal determination to coerce them into excessive spending on social policy, was soon transformed into a generalized hostility toward conditional grants, a position that hitherto had little support outside of Quebec. Ontario's Ministry of Treasury, Economics, and Intergovernmental Affairs (TEIGA) took the lead in expressing such sentiments. In 1972 it produced a lengthy staff paper which listed and described the shared-cost programs in which the province participated as well as their alleged disadvantages.[18] Over and above the usual rhetoric about provincial autonomy, the gist of the argument was that shared-cost programs lessened the ability of TEIGA to control the total volume of provincial expenditure, and, incidentally, to assert its authority over the program departments such as Health, Education, or Community and Social Services. Clearly there was some concern on the part of TEIGA at the tendency of conditional grants to increase the autonomy and expand the importance of the program departments, especially those concerned with social policy. On the other hand, J.A.

Corry had argued long before that this tendency could never go as far in Canada as in the United States because of the hierarchical and centralizing nature of parliamentary cabinet government.[19] The growing power of TEIGA and of co-ordinating agencies in other provinces, although it had other causes, seemed to lend substance to this view.

At the same time as the provincial governments were developing a generalized opposition to conditional grants, the federal government was also losing much of its enthusiasm for them. At the federal level, as at the provincial, the new perspective was largely motivated by the view that public expenditure on health, education, and welfare was growing too rapidly, and that public policy should be re-oriented toward a greater emphasis on the more traditional and congenial role of promoting the accumulation of capital. This theme was expressed in the Liberal election campaign of 1968, which proved highly successful, especially in high-income urban and suburban areas, and in the three "rich" provinces where Liberal members elected increased by almost half. It was given added emphasis by the evidence of an inflationary trend, which led to the formation of a Prices and Incomes Commission in 1969. The government could not escape from its commitment to medicare, but its subsequent promise of "no more medicares" was as much an expression of its own sentiments as a concession to the provinces.

So strong had this view become that the federal government was now prepared to propose a constitutional restriction on its own power to make conditional grants. This was done in a working paper entitled *Federal-Provincial Grants and the Spending Power of Parliament*, which was submitted to the Constitutional Conference in June 1969. The main recommendation of the paper read as follows:

> The power of Parliament to make general conditional grants in respect of federal-provincial programmes which are acknowledged to be within exclusive provincial jurisdiction should be based upon two requirements: first, a broad national consensus in favour of any proposed programme should be demonstrated to exist before Parliament exercises its power; and secondly the decision of a provincial legislature to exercise its constitutional right not to participate in any programme, even given a national consensus, should not result in a fiscal penalty being imposed upon the people of the province.[20]

This proposal must be interpreted in the light of two facts. In the first place, a subsequent working paper declared that health insurance and social services (although not family allowances or pensions) were, and should remain, under exclusive provincial jurisdiction.[21] In the second place, the "broad national consensus" as defined had nothing to do with the ordinary meaning of the term, but was a euphemism for a requirement that any proposed program must be supported by the governments of both Quebec and Ontario, and by at least four of the other provincial governments as well, including a minimum of two western provinces and two Atlantic provinces, not counting Prince Edward Island.

In 1971, the federal government commenced its efforts to escape from financial responsibility for hospital and medical insurance, to say nothing of postsecondary education. An ostensible reason for this move was to place Quebec on the same footing as the other provinces. The fact that only Quebec had opted out of hospital insurance seemed dangerously close to the heresy of "special status," but if the federal government itself opted out the other provinces would be placed in a similar position. A more important reason was to reduce the drain of health, education, and welfare expenses, all of which seemed to be increasing faster than tax revenues, on the federal treasury. In addition, if the provinces were forced to bear the full financial responsibility they would have a greater incentive to economize and reduce the overall rate of growth of expenditure on legitimization.

The first target of the federal effort to reduce the growth of expenditure was postsecondary education. In 1966 the federal government, while terminating any direct relationship with the universities, had agreed to pay the provinces an annual subsidy equivalent to half of university operating costs, presumably to be used for that purpose. Less than five years later, it informed the provincial governments that these subsidies would be allowed to increase by no more than 15 percent each year, regardless of the actual operating costs of the universities.

At the same time the federal government unveiled a new proposal for the financing of health insurance. Instead of being related to the actual costs of the programs, federal contributions would be allowed to increase no faster than the per capita GNP. To sweeten the pill, an additional sum of $640 million over five years would be made available for the improvement of health services. Since the costs of health insurance were more difficult for the provinces to control than the costs of running the universities, this suggestion met with firm and unanimous opposition. The provinces differed, however, as to what alternative should be proposed. Quebec and Ontario, with some support from Alberta and British Columbia, suggested that federal contributions to health insurance should be replaced by an abatement of the personal income tax. The smaller provinces, on the other hand, preferred the status quo. No agreement was reached, although the federal government indicated that it would be willing to consider the alternative of an abatement, provided that it retained enough control over the income tax to pursue Keynesian policies. (A brief explanation of Keynes' policies begins on page 182.)

In 1973 the federal government produced a new set of proposals.

Federal contributions to postsecondary education would be provided through a per capita grant based on the eighteen to twenty-four age group of the population of each province, increasing by 7 percent each year. Apparently this proposal was based on the curious assumption that all students attended a university in their own province. Federal grants for health insurance would be replaced by an income tax abatement of 6 equalized percentage points, removal of the federal excise taxes on liquor and tobacco so that the provinces could occupy this field, and a cash adjustment grant. This proposal proved no more acceptable than its predecessor, and the same division of opinion among the provinces as had existed earlier reappeared. Ontario and Quebec both demanded huge abatements, while most of the smaller provinces indicated a preference for the existing system. No province was interested in the liquor and tobacco taxes. The hostility of the federal NDP, on whose support the minority government depended, made it unwise for the federal government to insist on implementing its own proposal.

In 1974, however, the Liberals had regained their majority in the House of Commons. In the budget speech of 1975, the Minister of Finance, John Turner, announced the government's intention to terminate the cost-sharing agreement for hospital insurance in five years, the minimum period of notice required by the legislation. He also announced that a ceiling would be placed on the per capita rate of growth of federal contributions to medicare, regardless of its actual costs. The maximum increase allowed would be 13 percent in the first year, 10.5 percent in the second, and 8.5 percent in subsequent years. Legislation to provide for this was given first reading almost immediately and adopted the folowing year. Ontario offered to take full responsibility for both kinds of health insurance in return for 17 percentage points of the personal income tax, but the offer was rejected.

ESTABLISHED PROGRAMS FINANCING

Agreement with all provinces was finally reached in 1976 on a complex arrangement known as Established Programs Financing (EPF), which from April 1977 onward replaced the old cost-sharing arrangements for health insurance and postsecondary education. Federal contributions would no longer be directly related to the costs of the programs, but instead would escalate in accordance with population and gross national product, although the level of payments established for the first year was related to what the provinces had actually received in the second-to-last year of the old agreement. The extra revenue made available to the provinces in place of the old conditional grants was partly in the form of cash payments and partly in the form of abatements. Each province would receive a basic cash payment intended to provide approximately half of its total income under EPF.

The remainder was provided in the form of equalized abatements: 1 percent of corporation profits and 13.5 percent of personal income tax. The corporation tax abatement and 4.357 percent of the personal income tax merely perpetuated the abatements made in lieu of university grants a decade earlier, while 9.143 percent of personal income tax was actually a new abatement. In addition, there were so-called transitional payments equal to the difference between the basic cash grant on the one hand and the total of equalization plus abatement on the other. These were, in effect, a form of super-equalization bringing the yield for all provinces up to the level enjoyed by Alberta, the richest province. To complicate the picture further, there were small "levelling payments" intended to remove over five years the inequalities carried over from the old cost-sharing provisions. Special provisions were also needed for Quebec since it had opted out of hospital insurance years before; in effect, the proceeds from that earlier abatement were simply deducted from Quebec's basic cash payment. In addition to EPF, the provinces received grants for "extended health care services." Finally, one additional tax point and the equivalent in cash was added to the EPF payments in compensation for the termination of the revenue guarantee in the 1972 fiscal arrangements.[22]

The federal retreat from direct responsibility for social policy was pursued in other ways as well during the 1970s. In 1973, after years of agitation from the government of Quebec, the federal government agreed to channel family-allowance payments through the provinces, thus permitting Quebec to redistribute payments in an effort to encourage large families (so far without success), and permitting Alberta to implement a bizarre and regressive scheme by which payments would escalate as the children grew older. Federal plans to supplement the incomes of "the working poor" were abandoned in 1976, partly because of determined resistance by the government of Ontario. In the autumn of 1975, a number of existing federal programs devoted to legitimization were cut back or terminated as part of the anti-inflation program announced at that time. Finally, the federal government and the more influential provinces agreed in 1978, despite protests from Saskatchewan, to replace the Canada Assistance Plan with a single general-purpose block grant for the sake of greater "flexibility," an idea borrowed from Richard Nixon's administration in the United States. This was ardently desired by the Progressive Conservative provincial governments, which saw it as an opportunity to reduce overall expenditure on welfare.[23] Their expectation that the funding would be for all practical purposes unconditional proved to be mistaken, however, since the legislation placed before Parliament in May 1978 did provide for some federal control over how the provinces used the money. A predictable protest followed from the provincial welfare ministers assembled in conference.[24] In the end the federal government had second thoughts about the legislation, which was never enacted, and the Canada Assistance Plan continued to operate.

Little more than a year's experience with EPF was needed to demonstrate that its ill effects would be felt by the beneficiaries of the programs and not by provincial treasuries. Poor economic conditions provided provinces with either a reason or an excuse for parsimonious approaches to health, education, and social services. Medicare in particular was threatened by the increasing tendency of doctors either to withdraw from the program or to collect extra fees from their patients in addition to what they received from the provincial government. Provincial governments refused either to prohibit these practices or to increase disbursements to the doctors in proportion to increases in the rate of inflation. In 1978 Ontario proposed a 38 percent increase in its health insurance premiums, already by far the highest in Canada, but the opposition parties in the legislature forced the minority government to settle for an increase only half as large. In September 1979 Joe Clark's federal government appointed Emmett Hall, who had headed the Royal Commission on Health Services in the 1960s, to investigate the deterioration of health insurance under EPF. Hall's report in the following year recommended the prohibition of extra billing by physicians and the abolition of premiums in the provinces that still retained them.[25]

The situation of postsecondary education was similar. Since the EPF formula was not related to operating costs, the result in most provinces was that the percentage of university operating expenses provided by the province from its own resources declined sharply between 1976–77 and 1977–78. The exceptions were Alberta, where there was little change, and Quebec, whose distinctive position under the earlier fiscal arrangements made its data not strictly comparable to those of other provinces. In Prince Edward Island the federal contribution for postsecondary education under EPF was actually higher than the total operating costs of the universities, so that the province contributed no funds of its own. In New Brunswick the federal contribution was only about 90 percent of operating costs, but since some operating costs were covered by student fees, private donations, and endowments, that province probably made no contribution from its own funds either.[26] Most provinces soon discovered that they could starve their universities and pocket all the savings themselves, since the federal cash grants and the yield from the abatements continued to rise in any event. Ontario's fifteen universities, many of them opened in the 1960s amid much ballyhoo, were in such a state of crisis by 1980 that bankruptcies, mergers, and the closing of some campuses were all under consideration. Manitoba actually managed to spend less of its own money on universities in the fifth year of EPF than it had spent in the first year, despite a galloping rate of inflation.

Federal disquiet about EPF became more evident when the Liberals returned to office in 1980. Massive budgetary deficits and the increased cost of borrowing made disbursements for ungrateful and politically unfriendly provincial governments a tempting source of possible economies. The federal government seems to have discovered, belatedly, that by instituting EPF it had deprived itself of any influence over the programs without really reducing the drain on its finances. In the case of health insurance it was apparently powerless to prevent the piecemeal destruction of a program still regarded by Liberals as one of their major achievements. In the case of universities, it was paying an increasingly larger share of the costs and receiving no credit, while the provinces jealously guarded their jurisdiction and contributed little or no money from their own resources.

In February 1981 the federal government established the so-called Task Force on Federal-Provincial Fiscal Arrangements, actually a special committee of the House of Commons chaired by Herb Breau, a Liberal member from New Brunswick. The task force held hearings in all the provincial and territorial capitals and issued an informative report some six months after it had been established. It recommended retaining EPF in substance but separating the health and education portions thereof into two distinct programs, with approximately two-thirds of the funds allocated to health and the remainder to education. It affirmed the importance of protecting both health and postsecondary education against misguided economizing by either level of government. In the case of health insurance it recommended stricter federal conditions to prevent provinces from undermining the program, although in the case of postsecondary education it was inclined to be more permissive. The report, when it appeared in August, was generally regarded as having made it politically more difficult for the federal government to reduce funding under EPF.

In his budget speech of November 1981, three months after the Task Force had submitted its report, Alan MacEachen, the Minister of Finance, expressed concern about the effectively unconditional nature of EPF payments. "Federal ability to enforce basic health standards and to influence postsecondary education development has been far less than expected."[27] Nonetheless, EPF continued virtually unchanged in 1982–87, apart from a slight reduction in the cash payments to Alberta and British Columbia, which had been receiving more per capita than the other provinces. The compensation for the termination of the revenue guarantee was also discontinued, but that provision had no logical connection with EPF.

Two important recommendations of the Breau Task Force were implemented in 1984, shortly before the retirement of Prime Minister Trudeau. EPF was formally divided into two distinct programs, for health care and postsecondary education respectively. In addition Parliament adopted the Canada Health Act, which made health care payments genuine conditional grants. The Canada Health Act prohibited hospitals from imposing user charges for services covered by provincial health insurance plans and also prohibited doctors from charging patients more than the amount covered by provincial health insurance, a practice known as extra-billing. Any provincial government that tolerated either practice (which most of them did at the time) would have the cash portion of its health care payments from the federal government reduced by an amount equal to the total amount of user charges and extra-billing fees collected in that province. At the discretion of the federal cabinet, provinces could suffer additional financial penalties if their health insurance plans were deemed to fall short of the five conditions of the federal grant: public administration, comprehensiveness, universality, portability, and accessibility. They might even have their payments reduced if they failed to:

> . . . give recognition to the contributions and payments by Can-
> ada under this Act in any public documents, or in any advertis-
> ing or promotional material, relating to insured health services
> and extended health care services in the province.[28]

This was stronger language than the provinces had been accustomed to hearing from the federal government since the days of Louis St. Laurent. Furthermore, the Progressive Conservative opposition and their new leader Brian Mulroney, knowing that an election was only months away, abandoned their usual deference to the provincial governments and voted for the Act. The Canada Health Act was thus adopted unanimously in both houses of Parliament, a rare distinction for a statute of such importance. With varying degrees of reluctance, the provinces eventually abandoned user charges and prohibited extra-billing. In Ontario the prohibition of extra-billing led to a doctors' strike in 1986, the third in Canadian history. (The others had occurred in Saskatchewan in 1962 and in Quebec in 1970, to protest against the introduction of medicare in those provinces.)

The problem of postsecondary education proved considerably more difficult to resolve. While medicare was universally popular, postsecondary education was not. There was little reason to suppose that the public, apart from professors and students, would support a tough stand vis-à-vis the provinces, as it had done in the case of the Canada Health Act. The provincial governments, while more or less acknowledging that health insurance was a legitimate concern for both levels of government, rejected any federal involvement in postsecondary education. Although the view that the central government would wash its hands of this vital aspect of public policy would seem bizarre in any other country, it was sadly in accordance with Canadian tradition.

In the last days of the Trudeau government, a number of alternatives that would strengthen the federal role in postsecondary education were nonetheless considered. Perhaps the most radical of these ideas, which later surfaced in the report of the Royal Commission on the Economic Union and Development Prospects for Canada, was to eliminate payments to the provinces entirely and make payments directly to students in the form of "vouchers" that they could use to pay their tuition fees. In effect the distribution of funds among provinces and universities would thus be determined by the preferences of the students rather than by governments and civil servants. Since Canadians long ago rejected democracy and individualism in favour of tradition, provincialism, and deference toward the state, this was doubtless a utopian proposal, but it was an indication of how impatient the Trudeau government had become with the status quo.[29]

Meanwhile the Department of the Secretary of State commissioned A.W. Johnson, a former deputy minister in both the Saskatchewan and federal governments, to study the problem of funding postsecondary education. Johnson's report, released in March 1985 after the Liberals had left office, documented the underfunding of universities by the provinces, and recommended that increases in federal grants to the provinces be tied to increases in provincial grants to the universities.[30] This proposal was endorsed by the Association of Universities and Colleges of Canada and by the Canadian Association of University Teachers but was denounced by the provincial governments as an encroachment on their jurisdiction. The Mulroney government took no action on the proposal.

The reduction of the federal deficit appeared to be a higher priority for that government than the maintenance, let alone the improvement, of existing programs for income support, health, welfare, and education. In his budget speech of May 1985, the new Minister of Finance, Michael Wilson, foreshadowed an end to the universality of old age pensions, but the outrage that followed this announcement soon forced the government to beat an inglorious retreat on that front. Wilson also stated that the rate of growth in EPF transfers to the provinces would be reduced, beginning in 1986–87, with the objective of saving the federal treasury more than two billion dollars per annum by the end of the decade. Legislation adopted in the following year carried out this promise by modifying the "escalator" formula which automatically adjusts EPF payments from year to year in accordance with population increases and changes in the gross national product. Although concern over the deficit was entirely legitimate, this measure did not attack its real causes, although it did place the health and education of Canadians at risk.

Canadians and their governments have long been obsessed with their land and natural resources, which they erroneously believe to guarantee them a high standard of living. The desire of Ontario farmers and their spokesman George Brown for prairie land made Confederation politically feasible, although in the end it was immigrants from Europe and the United States who settled most of the land in question. John A. Macdonald and Oliver Mowat battled one another for nearly two decades over the ownership of a moose pasture that neither of them had ever seen. A century later the Mulroney government proposed to build the world's fourth most powerful navy, ostensibly to defend some Arctic islands and icebergs against imaginary threats to our "sovereignty." Yet Canada's *human* resources, which are of far greater importance, have received less attention from Canadian governments than the reputed wealth of lands, minerals, and forests. Programs to protect and develop those human resources, when undertaken by either level of government, have often been the targets of ill-conceived economies or the pawns of intergovernmental and partisan controversy. Each level of government seeks to gain the credit for itself while unloading the financial responsibility onto the other level. Federalism makes it convenient and easy to "pass the buck" and to obscure the real issues with appeals to provincialism, nationalism, partisanship or ethnic solidarity. Some real progress has nonetheless been made, notably in universal pensions and health insurance, but it has been an uphill struggle. Education, on the other hand, has fared less well. In a world where knowledge is power, and where even Australia has emancipated its universities from the forces of provincialism, will Canadians be satisfied indefinitely with the status quo?

NOTES

1. From Donald V. Smiley, *Constitutional Adaptation and Canadian Federalism since 1945*, 57. Published with permission of the Minister of Supply and Services Canada.

2. J.A. Corry, *Difficulties of Divided Jurisdiction* (Ottawa: King's Printer, 1939) 28–36.

3. Donald V. Smiley, *Constitutional Adaptation*, 66–67.

4. *Attorney General for Canada vs. Attorney General for Ontario and Others* (1937) *Appeal Cases* 335. This reference dealt with the Employment and Social Insurance Act.

5. Corry, *Difficulties of Divided Jurisdiction*, and Donald V. Smiley, *Conditional Grants and Canadian Federalism* (Toronto: Canadian Tax Foundation, 1963).

6. A good example of the argument is George E. Carter, *Canadian Conditional Grants Since World War II* (Toronto: Canadian Tax Foundation, 1971), especially pages 5–20.

7. See Trudeau's essay, "Federal Grants to Universities," first published in 1957 and reprinted in his *Federalism and the French Canadians* (Toronto: Macmillan, 1968).

8. R.M. Burns, *The Acceptable Mean: The Tax Rental Agreements, 1941–1962* (Toronto: Canadian Tax Foundation, 1980) 46–47.

9. Christopher Armstrong, *The Politics of Federalism: Ontario's Relations*

with the Federal Government, 1867–1942 (Toronto: University of Toronto Press, 1981) 124–25.

10. For a lengthy list of such grants, see *Federal-Provincial Programs and Activities: A Descriptive Inventory* (Ottawa: Federal-Provincial Relations Office, 1979).

11. See the table in Carter, *Canadian Conditional Grants Since World War II*, 114–16.

12. Kenneth Bryden, *Old Age Pensions and Policy-Making in Canada* (Montreal: McGill–Queen's University Press, 1974). Pages 61–101 have a good account of the 1927 legislation.

13. Bryden, 68.

14. Rand Dyck, "The Canada Assistance Plan: The Ultimate in Co-operative Federalism," *Canadian Public Administration*, XIX (1976): 587–602.

15. *Federal-Provincial Conference, Ottawa, July 19–25, 1965* (Ottawa: Queen's Printer, 1968) 15–16.

16. *Dominion-Provincial Conference 1960* (Ottawa: Queen's Printer, 1960) 31–32.

17. *Constitutional Conference, Proceedings, Second Meeting* (Ottawa: Queen's Printer, 1969) 161.

18. *Federal-Provincial Shared-Cost Programmes in Ontario* (Toronto: Ministry of Treasury, Economics, and Intergovernmental Affairs, 1972).

19. J.A. Corry, "Constitutional Trends and Federalism," *Evolving Canadian Federalism*, ed. A.R.M. Lower and F.R. Scott (Durham, N.C.: Duke University Press, 1958).

20. From Pierre Elliott Trudeau, *Federal-Provincial Grants and the Spending Power of Parliament*, 36. Published with permission of the Minister of Supply and Services Canada.

21. Pierre Elliott Trudeau, *Income Security and Social Services* (Ottawa: Queen's Printer, 1969) 102, 104, and 106.

22. For a detailed analysis, see George E. Carter, "Financing Health and Post-Secondary Education: A New and Complex Fiscal Arrangement," *Canadian Tax Journal*, XXV (1977): 534–50.

23. See Leonard Shifrin, "Horse sense loses out to politics of federalism," in *The Citizen* (Ottawa) 20 March 1978.

24. R.B. Byers and John Saywell, *Canadian Annual Review of Politics and Public Affairs 1978*, 71.

25. Health and Welfare Canada, *Canada's National-Provincial Health Program for the 1980s: A Committment for Renewal* (Ottawa, 1980).

26. Parliamentary Task Force on Federal-Provincial Fiscal Arrangements, *Fiscal Federalism in Canada* (Ottawa, 1981) 133.

27. *The Globe and Mail*, 13 November 1981.

28. Canada, Statutes, 1984, Chapter 6, Section 13(b).

29. In his book *Tug of War: Ottawa and the Provinces under Trudeau and Mulroney* (Toronto: Lorimer, 1986) 191, David Milne cites a press report that Trudeau had decided to proceed with this plan if he did not

retire and was re-elected to office. No specific citation is provided. As Trudeau himself used to say, "If my grandmother had wheels, she'd be a streetcar."

30.   A.W. Johnson, *Giving Point and Purpose to the Federal Financing of Post-Secondary Education and Research in Canada* (Ottawa: Minister of Supply and Services, 1985).

8 Federalism and Economic Policy

The persistent difficulty of adjusting institutions combining feudalism and modern capitalism, which characterizes the federal governments of the North American continent, in placing, according to feudal principles, control over natural resources and land in the hands of the provinces and the states, and, according to capitalistic demands, control of interstate and foreign trade in the hands of the federal government, involves a drain on economic energies and inability to direct them effectively.

HAROLD INNIS[1]

. . . the Canadian constitution is not concerned with timeless abstractions, but still remains — as it always was — a vehicle for the attainment of very practical ends. It cannot long stand if, instead of fostering those ends, it obstructs their attainment.

J.R. MALLORY[2]

Confederation occurred at a time when expectations regarding intervention by the state in the economy were very different from those of today. It is true that British colonies overseas, unlike the United Kingdom itself, never fully adopted Adam Smith's gospel of economic laissez-faire. An economy based on the extraction of natural resources and a small population scattered over vast distances required that the state intervene at least to manage the public domain and provide the necessary infrastructure of roads, canals, and railways. The tariff was used, even before 1867, both as a source of revenue and as an encouragement to industrialization. Nonetheless, the nineteenth century state had modest administrative resources and relatively few economic instruments at its disposal, and its economy itself was fairly simple. Most Canadians were still self-employed. Foreign direct investment scarcely existed. Coal was practically the only source of energy, apart from the muscles of human beings or of animals. There were not even accurate data regarding unemployment, inflation, rates of growth, or regional disparities, let alone the belief that the state could and should be responsible for improving these conditions.

In these circumstances economic policy required little co-

ordination between levels of government, and the elaborate distribution of legislative powers in Sections 91 and 92 seemed to correspond
closely to the needs of the new federal state. Subsequently the broad
interpretations of "property and civil rights" by the Judicial Committee of the Privy Council, and its more restrictive interpretations of
"Peace, Order and Good Government" and "the regulation of trade
and commerce" helped to undermine the original logic of the constitution. The centrifugal forces described in Chapter 4 of this book, and
the very large size of the two central provinces relative to the country
as a whole, reinforced the impact of the Judicial Committee. As the
Rowell–Sirois Commission recognized in the 1930s, Canada had
become an industrial society requiring active intervention in economic affairs by the state. However, the central government had been
deprived of much of the authority needed to provide such active intervention, and the smaller provinces at least lacked the power to do so
effectively. The reallocation of responsibilities and financial
resources that the Royal Commission recommended did not take
place, and the drift toward provincialism resumed after the Second
World War, which had temporarily reinforced the power of the central
government.

At the present time it is fair to say that the central government in
Canada has less effective power to make economic policy than that of
any other industrialized country. This may seem a paradoxical conclusion given the size and complexity of the federal bureaucracy, the
multitude of regulatory agencies and crown corporations, the impressive output of statutes and orders-in-council pertaining to economic
matters, and the fact that no less than twenty-two members of the
federal cabinet (as of 1987) were responsible for various aspects of
economic policy, compared with only eight in 1945. If size and complexity were synonymous with effectiveness, however, the dinosaur
would have been a highly effective animal. The almost continuous
reorganizations of the federal machinery for making and implementing economic policy since the Pearson government took office in 1963
have made the public sector more complex but not more effective. In
fact they are better understood as futile efforts to compensate for a lack
of effectiveness that has more fundamental causes than the inadequacies of administrative arrangements.

The output of an economy is based on three factors: land (including
natural resources), labour, and capital. The provinces in Canada own
all public lands and natural resources, apart from those located
beneath the sea or in the northern territories. Provincial schools, colleges, and universities train the labour force, and the provinces regulate industrial relations, collective bargaining, and related matters
except in a few federally-regulated industries such as railways, airlines, and banks. The provinces have the primary responsibility for the
health and welfare of the labour force while the federal government

has primary responsibility for immigration and exclusive responsibility for unemployment insurance. Capital, unlike land and labour, is mainly under federal jurisdiction, but the provinces exercise important powers over capital nonetheless. Like the federal government, they have virtually unrestricted power to tax incomes and property. While the federal government regulates the banks, the provinces regulate securities dealers and stock exchanges, credit unions, trust companies, and most insurance companies. Alberta and Ontario own and operate savings banks, known in Alberta as treasury branches. The Quebec and Alberta governments control two of Canada's largest pools of capital, La Caisse de dépôt et de placement and the Heritage Savings Trust Fund. Quebec, Alberta, and Nova Scotia offer tax incentives to investors who buy the shares of corporations with headquarters located in the province.

The normal powers exercised by a modern capitalist state over the economy are thus, to a very large degree, exercised in Canada by the provinces. The provinces are admittedly handicapped, albeit to varying degrees, by their relatively small size and openness of their economies to external influences. However, this is also true of the federal government, owing to the proximity and economic power of the United States and the high degree of integration between Canada and that country. Although monetary policy is a federal responsibility, interest rates set in Ottawa are heavily influenced by those set in Washington. The overwhelming majority of Canada's external trade is with the United States, and exports to that country account for about one-fifth of the gross national product. Canadian railways and airlines are really part of a continental network, as evidenced by the speed with which the deregulation of those industries in the United States affected their Canadian counterparts. Canada's most important manufacturing industry, the production of automobiles and parts, is integrated on a continental basis. For many purposes, in fact, it is more useful to think in terms of a North American economy than of a Canadian economy. Within that continental economy all eleven Canadian governments are in a sense "provincial," and the one located in Ottawa has few significant powers not enjoyed by the other ten.

Edmond Orban, a political scientist at the Université de Montréal, has recently argued that in modern federations the power to make economic policy is increasingly centralized, with the provincial or subnational governments becoming no more than agencies for the implementation of policies determined at the centre.[3] While this tendency appears to exist in the various European federations, and in the United States, the theory lacks credibility when applied to Canada, or at least to the four largest Canadian provinces. Those provinces, and to some degree even the smaller ones, retain the means to pursue economic objectives of their own. Furthermore, each responds to a different constellation of economic interests from its counterparts in other provinces and from the federal government, so that its objectives are likely to be different. The policies of the Canadian federal government may influence the parameters within which a provincial government pursues its own objectives (although the policies of the United States government may be even more important in that regard) but they do not determine the province's own policies or necessarily preclude their success, even if the two are in conflict.

"Province-building," an expression first used in 1966 by Edwin Black and Alan Cairns, is still a useful concept for understanding the economic activities of provincial governments, although other political scientists have recently disputed its relevance.[4] Black and Cairns emphasized the parallels between the "nation-building" of the central government, most explicitly formulated in the National Policy of John A. Macdonald, and the ability of provinces to influence their own economic environments and to pursue their own economic objectives, sometimes as responses to the policies of the central government or to external economic circumstances. Since Black and Cairns wrote, certain provincial governments, notably Quebec in 1979 and Alberta in 1984, have issued white papers formulating their economic goals and strategies.[5] Like the federal government, provincial governments have developed larger and more complex bureaucracies and more numerous regulatory agencies and state enterprises to pursue their economic policies. These policies are, in part, a consequence of the relatively specialized provincial economies and the fact that their relevant interdependencies are as much with the outside world (particularly the United States) as with one another, but province-building has also reinforced those tendencies. Ontario and Quebec are economically and geographically parts of a single region, as are Alberta and Saskatchewan, but in each case the economies of the neighbouring provinces have become more distinct from one another, and more self-contained, as a result of province-building.

Nation-building or economic nationalism, of which the National Policy was one example, is an effort to shape a socioeconomic entity which to some degree is self-contained and self-directed by intensifying internal patterns of interdependence and by restricting or regulating ties with the outside world. Another objective is often to increase the size of the nation's employed labour force and thus of the nation itself, even if this depresses the average per capita income.

Province-building or economic provincialism is very similar both in its objectives and its methods, even when it is not carried to its logical conclusion of outright separatism. Both nation-building and province-building invariably are promoted by those class fractions that are dominant within the relevant territorial jurisdiction but are frustrated by having to share their power with external economic interests. In order to achieve their goals, these class fractions must gain some degree of wider popular support (or at least acquiescence) by identifying their own needs with those of the whole society. Depending on the circumstances, they may describe their objectives as "catching up" with a more advanced economic unit (often the same one whose external impact on their own economy is resented), or as protecting some local economic advantage, like Ontario's hydro-electricity or Alberta's oil. The real objectives, and the methods used to achieve them are, in either event, much the same.

If economic nationalism and economic provincialism are pursued simultaneously by different class fractions within a federal country, conflict is almost certain to ensue. The economic nationalists want to strengthen interdependence across provincial boundaries and regulate or restrict links with the outside world. The economic provincialists want to regulate or restrict the province's links with the outside world (including other provinces). This conflicts with the first objective of the federal nationalists, and they may use external allies, such as multinational corporations or even foreign governments, to assist their province-building strategy, which conflicts with the second objective of the federal nationalists. It is significant that the power of disallowance, which was an important weapon used by nation-builders against province-builders, ceased to be employed at approximately the time when the National Policy was abandoned.

A central government that pursues no nationalist goals of its own can afford to be rather tolerant of province-building. The Clark government of 1979–80 was perhaps the most extreme instance of this phenomenon in Canadian history, but federal governments in the 1920s and 1960s were also cases in point. More nationalist and interventionist governments, like those of Macdonald (particularly after 1878) and of Trudeau (particularly after 1980) almost inevitably clash with the provinces. Province-building can also lead provincial governments into conflicts with one another, although this is less common.

Canadian economic policy must therefore be referred to in the plural, as the distinct and independent policies of several governments pursuing different objectives, responding to different sets of interests and circumstances, and competing to control the same resources, including the intangible resources of power, influence, and authority. Of course the goals of two or more governments may overlap or coincide, and when this happens the governments in question may cooperate or collaborate in making and implementing policy. (Some instances of this phenomenon are described below.) However, cooperation and collaboration may not always be possible if fundamental conflicts exist between objectives. Furthermore, they may not always be desirable. Albert Breton has pointed out that collusion between governments, often celebrated by political scientists who study federalism, may in fact lessen their accountability and responsiveness to their electorates.[6] Canadian experience suggests that it may also lead to incoherent and ineffective policies.

STABILIZATION

At least since the 1920s the two great preoccupations of governments throughout the industrialized capitalist world have been unemployment and inflation. Although prior to the First World War it seemed that both full employment and stable prices could be taken for granted, subsequent experience in Canada and elsewhere has indicated that this was no more than a comforting illusion. Public opinion polls almost always indicate that unemployment and inflation (usually but not always in that order) are perceived as the two most important problems facing the state and society. Governments, particularly the federal government, are held responsible if either unemployment or inflation increases or persists at too high a level. Quite apart from the problems of divided jurisdiction and external dependence that characterize Canada in particular, all capitalist states face two fundamental difficulties in responding to these concerns. Firstly, the sources of unemployment and inflation may lie in the private sector of the economy, which the state can influence but does not really control. Secondly, measures that reduce unemployment tend to contribute to inflation, and vice versa.

John Maynard Keynes suggested that both problems could be resolved through fiscal policy, which would allow governments to control both unemployment and inflation and to regulate the economy without seriously diminishing the freedom of private enterprise. The solution was to regulate the amount of demand in the economy. If unemployment was high, governments should tax less and spend more, increasing the demand for goods and services and thus putting people back to work. If inflation threatened, governments should tax more and spend less, reducing the demand and thus causing prices to fall.[7] Within a few years of its publication in 1936, this theory had been enthusiastically espoused by the Department of Finance in Ottawa. For three decades after the Second World War, Canadian governments pursued more or less Keynesian policies, with apparent success.

Keynesian economics had a considerable impact on Canadian federalism, and vice versa. Keynes had devised his theory for a unitary state, the United Kingdom, where taxes on incomes and profits were imposed exclusively by the central government. Canada's federal constitution provided otherwise, but the tax rental system, described in Chapter 6 of this book, made it possible to approximate the fiscal centralization of a unitary state. The Department of Finance thus hoped to prolong the tax rental system indefinitely after the war. Even after tax rental gave way to tax sharing, Keynesian officials hoped to slow down the gradual transfer of "tax points" to the provinces. If the federal government could not literally monopolize the personal and corporate income taxes, it might hope to maintain a large enough share of them to pursue some semblance of Keynesian fiscal policy. No one knew exactly how large a share would be sufficient, but it was reasonable to assume that the larger the federal share, the more effective would its policies be. Keynesianism thus provided a powerful argument for fiscal centralization.

The Keynesian rationale was disputed, not surprisingly, by Quebec's Tremblay Commission. Not only did the Commission suggest that the efficacy of Keynesian fiscal policy was unproven, but it argued that Keynesian fiscal policy did not necessarily require fiscal centralization. Instead, the Tremblay Commission suggested that the federal and provincial governments might co-ordinate their fiscal policies and jointly assume responsibility for stabilizing the economy.[8]

Whether co-ordinated counter–cyclical policies, as recommended by the Tremblay Commission, would have been feasible is impossible to determine since the experiment was never tried. At the time the suggestion was made, few if any provincial treasury departments would have had the expertise to devise or implement appropriate policies, and probably few provincial governments, apart from that of Saskatchewan under Tommy Douglas, would have been receptive to Keynesian ideas. A more fundamental problem would have been the fact that provincial governments are inherently predisposed to consider unemployment a more serious problem than inflation, so they probably could never have been persuaded to pursue deflationary policies even when the economy required them. This phenomenon is discussed below since it became apparent only after the federal government had abandoned Keynesian economics.

In any event, co-ordination was not tried, nor was centralization maintained. Instead, as described in Chapter 6, the St. Laurent government transformed the tax rental system into tax sharing, and the Diefenbaker, Pearson, and Trudeau governments gradually conceded more and more tax room to the provinces. In part this occurred because faith in Keynesianism among federal politicians was waning, although political expediency and fear of the independence movement in Quebec were the principal motives. On the other hand, it is difficult to avoid the conclusion that decentralization without co-ordination made Keynesian fiscal policies increasingly ineffective, and thus helped to undermine the belief in the Keynesian theory. Although the federal government continued to enjoy more revenue from income and corporation taxes than all provinces combined, a much larger part of its expenditure was devoted to statutory commitments, such as pensions, family allowances, and equalization payments, and thus could not be adjusted upward or downward for countercyclical purposes. Jacques Parizeau, who would later serve as Quebec's Minister of Finance in the Lévesque government, pointed out in 1964 that federal fiscal policies could not be effective because provincial and local governments accounted for three-fourths of all public capital expenditures and four-fifths of all purchases of non-defence goods and services. Parizeau, who had not yet become a separatist at that time, concluded as an economist that the Canadian public sector required more centralization.[9]

Keynesian policies were finally abandoned in the 1970s because they were no longer perceived to be effective, although fiscal decentralization was probably not the only, or even the principal, reason for their ineffectiveness. Whatever the reasons were, Canada began to experience relatively high levels of unemployment and inflation simultaneously, which, according to the theory, was not supposed to happen. Keynesianism had, at least implicitly, made the fight against unemployment a higher priority, and this seemed sensible because Canadian prices were remarkably stable in the two decades following the Second World War. Inflation began to increase in the late 1960s, and became really alarming after 1973, which caused the federal government to gradually shift its priority toward the fight against inflation. At the same time unemployment remained too high to be entirely disregarded, especially in the Atlantic provinces and in politically-sensitive Quebec. These circumstances seemed to require a new approach to policy.

Since this is a book about federalism and not about economic policy, the latter subject cannot be treated in detail, but the broad outlines of federal policy, and its impact on federal-provincial relations, are worth noting. As Keynes was discarded, his place was partly taken by John Kenneth Galbraith, who argued that modern economies no longer resemble the free market model of classical economics and that governments must control prices and incomes in those sectors where the conditions of a free market no longer prevail.[10] In 1969 the Trudeau government urged both business and labour to exercise restraint in seeking price or wage increases, and established a Prices and Incomes Commission which was supposed to observe trends in the economy and make recommendations to the private sector. The Commission was discontinued in 1972, but in the following year the government established a Food Prices Review Board, which lasted until 1975. At about the same time, the government began to control the price of oil and natural gas, a policy that lasted for more than a decade. Finally, in 1975, mandatory wage and price controls were imposed, and the Anti-Inflation Review Board, headed by former (and subsequent) cabinet minister Jean-Luc Pepin, was established to implement them. The Supreme Court ruled in 1976 that this program was constitutionally valid, and the controls lasted until 1978. Later still, in 1982, the government announced that salaries and wages of federal employees, as well as certain transfer payments to individuals and certain prices in federally regulated industries, would be limited to increases of 6 percent in the first year and of 5 percent in the year following, even though it had signed contracts with some of its employees providing for larger increases. Despite all of these measures, it may be noted that the dollar lost 60 percent of its purchasing power between 1973 and 1983, and that this was by far the worst episode of inflation in Canadian history.[11]

Almost inevitably, the shift from a Keynesian to a Galbraithian approach involved the provincial governments in macro-economic policy, although perhaps not as much as those governments would have liked. It was very doubtful at first whether Parliament had the legal authority to control wages and prices in the private sector, and the Supreme Court decision, upholding its authority in 1976, was based on the narrow grounds that inflation had attained the status of an emergency. Apart from the private sector, the provincial and local governments and their agencies employ a significant proportion of the labour force, and it was clear that the wages of those persons could only be controlled with the consent and participation of the provinces. That consent had to be sought at an early stage if controls were to have any chance of being effective.

A few days after the imposition of mandatory controls, the Minister of Finance met with his provincial counterparts to seek their approval of the anti-inflation program, and their agreement to apply it to their own employees. All provinces except Quebec agreed to bring their employees under the jurisdiction of the Anti-Inflation Review Board. Ontario, whose government had been reduced to a minority position in the legislature, did so by executive decree, a procedure which the Supreme Court later ruled to be improper. Quebec established its own anti-inflation board but generally co-operated with the federal program. The agreements with the provinces were scheduled to expire in April 1977. Meetings of the finance ministers and treasurers in February, May, and October of that year failed to produce consensus on whether controls should continue. At the annual conference of provincial premiers that summer, the premiers urged the federal government to announce a date on which controls would end and also demanded that the federal government agree to recognize a permanent provincial role in macro-economic policy. The unspoken implication was that the provinces would be more likely to co-operate with the anti-inflation program if this recognition were granted. There was no explicit recognition, but in February 1978 the Prime Minister and the ten premiers held what was described as a conference on the economy. Mandatory wage and price controls ended in October of that year.

It soon became apparent that the premiers did not intend the February conference on the economy, with its implication that the two levels of government shared responsibility for economic policy, to be the last of its kind. In both 1980 and 1981 the annual premiers' conference urged that another such conference be convened, and Premier Davis of Ontario sent several letters to the Prime Minister making the same recommendation. Prime Minister Trudeau reluctantly agreed to a second conference on the economy in February 1982. Most of the premiers used that occasion to express harsh criticisms of federal economic policy, and particularly of the high interest rates which the Bank of Canada had introduced as an alternative (and apparently more successful) weapon in the fight against inflation. The premiers demanded that unemployment (which had worsened due to high interest rates) replace inflation as the main target of the government's economic policy and that the Canadian dollar be allowed to decline indefinitely in relation to that of the United States. Federal officials were heard afterward to express the hope that there would be no further conferences on the economy.[12]

Despite the general atmosphere of discord, the premiers had agreed with the Prime Minister on the desirability of restraining wage increases in the public sector. This fact may have encouraged the federal government to proceed with the "six and five" guidelines introduced in June of the same year. On 30 June 1982 the Prime Minister again met with the premiers to discuss the recently announced guidelines, and to urge them to impose similar restraints on their own employees. Premier Lougheed of Alberta predictably complained that the premiers had not been consulted before the guidelines were announced, and the conference refused to endorse the guidelines explicitly.[13] Nevertheless, by the end of the year most of the provinces had introduced wage restraints of one kind or another. In 1983 Prime Minister Trudeau refused to hold another first ministers' conference on the economy, but such conferences have become an annual event under Prime Minister Mulroney, normally occurring in February so that they precede the introduction of federal and provincial budgets.

Federal-provincial conferences on the economy may turn out to have been the only lasting consequence of the Trudeau government's experiment with wage and price controls: an ironic legacy for a Prime Minister who entered federal politics in order to reassert the supremacy of the central government. The legacy is not only ironic but unfortunate, as Trudeau himself seems to have realized after the conference of February 1982. Since there is no provision for a majority vote, and since a majority that excluded the central government would be meaningless, federal-provincial conferences can only make economic policy when there is complete consensus among the eleven governments, and in that unlikely event a conference would not really be necessary. On the other hand, the conferences undermine the legitimacy of the central government, lessen the accountability of all governments to their respective legislatures, and provide provincial premiers with an irresistible temptation to indulge in irresponsible criticism. It is usual in Canada for at least half of the provincial governments to have different party labels from the central government, and they thus have what should be an obvious interest in discrediting its policies. A more fundamental problem, however, is the fact that conferences on the economy give the provincial governments power, or at least influence, with no corresponding responsibility. This was most dramatically illustrated in February 1982 when the provincial premiers argued, in apparent seriousness, that inflation, which had reached the catastrophic level of 12.5 percent in the previous year, was not Canada's major economic problem. Canadians tend to blame both levels of government for unemployment, while they blame only the central government for inflation, so that the behaviour of the premiers was politically rational. Nonetheless, no federal government could possibly have taken their advice, unless it wished Canada to repeat the unhappy history of Argentina.

Professional economists no longer seem to have a model of the modern economy as convincing as the models of Smith and Keynes were in their time. Some neo–Marxists now make the plausible, although unproven, assertion that "the crisis" of contemporary capitalism is irreversible and that stabilization policies are thus futile. Whether or not one accepts that argument, few would deny that striking the appropriate balance between policies to combat inflation and unemployment is the most difficult task facing the modern capitalist state. It is particularly difficult in an economy as open to external influences as that of Canada. If stabilization policies are to have any chance of success they will have to be made by one government which accepts responsibility for their outcomes, and not by a federal–provincial conference.

REGIONAL AND INDUSTRIAL DEVELOPMENT

Stabilization policies treat the national economy as a single entity and use national economic indicators to measure the degree of success achieved. Canada, however, is less a single economy than a number of regional economies based on different industries and as closely tied to neighbouring regions of the United States as they are to one another. These circumstances have contributed to interregional disparities of economic and population growth, employment rates, and per capita incomes that are more acute than those of most other industrialized countries. An increasing awareness of this fact contributed to the declining popularity of the federal government's Keynesian policies in the 1960s.

The relative decline and increasing capital intensity of agriculture, wartime industrialization in the corridor from Windsor to Sorel, and the concentration of postwar growth around a handful of American-oriented resource projects caused a redistribution of population that endangered a variety of political and economic interests. Albert Breton has argued that a desire to preserve the existing spatial distribution of population is a rational expression of self-interest for politicians and explains a large part of their activity.[14] It is evident that loss of population could threaten the livelihood of retailers, professionals, building contractors, insurance agents, and other such persons who tend to serve interchangeably as political and economic elites in the less developed regions of Canada. This fact explains the basis of such enterprises as the Manitoba Development Corporation and Industrial Estates Limited in Nova Scotia.

Although the efforts which they represent were intensified after the Second World War, these organizations followed in a long tradition of provincial and local incentives to direct investment.[15] The ability of provincial governments to offer incentives was increased in the 1960s by their rapidly increasing tax revenues supplemented by federal equalization payments for all but the richest provinces. The incentives offered have included loans, tax holidays, guarantees for corporate borrowing in the private sector, and even direct equity participation by the provincial government, which is usually content to act in such cases as a silent partner exercising little or no influence over the management of the enterprise. Where a development corporation or similar entity is formed, it is usually managed by persons recruited by the private sector and given virtual freedom from any control by the provincial cabinet, let alone the legislature.

In addition to direct financial aid, incentives offered to industrial enterprises by provincial governments can include the provision of infrastructure at public expense, unusually favourable terms for the exploitation of crown timber and other resources, or promises to deal firmly with the labour force. The combination of interprovincial competition to attract industrial investment and provincial jurisdiction over labour–management relations has almost certainly exposed Canadian wage earners to more frequent and obvious intervention by the state on behalf of their employers than they would otherwise have experienced. In most provinces the intervention of the police to support those attempting to cross a picket line is an accepted routine. It may be significant to note that the unusually harsh reaction of Premier J.R. Smallwood to the Newfoundland woodworkers' strike of 1959 occurred at a time when he was attempting to negotiate a major deal with the Crown Zellerbach paper company.[16]

Nova Scotia, under two different governments, twice adopted labour legislation designed specifically to meet the needs of Michelin Tire, a firm controlled in France and notorious for its hostility to unions. The second bill, which made it impossible for a union to organize any Michelin plant unless it was able to organize them all simultaneously, was followed within twenty-four hours by an announcement that Michelin would build a third plant in the province and enlarge the two already in operation.[17]

How successful provincial industrialization strategies have been in achieving their objectives is a matter on which opinions may differ. The media and the general public probably underestimate their success, since they persist in the erroneous belief that the original intention was to increase per capita incomes in the poorer provinces; a goal quite distinct from, and even contrary to, the real objective of increasing the population. Conversely there have been a number of negative effects. Even when the enterprises attracted were legitimate and successful, the effect of ten different industrial strategies has been to fragment even further an industrial sector which is already too fragmented for the size of the Canadian market. Politically inspired locational decisions are likely to decrease the international competitiveness of Canadian industry, and considerations of comparative advantage have been ignored in the desire of each province to emulate the industrial structure of Ontario on a smaller scale. Moreover, incentives have redistributed income away from provincial taxpayers for the benefit of already profitable firms, many of which are owned and controlled outside of Canada. The poorer the province's natural advantages, the larger the incentives it must offer, and the greater the regressive effect. Since the size of incentive needed to attract investment can never be estimated precisely, the incentives must be too generous if they are to be successful.

Finally, one must note the many spectacular disasters that were the result of provincial industrialization strategies. The Come by Chance oil refinery in Newfoundland and the Bricklin automobile factory in New Brunswick suspended operations soon after they were launched, and the Churchill Forest Industries project in Manitoba disappeared in a thicket of numbered Swiss bank accounts as impenetrable as the northern forest itself.

In the heyday of Keynesianism, from the early 1940s to the early 1960s, the federal government did not devote much attention to the problem of regional disparities. In 1957 the Royal Commission on Canada's Economic Prospects recommended various measures to assist the lagging economies of the Atlantic provinces, but the regional programs instituted by the Diefenbaker and Pearson governments were modest and mainly oriented toward agriculture and renewable resources. The attack on regional disparities became a much higher priority after 1968, since it was viewed as a major element of the Trudeau government's efforts to counteract the force of Quebec nationalism. Quebec was by this time widely perceived as an economically deprived province, and the accusation that federal policies systematically favoured Ontario was becoming popular there. Many individual Canadians have "solved" the problem of regional disparities by moving to a different province but this is obviously more traumatic for Quebec francophones than for other Canadians, since it means moving from an environment where their own language is dominant to one where it may be almost non-existent. Although the Trudeauvian approach to Quebec's grievances generally emphasized the goal of individual rather than collective well-being, the strengthening of the Quebec economy nonetheless had to be a high priority for this reason. At the same time the even more deprived

Atlantic provinces could not be ignored without exposing the government to credible charges of discrimination.

The result was the formation of the Department of Regional Economic Expansion, initially headed by Trudeau's friend and confidant Jean Marchand. This department inherited the existing programs of agricultural and rural development but also conducted two other kinds of programs: investment in infrastructure, such as highways, and industrial incentives or financial aid to private enterprise in return for a promise to create jobs in a depressed province or locality. The infrastructural programs almost inevitably involved some collaboration with provincial and local governments. The industrial incentives, which parallelled and occasionally counteracted similar efforts by most of the provinces, were an exclusively federal program. In the early years of DREE, industrial incentives accounted for the largest portion of its budget, but they proved to be conspicuous, unpopular, controversial, and not particularly effective. In the rich provinces they were viewed as "corporate welfare" and robbing Peter to pay Paul, while the governments of the poorer provinces appeared to resent the lack of consultation.[18] The United States, after 1971, took a dim view of direct Canadian subsidies to firms that in some cases competed with American producers in the American market.

After the 1972 election, in which Liberal support west of the Ottawa River declined sharply, industrial incentives were de-emphasized and co-ordination of federal and provincial efforts became a higher priority. The geographical scope of DREE's activities was extended to cover almost the entire country. General Development Agreements were negotiated and signed with every province except Prince Edward Island, which had already been the beneficiary of a long-term federal-provincial development plan beginning in 1969. While the Prince Edward Island plan covered a period of fifteen years, the GDAs were for periods of ten years. In effect this meant that the specific priorities of federal spending on regional development would be determined by, or at least in consultation with, the provincial governments; that projects selected in this way would be jointly funded in varying proportions by the two levels of government; and that all provinces would have a share in the DREE budget, although the poorer provinces naturally received a disproportionate share. Some of the programs and projects included in the GDAs were funded and administered by other federal departments such as Transport, Agriculture, and Environment.[19]

The GDAs and the Prince Edward Island Development Plan all expired in 1984, which, by coincidence, proved to be the year of Prime Minister Trudeau's retirement. By this time DREE had ceased to exist, with most of its programs and personnel having been transferred to a new Department of Regional Industrial Expansion, which also incorporated much of the old Department of Industry, Trade and Commerce. Economic and Regional Development Agreements, replacing the old agreements and covering the years from 1984 to 1994, were negotiated and signed with all ten provinces. Manitoba was the first province to sign an agreement, in November 1983, while Quebec was the last, in December 1984. The agreements with Ontario, British Columbia, and Quebec were all signed after the Progressive Conservatives took over the federal government in September. Outside the framework of the GDAs and ERDAs, the federal government has continued to subsidize a wide variety of industrial sectors and enterprises, either directly or through the tax system. Most of these efforts are made for political reasons in response to threats of increased unemployment in particular provinces or regions, and often in collaboration with the province concerned. For example, in 1987 the federal and Quebec governments jointly made an interest-free loan of $220 million for thirty years to the world's largest industrial corporation, General Motors, in return for a pledge that the firm would not close its assembly line at Ste. Thérèse.

Federal and provincial programs of regional development have thus been generally harmonized, essentially by the easy device of having the federal government subsidize provincial programs and objectives rather than pursuing objectives independently. There has been no overall national economic plan or industrial strategy, although the Science Council of Canada has repeatedly urged the government to adopt one.

Efforts to devise an industrial strategy in the 1970s accomplished nothing, mainly because the provinces could not agree with the federal government, or with one another, on anything but the vaguest of generalities. Since the residents of every other province consider it axiomatic that federal policies are systematically biased in favour of Ontario, there are serious political risks involved in any overt encouragement of the industrial sectors that have a chance to be internationally competitive (most of which are located in Ontario), or even of secondary manufacturing in general. Any initiatives in this direction must, for political reasons, be counterbalanced by measures to favour the natural resource industries and agriculture of the western provinces or to prop up the moribund steel industry of Nova Scotia, the textile industry in Quebec, or the inshore fisheries of Newfoundland. The Canadian economy thus pays a heavy price for the obsessive jealousies between the provinces. As Harold Innis commented in 1946:

The hatreds between regions in Canada have become important vested interests. Montreal exploits the hatred of Toronto and Regina that of Winnipeg and so one might go through the list. A native of Ontario may appear restive at being charged with exploitation by those who systematically exploit him through their charges of exploitation, but even the right to complain is denied to him.[20]

NATURAL RESOURCES AND ENERGY POLICY

Of all the various means by which Canadian provincial governments have pursued provincialist goals, the most frequently used, most successful, and most fully documented has probably been the exercise of the province's ownership rights with regard to natural resources. Not coincidentally, this has been the most difficult strategy for opponents of provincialism (including the federal government) to attack, since it has been explicitly accorded at least a degree of legitimacy by the terms of the BNA Act. Section 109 of the Act provided that "All Lands, Mines, Minerals, and Royalties, belonging to the several Provinces of Canada, Nova Scotia, and New Brunswick at the Union" would belong henceforth "to the several Provinces of Ontario, Quebec, Nova Scotia, and New Brunswick in which the same are situate or arise." British Columbia, Prince Edward Island, and Newfoundland subsequently entered Confederation on similar terms, qualified in British Columbia's case by the fact that the federal government took over certain lands and resources which it intended to use to subsidize the construction of the Pacific Railway. The three Prairie provinces, on the other hand, were formed out of territory which already belonged to the federal state, and the governments of Macdonald and Laurier followed the American practice of retaining their lands and resources in federal hands after provincial status was granted. In the 1920s, pressure from the Prairie provincial governments, and from the federal Progressive party which represented the same class interests and held the balance of power in Parliament, led Mackenzie King to promise the "return" of these lands and resources to provincial hands. This transaction was finally completed in 1930, and at the same time British Columbia regained that portion of the "railway belt" that had not already been handed over to the CPR.

Section 109 was mainly intended as a means of assuring revenues to the provincial governments, a fact suggested by its inclusion in the part of the Act headed "Revenues; Debts; Assets; Taxation." Its other implications may not have been appreciated, although Macdonald did complain in 1872 that the Ontario government's control over timber licences enabled it to extract campaign funds from the lumber industry for the Liberal Party.[21] The real significance of Section 109, however, lay in its possible use as a means of promoting industrialization and economic diversification, at least in those provinces that were well-endowed with resources. Since resources are, in practice, very unevenly distributed, Section 109 has made a major contribution to the much-discussed phenomenon of regional disparities.

As H.V. Nelles has shown in his outstanding study, Ontario was the first province whose government understood and exploited these possibilities.[22] Beginning with the forests, which were the most important resource industry in the nineteenth century, Ontario originated the "manufacturing condition," by which permits to cut wood on the crown lands were only granted on condition that the wood be sawed into lumber before being exported. Neither the federal government nor the largely American lumber companies were particularly enamoured of this policy, but they could do little to prevent it since the provincial government owned practically all of the forested land in the province. It would have been difficult to argue that a provincial government should enjoy less freedom than a private citizen in disposing of its own property. Because of the more complex nature of the industry and the technology involved, Ontario had somewhat greater difficulty later on when it tried to extend the manufacturing condition to mineral resources, but even in this area a considerable degree of success was eventually achieved, although by more devious methods.

Ontario was a pioneer in policies of this kind not so much because its resources were important, but because they were relatively unimportant. If the resource interests had been the dominant class fraction they would probably have been able to prevent the imposition of any restraint on their freedom to export without processing. The Ontario government did impose restraints because it was dominated by industrialists who wanted to improve their competitive position in relation to Quebec and the United States, and who understood the importance of backward and forward linkages from the resource industries in strengthening and diversifying the provincial economy. In strengthening Ontario they strengthened themselves, and vice versa.

While forests and metallic minerals have at times been the instruments of province–building strategies in Ontario and elsewhere, energy resources, an essential input for any kind of manufacturing, have been far more useful for this purpose, and have decisively affected Canadian federalism. Energy resources were a concern of Canadian governments many decades before the petroleum crisis of the 1970s. In the age of steam Canada was handicapped by the fact that its coal resources were at the extremities of the country and its industry in the centre. Federal governments from Macdonald to Mackenzie King explored and devised various policy options to overcome this problem. Nova Scotians, the original blue-eyed sheiks, derived almost a third of their provincial revenues from coal royalties in the last years of the nineteenth century, at a time when other provinces relied mainly on federal handouts.[23] Like their counterparts in Alberta almost a century later, they also flirted with separatism. Canada's most important energy resource, however, proved to be not coal but hydro-electricity. Unlike coal, oil, and gas, hydro-electricity is endlessly renewable. Like them, it falls under provincial ownership and control but is unevenly distributed among the provinces. Its virtual absence in the Maritime provinces and on the island of Newfoundland is an important reason why Atlantic Canada has lagged economically behind the rest of the country.

The Ontario government was the first in Canada, and one of the first in the world, to enter the electric power business. The establishment of Ontario Hydro, as Nelles has demonstrated, had little to do with any "collectivist" ideology. Rather it represented, like the manufacturing condition, the use of the provincial state to support the objectives of industrial capitalists. The significant fact that this initiative took place at the provincial level reflects the fact that the industrial capitalists were concentrated in Ontario, with the result that the Ontario government was the one over which they exerted the greatest influence. In the United States and Australia, by contrast, major hydro-electric projects were undertaken by the federal government.

Ontario Hydro was used from the outset, and with considerable success, to provide power at low rates to improve the competitive position of Ontario industry in relation to that of Quebec and the United States. It also lessened, although it did not completely eliminate, Ontario's reliance on imported sources of energy, chiefly American coal. Ontario Hydro increased the self-reliance of Ontario and also reinforced the uneven development and concentration of Canadian industry in one province that had made it possible in the first place. Simultaneously, it transformed the character of the provincial state by increasing its share of capital investment and its impact on the economy; decisively influencing its relations with the federal government; involving it to some degree in Canadian-American relations; and strengthening its identification with the interests of industrial capital in Canada. Low power rates became as important to Ontario industry as high tariffs. The National Policy became the "Provincial Policy."

Partly because manufacturing industry was less influential in the other provinces, they were slower to follow in Ontario's lead, although all but Alberta and Prince Edward Island eventually did so. Because it was less capital-intensive, thermal generation of electricity remained longer in the hands of private enterprise than did hydro, a pattern that has also been visible in the United States. The relative importance of the two sources of power in each province influenced the chronological order in which provincial governments entered the field. Farmers as well as industrialists learned the virtues of cheap power, a fact that led Saskatchewan to take over not only electricity, but natural gas distribution as well. Manitoba and New Brunswick moved fairly quickly into hydro. Quebec made a promising start in 1943, but did not complete the process until twenty years later, at about the same time that British Columbia purchased control of its American–owned utility. Nova Scotia and Newfoundland waited until the 1970s.

Electricity, which was the major instrument of industrialization in the twentieth century as steam was in the nineteenth, ended up in provincial hands and as an instrument of provincial purposes. By 1960 it was evident that the Diefenbaker government could not implement its campaign promise of a national power grid, which would have assisted Saskatchewan and the Maritime provinces to industrialize, because of the firm control of hydro–electricity by a few of the more fortunate provincial governments. Who controlled the power, in both senses of the word, was soon demonstrated even more conclusively by the humiliating fiasco of the Columbia River Treaty, one of the most significant episodes in the history of Canadian federalism.

The Columbia River Treaty, signed by Canada and the United States in January 1961, was actually a second-best solution for Canada, like the St. Lawrence Seaway agreement a few years earlier. General Andrew McNaughton, the Canadian co-chairman of the International Joint Commission, had argued that Canada should develop the Columbia itself, and divert some of its water into the Kootenay River, rather than sharing it with the United States.[24] Thanks to Premier W.A.C. Bennett of British Columbia, Canada did not even get the second-best solution. By expropriating the B.C. Electric Company, Bennett prevented first the Diefenbaker and then the Pearson government from implementing the treaty until it had been rewritten to give the United States all of the power, rather than merely half, in return for a cash payment. In the end the payment barely covered Canada's share of the expenses. Moreover, the surrender to Bennett's demands ended a traditional federal policy of refusing to allow long-term power exports to the United States.

Quebec and Manitoba soon entered the export business also, and the dream of a national power grid was replaced by the reality of a series of links from north to south. Electricity tied the provinces to the United States in another way as well, since they relied increasingly on the New York bond market to finance their hydro-electric projects. Concern for their credit ratings in New York became an overriding factor affecting provincial policies toward foreign ownership and related matters.

Another episode which revealed how provincial control over hydro–electricity has balkanized the country was the protracted controversy between Quebec and Newfoundland over the latter province's share of the power from Churchill Falls. Quebec refused to allow Newfoundland to build a transmission line across its territory, leaving Newfoundland little choice but to sell its share to Quebec at a low price. Quebec then resold the power in the United States at a considerably higher price. Premier Smallwood's successors, like those of Premier Bennett at the other end of the country, inherited a bad contract made worse by the rapid inflation of the 1970s. Smallwood, unlike Bennett, at least had the excuse that the action of a larger and more influential province left him with little choice. His successors continued without success to urge Quebec to renegotiate the agreement. In June 1981, federal Energy Minister Marc Lalonde unveiled draft legislation which would allow the federal government to expropriate land in a province for interprovincial transmission lines. Premier Léves-que's response was to brand the legislation "stupid" and "not feasible" and to predict that a power line built under such circumstances would be destroyed, although he did not specify by whom.[25] The federal government did not proceed with its legislation.

To many western Canadians the relative inactivity of the central government in relation to hydro–electricity, and its more intervention-ist policies in relation to oil and natural gas, suggest that it is biased against their interests and in favour of Ontario and Quebec. The accu-sation is plausible, but it must be remembered that British Columbia (as noted above) and Manitoba have benefited from federal passivity toward the hydro–electric industry; that Alberta and Saskatchewan have sometimes benefited from federal intervention in the petroleum industry; and that the Canadian government's obsession with oil and gas in the 1970s and early 1980s was shared by central governments throughout the world at that time. A more credible accusation would be that federal energy policies have been usually misguided and based on faulty information or on the assumption that existing short term trends would continue indefinitely. H.V. Nelles suggested in 1980 that this was the case, and subsequent events have done nothing to dis-prove his judgment.[26]

Although the production of crude oil in Canada began before Con-federation (George Brown was one of the early investors in what became Imperial Oil), the modern history of the industry is usually dated from February 1947, when the Leduc field near Edmonton began production. Since that time Alberta has consistently provided more than 80 percent of Canada's production of both oil and natural gas, with Saskatchewan's oil and British Columbia's gas accounting for most of the remainder. For more than two decades after Leduc, the federal and Alberta governments shared a common interest in deve-loping and finding markets for the province's petroleum resources, and relations between the two governments were generally harmoni-ous. If the theories of the classical economists had been followed at that time, Canada should not have had a crude oil industry, since imported oil was cheaper than the domestic product. Nonetheless, the Diefenbaker government instituted a policy of reserving the entire Canadian market west of Ottawa and Brockville for Alberta oil. Sur-pluses of both oil and gas were exported to the United States, while refineries in Quebec and the Atlantic provinces continued to use imported oil.

Policies changed drastically in the 1970s, when Canadians became aware that their proven reserves of oil and gas were limited in quantity, and when the major oil producers of Africa and the Middle East successfully concerted their efforts to control the price and supply of crude oil throughout the world. The price of a barrel of oil in U.S. dollars increased more than tenfold during the decade. This led to international conflict between producing and consuming nations. Within Canada the same conflict occurred in microcosm, between producing and consuming provinces, with the federal government generally supporting the latter. Animosity between Alberta and the federal government rose to levels not seen since the early days of the Social Credit movement in the 1930s.

In Alberta the Progressive Conservative provincial government, newly elected in 1971, saw the global energy crisis as an opportunity to pursue province-building on a grander scale than any previous Canadian provincial government had imagined. Rapidly rising prices could simultaneously provide higher profits for the oil companies, higher royalties for the provincial government, lower taxes for the voters, and more business for the assortment of local entrepreneurs who provided goods and services to the petroleum industry, and who were the social base of the governing political party. There was also vague talk of diversifying the provincial economy (which came to nothing) and reorganizing Canadian federalism to benefit "the West" and the petroleum industry. Regrettably, there was some progress in the latter direction, as described in Chapter 10.

The federal government, however, had other plans. It had begun to restrict exports of natural gas in 1970, and it imposed an export tax on crude oil in 1973. It also decided in 1973 that the domestic price of oil should be kept below the rapidly rising international price to reduce the costs of heating and transportation for Canadian consumers. Initially the latter policy was supported by the provincial governments of Ontario, Quebec, Manitoba, British Columbia, and the Maritime provinces. Faced with this opposition, Alberta and the oil companies were persuaded to accept a lower price than the international price, although still considerably higher than the price before 1973. They were mollified slightly by the addition of the Montreal refineries to their protected market, beginning in 1976 when the necessary pipeline was completed. Eastern Quebec and the Atlantic provinces continued to use imported oil, but an elaborate system of federal subsidies ensured that consumers in those areas would also pay the low domestic price for oil products. In 1975 Parliament adopted legislation allowing the federal cabinet unilaterally to set the price of any oil that was transported across a provincial boundary and to ration supplies in the event of scarcity. Exports of crude oil to the United States were virtually ended, apart from some low-grade oil that could not be processed by Canadian refineries.

For the next several years increasingly technical and unintelligible arguments about the price and supply of oil and gas appeared to dominate the Canadian political agenda. Alberta achieved the highest rates of economic growth and population increase in Canada, reduced its already low levels of taxation, rapidly increased its public expenditures, and still accumulated a Heritage Savings Trust Fund consisting of reinvested oil and gas revenues that exceeded $10 billion by the end of the decade. It nonetheless complained that the federal government was not allowing the price of oil to rise quickly enough, even though substantial increases did take place. Alberta and the old companies also insisted that Canada could only be "self-sufficient" if the price was high enough to give producers an incentive: a classic case of business putting pressure on the state by threatening to withhold investment. Why Canada needed to be self-sufficient in this one commodity was never explained, but since most Canadians harboured racist sentiments toward the Middle Eastern producers, the argument appeared to be convincing.

As the decade drew to a close, the federal government was caught in a difficult situation. Low prices were popular with the electorate (except in Alberta and Saskatchewan), and an even more important consideration was the fact that increases in Alberta's revenues threatened to make the formula for distributing equalization payments unworkable, as described in Chapter 6. On the other hand, the subsidies to users of imported oil were increasingly costly and would become more so if domestic production were allowed to decline. Most of the provincial governments, with the significant exception of Ontario, now sided with Alberta, either because they hoped to become oil producers themselves or because they objected in principle to federal interference with natural resources. The Canadian Manufacturers Association also became an advocate of allowing the market to set the price of oil, since the steel companies and other influential members hoped to profit from any increased demand for oil rigs and pipelines.

In December 1978 there was a second surge of world oil prices following the revolution in Iran. The Clark government, although committed to "self-sufficiency" and a more decentralized federalism, was no more successful than the Trudeau government in reaching an agreement with Alberta on the domestic price. Clark's defeat, in Parliament and at the polls, was widely attributed to his pledge to sell the national oil company, Petro-Canada, and to the perception that he favoured a higher price for oil. The Liberals returned in March 1980, and in October they unveiled the National Energy Program. It provided that the system of controlled but gradually increasing prices would continue, with or without Alberta's approval. It also provided for special federal taxes on the output of natural gas and on the profits of oil and gas companies. Complicated tax incentives were offered to encourage the substitution of gas for oil, the growth of Canadian ownership in the petroleum industry, and the shift of exploration and production away from Alberta toward the northern and offshore areas (described as "Canada lands") where the federal government would collect the royalties. Finally, the NEP provided that the Crown (meaning Petro-Canada) would automatically acquire a 25 percent interest in any petroleum discovered on "Canada lands."

Alberta reacted with outrage. Right-wing separatist organizations held mass meetings and the provincial government announced that oil production would be gradually reduced until the federal government agreed to negotiate a new price. The Premier appeared on prime-time television to warn of an impending crisis, and urged Albertans to tell their friends and relatives in other provinces about Alberta's concerns. More effective pressure came, after January 1981, from the newly elected Reagan administration in the United States, which found the National Energy Program offensive to a variety of American interests. The federal government began to retreat. In September the federal and Alberta governments signed a new agreement on the price of oil, to the evident chagrin of the western separatists. Less than two months later they also reached agreement on constitutional issues, as described in Chapter 10. Abandoning earlier visions of an "industrial strategy," the federal government now argued that Canada's future growth should be based on its natural resources, and specifically on energy-related "mega-projects" like the extraction of synthetic oil from Alberta's tar sands. This was music to the ears of the Alberta government, and also a conscious decision to perpetuate the staple dependency that Harold Innis deplored in his writings on Canadian economic history.

The ironic sequel to all this unpleasantness was that both the federal and Alberta governments were wrong in their shared assumption that the international price of oil would continue to rise indefinitely. In fact it began to decline in 1981, frustrating the plans of both governments, but giving them less to fight about. The last vestiges of the National Energy Program were abandoned after the Mulroney government took office, and the so-called Western Accord of March 1985 was a complete federal surrender to the demands of the petroleum-producing provinces. By this time, however, falling oil prices had thrown Alberta's economy into recession, and the provincial government soon had the temerity to demand that the federal government again control the price of oil, only this time with the objective of keeping it *above* the world price. Alberta also continued to beat the drums for "self-sufficiency" and to plead for federal aid to assorted energy projects, none of which was economically justified at current prices but all of which would create employment in Alberta at the Canadian taxpayer's expense. Since the province still refused to institute a retail sales tax, it neither deserved nor received much sympathy for the woes of its over-expanded public sector.

The definitive history of Canada's "energy crisis" has yet to be written, but when it is it will probably reflect little credit on either governments, private enterprise, or the Canadian people. Both the federal and Alberta governments vastly overestimated the ability of energy resources to contribute to their respective goals. Both acted as though they expected the temporary rise in the price of oil to last forever. Voters in both producing and consuming regions followed the example of their governments and allowed short-sightedness and cupidity to triumph over common sense. As Canadians are wont to do, they ignored the fact that the mere possession of natural resources guarantees neither lasting wealth nor political power, and that human resources are the only ones which count in the long run. The behaviour of all concerned, the concentration of petroleum resources in a single province, and the ownership rights given to the provinces by Canada's constitution combined to place unusual strains on Canadian federalism. That the Canadian state survived the ordeal, as well as the simultaneous trauma of the sovereignty-association movement in Quebec, is perhaps the best tribute to its durability.

TRANSPORTATION

Canadian public policy has probably been more concerned with transportation than that of any other country. The promise of railways lured the outlying provinces into Confederation, and railways were the most important preoccupation of the central government for at least another sixty years. Interprovincial railways were assigned to Parliament's jurisdiction, and most other railways were either absorbed by one of the transcontinental systems or declared to be "works for the general advantage of Canada." At the end of the First World War, about half the railway system was nationalized, and the entity that resulted, Canadian National, is still the largest federal crown corporation.

Nonetheless, the provinces have not been totally absent from the field of rail transport policy. Every province except Saskatchewan has at one time or another owned a railway. Nova Scotia, New Brunswick, Prince Edward Island, and Newfoundland all turned their railways over to the federal government when they became Canadian provinces. Quebec sold its provincial railways to the expanding CPR not long after Confederation. Manitoba's efforts to build or sponsor railways competitive with the CPR were repeatedly disallowed by the Macdonald government. More recent provincial railways have been intimately associated with resource development. Ontario built the Timiskaming and Northern Ontario (later renamed Ontario Northland) in 1908. It failed in its original objective of encouraging agricultural settlement but assisted greatly in the development of mineral resources. When important mineral deposits were discovered at Noranda in northwestern Quebec, Ontario built a branch line to that locality in 1928, thereby bringing it into the economic orbit of Toronto, rather than Montreal.

British Columbia's provincial railway had had a long and somewhat ridiculous history, but it became important for the first time when

W.A.C. Bennett was premier of the province. Besides completing the southern extension to North Vancouver, he extended it north to Fort St. John in the Peace River country, strengthening that area's links with Vancouver and weakening its ties with the much closer metropolis of Edmonton. Not to be outdone, the Alberta government built the Alberta Resources Railway in the same general direction; this remained a white elephant for several years until it was rescued by the discovery of an important coal deposit near its northern terminus. British Columbia meanwhile extended its railway all the way to Fort Nelson with such disastrous financial results that a provincial Royal Commission was eventually set up to investigate.

Provinces also attempt to promote their own economic interests by influencing the railway policies of the federal government. Freight rates have been a traditional subject of concern for both the Maritime provinces and the West.[27] The absorption of the Intercolonial Railway by Canadian National produced higher freight rates which, in the judgment of many Maritimers, impeded the industrial development of their region. Lobbying by the provincial governments led to the Maritime Freight Rates Act of 1927 which provided subsidies to the railways and permitted them to lower their rates between the Maritimes and central Canada. The operation of this act was later extended to cover the trucking industry as well. In Western Canada accusations that freight rates are discriminatory have been repeated for a hundred years and have become part of the region's political culture. Provincial governments have demanded compensation for these alleged iniquities before a succession of Royal Commissions and at the Western Economic Opportunities Conference of 1973. In fact the region, and particularly its agriculture, has been treated generously. From 1925 until 1983 an act of Parliament prevented the railways from increasing their rates on the movement of export grain, a traffic which thus became highly unprofitable. The so-called Crow Rate was eventually abolished by the Trudeau government but was replaced by massive subsidies, divided between the grain producers and the railways. In response to western pleas the federal government has also made it extremely difficult for the railways to abandon any branch line that carries prairie grain, and has incurred enormous expenditures to rehabilitate the branch lines in question and to re-equip the railways with freight cars used for grain traffic. (Some freight cars have also been purchased by the Manitoba, Saskatchewan, and Alberta governments.) Similarly, the government of Newfoundland has successfully opposed Canadian National's efforts to abandon railway service in that province.

In recent years the provinces have also begun to play a role in air transport policy. All except New Brunswick and Prince Edward Island now have officials in their Departments of Transport who are concerned with civil aviation. Until the industry was deregulated they intervened frequently before the Canadian Transport Commission on behalf of, or sometimes against, air carriers that were seeking permission to establish new services. In doing so they were motivated partly by concern for the users of airline service and partly by a desire to increase the number of aviation-related jobs within their respective provinces. Thus they usually favoured airlines whose headquarters were within the province concerned over those located elsewhere. Alberta purchased control of Pacific Western Airlines in 1974 and kept it for ten years. Soon after the purchase, the airline's headquarters and maintenance facilities were moved from Vancouver to Calgary. In 1983 Quebec purchased Quebecair, the only major francophone airline, to prevent it from going bankrupt or being absorbed by a larger carrier. After the Liberals defeated the Parti Québécois, it was re-sold to the private sector. Another regional airline, Nordair, was owned by Air Canada from 1978 until 1984. For most of that period it was the object of conflict between the Quebec and Ontario governments, each of which urged the federal government to ensure that Nordair would be sold to owners within its own province. Ontario has created another airline, Norontair, to serve its remote regions. The aircraft are owned by the provincial government but operated on its behalf by private enterprise.[28]

The provincial impact on transportation, however, is greatest in relation to highways. Highway building became an important provincial activity after the First World War. It provided provincial governments with vast opportunities for patronage, corruption, and the collection of party campaign funds, just as railway building had earlier provided similar opportunities to the federal government. Intercity truck and bus transportation gradually gained in importance at the expense of the railways, and for a long time it appeared that it fell under provincial jurisdiction. In 1951, however, the Supreme Court of Canada ruled that New Brunswick had no jurisdiction to regulate a bus operation which ran through the province on its way from the United States to Nova Scotia.[29] This finding was upheld by the Judicial Committee of the Privy Council three years later in the last Canadian case which it ever decided.[30] The Judicial Committee actually went further than the Supreme Court in placing highway transportation under federal authority, since it held that the interprovincial and intraprovincial aspects of the bus line could not in practice be separated. Poetic justice was thus visited on the province that had prevented a reference to highways from appearing in the BNA Act.

The federal response to what should have been a welcome decision was a curious one: it proceeded to delegate the power it had just won back to the provinces, on the rather lame excuse that it lacked the administrative machinery to regulate highway transportation. The rather questionable device of delegating federal powers to a provincial board had recently been endorsed by the Supreme Court in a case involving the marketing of potatoes, and was pressed into service on this occasion.

The federal government's failure to accept its responsibilities allowed a situation to persist in which regulations such as those concerning the weights and dimensions of trucks varied from one province to another; a serious inconvenience to firms operating across provincial boundaries. There was also the possibility that provinces could discriminate against carriers located in other provinces in awarding licences. Beginning in 1959 the trucking industry urged the provinces at least to standardize their regulations, and beginning in 1965 it urged the federal government to put pressure on them to do so.

Meanwhile the MacPherson Royal Commission on Transportation had reminded the federal government that trucks and trains were now directly competitive, and that a coherent and rational transportation policy could not be constructed on the assumption that they were unrelated. The National Transportation Act, adopted by Parliament in 1966, was based on this philosophy, and Part III of the Act provided for the federal government belatedly to assume the responsibility, which the courts had assigned to it more than a decade before, of regulating highway transportation. However, the implementation of Part III was repeatedly postponed because of opposition from provinces, particularly Quebec and Ontario, and hesitation within the federal bureaucracy. The provincial governments believed that control over trucking could be used for "province-building" objectives, in opposition to the nation-building associated with the railways. Quebec threatened to turn the main highway across southern Ontario into "a parking lot" by stopping federally regulated vehicles at the provincial border.[31] Other provinces proposed complex regulatory schemes that would provide the appearance of federal jurisdiction but the reality of provincial veto power over decisions. The trucking industry itself twice reversed its position on the desirability of federal control but appears to have had little influence on the outcome. In 1973 the federal government capitulated and abandoned its efforts, such as they were, to assume control over highway transportation. In 1987 a new National Transportation Act provided for deregulation of interprovincial trucking after consultation with the provinces, most of which were in the process of deregulating their internal trucking industries at the same time.

CANADA AS AN ECONOMIC UNION

An economic union is a geographical space within which there are no political or administrative barriers to the free movement of labour, capital, commodities, and services. It might be assumed that any country united under a common government for well over a hundred years would meet this criterion, even if the common government were a federation rather than a unitary state. However, the extensive economic powers and activities of Canadian provincial governments mean that it cannot be assumed in Canada's case. Provincial tariffs were prohibited after Confederation, but other means of restricting or deflecting the flow of commodities were implicitly allowed by the constitution. The constitution did not prohibit restrictions on the movement of labour between provinces until 1982, and even then the restriction was qualified. The provinces still have almost complete freedom to restrict the movement of capital, and possibly of services. Furthermore, the federal government, sometimes with the collaboration of the provinces, has itself at times violated the principle of a Canadian economic union.

Resource policies that require processing within the province, or that restrict exports for the sake of "conservation" or giving priority to local needs are one type of provincial interference with the movement of commodities. On occasion they have been struck down by the courts on the grounds that they trespassed on the federal field of trade and commerce, but the addition of Section 92A to the constitution in 1982 has actually strengthened the legal authority of provinces to pursue such policies.

Provincial governments and their various enterprises and agencies can also discourage interprovincial trade by giving preference to local suppliers of goods and services. Since provincial and local governments collectively are far more important purchasers of goods and services than is the federal government, this power is important. Hydro-Quebec, Canada's largest industrial enterprise in terms of assets, has an explicit policy of giving preference to Quebec-based suppliers, and it is not unique in this respect. In addition to the hydro authorities, urban transit systems and the government-owned telephone systems of the prairie provinces are important purchasers of capital goods. Construction and service industries, which tend to be localized in any event, are heavily dependent on provincial and local governments. Partly for this reason, small business proprietors are often directly involved in provincial politics and usually support their respective provinces in disputes with the federal government.

Provincial monopolies or near-monopolies over the retail sale of alcoholic beverages are impediments to the economic union as well as important sources of provincial revenue. Individuals are not permitted to transport alcoholic beverages from one province to another. Provincial liquor control boards refuse to import beer from other provinces, although they do import it from foreign countries, and the brewing firms must therefore sacrifice economies of scale by operating a brewery in each province. Ontario and British Columbia, the two provinces where grapes can be grown, discriminate in favour of local wines by imposing higher markups on those produced elsewhere, or simply refusing to sell them at all. In some provinces it is a long-established tradition that the listing of any product for sale by the liquor control board requires a contribution by the beverage company to the campaign funds of the governing party.

The marketing of agricultural products is another area in which discriminatory policies have been pursued. Because independent commodity production has continued to predominate in agriculture, individual producers have little power in the market. Because the protection of farmers is considered socially and politically desirable, governments in many parts of the world have intervened to rectify this situation, a tendency that in federal countries can cause legal and political complications. In Canada the effort by the federal government to regulate the marketing of agricultural commodities through a Dominion Marketing Board was declared unconstitutional by the Judicial Committee of the Privy Council in 1937.[32] The provinces then created their own boards, and in 1949 Parliament adopted an act permitting the delegation to the provincial boards of powers to regulate the marketing of produce destined for markets outside the province where it was produced. Two decades elapsed before the question arose as to whether the provinces could legally discriminate in favour of their own producers.

In 1970 the government of Quebec responded to pressure from Quebec egg producers by giving their association, known as FEDCO, the power to control the sale of all eggs within the province. This was bad news for Ontario and Manitoba egg farmers who had enjoyed a substantial share of the Quebec market. FEDCO prohibited imports and raised the price of eggs to a level far above that prevailing in other provinces, permitting less efficient Quebec producers to expand their own production and replace the imports. The Manitoba government responded with a curious but effective use of its power to refer legislation to the provincial Superior Court for a ruling on its validity. It drafted a bill identical to the Quebec legislation of 1970, which it then referred. The bill was declared invalid by the Superior Court and, on appeal, by the Supreme Court of Canada, with the obvious implication that the Quebec legislation also violated the constitution.[33]

Meanwhile a somewhat similar situation had arisen with regard to broiler chickens, except that Quebec in this case was the victim rather than the instigator of protectionist policies. Ontario gave its broiler board, controlled by the poultry farmers, similar powers to those which the Quebec legislation gave to FEDCO in relation to eggs. The broiler board used its power to prevent imports from Quebec, which produced a surplus of broiler chickens. In both provinces boards were authorized to confiscate products imported without their approval, since a considerable illicit trade in both types of poultry products was taking place across the Quebec–Ontario border. The confusion finally had to be terminated by the intervention of the federal government. In 1972 Parliament adopted the National Farm Products Marketing Act, which permitted the establishment of federal boards and marketing schemes for such products as chickens and eggs, and the allocation of production quotas among the provinces. It is not clear that this initiative improved matters from the viewpoint of the consumer, but at least it ended bickering among the provinces and provided protection to all producers.[34]

As well as restricting the movement of goods and commodities, some provincial governments have tried to restrict the movement of capital into or out of their provinces. Saskatchewan and Prince Edward Island limit the purchase of land by non-residents. British Columbia used its power over timber rights to force Macmillan Bloedel to refuse a takeover bid from Canadian Pacific. Quebec used the *Caisse de dépôt et de placement* to prevent a takeover of Quebec-based Power Corporation by Ontario-based Argus Corporation. It also provides tax benefits to Quebec residents investing in Quebec-based corporations, thus providing a deterrent to the export of capital from the province. Alberta and Nova Scotia have subsequently imitated this practice.

At least until 1982, provinces could also restrict the mobility of labour by such means as lengthy residence requirements for the practice of certain professions, refusal to recognize professional and educational qualifications acquired elsewhere, and local preferences in the hiring of public sector employees. In 1978 Quebec introduced new regulations for the construction industry which denied employment to many residents of eastern Ontario who had traditionally worked in the province. Some provinces also required companies exploring for or extracting their natural resources to discriminate in favour of indigenous labour.

In the 1970s the federal government and certain elements of the central Canadian bourgeoisie became concerned that the proliferation of such practices might be detrimental to economic growth and to Canada's ability to compete internationally. Similar concerns were expressed by the Pepin-Robarts Task Force on Canadian Unity and by the Constitutional Committee of the Quebec (provincial) Liberal Party in its so-called "beige paper."[35] Studies of economic barriers between the provinces were sponsored by various federal agencies, and a 1980 discussion paper published under the by-line of the Minister of Justice proposed measures for "securing the Canadian economic union in the Constitution."[36] During the constitutional discussions then in progress the federal government, with lukewarm and partial support from Ontario and Saskatchewan, placed this item on the agenda. Specifically it wanted the constitution to prohibit discriminatory purchasing policies and barriers to the movement of labour, services, and capital. It also wanted Parliament to have explicit jurisdiction over product standards and competition policy. Provincial opposition was so intense that none of these ideas was pursued, apart from the prohibition of barriers to the movement of labour. This eventually became the "mobility rights" section of the Canadian Charter of Rights and

Freedoms, although at the behest of Newfoundland it was qualified to permit discriminatory policies in provinces whose rates of unemployment were above the national average.

In November 1982, following the patriation of the constitution, the federal government appointed the Royal Commission on the Economic Union and Development Prospects for Canada, headed by former cabinet minister Donald S. Macdonald. The Royal Commission's terms of reference, as well as its name, referred to the issue of economic union, and it was widely expected to recommend measures that would eliminate some of the barriers and prohibit the provinces from establishing new ones. However, on the basis of extensive research studies, the Royal Commission concluded that the economic costs of existing barriers were relatively low and that constitutional amendment to secure the economic union was not a high priority. Their main recommendation in regard to the economic union was that federal and provincial governments should jointly develop a Code of Economic Conduct, which would not be entrenched in the constitution.[37] On the other hand, the issue of economic union is relevant to the Royal Commission's principal objective: a free trade agreement with the United States. Some of the policies and activities of Canadian governments that are often cited as obstacles to the economic union could also be considered non-tariff barriers to free trade between Canada and the United States, and would thus be objectionable to the latter country in the context of a free trade agreement. It is possible, therefore, that the extent to which Canada approximates an economic union will not be determined by Canadians alone. If the outcome is decisively influenced by the demands of the United States, it will be an ironic sequel to the "patriation" of Canada's constitution from the formal authority of the United Kingdom.

NOTES

1. Harold Innis, *Essays in Canadian Economic History* (Toronto: University of Toronto Press, 1956) 277–78.

2. J.R. Mallory, *Social Credit and the Federal Power in Canada* (Toronto: University of Toronto Press, 1976) 198.

3. Edmond Orban, *La dynamique de la centralisation dans l'Etat federal: un processus irreversible?* (Montreal: Editions Quebec/Amerique, 1984).

4. E.R. Black and A.C. Cairns, "A Different Perspective on Canadian Federalism," *Canadian Public Administration* IX (1966) 27–45. See also R. Young, P. Faucher, and A. Blais, "The Concept of Province-Building: A Critique," *Canadian Journal of Political Science* XVII (1984): 783–818.

5. Gouvernement du Québec, *Batir le Québec: Énoncé de politique économique* (1979); Government of Alberta, *White Paper: Proposals for an Industrial and Science Strategy for Albertans, 1985 to 1990* (1984).

6. Royal Commission on the Economic Union and Development Prospects for Canada, *Report* (Ottawa, 1985) III, 486–526.

7. John Maynard Keynes, *The General Theory of Employment, Interest and Money* (London: Macmillan, 1936).

8. Quebec, *Report of the Royal Commission of Inquiry on Constitutional Problems* (1956) II, 273–328.

9. Jacques Parizeau, "Prospects for Economic Policy in a Federal Canada," in *The Future of Canadian Federalism*, ed. P.A. Crepeau and C.B. Macpherson (Toronto: University of Toronto Press, 1965) 45–57.

10. John Kenneth Galbraith, *The New Industrial State* (Boston: Houghton Mifflin, 1967), especially chapter XXII.

11. Calculated from the consumer price index data in *1984 Corpus Almanac and Canadian Sourcebook* (Don Mills: Southam Communications, 1984) I, 11–19.

12. R.B. Byers, ed., *Canadian Annual Review of Politics and Public Affairs 1982* (Toronto: University of Toronto Press, 1984) 51.

13. Byers, 135.

14. Albert Breton, *Discriminatory Government Policies in Federal Countries* (Montreal: Private Planning Association of Canada, 1967) 53–73.

15. R.T. Naylor, *The History of Canadian Business*, (Toronto: Lorimer, 1976) II, 104–60.

16. J.R. Smallwood, *I Chose Canada* (Toronto: Macmillan, 1973) 438–39.

17. Stephen Kimber, "Michelin Tire Rolls On," *Financial Post Magazine* 26 April 1980.

18. A.G.S. Careless, *Initiative and Response: The Adaptation of Canadian Federalism to Regional Economic Development* (Montreal: McGill-Queen's University Press, 1977).

19. Donald J. Savoie, *Federal-Provincial Collaboration: The Canada-New Brunswick General Development Agreement* (Montreal: McGill-Queen's University Press, 1981) is a useful account of one GDA.

20. Harold A. Innis, *Political Economy in the Modern State* (Toronto: McGraw-Hill Ryerson, 1946) xi.

21. Joseph Pope, *Correspondence of Sir John Macdonald* (Toronto: Oxford University Press, 1921) 176.

22. H.V. Nelles, *The Politics of Development: Forests, Mines and Hydro-Electric Power in Ontario, 1849–1941* (Toronto: Macmillan, 1974).

23. J. Murray Beck, *Politics of Nova Scotia, Volume One 1710–1896* (Tantalon, N.S.: Four East Publications, 1985) 260.

24. John Swettenham, *McNaughton, Volume III 1944–1966* (Toronto: Ryerson, 1969) 232–320.

25. *The Globe and Mail*, 26 June 1981.

26. H.V. Nelles, "Canadian Energy Policy 1945–1980: A Federalist Perspective," in *Entering the Eighties: Canada in Crisis*, ed. R.K. Carty and W.P. Ward (Toronto: Oxford University Press, 1980) 91–117.

27. For an excellent account see Howard Darling, *The Politics of Freight Rates* (Toronto: McClelland and Stewart, 1980).

28. The subject of this paragraph is treated more extensively in Garth Stevenson, *The Politics of Canada's Airlines: From Diefenbaker to Mulroney* (Toronto: University of Toronto Press, 1987).

29. *Winner vs. SMT Eastern* S.C.R. (1951) 887.

30. *A.G. Ontario vs. Winner* (1954) in R.A. Olmsted, *Decisions of the Judicial Committee of the Privy Council relating to the British North America Act, 1867*, Vol. III, 775–820.

31. Richard Schultz, *Federalism, Bureaucracy and Public Policy* (Montreal: McGill-Queen's University Press, 1980) 65.

32. *A.G. British Columbia vs. A.G. Canada* (1937) in Olmsted, III, 228–52.

33. *Manitoba Egg Reference* (1971), S.C.R. 689.

34. For a fuller account see A.E. Safarian, *Canadian Federalism and Economic Integration* (Ottawa: Information Canada, 1974) 48–54.

35. The Task Force on Canadian Unity, *A Future Together: Observations and Recommendations* (Ottawa: Supply and Services, 1979) 63–79. The Constitutional Committee of the Quebec Liberal Party, *A New Canadian Federation*, (Montreal, 1980) 101–08.

36. Jean Chrétien, *Securing the Canadian Economic Union in the Constitution* (Ottawa: Supply and Services, 1980).

37. Royal Commission on the Economic Union and Development Prospects for Canada, *Report* (Ottawa, 1985) III 97–141, 391–93.

9 Federal-Provincial Conflict and Its Resolution

The Canadian politician must operate, therefore, at two levels, concerning himself, on the one hand, with the variety of sentiments which are rooted in the past of the people and, on the other, with the tensions and conflicts of an industrial society as it exists in the present. The tensions of the second description may, and often do, express themselves in terms of the differences of the first, but an independent zeal for race and religion may also interfere with the functioning of the complex industrial mechanism. What is the order of the importance of the problems of Canadian politics and from where are they derived? These are the questions which any serious Canadian politician must answer, for the battlefield of Canadian political life is strewn with the corpses of leaders who did not know the answers to them.

H.S. FERNS AND B. OSTRY

Conflict between federal and provincial governments has been an enduring feature of Canadian political life for more than a century. Indeed it has been so ubiquitous that it tends to be taken for granted or treated as almost synonymous with federalism, rather than as a distinct phenomenon to be analysed in its own right. Consequently, there have been no systematic studies of federal-provincial conflict, and not much attention has been paid by students of the political system to the mechanisms by which federal-provincial conflicts are managed and resolved.

Some degree of conflict between the two levels of government is probably best viewed as an endemic and almost universal condition, but its incidence has none the less been unevenly distributed, both in space and in time. Certain episodes and sources of controversy stand out conspicuously in the history of federal-provincial relations, from Macdonald's conflicts with Mowat over navigable rivers and provincial boundaries to the recent struggles over economic, fiscal, and constitutional issues. Certain periods in Canadian history appear to have been relatively lacking in federal-provincial controversy, while during other periods, such as the 1960s and the 1970s, it seems to have been unusually intense. Certain provinces, like Ontario and British Columbia in the past, or Quebec and Alberta more recently, have seemed particularly prone to become involved in conflict with the federal authorities over a variety of issues, while others have appeared more docile and passive in their disposition.

CAUSES OF FEDERAL-PROVINCIAL CONFLICT

If the study of federal-provincial conflict had been pursued as extensively and as systematically as the subject of international conflict, there doubtless would be as many competing and conflicting explanations for the phenomenon as the students of international relations have devised to explain the causes of war. In both cases it seems likely that no single explanation will suffice, and in other ways, too, it would not be unduly fanciful to draw a parallel between them. Provincial policies toward the federal government, like the foreign policies of sovereign states, seem to have elements of continuity that survive regardless of parties, issues, and personalities. Alberta has always been remote, suspicious, and politically unorthodox, the Maritimes concerned with their poverty, and Quebec conscious of its distinctiveness and fearful of the anglophone majority. Mackenzie King once said that Canada had too much geography rather than too much history, but there often seems to be too much of both in federal-provincial relations, and both affect the behaviour of individual provinces in ways that are not easily changed.

Conflict with the federal government seems also to affect the provinces in the same ways that war and cold war affect the development of sovereign states. Local chauvinism and hostility toward the external adversary are stimulated by enhancing the ceremonial and symbolic aspects of political life. Administrative resources are expanded and strengthened, the power of the legislature to control the executive is curtailed, and the state intervenes more directly in economic life to shape it for its own purposes. Powerful, combative, and effective leaders emerge and become symbols of the province's determination to defend its interests. Just as war and external danger produced a Lloyd George, a Churchill, a Stalin, or a de Gaulle, so federal-provincial conflict seems to produce a Mowat or a Mercier, a Duplessis or a Drew, a Lesage or a Lougheed.

Provincial governments can stir up conflict with the federal government to distract attention from internal conflicts or to release the tension that arises from them, much as European powers used to use imperialist adventures for the same purpose. Martin Robin's history of British Columbia politics suggests that this has been an enduring syndrome in that province's behaviour; perhaps because the character of the provincial economy makes class conflict more acute and more dangerous to local vested interests there than in most other parts of

Canada. Quebec nationalism from Mercier to Duplessis and from Duplessis to Lévesque has also attempted with some success to sublimate class conflict into hostility toward the supposedly nefarious designs of the federal authorities. Ontario, under Mitchell Hepburn from 1934 until 1943, and Alberta, under Peter Lougheed from 1971 until 1985, also illustrate the success with which federal-provincial conflict can be promoted and manipulated to distract attention from internal class conflicts.

Class conflict can also lead to federal-provincial conflict more directly if a provincial government represents a different class or a different combination of class interests from the federal government. The best examples of this situation in Canadian history are the conflicts between farmer-dominated provincial governments in the Prairie provinces and federal governments that represented the commercial, financial, and industrial interests of the central Canadian bourgeoisie. After the First World War, Prairie farmers rejected the traditional two-party system and launched a number of distinctive populist parties and movements. With the diversification of the prairie economy and the transformation of the surviving farmers into large-scale entrepreneurs, the region has lost its political distinctiveness. A more recent example would be the government of Quebec from 1976 until 1985, which represented an alliance between the salaried new middle class, some elements of the working class, and some francophone small entrepreneurs. The objectives of this government— political sovereignty for Quebec and stringent restrictions on the use of the English language in the private sector of the economy—were vigorously opposed by the Canadian bourgeoisie and the federal government.

More frequently, federal-provincial conflict has represented the conflict between different class fractions within the dominant world of corporate capitalism. Christopher Armstrong has documented a number of such struggles in early twentieth-century Ontario: between electric utilities and manufacturers, between the promoters of electric and steam railways, between different sectors of the insurance industry, and between a variety of natural resource interests.[2] Each fraction identifies its interests with a level of government where it finds a sympathetic hearing, and the economic conflict becomes institutionalized as a federal-provincial one, complete with the usual ideological justifications on both sides. More recent examples have been the efforts of Premier John Robarts to protect the insurance industry (particularly influential in his own city of London) against the competition of government pensions and medicare; the lobbying of western provincial governments against federal tax reforms that threatened the privileges of the mining industry; and the recent disposition of several provincial governments to participate in the making of tariff policy.

Conflicts of this kind exist in virtually all countries, with or without federal institutions, and intergovernmental conflict is not the only form they could take, even in Canada. There are a number of reasons, however, why in Canada they are particularly likely to develop as such. The regionalized nature of the Canadian economy increases the probability that a particular sector of the economy will be largely concentrated in one province and will exercise significant economic and political power within that province. The fact that the provinces are few in number and that most of them are relatively large increases the likelihood that a determined provincial government can influence federal policy or place obstacles in the way of federal initiatives.

It would be wrong, however, to view the provincial governments only as the direct representatives of specific interests or to view federal-provincial conflict entirely as an expression of economic rivalry. The modern capitalist state has a certain degree of autonomy (which seems to be increasing) in relation to the specific interests whose collective purposes it serves, and it can only be effective insofar as this is the case.[3] The provincial level of Canadian government is no exception to this rule. To a large degree the increasingly complex and sophisticated apparatus of provincial government, like any organization, has its own interests to protect, although it may or may not serve other interests as an incidental consequence of doing so.

Thus a large part of federal-provincial conflict is really no more than conflict between competing organizations, each with its own imperatives of expansion, survival, and self-defence. No class analysis is needed to explain why provincial governments seek to expand their revenues through equalization or abatement, as the case may be, or to exclude the other level of government from functional areas of jursidiction over which they have already staked a claim. Nor is class analysis needed to explain why politicians quarrel over patronage or campaign funds, although the expansion and bureaucratization of government at both levels has made this kind of conflict far less important than it was in the days of Mitch Hepburn.

Federal-provincial conflict thus has a number of different causes, each of which has a long history in Canada and none of which is capable of being removed except through very fundamental changes in the society. Moreover, the institutional type of conflict is really an inevitable consequence of the existence of federalism, whose rationale is that it is the only basis on which even a semblance of national unity can be achieved in the face of the other types of conflict. Despite this rather paradoxical dilemma, federal-provincial conflict has historically been managed, and at times resolved, with a fair degree of success. Various institutional mechanisms or procedures have been employed for this purpose, although not all of them seem equally suitable for every circumstance or every type of conflict. In the next section these mechanisms or procedures will be examined in roughly the chronological order in which they emerged to a position of importance. The progression begins with the quasi-federal devices of disallowance and reservation, continues through political, judicial, and administrative approaches to conflict management and resolution, and concludes with the phenomenon variously described as executive federalism or federal-provincial diplomacy.

DISALLOWANCE AND RESERVATION

Enough has been written concerning the powers of disallowance and reservation that it is not necessary in this context to describe them in detail. In theory they offered a means of "resolving" federal-provincial conflicts through an assertion of the federal authority against which the province had no redress. In so doing they accorded both with the monarchical and hierarchical philosophy of the Fathers of Confederation and with the apparently overwhelming strength of the economic interests that favoured a centralized and quasi-federal union in 1867.

Yet in practice the use of these powers was not particularly convenient or successful, with the result that they were used only rarely and with decreasing frequency even against the new and supposedly immature provinces of the West. Almost half the acts that have been disallowed or reserved since the death of John A. Macdonald were from the single province of British Columbia, and after Laurier's defeat in 1911 both powers became virtually extinct, apart from the brief revival of disallowance in relation to the Alberta Social Credit legislation between 1937 and 1943.

One reason for this was the fact that with the gradual growth of democratic sentiment the use of these powers, particularly that of reservation, came to appear increasingly illegitimate and anachronistic. The Judicial Committee's opinion in the Maritime Bank case also conferred the ideological support of the imperial connection on the notion that the provincial legislatures should enjoy equal dignity and status with the federal Parliament. Moreover, it was politically hazardous to use disallowance and reservation, especially against the larger provinces whose support was crucial in federal elections. If the provincial government affected was of the same party as the federal one it might refuse its assistance, while if it was of the other party it might redouble its efforts in support of the federal opposition. In either case the provincial electorate would be unlikely to look favourably on the disallowance or reservation of acts approved by their elected representatives in the legislature. In fact it is possible that the peculiar Canadian tendency for the party that holds office in Ottawa to enjoy little success in provincial elections is in part a legacy of resentment against the frequently partisan interventions of federally appointed lieutenant-governors.

An additional defect of disallowance and reservation was that there was nothing to prevent the provincial legislature from adopting the same act, or a practically identical one, a second time, thus forcing the federal government or the lieutenant-governor either to admit defeat or to repeat the process, again with no assurance of ultimate success. There were some notable cases of provincial defiance, such as Mowat's Rivers and Streams Acts which the Macdonald government disallowed on three occasions, or the repeated attempts by the Manitoba government to charter railways in competition with the CPR. Such protracted episodes could only increase popular sympathy for the provincial government and give the federal government an appearance of heavy-handed ineptitude and callous disregard for the principles of representative government. Thus it is not surprising that the powers eventually fell into disuse.

Disallowance and reservation seem to have been used successfully in some cases, although the overall record was not particularly encouraging to their proponents. In some cases the provincial government did not persevere with its intention, and the federal initiative was successful. It is not clear exactly what variables contributed to success or failure in the use of the federal powers. It does appear that they were used in response to several types of federal-provincial conflict. In a very large number of cases the federal government seems to have acted on behalf of either transcontinental railways or financial institutions when it disallowed provincial acts. Examples of disallowed acts that offended these interests would include the Manitoba railway charters, three efforts by Saskatchewan to incorporate trust and loan companies, anti-Oriental legislation in British Columbia (which threatened to interfere with construction of the CPR and later the Canadian Northern), and the Social Credit legislation in Alberta. Some of these episodes can certainly be regarded as cases of class conflict (capitalists versus farmers), while others were conflicts between fractions of the dominant class. Still other cases of disallowance resulted from expressions of institutional self-interest on the part of the two levels of government. This category would include such episodes as the Rivers and Streams Acts in Ontario, the Alberta Mineral Tax Act of 1923 (which was disallowed because it seemed to threaten the federal ownership of lands and resources in the province), or the disallowance at about the same time of a Nova Scotia private bill that attempted to reverse a decision of the Supreme Court of Canada.

It would be foolhardy to predict that the powers of disallowance and reservation will never again be used, but certainly they have become unpopular and recent federal governments have shown little or no disposition to use them. The Trudeau government more than once suggested their abolition during constitutional discussions, but the fact that no province apparently regarded this as a major priority testifies to the almost universal expectation that the powers will never again be exercised.

POLITICAL PARTIES AND CONFLICT RESOLUTION

A less contentious response to federal-provincial conflict, and one
that could conceivably have been used, would be to seek accommodation through the machinery of a political party. By definition, of
course, this method of resolving conflict would only be available
when the same party held office both federally and provincially. There
are, however, more fundamental reasons why it has become relatively
insignificant.

Donald Smiley's lament that Canadian political scientists have
ignored the subject of federal-provincial party relations is still largely
justified, although a major gap in our knowledge has since been filled
by Reginald Whitaker's outstanding work on the Liberal party under
King and St. Laurent.[5] Most students of Canadian federalism have
dismissed parties as being of little importance, in contrast to non-
Canadian writers on federalism such as K.C. Wheare and W.H. Riker,
both of whom attribute to parties a decisive role in facilitating the
operation of a federal system. Smiley concludes that Canadian parties
and the party system are too loosely integrated or, as he puts it, "confe-
deral" to have any impact on federal-provincial relations. By this he
means that Canadian voters do not typically support the same party at
both levels and that federal and provincial parties, even if they bear the
same name, have separate organizations, elites, platforms, and sources
of financial support.[6]

While few would argue today with Smiley's description of the
Canadian party system, it did not always have the characteristics he
describes. At least until 1917, when the federal Liberal party split over
conscription and a coalition government was formed, the party system
was in fact quite integrated according to Smiley's criteria. It also
appears that party had a significant impact on federal-provincial relations, in the sense that relations were much more cordial when the
same party held office at both levels.

Relations between the federal government and the two central provinces were very close in the first few years when the provincial governments were controlled by allies of Macdonald and Cartier. The
Interprovincial Conference of 1887 was basically a meeting of Liberals
to denounce a Conservative federal government, apart from the pres-
ence of the nominally Conservative Premier Norquay of Manitoba.
British Columbia and Prince Edward Island, both governed by more
orthodox Conservatives, were not represented at the conference. The
bitter struggles between Ontario and the federal government occurred
between 1878 and 1896, when the former was Liberal and the latter
Conservative. Between 1905 and 1911, when the positions were
reversed, relations again deteriorated. Federal politicians depended
on the organizational support of friendly provincial governments to
win elections, and the provincial allies were rewarded with "better

terms" and sometimes with appointments to the federal cabinet. It seems reasonable to conclude that many conflicts were avoided or quietly resolved through political channels.

However, this method of resolving and managing conflicts had its limitations. In some cases, Norquay's experience as Premier of Manitoba being a good example, the objective conflicts of interest between a provincial government and the federal authorities were too serious to be accommodated within the party machinery. The provincial government was forced to disagree publicly with the federal one and thus fell between two stools, being regarded by the federal government as untrustworthy and by the electorate as too closely tied to the federal government. It is not accidental that Ontario, with its long history of federal-provincial conflict, has usually been governed by the federal opposition party, but it is arguable that the latter fact is more the result of conflict than the cause of it. Ontarians may have believed that the federal government and, by implication, the party that controlled that government were too closely tied to the economic interests of Montreal. The use of anti-French bigotry in Ontario by both nineteenth-century Liberals and twentieth-century Conservatives could be viewed as an ideological smokescreen to conceal what was basically an economic rivalry between Toronto and Montreal. Significantly, the bigotry ceased to be respectable because it was no longer necessary once Toronto replaced Montreal as the major economic centre.

There were, however, other reasons why the partisan method of dealing with federal-provincial conflict became obsolete. The events of 1917 disintegrated the party system and produced, as one consequence, the formation of provincial governments in Alberta, Manitoba, and Ontario by parties that had no realistic chances of success at the federal level. The Saskatchewan Liberals remained in office, but at the cost of loosening their ties with the federal party. With the rapid disappearance of the federal Progressive party, the governments of the Prairie provinces, in effect, adopted a position of quasi-neutrality with respect to federal politics, and were able to deal impartially, although not always cordially, with federal governments of either party.[7] The ambiguity was increased when Manitoba's Progressive government became a coalition including the Liberals and eventually even the Conservatives. A coalition of the two major parties also governed British Columbia between 1942 and 1952, largely to keep the CCF out of office.

Another milestone in the transformation of the party system was reached in 1935, when Maurice Duplessis formed his Union Nationale, the first major Canadian political party, apart from Mercier's short-lived Parti National, to operate exclusively at the provincial level. Quebec continued to support the Liberal Party in federal elections while giving the Union Nationale the largest share of its votes in provincial ones. Subsequently the Union Nationale's practice of operating exclusively at the provincial level has been imitated by the Social Credit party in British Columbia and by the Parti Québécois.

This peculiar separation of the party system into federal and provincial layers is perhaps, in part, a consequence of the intensity of federal-provincial conflict, which makes it difficult for a party affiliated with the federal government to appear as a credible defender of provincial interests. Significantly, the traditional two-party system has survived at the provincial level only in the Atlantic provinces, which are so dependent on federal largesse that affiliation with the federal government is still an electoral asset. At the same time, the separation of the federal and provincial party systems was facilitated by, and might not have been possible without, the bureaucratization and depoliticization of government at both levels, especially the federal, which limited the functions of parties to recruiting candidates and conducting election campaigns. The conduct of federal-provincial relations was one of the functions that was largely transferred from the parties to the non-partisan bureaucracy.

Whitaker's account shows the extent of this process in the federal Liberal Party, which remained in office for so long that it became virtually a part of the machinery of state and, in a sense, the political and electoral arm of the federal bureaucracy. The bureaucracy supplied the party with ideas, programs, and even personnel such as Pearson and Pickersgill. In return the federal party's behaviour in federal-provincial relations was determined by bureaucratic rather than partisan considerations. It ruthlessly undermined its faltering provincial affiliates to improve relations with the non-Liberal governments of Quebec, Ontario, Alberta, and British Columbia (as in the episode of the Quebec income tax discussed in Chapter 6). Interestingly enough, this did not happen in Saskatchewan; apparently it was considered more important to maintain a viable "free enterprise" party there than to develop a friendly relationship with Tommy Douglas. In the four largest provinces, however, the indifference of the federal Liberal party to the fate of its provincial affiliates was both a cause and a consequence of the perceived irrelevance of party ties to federal-provincial relations.

The federal Liberals rebuilt their organization during their sojourn in opposition from 1957 to 1963 in a way that made the federal party virtually independent of the various provincial Liberal parties, most of which were still languishing in opposition when the federal Liberals returned to office. Quebec's provincial party, still smarting from the slights it had endured at the hands of Louis St. Laurent, established a parallel organization completely separate from the federal party in 1964. The tendency of the federal Liberals to ignore and bypass the provincial organizations antagonized provincial Liberals like Ross Thatcher (Premier of Saskatchewan from 1964 to 1971), and contributed to the rapid decline of both federal and provincial Liberal parties in the western provinces.[8] In 1980 the federal Liberals achieved a feat without precedent in Canadian politics: they returned to office with a convincing majority even though there was not a single provincial Liberal government in the country.

The other two federal parties, the Progressive Conservatives and the New Democrats, have retained a much greater degree of integration between their federal and provincial organizations. This may be partly a consequence and partly a cause of their lack of success at the federal level. The Progressive Conservatives do not contest provincial elections in Quebec, and the New Democrats have been a negligible factor in that province until very recently, but elsewhere both parties rely on essentially the same organizations and personnel in federal and provincial politics. This is also largely true of the Liberals in the Atlantic provinces. This more traditional, or integrated, kind of party organization may occasionally facilitate the resolution of intergovernmental disputes if the same party is in office at both levels. However, it is not guaranteed to do so, and it may expose the federal party to conflicting pressures from its various provincial affiliates. During the bitter conflicts over energy and the constitution in the early 1980s, both the Progressive Conservative and New Democratic parties in Parliament experienced difficulty in maintaining harmony between their Ontario members and those from the West. Several NDP members of Parliament from Saskatchewan publicly opposed their leader and supported their provincial government on the constitutional issue.

In relation to federalism, as to most other subjects, the two major federal parties have at times expressed different opinions from one another, but the differences seem to have been usually based on expediency and circumstance rather than on fundamental philosophical differences. No major party leader, apart from John A. Macdonald, Pierre Trudeau, and possibly Edward Blake, appears to have given much thought to theories of federalism. Macdonald was clearly more of a centralist than his political opponents. Trudeau, although not much of a centralist by Macdonaldian standards, was clearly more so than Joe Clark, who led the Progressive Conservatives from 1976 to 1983, served briefly as Prime Minister, and once described Canada as "a community of communities."[9] Generally speaking, the governing federal party tends to be more centralist than the opposition, and long-established governing parties or experienced prime ministers tend to be more centralist than those who have recently taken office. Partly this reflects the truth of the American aphorism, "Where you stand depends on where you sit" and partly the fact that newly elected governments often have to repay political debts to their provincial allies. There is also a tendency for opposition caucuses to consist disproportionately of farmers and small entrepreneurs, who tend to be more provincialist in their orientations than most other Canadians.

JUDICIAL CONFLICT RESOLUTION

Since judicial interpretation of the constitution is discussed at length
in Chapter 3, no extensive treatment of the subject is necessary in the
present context, but its usefulness may be noted. The courts can contribute to the resolution of federal-provincial conflicts by clarifying
the legal authority of the contending parties, and a decision by the
Supreme Court may permit a face-saving withdrawal by the losing
side. Of course, not all judicial interpretations of the constitution arise
from intergovernmental disputes; more frequently a case is initiated
by a private litigant. Even a case of this kind, however, may contribute
to the settlement of an intergovernmental dispute. Much more significant in this regard are reference cases, which are relatively common in
Canada although the courts in both Australia and the United States
have refused to hear them. A government may refer its own legislation,
or that of the other level of government, to the courts for advice in an
effort to strengthen its own bargaining position or to accelerate the
process of resolving the dispute. Numerous reference cases involving
the control of alcoholic beverages, insurance regulation, agricultural
marketing, offshore mineral resources, and the process of constitutional amendment can be cited in illustration. As was noted in Chapter 3, the publicity and controversy that have surrounded the Supreme
Court in recent years are in marked contrast to the situation in the
1950s and 1960s: it was then often alleged that the judiciary was no
longer of decisive importance in defining the shape of Canadian federalism. The reasons for the change appear to have less to do with the
personalities or preferences of the justices than with the changing
agenda of intergovernmental relations. At a time when the main priorities of governments were expenditures on health, education, and welfare, and in the case of the federal government on military defence,
their disputes were largely over the sharing of revenues, which is more
readily determined by political compromise than by judicial decision.

In recent years both levels of government have attempted to restrain
the growth of expenditures, but both have become more interventionist in seeking to regulate the activities of the private sector. This inevitably provokes conflicts of a different kind, with which the courts are
well suited to deal. Disputes over money can often be resolved by
"splitting the difference," regardless of the legal situation, but disputes over the regulatory powers of the state require a precise determination of who has the legal authority. If one level of government can
regulate a particular activity, the other cannot, and should be discouraged from attempting to do so.

Arguments that the courts should somehow stand aside and leave
the resolution of disputes to "the political process" are thus unper-
suasive, and in most cases amount to little more than special pleading
on behalf of provincial governments whose empire-building schemes

would not survive any serious test of their legal validity. The political process, which in this context is really a euphemism for intergovernmental bargaining, is no more democratic, and certainly less dignified and less rational, than the judicial process. In fact an effective political settlement may actually be facilitated if the courts have clearly determined the legal authority of the governments involved before bargaining begins. Furthermore, a political agreement that takes place before the legal issues have been resolved may be built on sand if it results from false assumptions concerning the legal authority of the parties. If the true legal situation is revealed as a result of private litigation, or because a subsequent government decides to refer the question to the courts, the premature political compromise is likely to collapse.

A judicial decision also does not totally determine the terms of the political settlement that may follow. Federal governments in Canada have at times proved willing to surrender at the bargaining table some of the advantages that they won in the courtroom. The concession of regulatory power over highway transport to the provinces after the Judicial Committee had granted authority to the federal government noted in the preceding chapter is an example of this. A more recent and equally striking instance concerns the control over offshore mineral resources in the vicinity of Newfoundland. For years after the Supreme Court upheld federal ownership and jurisdiction on the Pacific coast, the government of Newfoundland claimed that it, in contrast to other coastal provinces, was the owner of its continental shelf by virtue of its alleged status as a self-governing dominion before 1949. The Supreme Court finally rejected this claim in 1984, two years after the federal government had referred the question to the Court for decision.[10] In 1985 a new federal government reached an agreement with Newfoundland, giving that province practically all the benefits it would have received had the Court found in its favour.[11]

CO-OPERATIVE FEDERALISM

The administrative approach to managing and resolving intergovernmental conflicts did not really begin to develop before the turn of the century, and it reached its fullest development in the period roughly from 1945 until 1970. During the two decades following the Second World War, it was the predominant method of dealing with federal-provincial conflict, largely supplanting both the party-political and the judicial approaches. This was the heyday of "co-operative federalism," a phrase borrowed from the United States, which both celebrated, and purported to describe, the way in which the federal system operated at that time. By the late 1960s, however, administrative or "co-operative" federalism was already being transformed into executive federalism, which will be considered subsequently.

Administrative or co-operative federalism, its proponents like to argue, was based on the virtues of compromise, flexibility, and pragmatism.[12] It was also based on the assumption that all disputes and problems could be resolved through the application of these virtues, and that some mutually acceptable position could always be discovered. Certainly the administrative approach to the resolution of conflict contrasted with the judicial approach in that it did tend to promote such compromises and was thus more effective in resolving certain kinds of dispute, such as those over fiscal matters. The administrative approach also appealed to governments which, for one reason or another, preferred not to seek a clear definition of jurisdictional boundaries, or which did not believe it was possible to find one.

While it had certain advantages over the judicial approach, the administrative approach tended to replace the party-political approach to conflict resolution for somewhat different reasons. As bureaucracies became larger, more powerful, more functionally specialized, and more removed from partisan influence and pressure, they assumed increasingly autonomous roles in seeking accommodation with their counterparts at the other level of government. As specialists of various kinds came to predominate in certain sectors of the public service, they tended to discover that they held interests, goals, and assumptions in common with similar specialists at the other level of government, and that these took precedence over considerations of intergovernmental competition, party rivalry, or even constitutional propriety. Thus administrative methods of problem-solving were preferred. Politicians acquiesced in this, partly by necessity (since they could no longer control all the detailed activities of their departments), partly because it lacked the risks of the judicial approach, and partly because they were themselves acquiring bureaucratic perspectives. It is significant that the administrative character of federalism became most pronounced under the St. Laurent government, at a time when the governing federal party had become almost a part of the bureaucratic machinery.

The growth of administrative or co-operative federalism was very closely associated with the growth of conditional grants and shared-cost programs, a phenomenon discussed in the preceding chapter. Inseparable from both was the proliferation of federal-provincial committees, councils, meetings, and other forms of contact at various levels of officialdom, which served as the mechanisms by which problems were resolved in an administrative manner.

These bodies have been catalogued and described by a number of writers. Gerard Veilleux discovered in the 1960s that about four-fifths of them were concerned with the areas of general government (including finance), statistics, health and welfare, natural resources, and agriculture.[13] This list suggests the areas in which administrative approaches to the resolution of intergovernmental conflict were generally successful and popular. Finance is the area least amenable to solutions achieved through the judicial process; health and welfare, for reasons already described, was the area where conditional grants and shared-cost programs were most important; agriculture is a shared jurisdiction under the BNA Act. The inclusion of resources appears anomalous from our present perspective, but at the time Veilleux wrote they would have been mainly renewable resources, which are closely associated with agriculture.

Donald Smiley has suggested some of the circumstances under which co-operative federalism is most likely to be successful. The officials who do the negotiating should have real authority to speak on behalf of their governments; they should have a common frame of reference, such as might result from shared professional training and expertise; they should be more committed to the success of the program than to other types of goals; they should be willing to compromise, and also to share confidential information with one another. Finally, there should not be too much public interest or involvement in the matters at issue.[14]

Viewed in a somewhat different way, co-operative or administrative federalism seems to be a fairly effective remedy for the types of conflict that arise from the organizational imperatives of different levels of government. It can prevent or resolve such conflicts, at least to some degree, through the countervailing impact of professional or programmatic goals that cut across, instead of reinforcing, the jurisdictional rivalries between the two levels. Co-operative federalism cannot, however, deal very successfully with the conflicts that originate outside the governmental and bureaucratic milieu and that result from more fundamental antagonisms between the interests of different classes or class fractions. Whether producers or consumers benefit from resource developments, whether industries are established in the East or in the West, whether jobs go to anglophones or francophones—these are not the types of question to which co-operative federalism provides answers. This is one reason for its obsolescence.

EXECUTIVE FEDERALISM

In recent years the term "executive federalism," first coined by Donald Smiley, has come to be used more frequently than "co-operative federalism."[15] Although the fact may not always be explicitly stated or even recognized, the change in terminology corresponds to a real change in the nature of intergovernmental relations, and one that began to take place a few years before the terminology was changed to correspond with it. Although one cannot state any precise date at which it occurred, the change was in fact fundamental. Co-operative federalism was characterized by the fragmentation of authority within each level of government, the absence of linkages between different issues and functional domains, the forging of specific intergovernmental links by different groups of specialized officials, and the lack of publicity or public awareness of what was happening.

Executive federalism, on the other hand, is characterized by the concentration and centralization of authority at the top of each participating government, the control and supervision of intergovernmental relations by politicians and officials with a wide range of functional interests, and the highly formalized and well-publicized proceedings of federal-provincial conference diplomacy. While co-operative federalism tended to subordinate the power, status, and prestige of individual governments to programmatic objectives, executive federalism does exactly the opposite.

Despite its recent rise to prominence, the origins of executive federalism and its most characteristic institutional manifestation, the first ministers' conference, can be traced back fairly far in Canadian history. Contacts between the Prime Minister and individual premiers were fairly frequent in the early period when partisan political considerations exercised a decisive influence on federal-provincial relations. Laurier summoned all of the premiers to a conference in 1906 to discuss the proposed changes in statutory subsidies to the provinces. There was a one-day conference in 1910 to discuss company law reform and a longer one in 1918, mainly to discuss problems of postwar reconstruction. In 1927 Mackenzie King organized a major conference to commemorate the sixtieth anniversary of Confederation, at which an extensive agenda was discussed. There were four more conferences during the Depression, mainly to discuss problems of relief and federal-provincial-municipal finance, an abortive conference to discuss the Rowell–Sirois Report in 1940, and a conference on postwar reconstruction and fiscal arrangements in 1945. As it turned out, the postwar pattern of federal-provincial finance required a first ministers' conference to discuss the arrangements at least every five years, and two additional conferences were also held in 1950 to consider the amendment of the constitution, a topic that had also been discussed in 1927 and 1935.

Federal-provincial first ministers' conferences were thus by no means unknown, but they took place at fairly infrequent intervals and could hardly be considered the predominant mechanism of interaction between the two levels of government, at least when considering the more mundane topics that dominated the federal-provincial agenda. Only for major changes in fiscal arrangements or for the consideration of amendments to the BNA Act were they considered essential. For the most part federal-provincial relations in the postwar period remained fragmented, specialized, unco-ordinated, and dominated by officials. Gerard Veilleux estimated in his book that only one-tenth of federal-provincial meetings and conferences involved elected politicians as participants.[16] By contrast, a study done for the government of Alberta in 1975 found that by that time politicians participated in almost one out of every four meetings.[17] It is also significant that at least one first ministers' conference took place almost every year from 1963 onward. The federal government in fact proposed in its "Victoria Charter" that the obligatory requirement of an annual conference be written into the constitution, corresponding to the requirement that there be an annual session of Parliament.

The most important reason for the shift from co-operative to executive federalism was that federal-provincial conflicts were becoming too serious, too profound, and too sensitive to be safely entrusted to the diplomatic and managerial skills of subordinate officials. In particular the evident dissatisfaction of Quebec during the Quiet Revolution could not be accommodated by traditional means. Federal-provincial relations had to be politicized and conducted at the highest level, as in the case of the Pearson-Lesage negotiations over the Canada and Quebec pension plans. At the same time or subsequently a number of other serious conflicts emerged which involved provinces other than Quebec: conflicts over tax-sharing and the financing of health, education, and welfare, over economic relations with the United States, over regional development and the competitive scramble for investment, and over the division of benefits from mineral resources. All of these matters were clearly "political" rather than "administrative" in the sense that large numbers of people outside the bureaucracy were aware of their significance and deeply interested in their outcomes. In fact the complex of problems, and particularly the situation in Quebec, provided grounds for apprehension that the survival of the federal state itself might be called into question.

This exacerbation of conflict led to a renewed emphasis on intergovernmental competition and to a tendency to give the institutional interests of governments priority over functional or programmatic objectives. A distrust of co-operative federalism followed, accompanied by a belief that the fragmentation of authority and the lack of co-ordination that it entailed were luxuries that no self-respecting government could afford. Quebec nationalists had always argued, correctly from their point of view, that the proliferation of specialized and fragmented intergovernmental relationships, such as those that arose from shared-cost programs, was a potential menace to the integrity of their provincial state and its ability or willingness to defend its own interests. This belief had caused Maurice Duplessis to refuse some conditional grants and had caused a later generation of Quebec nationalists to denounce the co-operative federalism of the 1960s as a fraud and a delusion.[18] Similar reasoning became increasingly apparent on the part of other provincial governments, and even of the federal government itself. This led to the development of new mechanisms for the conduct of intergovernmental relations.

These sentiments arising out of intergovernmental competition reinforced certain incentives toward centralization and concentration of power within each of the eleven governments that had arisen simultaneously from other causes. There was a widespread conviction in the 1960s that administrative structures and procedures could and should be reformed to make them more "rational." The centralized setting of priorities and the control of expenditure, through a process that related decisions on expenditure to more fundamental decisions on objectives, were viewed as fundamental to successful administration and policy-making. The desire to control expenditure was particularly strong on the part of Canadian provincial governments, which saw themselves after 1966 as faced with mounting expenditures on legitimization coupled with the diminishing likelihood that the "tax room" made available to them by the federal government would increase proportionately.

All of these pressures to centralize and concentrate authority were manifested in organizational changes at both the federal and provincial levels. Intergovernmental competition certainly played a part in promoting these changes, although they occurred so rapidly that it is not easy to determine which level of government initiated the trend and which level responded. At the federal level the establishment of the Treasury Board as a separate department and the proliferation of cabinet committees and support staff took place under Prime Minister Pearson. It was followed under Prime Minister Trudeau by a dramatic expansion of the Prime Minister's Office and the Privy Council Office, and by the creation in 1974 of a separate Federal-Provincial Relations Office reporting directly to the Prime Minister. From 1977 to 1980 there was also a Minister of State for Federal-Provincial Relations.

At the provincial level there has also been a tendency to expand and improve the machinery for co-ordinating intergovernmental relations. Until the 1960s such machinery was practically non-existent. In 1961 Quebec established a Ministry of Federal-Provincial Affairs, and in 1967 the name of the ministry was changed to Intergovernmental Affairs. Until 1976 this portfolio was always held by the Premier, but in that year Claude Morin, who had been the deputy minister under Lesage and Johnson, became a full-time Minister of Intergovernmental Affairs. From the outset the ministry was responsible for Quebec's international activities as well as its relations with other Canadian provinces, but in 1984 these functions were separated and placed under different ministers. After the change of government in 1985, both portfolios were held by Gil Remillard.

Quebec's example in establishing a department to conduct its intergovernmental relations was followed by Alberta in 1972, Newfoundland in 1975, Ontario in 1978, and both British Columbia and Saskatchewan in 1979. The Saskatchewan department lasted only four years before it was abolished, but the others have continued. In New-foundland, and since 1985 in Ontario, the intergovernmental affairs portfolio has been held by the Premier. The Alberta and Ontario departments follow the original Quebec model most closely in that they combine responsibility for international and federal-provincial activities. Ontario's was also responsible for the province's relations with its municipalities until 1981, when a separate department was organized for that purpose.[19]

Opinions differ on the question of whether the proliferation of intergovernmental affairs departments and other central agencies has made federal-provincial relations better or worse. Their detractors argue that they have contributed to the erosion of co-operative federalism by reducing the autonomy of the functional departments such as agriculture, health, and welfare, and that they have a vested interest in intergovernmental competition and conflict. Their defenders respond that the intergovernmental affairs departments are at most a symptom, and certainly not a cause, of the transition from co-operative to executive federalism, and that the nation-wide network of intergovernmental affairs specialists is itself, like the functional networks that it partly replaced, a contributor to national unity.

Whatever the truth of these assertions, it seems indisputable that the success of executive federalism in resolving problems has not been impressive. When the sessions are televised, participants tend to read speeches to the cameras rather than negotiating seriously, but when negotiations take place in secret the governments cannot be held accountable for the results. Consensus is rarely achieved among governments representing different regions, political parties and jurisdictional interests. When it is not achieved the public demands a scapegoat, and each government argues that some other government is at fault. Even the Pepin-Robarts Task Force, in a report otherwise distinguished by an excessive sympathy for the provincial governments, expressed awareness of the dangers:

> The spectacle of Canadian governments wrangling constantly among themselves has done nothing to reduce cynicism about public affairs and it has presented Canadians with the image of a country deeply divided against itself.[20]

Media coverage of the conferences, portraying the federal government as merely one of "eleven senior governments," has undermined its legitimacy and has dangerously elevated the status of the premiers, who increasingly tend to argue that they collectively represent the national interest. Although Richard Simeon's observations of executive federalism in the 1960s led him to conclude that there was an

unwritten rule against provinces "ganging up" on the federal government, this has not been evident recently.[21] Yet when most or all of the
provinces attend the conference armed with a common set of demands
agreed upon in advance, there can be little hope of serious negotiation.

Another problem with executive federalism is its tendency to erode
the power and influence of the legislature at both levels. Legislatures
are weakened when they must legislate within the parameters of executive agreements arrived at in secret without their participation.
Opposition parties, especially at the federal level, are placed in the
position of being forced either to acquiesce in the agreements arrived
at or to criticize the members of their own party who have participated
in making them. Accountability also suffers when each government
involved in an agreement can deny responsibility by claiming that
undesirable features of the agreement were insisted upon by one of the
other governments involved. At the same time executive federalism is
arguably a consequence, as much as a cause, of the domination of
legislatures by cabinets, or more precisely, of a parliamentary form of
government. Certainly in the United States, with its separation of
powers, nothing of the sort would be possible. Neither the President
nor state governors could assume that an executive agreement would
be acceptable to Congress or the state legislatures.

As discussed below, Canada's federal institutions, particularly Parliament, have recently borne the brunt of much criticism to the effect
that they do not adequately reflect the diversity of regional interests
and that conflicting interests are, therefore, almost inevitably
expressed as conflicts between the two levels of government. While
there is some truth to this impression, it really explains only half the
problem. The other half is the impact of parliamentary institutions
and party discipline at the provincial level, where majorities and
governments are subjected to even fewer checks and balances than they
are at the federal level. Unlike an American state, a Canadian province
does not have separation of powers, nor a rigid constitution, nor an
upper house. The government's majority in the legislature is often
overwhelming, and the legislature is typically in session for only a few
months of the year. Natural resource revenues, external borrowing,
and profit-making ventures such as provincial liquor boards weaken
the legislature's control over the public purse. The checks and balances which the BNA Act provided by establishing the office of
lieutenant-governor are now widely viewed as illegitimate, and are
practically never used. Electoral campaigns focus on the premier's
leadership, particularly his role in federal–provincial relations, so
that members of the legislature are elected on the party label as docile
members of a "team" and are not expected to have independent
thoughts on important issues. Far more than at the federal level, and
more than in any other liberal democracy, power is concentrated in the

hands of a few persons or even one person. The illusion that what the premier wants is what the province wants is easily perpetuated. This in turn makes Canada appear like a collection of ten private fiefdoms, in which the provincial boundary is the most significant basis of political interest or allegiance. The diversity of interests within each province, and the many interests and associations that unite individuals and groups across provincial boundaries, are given little expression.

INTRASTATE FEDERALISM

Although federalism was defined in the first chapter of this book in a way that emphasized the co-existence of two distinct levels of government, some recent writing on the subject, particularly in Canada, has emphasized another aspect of federalism, namely the representation of the provinces or sub-national states and their interests within the institutions of the central government. The terms interstate and intrastate federalism have been devised to distinguish between these two aspects, with interstate federalism referring to the relations between two distinct levels of government and intrastate federalism referring to the representation of the component parts within the central institutions. While both the academic study of and popular impressions of Canadian federalism have traditionally emphasized the interstate aspect, recent years have seen an increasing emphasis on intrastate federalism.

Students of intrastate federalism argue that the central institutions of the Canadian state, and particularly the House of Commons and the Senate, fail to provide adequate representation of the diversity of provincial and regional interests. As a result, those interests must seek representation through the provincial governments and the accommodation of interests can only take place through intergovernmental bargaining or, if that fails, through intergovernmental conflict. This line of argument, while increasingly popular, is rather ambiguous in its motives and conclusions. As Donald Smiley and Ronald Watts point out in a useful book on the subject, proponents of institutional reform along the lines of intrastate federalism may be seeking either to strengthen or to weaken the federal level of government, and the two motives are not always clearly distinguished.[22] Intrastate federalism might strengthen the federal level by increasing its legitimacy and by persuading regionally concentrated interests to seek their objectives through it rather than through the provincial governments. On the other hand, it might weaken the federal level by making it increasingly difficult to devise coherent and effective policies, by promoting political instability, and by encouraging the provincial governments to meddle in national politics. While many intrastate federalists are no doubt sincerely devoted to the first objective, the fact that the governments of Alberta and British Columbia have been among the most enthusiastic proponents of the concept gives considerable grounds for apprehension.

Elements of intrastate federalism are, of course, to be found in the status quo, and there is some evidence that they were more effective in the early years of Canadian federalism than they are today. The Fathers of Confederation seem to have taken the Senate seriously as a means of representing regional diversities, if one is to judge by the amount of time devoted to discussing that institution at the conferences that preceded Confederation. Party discipline in the House of Commons was less rigid in the nineteenth century than it is now; members often broke ranks with their party on regionally sensitive issues like the Riel affair, the Pacific railway, or Catholic education in New Brunswick. The federal civil service, being recruited through political patronage, could be influenced by the regional concerns of ministers and members of Parliament. Most importantly, the cabinet consisted of persons closely tied to provincial party organizations, and often with political experience at the provincial level, who ensured that their own province received its fair share of patronage and public expenditure. To some extent the cabinet is still an agency of intrastate federalism even today, as suggested by the rigid convention requiring at least one minister from each province. Its effectiveness in this regard has been eroded, however, by the technocratic background of many ministers, the extent to which ministers are influenced by the non-political bureaucracy, and the increasingly complex organization and processes of the cabinet itself.

Since few seem to wish a return to the type of cabinet and civil service that existed under Macdonald and Mackenzie, recent proposals to strengthen intrastate federalism have concentrated on the House of Commons and the Senate. The two major complaints about the Commons have been in relation to the rigid party discipline and the electoral system. Party discipline means that members, particularly on the government side of the house, must defer to the collective decision of their party rather than speaking out publicly for regional interests. Since the collective decision will naturally reflect mainly the interests of the provinces with the largest number of representatives, the interests of small provinces, or of provinces where the party in question has little support, will receive inadequate representation.

The electoral system, as Alan Cairns argued in a classic article in 1968, worsens the problem by magnifying regional variations in the support of the different parties, and creating the possibility that the caucus of the governing party will seriously underrepresent certain provinces.[23] Thus the Progressive Conservative caucus elected in 1979 contained only two members from Quebec and the Liberal caucus elected in 1980 contained only two members from the West, both of whom were from Winnipeg. The absence of representatives from petroleum producing provinces seemed to many westerners a credible explanation for the subsequent introduction of the National Energy Program by the Liberal government.

Party discipline is a complex phenomenon that goes to the heart of responsible government, and criticism of it leads logically to the rejection of the parliamentary system itself, something which relatively few Canadians seem willing to contemplate. The electoral system is a more tempting target of criticism. The Task Force on Canadian Unity, which reported at a time when Quebec had only two representatives in the government caucus, recommended that about sixty additional members of the House of Commons should be elected by proportional representation. A few months later the Quebec Liberal Party's "beige paper" suggested more cautiously that the idea of proportional representation should be considered. The federal New Democratic Party supported a proposal similar to that of the task force. However, the election in 1984 of a government with substantial support from every province caused interest in the idea to subside, at least temporarily.

The principal target of intrastate federalists has always been the Senate. This is so, in part, because the institution itself is unpopular, but also because it was ostensibly designed to represent regional diversities, and because the second chambers of other federal countries, particularly the United States, appear to do so more effectively. Proponents of Senate reform, who seem to be heavily concentrated in western Canada, have a more specific motive; they believe that a revitalized Senate would counteract what they consider to be the excessive influence of Ontario and Quebec in the House of Commons.

There are almost infinite possible variations of a hypothetical reformed Senate, and the subject cannot be pursued in detail here. Generally speaking, proposals can be placed in one of two categories: a Senate that would be wholly or partially appointed by the provincial governments or legislatures, and one that would be elected by the people of each province. Germany, India, and the United States before 1913 provide possible prototypes of the first version, while Australia and the present-day United States are the prototypes of the second. Switzerland combines elements of both.

When intrastate federalism first became fashionable in the 1970s, the first version appeared to have more support, presumably because it was less of a break with Canadian tradition and with the elitist strands in our political culture. (It might be noted in passing that the interprovincial conference of 1887 called for provincial appointment of half the senators, so the idea is far from new.) In 1978 the Trudeau government introduced Bill C-60, which would have provided for half the senators to be elected by the House of Commons and half by the provincial legislatures. A second chamber modelled after the German Bundestag, with all its members appointed as delegates from the provincial governments, was proposed by the government of British Columbia, the Task Force on Canadian Unity, and the Quebec Liberal

Party's "beige paper." The government of Alberta belatedly climbed on the bandwagon in 1982, but changed its mind three years later. All these proponents of the German model were probably more interested in weakening rather than strengthening federal institutions, a fact which undermined their credibility. Critics pointed out that the Bundestag only works in Germany because the main role of the states is to implement and administer federal legislation. In Canada the combination of federal legislation with provincial administration exists only in the field of criminal law.

In 1984 a joint parliamentary committee on Senate reform, after considering the various alternatives, recommended a Senate that would be directly elected by the people.[24] Subsequently a committee of the Alberta legislature reached the same conclusion and the government of Alberta, possibly because polls showed that most Albertans favoured an elected Senate, soon abandoned its flirtation with the German model. Instead it began to promote what it called a "triple E" Senate, meaning elected, equal, and effective. By "equal" it meant that each province should have the same number of senators regardless of population, a view that is an article of faith in most of western Canada. As anyone who has lived there can attest, almost any real or imagined misfortune suffered by the West is attributed to the fact that Ontario and Quebec together have a majority of the seats in the House of Commons.

In the Meech Lake accord of 30 April 1987, Prime Minister Mulroney and the ten provincial premiers agreed to pursue the subject of senate reform as the first priority of constitutional conferences to be held at least once a year beginning in 1988.[25] The Prime Minister agreed that until reform was achieved, he would select senators only from lists of candidates provided by the provincial governments. At the same time the modified amending formula proposed at Meech Lake would require the approval of every province before reform could take place. It is at least possible that the experience of sharing in the patronage that results from an appointed Senate will dampen any enthusiasm that the provincial governments, including Alberta, might have for the prospect of an elected one.

In any event, the "triple E" proposal deserves very critical examination. Australian experience, including a constitutional crisis in 1975 that led the governor general to dismiss the elected government, suggests that an elected second chamber works badly in a system of responsible government, unless the same party has a majority in both houses. Australian experience also suggests that a "triple E" Senate would not seriously reduce the discontent of Canada's peripheries. Tasmania, Queensland, and Western Australia complain about the domination of New South Wales and Victoria just as much as western and Atlantic Canada complain about the domination of Ontario and Quebec.[26] Equal representation for Ontario and Prince Edward Island, despite the hallowed example of the United States, would be difficult to justify in a liberal democracy. The authors of the U.S. constitution were not liberal democrats in the modern sense (Thomas Jefferson was, but he did not attend the convention), and the disproportion in size between the larger and smaller states at that time was far less than the disproportion between the larger and smaller provinces in present-day Canada. An additional reason for rejecting the "triple E" proposal is that it would reduce francophones to a minority of about 10 percent in an important federal institution.

When Australia was drafting its federal constitution, the view was expressed that responsible parliamentary government on the British model was inappropriate in a federal country. The question raised by that comment is a real one and should be considered rationally, not through appeals to imperial history, ethnic solidarity, or anti-Americanism. Nonetheless, the worst possible solution would be to Americanize our institutions in Ottawa while retaining the present authoritarian and centralized institutions in the provincial capitals. If there is a problem, it must be dealt with at both levels simultaneously.

NOTES

1. From *The Age of Mackenzie King: The Rise of the Leader* by H.S. Ferns and B. Ostry (London: Heinemann, 1955). Reprinted by permission, 4.

2. Christopher Armstrong, *The Politics of Federalism* (Toronto: University of Toronto Press, 1981).

3. This argument is persuasively presented in Leo Panitch, "The role and nature of the Canadian state," in *The Canadian State: Political Economy and Political Power*, ed. Leo Panitch (Toronto: University of Toronto Press, 1977).

4. A brilliant analysis and interpretation of the latter episode is J.R. Mallory, *Social Credit and the Federal Power in Canada* (Toronto: University of Toronto Press, 1954). See also Eugene Forsey, "Canada and Alberta: the Revival of Dominion Control Over the Provinces," in his *Freedom and Order: Collected Essays* (Toronto: McClelland and Stewart, 1974).

5. Reginald Whitaker, *The Government Party: Organizing and Financing the Liberal Party of Canada, 1930-1958* (Toronto: University of Toronto Press, 1977).

6. Donald V. Smiley, *Canada in Question, Federalism in the Seventies*, 3rd ed. (Toronto: McGraw-Hill Ryerson, 1980) 120–57.

7. An argument that this fact was an essential "safety valve" for regional conflict is presented in Steven Muller, "Federalism and The Party System in Canada," in *American Federalism in Perspective*, ed. Aaron Wildavsky (Boston: Little Brown, 1967).

8. This is explored more fully in David Smith, *The Regional Decline of a National Party* (Toronto: University of Toronto Press, 1981).

9. According to a former colleague, who knows Clark personally, this

phrase was borrowed from Benjamin Disraeli. Possibly some reader can supply a specific reference.

10. *Reference re Newfoundland Continental Shelf* 1 S.C.R. (1984) 86.

11. For details see David Milne, *Tug of War: Ottawa and the Provinces Under Trudeau and Mulroney* (Toronto: Lorimer) 99–107.

12. See for example Jean-Luc Pepin, "Co-operative Federalism," in *Canadian Federalism: Myth or Reality*, 1st ed., ed. J. Peter Meekison (Toronto: Methuen, 1968) 320–29.

13. Gerard Veilleux, *Les Relations intergouvernementales au Canada, 1867–1967* (Montreal: Les Presses de l'universite du Quebec, 1971) 90.

14. Donald V. Smiley, *Constitutional Adaptation and Canadian Federalism Since 1945* (Ottawa: Queen's Printer, 1970) 111–18.

15. Smiley, *Canada in Question*, 91–119.

16. Veilleux, *Les Relations intergouvernementales au Canada*, 73.

17. R.D. Olling, "Canadian Conference Activity 1975: Alberta Participation," in *Canadian Federalism: Myth or Reality*, 3rd ed., ed. J. Peter Meekison (Toronto: Methuen, 1977) 229–38.

18. See for example Jean-Marc Leger, "Le Federalisme co-operatif ou le nouveau visage de la centralisation," in Meekison, *Canadian Federalism*, 1st ed., 317–20, and Claude Morin, *Quebec versus Ottawa: The Struggle for Self Government, 1960–1972* (Toronto: University of Toronto Press, 1976).

19. Further details on intergovernmental relations machinery may be found in Bruce G. Pollard, *Managing the Interface: Intergovernmental Affairs Agencies in Canada* (Kingston: Institute of Intergovernmental Relations, 1986).

20. From *A Future Together: Observations and Recommendations*, page 95. Published with permission of the Minister of Supply and Services Canada.

21. Richard Simeon, *Federal-Provincial Diplomacy* (Toronto: University of Toronto Press, 1972), 229–30.

22. Donald V. Smiley and Ronald L. Watts, *Intrastate Federalism in Canada* (Toronto: University of Toronto Press, 1985).

23. Alan C. Cairns, "The Electoral System and the Party System in Canada, 1921–1965," *Canadian Journal of Political Science* I (1968): 55–80.

24. Canada, Parliament, *Report of the Special Joint Committee of the Senate and the House of Commons on Senate Reform* (Ottawa: Supply and Services, 1984).

25. The text of the accord is in *The Globe and Mail*, 2 May 1987.

26. Donald Smiley, *An Elected Senate for Canada? Clues from the Australian Experience* (Kingston: Institute of Intergovernmental Relations, 1985), discusses this subject in more detail.

10 Federalism and Constitutional Change

*Changing a constitution confronts a society with the most impor-
tant choices, for in the constitution will be found the philosophical principles and rules which largely determine the relations of
the individual and of cultural groups to one another and to the
state. If human rights and harmonious relations between cultures are forms of the beautiful, then the state is a work of art that
is never finished.*

FRANK R. SCOTT[1]

*The law is like sausage; if you love it, you wouldn't want to see
how it is made.*

HORACE A. (BUD) OLSON

In all of the federations that have lasted for any extended period of time
— and Canada is no exception — the way in which federalism operates
has been altered more extensively and more frequently by informal
changes in practice than by formal amendments to the constitution.
Occasionally federal constitutions may have to be amended because
the judicial interpretation of the existing constitution imposes an
obstacle to necessary adaptation, but such occasions are in fact quite
rare. In Canada the only real case of this kind was the unemployment
insurance amendment of 1940. The BNA Act has in practice been
remarkably adaptable (some would say too adaptable) to shifts in the
distribution of political and economic power.

Constitutional amendment, however, plays an important role in the
politics of federal countries, and ironically this is more true in Canada, whose constitution was drafted without specifying a procedure
for its amendment, than almost anywhere else. One suspects that the
reason why constitutional amendment is so important, especially to
politicians, is that it brings with it symbolic benefits that no mere
informal change in practice can provide. Constitutional amendment is
not so much a cause of changes in the distribution of political power as
it is a means of legitimizing and giving explicit recognition to changes
that have already taken place. Yet the substance of change may often be
more easily achieved than the symbol. The provincial government of
Quebec, and the class fractions which it represents, have greatly

enlarged their freedom of action in practice since 1963, but they were unsuccessful in securing symbolic recognition of the fact through constitutional changes, at least until 1987.

Constitutional controversy is none the less important for an understanding of Canadian federalism since it draws attention to the issues that politicians consider important and to the economic and social forces that they represent. Although frequently expressed in arcane language, the controversies can be related to the familiar complex of conflicts and cleavages between different sectors of the economy — between English and French, metropolis and hinterland, large and small provinces, rich and poor provinces — that has shaped the evolution of Canadian federalism. If formal changes have been rare, it is because these forces have usually been too evenly balanced to allow the imposition of any proposed amendment.

EARLY CONSTITUTIONAL AMENDMENTS

It is generally known that the British North America Act of 1867 contained no procedure for its own amendment. This fact appears more anomalous and unsatisfactory today than it presumably did in 1867. The Act, after all, was a statute of the Parliament at Westminster, one out of many, before and since, that have made provisions for the government of various colonies. Presumably if it ceased to be suitable for its intended purpose it could be modified or repealed by the body that enacted it, a fate that had already overtaken such previous enactments as the Constitutional Act of 1791, which created Upper and Lower Canada, or the Union Act of 1840, which united them into a single province.

Admittedly, the convention had become established after the middle of the nineteenth century that the colonies populated mainly by British settlers would have virtually complete control over their internal affairs, and the corollary of this was that their internal constitutions would only be changed by Westminster at the request of the colonial politicians concerned, and would be changed whenever such a request was made. Presumably this meant that if the government of Canada subsequently requested an amendment to the BNA Act, Westminster would make the amendment with as little difficulty or hesitation as it had shown in adopting the original Act in 1867. Since the Fathers of Confederation were generally not very concerned with symbolic matters, they saw no reason to specify the procedure more precisely.

It is hindsight to say that this ignored the complexities of federalism, since the men of 1867 thought they had avoided those complexities by discarding the unwanted features of the American model. As discussed in Chapter 2, John A. Macdonald expressed the view that a province's representatives in the federal Parliament at Ottawa were the only "constitutional exponents of the wishes of the people" with regard to federal-provincial relations, and that the provincial legislatures should not be concerned with such matters.[2] Logically, this could only mean that a request to Westminster for a constitutional amendment would be a unilateral act by the federal government or Parliament. As long as the Macdonald view of federalism prevailed, the question of involving provincial governments or legislatures in the process of amendment could not arise.

F.R. Scott suggested an additional although related reason why the BNA Act was not provided with an amendment formula of the kind normally found in federal constitutions.[3] The reason was the belief held by the Fathers of Confederation that their distinctive and un-American approach to the problem of dividing legislative powers between the two levels of government had ensured that amendments would be largely unnecessary. In the United States, and subsequently in Australia, the national government was given only a few specified legislative powers, with the residue being left to the states. As time went on and the national government required legislative authority over new subjects, the constitution had to be amended accordingly. In Canada, on the other hand, the national government was supposedly given from the outset almost complete legislative powers, and any authority over unspecified or unanticipated matters was contained in the general power to make laws for the peace, order, and good government of Canada. Thus there was little reason to suppose that many amendments would be necessary.

For these reasons the question of adding an American-style amending procedure to the BNA Act only arose in the twentieth century, after Lord Watson and other members of the Judicial Committee of the Privy Council had placed their official stamp of approval on an American-style theory of federalism. In the nineteenth century several amendments were made, but the only procedural question that was raised concerning them was whether the federal cabinet could make the request without reference to the federal Parliament. Thus the Liberals protested because Parliament was not involved in the request for the amendment of 1871, an amendment that ratified the rather hasty creation of Manitoba in the previous year and also authorized Parliament to create additional provinces out of federal territories. However, a Liberal government four years later secured without reference to Parliament an amendment to Section 18 of the BNA Act (dealing, ironically, with parliamentary privilege) and this time it was the Conservatives who protested. In 1886 a formal address by both houses of Parliament was used to secure the amendment allowing for the parliamentary representation of territories not included in any province.

The practice of consulting the provincial governments before making such an address was not invented until as late as 1906, when it was used prior to the amendment that revised the provisions for financial subsidies to the provinces. Alexander Brady was almost certainly right in attributing the practice to political expediency rather than constitutional principle.[4] Even then, Wilfrid Laurier's government did not consider it necessary to secure the unanimous consent of the provincial governments. The request was made despite the vigorous objections of the government of British Columbia, which made its own representations to Westminster and was only partly placated by the latter's decision to delete from the amendment a statement to the effect that the new terms would not be subject to further revision.

Subsequent practice was not entirely consistent, confirming the validity of Brady's observation about political expediency. The provincial governments were not consulted about the amendment of 1915, which revised the formula for representation of regions in the Senate and also enacted the rule that no province should have fewer members in the lower than in the upper house of Parliament. They were also not consulted the following year about the amendment which allowed Parliament to extend its own term beyond the five years permitted by the BNA Act. The BNA Act of 1930, transferring natural resources to the western provinces, was preceded by consultation only with the provincial governments directly concerned, although the others had agreed in principle when the idea was mentioned at the federal-provincial conference of 1927. The amendment of 1940, which added unemployment insurance to the list of subjects on which Parliament could legislate, was the first that was clearly accepted in advance by all provincial governments. Whether the federal government of the day considered this to be a necessary requirement is not entirely clear. Mackenzie King's statement on the subject was so characteristically ambiguous that it can be used to support either an affirmative or a negative response to this question. Indeed in 1981, when the Supreme Court of Canada divided on the question of whether a convention requiring provincial consent existed, both the majority and minority opinions quoted the same portion of King's speech to support their respective conclusions.[5]

THE SEARCH FOR AN AMENDING FORMULA: 1927–65

It was not the practical necessity of amending the BNA Act so much as the progress toward Canadian independence after the First World War that began the long search for an explicit amending formula. Canada had joined the League of Nations and was beginning to conduct its own relations with the United States and other foreign countries. In 1926 a conference of Commonwealth Prime Ministers agreed that Great Britain and the dominions were "equal in status, in no way subordinate one to another in any aspect of their domestic or external

affairs, though united by a common allegiance to the Crown."⁶ The fact
that the United Kingdom Parliament retained the power to amend the
BNA Act was a conspicuous and anomalous exception to this general
principle. Not surprisingly, the first discussion of "repatriation" at a
federal-provincial conference took place one year later.

Westminster could not divest itself of the power to amend the BNA
Act without stating where that power would henceforth reside, but by
1926 this had become a rather delicate point that was far more conveniently left to the imagination. Unfortunately, it had become both
politically inexpedient and unrealistic by that time to state what Sir
John A. Macdonald would have considered obvious under the circumstances, now that the power resided in the federal Parliament. Provincial governments, particularly those of Quebec and Ontario, revived
the "compact theory" of Mowat and Mercier and used it to argue that
the unanimous consent of all nine provincial governments should be
both a condition of "repatriation" and a requirement written into the
subsequent amending procedure itself. Mackenzie King's Liberal government, which began the discussion of "repatriation" in 1927,
depended for its electoral success on the Liberal provincial government of Quebec. The federal Conservative government of R.B. Bennett, which continued the discussions after 1930, was in a similar
position vis-à-vis the Conservative provincial government in Ontario.
Thus neither Prime Minister dared to challenge the compact theory as
Macdonald would have done. Underlying these political facts, of
course, were the economic developments discussed in Chapter 4 of the
present volume.

The result was a series of federal-provincial conferences which,
like the woes inflicted on sinners by the God of the Old Testament,
have lasted unto the third and fourth generation. It soon became
apparent that the procedures used in other federations, which typically require that a majority (but not all) of the provinces or states give
their approval either through their legislatures, special conventions,
or referenda, were not easily adaptable to Canadian circumstances. In
the first place, the two central provinces, with more than three-fifths of
the population and an even more overwhelming concentration of economic and political power, would settle for nothing less than a power
of veto. This meant that any formula would either have to extend the
same power to all the provinces, producing an unprecedented degree
of constitutional rigidity, or else explicitly concede that the provinces
were unequal in status. In the second place, the BNA Act itself contained a remarkable variety of provisions, some not really of constitutional significance, others pertaining to only one or a few provinces, so
that no single procedure seemed appropriate for all types of amendment.

In response to these problems the idea emerged in 1927 of classifying the sections of the BNA Act into categories that would be subject to different procedures of amendment. It was hoped that Ontario and Quebec would thus be persuaded to confine their insistence on unanimity to a few selected sections, which were so unlikely to need modification that a requirement of total unanimity would be acceptable. Thus the need to make invidious distinctions between the provinces would not arise. Other sections would be amendable by procedures similar to those used in other federations, or even by the federal Parliament alone in the case of sections that did not really pertain to provincial interests. The classification of specific sections into categories proved to be controversial, and consensus among the provincial and federal governments could not be achieved either in 1927 or in 1936. In 1931 the British Parliament declared Canada and the other dominions of the Commonwealth to be formally independent, but at Canada's request this enactment, known as the Statute of Westminster, included a clause stating that the British Parliament would retain the power to amend Canada's constitution.[7]

In 1949 Louis St. Laurent's government, without the assent of the provinces, secured from Westminster an amendment to the BNA Act which gave the Parliament of Canada the power henceforth to amend the Act, except in relation to the exclusive powers, rights, and privileges of the provinces, the educational guarantees for religious minorities, the use of the English and French languages, the requirement for an annual session of Parliament, and the maximum interval between federal general elections. This list of exceptions included all the matters of fundamental importance, and events were to show that the 1949 amendment had little significance. It was repealed in 1982.

St. Laurent's initiative was presumably intended to stake out a bargaining position and thus to precipitate an early decision on a formula to amend the excluded sections. Its chief effect, however, was to antagonize the provincial governments. A series of discussions in 1950 made little progress, with Ontario and Quebec insisting that the whole division of legislative powers be "entrenched." Saskatchewan expressed vigorous opposition to this idea since the CCF government led by Tommy Douglas insisted that the national Parliament should have the power to resolve economic and social problems of national scope.

Almost another decade elapsed before constitutional discussion was resumed by the Progressive Conservative government of John Diefenbaker. In the Fulton formula of 1961, named after the federal Minister of Justice, Ontario and Quebec achieved their objective of entrenching the whole division of legislative powers, as well as the educational and linguistic guarantees. The requirement of unanimous consent for amendment was also extended to the "Senate rule" which guaranteed each province a fixed minimum representation in the House of Commons, but it was not extended to the provisions for an annual session and a dissolution every five years. Most of the other important sections would be amendable with the consent of seven provinces comprising at least half of the population. There was also a provision for the delegation of powers between one level of government and the other. The Fulton–Favreau formula of 1964 was almost identical, but differed from both the 1949 amendment and the 1961 formula in that Parliament would no longer be able unilaterally to abolish the monarchy or to alter the scheme for allocating seats in either house among the provinces.

In 1961 Saskatchewan rejected the Fulton formula, as it had opposed Quebec and Ontario demands for a veto in 1950, on the grounds that the formula would make it too difficult for Parliament to acquire the necessary powers to deal with national problems. By 1964 Saskatchewan's CCF government had been defeated, and unanimity seemed to have been achieved at the federal–provincial conference in October of that year. When Premier Jean Lesage returned to Quebec, however, he encountered a well-orchestrated nationalist campaign against the formula, which was described as a strait-jacket that would hinder Quebec's evolution toward quasi-independence. In 1965 he had to withdraw his support for the formula, a humiliation from which the prestige of his government never recovered.

Quebec's rejection of the Fulton–Favreau formula was an indication that the parameters of the constitutional debate had shifted radically since the days of St. Laurent and Duplessis. The province traditionally most committed to a rigid constitution and to the compact theory had rejected a formula apparently designed to its own specifications on the grounds that it was too rigid. With the forces conducive to provincial autonomy on the rise, flexibility and centralization were no longer considered synonymous. In the next phase of constitutional discussion, proposals for substantive change would overshadow the search for an amending formula.

CONSTITUTIONAL POLITICS: 1965–79

Canada is probably unique among federations in that the procedures of constitutional amendment have been the subject of more discussion and controversy than the substantive content. Yet concern for the latter has not been absent, and implicit assumptions about the kinds of amendment that are desirable can usually be discovered lurking behind the procedural discussions. At times of crisis or breakdown they have emerged in demands for wide-ranging constitutional review. Thus in the 1930s changes were desired that would extend the legislative powers of Parliament; those who wished to do so were emboldened by the evident inability of the provincial governments to respond to the consequences of the Depression and the loss of legitimacy and power that they suffered as a result. It was these types of change, some of which would soon be proposed by the Rowell–Sirois Commission, that provided the incentive to seek an amending formula in 1935–36.

The next crisis that intervened to produce a renewal of interest in constitutional reform was Quebec's Quiet Revolution in the 1960s. This series of events, described in Chapter 5 of the present work, produced four distinct although related tendencies conducive to constitutional change. First Quebec's neo-nationalists, apart from the minority who favoured outright independence, proposed a variety of schemes to transfer powers from the federal government to the Quebec government, while retaining at least a semblance of the federal ties between Quebec and the rest of the country. Secondly, many persons in other provinces, well-intentioned or otherwise, argued that conceding some of the demands of the Quebec nationalists would persuade the nationalists to forget their other demands, and thus unite all Canadians around a new and more decentralized federalism. Thirdly, the Quebec anti-nationalists led by Pierre Elliott Trudeau and their allies in other parts of Canada promoted bilingualism, "French power" in Ottawa, and constitutional entrenchment of individual rights as alternatives to the transfer of powers sought by the Quebec nationalists. Finally, and perhaps inevitably, other provincial governments followed Quebec's example by presenting their own lists of constitutional demands.

These four sets of forces, and the shifting pattern of conflicts and alliances that resulted from them, produced almost a quarter of a century of conferences, meetings, committees, agendas, proposals, ultimatums, compromises, manifestoes, and general unpleasantness. Even in Quebec, and certainly elsewhere, the whole subject preoccupied politicians, officials, and political scientists considerably more than it did the general public, and it is at least arguable that constitutional politics diverted attention from subjects that should have been of more immediate concern. On the other hand, conflict between distinct and well-organized ethnic communities sharing a single state is never a trivial matter, however remote it may seem from the everyday concerns of Corner Brook and Moose Jaw. While Canadian constitutional politics had their share of absurdity and folly, the country at least avoided the various fates of Nigeria, Pakistan, and Northern Ireland.

The credit or the blame for precipitating the whole chain of events must go to the Quebec neo-nationalists, but even they were relatively slow off the mark. The Lesage government displayed little interest in constitutional reform at the outset. This was partly because it had more immediate priorities, partly because there were few votes to be won by emphasizing constitutional issues, and partly because Lester Pearson's federal government, which took office in April 1963, postponed a showdown by giving Quebec additional tax revenues and allowing it to opt out of assorted social programs. By 1965, however, the Quiet Revolution was beginning to run out of steam. The worst abuses of Duplessism had been eliminated and a modern public sector had been created at the provincial level. The population was increasingly polarized between those who had had enough reform and those who wanted even more. Nationalist rhetoric was an inexpensive and easy way of uniting both groups, and one that presented no threat to the privileges of the intelligentsia. Economic and social reforms were costly and controversial. Visits with General de Gaulle and proposals to rewrite the constitution were neither, and the alarm which they caused in Ottawa could be viewed as an additional benefit rather than a disadvantage. Duplessis would have understood.

Nationalist demands thus followed a predictable trajectory. As early as 1964 the Societé St. Jean Baptiste de Montréal demanded the revision of the constitution to reflect the existence of "two nations." A year later Daniel Johnson repeated the same demand in a book that posed the choice of "equality or independence."[8] As Premier from June 1966 until September 1968, Johnson coupled this ultimatum with a more specific, although equally utopian, suggestion that the federal government withdraw from the field of direct taxation. In 1967 a gathering of middle-class notables, picturesquely styling themselves the Estates General of French Canada, proclaimed that Quebec had the right of "self-determination." In the same year René Lévesque resigned from the Liberal Party to form his sovereignty-association movement, which in 1968 became the Parti Québécois. By 1973 the Parti Québécois was the official opposition in Quebec and by 1976 it was the government. The provincial Liberals concluded that their soft-pedalling of the constitutional issue had not been productive. In 1977 they began to prepare their own blueprint for a decentralized federalism, which they finally published in January 1980.[9] In fairness it must be said that this document, the so-called "beige paper," was relatively moderate by the standards of the time.

These events might have attracted little attention in other provinces, but episodes of FLQ terrorism, General de Gaulle's visit in the summer of 1967, and the disruption of the St. Jean Baptiste Day parade by bottle-throwing separatists a year later were more difficult to ignore. In Canada, as elsewhere, the intelligentsia love to discover problems that they can promise to resolve. Canada seemed strangely deficient in the 1960s since it had neither a black civil rights movement nor a war in Vietnam. The "Quebec problem" made up for these deficiencies and reassured us that we were almost as interesting as our American neighbours. The question "What does Quebec want?" soon became an anglo-Canadian cliché. If Quebec itself could not make up its mind, there was no shortage of suggestions as to what it *should* want. Everyone from the *Canadian Forum* to the Canadian Bar Association had an idea for a new constitution. The president of the Canadian Pulp and

Paper Association co-authored a dismal book on the subject, which included the text of the proposed constitution as an appendix.[10] The Royal Commission on Bilingualism and Biculturalism, following the death of its co-chairman André Laurendeau, abandoned its plans to produce constitutional proposals, but the task was obligingly undertaken by a Parliamentary Joint Committee (1970–72) and subsequently by a Task Force on National Unity (1977–79).[11] A few months after the Parti Québécois took office, a group of distinguished anglophone writers and academics signed a manifesto calling for complete capitulation to the Quebec government's demands, even though the Quebec government had not as yet made any demands.[12]

The common denominator of all these proposals and suggestions was that they recommended giving the government of Quebec more powers, but the details were as varied as the motives of the originators. For Progressive Conservatives, in opposition for all but one of the years between 1963 and 1984, provincial autonomy was a convenient stick with which to beat the governing Liberals, and an outlet for understandable frustrations. It might also benefit Progressive Conservative provincial governments, of which there were several, and reduce the ability of federal Liberal governments to interfere with the sacred free market. For some New Democrats who supported constitutional reform, the motivation was precisely the opposite. They believed that giving "special status," or perhaps even independence, to Quebec would allow the federal government to exercise more powers over the rest of the country. Some anglophones secretly hoped that Quebec would go its own way so that they could eliminate bilingualism and other unwelcome evidence of the French connection. Others regarded Quebec as an oppressed "nation" and viewed it with a curious mixture of guilt, envy, romantic sympathy, and prurient fascination. While the former attitude was more conspicuous on the right and the latter on the left, they co-existed among the rank and file of both opposition parties.

The process of Canadian constitutional politics is managed and the outcomes determined by governments, not by academics, interest groups, or opposition parties. The federal government's response to these shifting currents and crosscurrents of opinion was largely the work of Pierre Elliott Trudeau, Minister of Justice from April 1967 until July 1968, and Prime Minister from April 1968 until June 1984, apart from a nine-month interlude in 1979–80. Most of Trudeau's ideas on Quebec, the constitution, and related subjects may be found in his essays, originally written between 1954 and 1967 and republished in the latter year under the title of *Federalism and the French Canadians*.[13] Trudeau had a somewhat romantic belief, which he derived from the English political philosopher Lord Acton, that federal governments and multicultural societies provided the best environments for individual freedom. He despised Quebec nationalism because it repudiated these principles and because he believed that it served the self-interest of the elites who promoted it, rather than the well-being of the entire population. He believed that Quebec nationalism could be rendered harmless not by making concessions to it, but by absorbing it into a larger and less exclusive Canadian nationalism, an idea that Henri Bourassa had preached without much success in the early part of the twentieth century. Like Bourassa, Trudeau believed that this would require a redefinition of the Canadian identity to make it less exclusively "British," increased participation of francophones in federal institutions, equal status for the two official languages from coast to coast, and a federalism that respected the exclusive jurisdictions of both levels of government.

These ideas, of which the preceding paragraph is a rather inadequate summary, involved a redefinition of the parameters of constitutional discussion rather than a Pearsonian (and characteristically Anglo-Saxon) search for the elusive compromise between "centralist" and "provincialist" positions. Instead of providing more powers for provincial governments, a revised constitution should entrench the rights of individuals, should guarantee the equal status of the English and French languages, and should reform federal institutions such as the Senate and the Supreme Court to more adequately reflect the diversity of the country.

Fairly detailed proposals along these lines were presented to a constitutional (i.e. intergovernmental) conference which the federal government convened in February 1968, shortly before Trudeau became Prime Minister.[14] The early sessions of the conference highlighted the diametrically opposed constitutional visions of Premier Daniel Johnson and Minister of Justice Pierre Trudeau. Robarts of Ontario, who disliked the federal government's fiscal and social policies, gave some support to Johnson. Most of the Premiers from the eastern and western hinterlands displayed a mixture of bewilderment and indifference that probably represented the views of their electorates accurately.

The constitutional conference continued intermittently until 1971, at which time agreement seemed near on a document known as the Victoria Charter, so-called because what proved to be the last meeting of the conference was held in Victoria, British Columbia. The Victoria Charter included elaborate provisions for the constitutional entrenchment and reform of the Supreme Court, entrenchment of linguistic rights, some concessions to Quebec's demand for more power over "social policy," a constitutional guarantee that equalization payments to the poorer provinces would continue, and a formula that would require approval of Quebec, Ontario, two western provinces, and two Atlantic provinces for subsequent constitutional amendments.[15] At the last moment Quebec Premier Robert Bourassa, presumably remembering Lesage's experience with the Fulton-Favreau formula, refused his consent.

The 1972 election reduced the federal Liberals to a minority in the House of Commons, although they remained in office. After their majority was restored in 1974 constitutional discussions were resumed, first only with Quebec and then with all the provinces. As early as 1975 Trudeau hinted that constitutional changes, including a new amending formula, might be adopted without securing provincial consent. In 1978 his government introduced a constitutional amendment bill, Bill C-60, which proposed certain changes to federal institutions, including provincial involvement in the selection of senators and justices of the Supreme Court. When witnesses before a parliamentary committee argued that Senate reform would require an act of the British rather than the Canadian Parliament, the government referred the question to the Supreme Court. In 1979 the Court ruled that the witnesses were correct, despite the BNA Act of 1949 that had supposedly given the Canadian Parliament the power to amend most parts of the constitution of Canada.[16]

The fourth, and ultimately the decisive, factor in the constitutional equation was the discovery by the other nine provincial governments that they could use the "Quebec problem" to gain additional powers for themselves. At the time of the negotiations leading up to the Victoria Charter, the governments of the predominantly anglophone provinces, with the possible exception of Ontario, did not seem much interested in this possibility. Gaining additional revenue, whether in the form of tax room or equalization payments, was clearly a much higher priority for them than increasing their legislative powers. The situation was different in the second phase of the constitutional negotiations from 1975 onward. The federal government was facing its own fiscal crisis and was no longer inclined to surrender tax room to the provinces, while the three westernmost provinces enjoyed dramatic increases of revenue because of the energy crisis. Rather than having too little revenue to carry out their legislative responsibilities, some provincial governments now seemed to have too few legislative powers in relation to their revenues and their economic importance. This impression was reinforced by a number of Supreme Court decisions striking down provincial statutes on the grounds that they trespassed on fields of federal jurisdiction, particularly indirect taxation, criminal law, or the regulation of trade and commerce. Quebec, Manitoba, and Saskatchewan were the provinces most directly affected by these judicial decisions but the other provincial governments felt threatened to varying degrees. The idea that constitutional amendments were needed to enlarge provincial legislative powers, and thus to protect provincial legislation against the unwelcome attentions of the courts, became increasingly popular.

While these developments gave certain provinces the motives to pursue their own constitutional demands, circumstances also gave them the opportunity. The energy crisis temporarily increased the bargaining power of petroleum-producing provinces, particularly of Alberta which was attracting an increasing share of the country's wealth and population during those years. Alberta's loans to the poorer provincial governments from its Heritage Savings Trust Fund facilitated the building of interprovincial coalitions, which were also reinforced by partisan hostility to the federal Liberals, and by the hopes of Newfoundland and Nova Scotia that they would soon become producers of petroleum themselves.

Even more important were the dynamics of the Quebec situation. Prime Minister Trudeau was determined to pursue his own constitutional agenda, which he believed would undermine the popularity of Quebec nationalism and thus achieve the objective which had led him to enter federal politics in 1965. The rising popularity of the Parti Québécois, the electoral victory of that party in 1976, and the subsequent announcement that a referendum would be held on sovereignty-association all added urgency to this determination. Since some or perhaps all of the constitutional changes which he contemplated were widely assumed to require provincial consent, this urgency increased the bargaining power of the anglophone provincial governments. The support of the anglophone premiers, and particularly their public statements to the effect that they would oppose negotiating economic association with a sovereign Quebec, would also be an important asset to the federalist forces in the referendum campaign. In effect the anglophone premiers could make their support for Trudeau's constitutional goals and for the federalist forces in Quebec conditional on the satisfaction of their own constitutional demands. This was popular with their electorates, given the widespread perception in anglophone Canada that Quebec had received an undue share of the federal government's attention, and the even more widespread belief that no province should be "more equal than the others."

Evidence of this fundamental change in the constitutional equation soon became apparent. By 1975 both British Columbia and Alberta were insisting that any constitutional amending formula must give them a veto, in contrast to the Victoria Charter formula. (Conservative Alberta particularly feared the Victoria Charter formula because of the possibility that the other three western provinces might all be governed by the "centralist" NDP.) In August 1976 the annual meeting of the ten premiers, which took place that year in Edmonton, presented a long list of constitutional demands, including increased powers over culture, communications, immigration, and natural resources as well as a provincial veto over the exercise of Parliament's power to declare that works and undertakings were for the general advantage of Canada and thus subject to federal regulation.

The constitutional conference, defunct since 1971, was revived in the autumn of 1978, and negotiations continued through the winter. The lengthy agenda included resources and interprovincial trade, indirect taxation, communications, family law, fisheries and offshore resources, the Senate, the Supreme Court, the Monarchy, equalization, a charter of rights, the spending power, the declaratory power, and the amending formula. Prime Minister Trudeau was now willing to make substantial concessions on legislative powers. Nonetheless, progress toward agreement was slow. Federal concessions were rejected as insufficient by the most extreme provinces — Quebec and Alberta — while the more cautious provinces criticized them for going too far. An elaborate document known as the "best efforts" proposal was put together in the course of the discussions, but the "concensus" which it allegedly represented was a polite fiction since Quebec and Alberta regarded most of its provisions as inadequate. By March 1979, when the federal Liberals focussed their attention on the more immediate task of attempting to survive the impending general election, genuine consensus had been achieved on only two of the thirteen items on the agenda. One of these was the retention of the monarchy, while the other was family law, which the federal government proposed, for no obvious reason, to transfer to provincial jurisdiction.

Entrenchment of individual rights was, as usual, a source of profound disagreement. Most provinces initially opposed any kind of a charter. By February 1979 all except Manitoba were prepared to accept the entrenchment of fundamental freedoms, democratic rights, and language rights, but only within areas of federal jurisdiction. Since democratic rights at the federal level were already entrenched in Sections 20 and 50 of the BNA Act, and since violations of language rights and fundamental freedoms in Canada have almost always taken place at the provincial level, this was not a particularly magnificent concession. Alberta, British Columbia, Manitoba, and Nova Scotia refused to concede educational rights to their francophone minorities; paradoxically their intransigence was supported by Quebec, which feared any threat to the educational provisions of Bill 101. Entrenchment of legal rights, equality rights, and mobility rights proved even less popular with the provincial governments.

The amending formula was an equally, if not more, controversial item on the agenda. Each government seemed to have a different preference, with Manitoba proposing to resurrect the Fulton–Favreau formula of 1964. The federal government in August 1978, and the Task Force on Canadian Unity a few months later, suggested that constitutional amendments might be adopted by referendum, as they are in Switzerland and Australia, but this democratic idea was objectionable to all of the provincial governments. Alberta, which wanted a veto for itself but did not want "centralist" Ontario to have one, resolved its dilemma by suggesting that amendments could be made with the approval of seven provinces having 50 percent of Canada's population, but that individual provinces could opt out of amendments reducing their powers. This bizarre idea attracted little interest or support out-side of Alberta in 1978. No one could have foreseen that it would be accepted by nine provinces and by the federal government in 1981.

THE PATRIATION INITIATIVE: 1980–82

Constitutional discussion was suspended during the brief interlude of Joe Clark's government, but it resumed in 1980, after the Quebec refer-endum, with a slightly different agenda. Three federal concessions which Quebec had contemptuously spurned in the course of the ear-lier discussions (restrictions on the declaratory and spending powers and provincial access to indirect taxation) had now been withdrawn. The monarchy appeared to be no longer an issue. The federal govern-ment also wanted to discuss a preambular "statement of principles" for the revised constitution.

The most significant change in the agenda was the inclusion, for the first time, of an item entitled "powers over the economy." This reflected the increasing concern of the federal and Ontario govern-ments and of industrial capital over the balkanization of the Canadian economy as a result of "province–building" activities in the hin-terlands.[17] Even Ontario, however, was ambivalent about some of the federal proposals, which included the addition of competition policy and product standards to the list of federal powers as well as a proviso that "trade and commerce" referred to the interprovincial movement of services and capital as well as commodities. Also proposed was an elaborate extension of Section 121, which forbids interprovincial tariff barriers, so that it would also preclude discriminatory purchasing policies and barriers to the movement of services and capital. Provin-cial support for such changes was predictably minimal although Sas-katchewan, in a rare triumph of social democratic philosophy over provincial expediency, supported the proposals concerning competi-tion policy and product standards.

These proposals added new elements of disagreement to the more traditional and equally intractable problems of natural resources, fisheries, communications, human rights, and amending formula, and the upper house. The supposition that eleven governments repre-senting different political parties and economic interests, as well as the institutional interests of powerful bureaucracies, could ever reach unanimous agreement on such a list of topics should have strained the credulity of even the long-suffering Canadian public. Positions were in fact more polarized than ever, with the Quebec and Alberta govern-ments committed to emasculating the federal state while the federal government, cautiously supported by Ontario, appeared for the first time in twenty years to be interested in extending its powers, or at least in making the provinces pay dearly for any concessions.

Finally, on 19 September 1980 Prime Minister Trudeau terminated the conference by announcing that agreement was impossible and that his government would proceed to patriate the constitution and entrench a charter of rights without waiting for provincial agreement. An end to the constitutional logjam was in sight, or so it seemed.

The decision to patriate the constitution and entrench a charter of rights without provincial agreement was an unprecedentedly bold step for a Canadian government. Since the days of Mackenzie King it had apparently been assumed that agreement of all provinces on an amending formula was a prerequisite for patriation. In 1965 and again in 1971 patriation had been postponed indefinitely because of Quebec's refusal to endorse an amending formula, although it is not certain that the refusal of one of the smaller provinces would have been equally decisive. Although Prime Minister Trudeau had raised the possibility of unilateral patriation as early as 1975, the threat does not seem to have been taken seriously by anyone at the time.

Several circumstances probably contributed to the government's uncharacteristically forceful behaviour in 1980. The decisive electoral defeat of Joe Clark with his "community of communities" approach to federalism, and the rejection of sovereignty-association in the Quebec referendum, may have suggested that public opinion was moving toward a centralist position. There was evidence that some sectors of the central Canadian business community were becoming concerned about excessive provincialism. The Ontario government's support for patriation, and its generally moderate approach to federal–provincial relations since 1971, seemed to confirm this tendency, given that government's traditional sensitivity to the preferences of big business. It was also easier to proceed over the objections of a Parti Québécois government, whose opposition could be discounted on the grounds that it was committed to the destruction of the federal state, than to do so if the Quebec provincial Liberals were in office. The defeat of the Parti Québécois in a succession of by-elections seemed to suggest that Lévesque would not hold office much longer, so that the opportunity must be seized while it was available.

The Trudeau government's plan, obviously prepared long before the breakdown of negotiations with the provinces, was to request the Queen (in effect, the British government) to secure the passage through the British Parliament of a bill terminating that Parliament's power to amend the Canadian constitution. Simultaneously the British Parliament would enact an amending formula for Canada, a charter of rights and freedoms, and a somewhat obscure provision entrenching the principle of equalization. A resolution to this effect, and the text of the changes that the British Parliament would be asked to enact, were promptly introduced in the Canadian House of Commons. The plan, of course, depended on British co-operation, but past experience led Trudeau to assume, erroneously, that this could be taken for granted. Effective provincial lobbying at Westminster, and the ideological and cultural rapport between the British Tory government and the Canadian Tory opposition, ensured that this would not be the case. One of the ironies of the whole affair is that British members of Parliament displayed considerably more interest in Canada's constitution in 1981 than their predecessors had done in 1867.

The proposed charter of rights and freedoms was a considerable advance over the minimal one that had been discussed at Victoria in 1971. Like the earlier document, it established the right to use either English or French in the federal courts or in dealing with the federal administration, included provisions for fundamental freedoms,and also extended to the provincial level the requirement for annual legislative sessions and elections at least every five years. Unlike the Victoria Charter, the 1980 version would also establish legal rights related to the administration of justice, the right to move freely and to take up a livelihood in any province, the right not to be discriminated against on grounds of race, ethnicity, religion, age, or sex, and the right of Canadians in any province to have their children educated in either English or French, depending on the mother tongue of the parents. However, it did mark a retreat from the Victoria Charter insofar as it did not provide for official bilingualism at the provincial level in Ontario and the Atlantic provinces, as the earlier document had done.

The proposed amending formula was the same as in the Victoria Charter, except that amendments could not be blocked by the Senate and would require the support of Atlantic provinces containing at least 50 percent of the Atlantic region's population. In addition, approval by the requisite majority of provinces voting in a referendum could be substituted for approval by the provincial legislatures. For the first two years after patriation, however, amendments would require the approval of all the legislatures, and if the governments of seven provinces comprising 85 percent of the population agreed on an alternative formula during that period, the people of Canada would be asked to choose in a referendum between the federal formula and the provincial formula. In this referendum a majority in the whole country would decide, regardless of how the vote was distributed between provinces.

This package of constitutional changes was supported from the outset by the government of Ontario and, after some hesitation, by that of New Brunswick. NDP leader Ed Broadbent courageously supported the proposals despite the refusal of Saskatchewan's NDP government to do so. Several members of the NDP caucus from Saskatchewan publicly broke ranks with their leader. Broadbent's predecessor, David Lewis, who died soon afterward, privately urged the Liberal government to stand firm in defence of its proposals.[18] Most Canadians, according to public opinion polls, wanted a charter of rights and freedoms. At least initially, most were indifferent to the argument that Trudeau had violated a "convention" by proceeding without the consent of all the provincial governments.

The opposition to the government's proposals, orchestrated by the federal Progressive Conservatives, the other eight provincial governments, and most of the major newspapers, quickly achieved levels of invective, slander, hysteria, and outright absurdity that had not been attained in Canadian politics since the First World War. In 1917 conscriptionist candidates had argued that a vote for Laurier was a vote for Kaiser Wilhelm. In 1980–81 their ideological successors argued, on equally reliable evidence, that a vote for Trudeau's proposals was a vote for confiscation of private property, domination of the smaller provinces by Ontario, and a unitary state. Since the charter of rights and freedoms was generally popular, and since the proposed amending formula differed little from the one that the provinces had accepted in 1971, the repertoire of rational arguments that could be used against the proposals was somewhat limited. Undaunted by this fact, the opponents resorted to the more congenial task of stirring up hatred against the Prime Minister with the aid of any argument that came to hand. On the pathological fringe of the political spectrum, particularly conspicuous in the western provinces, the amending formula and the charter were portrayed as elements of a diabolical plan that included "French" metric measurements, the state-owned oil company Petro-Canada, foreign policies that occasionally differed from those of the United States, removing the crown from RCMP patrol cars, and "forcing French down our throats."[19] Quebec nationalists alleged, even more absurdly, that the charter of rights and freedoms would open the doors to assimilation and unitary government, as proposed by Lord Durham in 1839.

Despite the posturing of the Official Opposition and *The Globe and Mail* (which had recently launched a "national edition" aimed at business and professional persons in the West), the hard core of resistance to the proposals consisted of the eight premiers whom journalists promptly dubbed "the gang of eight." Edward McWhinney described them more precisely as "an unholy alliance of mutually incompatible personalities, with quite disparate political, social, and economic interests and linked only by a common dislike of Prime Minister Trudeau."[20] The real source of their dismay was the fact that Trudeau had unexpectedly blown the whistle on their game of demanding increased legislative powers as the price for their support of patriation and a charter of rights and freedoms, a game that had seemed close to succeeding as recently as 1979. The anglophone premiers, although not Lévesque, were further scandalized by the proposal to let the voters choose an amending formula through a referendum. Some of them, notably Sterling Lyon of Manitoba, also regarded a charter of rights and freedoms as a dangerous departure from the British tradition of parliamentary supremacy.

Between October 1980 and January 1981, the government's proposals were considered by a special joint committee of the Senate and the House of Commons, which heard testimony and received written submissions from a variety of individuals and groups. Most of the delegations, apart from those representing provincial governments, were mainly interested in the charter of rights and freedoms. Partly in response to their representations, the government agreed to a number of improvements in the charter. In doing so, it gained broader support for its constitutional proposals but moved even further away from the position taken by the dissident provincial governments.

The improvements that resulted were significant: the charter was provided with an explicit mechanism of enforcement through the courts; a preliminary statement which appeared to limit its scope was considerably weakened; the provisions for legal rights were greatly strengthened; discrimination on grounds of age or mental and physical disability was prohibited; minority language education rights were extended to children whose parents had been educated in English or French, even if their mother tongue had been another language; and existing denominational education rights were reaffirmed. A completely new section was added entrenching aboriginal and native treaty rights, including the aboriginal rights of the Inuit and Métis. Meanwhile New Brunswick agreed to provisions entrenching official bilingualism in its provincial institutions. (The federal government's other ally, Ontario, was urged to do so but refused.)

Other, and in some cases regrettable, changes were made in an effort to gain the support of Saskatchewan, which did not formally join the "gang of eight" until February. These changes included a lengthy section extending and clarifying provincial powers over natural resources; a more explicit reference to equalization payments, restrictions on the use of referenda for constitutional amendment, and a provision that amendments could be initiated at the provincial level. The amending formula was made more flexible and less invidious to Prince Edward Island and Saskatchewan as the smallest provinces in their respective regions by removing the requirements that provinces agreeing to an amendment comprise 50 percent of the population in each region.

Meanwhile the provinces that opposed the constitutional package were lobbying against its passage at Westminster, with some success. The idea of an entrenched charter of rights and freedoms was contrary to British traditions of parliamentary supremacy, and was thus viewed with suspicion. The British also have a romantic fascination with the Canadian West, where anti-charter and anti-Trudeau sentiment was strongest, and the governments of the Prairie provinces had fraternal

ties with the major British political parties. Some British parliamentarians were apparently so ignorant of the issues that they believed
patriation to be a francophone plot against "British" Canadians and
were surprised to discover that Quebec was part of the "gang of
eight."[21] In January 1981 the Foreign Affairs Committee of the British
House of Commons released a report arguing that Westminster had no
obligation to approve the Canadian government's request.

In April 1981 the "gang of eight" announced that they had reached
agreement on a version of the amending formula first proposed by
Alberta almost three years earlier. Because the premiers had met in
Vancouver, and possibly in an effort to promote confusion with the
federal government's "Victoria formula," this came to be known as the
"Vancouver consensus." It provided that most amendments could be
made with the support of seven provinces having at least 50 percent of
the population but that any province could opt out of an amendment
reducing provincial powers. A few types of amendment, including
changes to the amending formula itself, the monarchy, the minimum
representation of each province in the Commons, and the status of the
two official languages, would require unanimity. At the request of
Quebec, the proposal also provided that a province opting out of an
amendment might receive financial compensation in lieu of any federal spending that took place in other provinces as a result of the
amendment.

The "Vancouver consensus" seemed an exercise in futility at the
time it was announced, and for some months afterward. Ironically, the
provincialist cause was rescued by the Supreme Court of Canada, so
often and unfairly accused of centralist bias. In late 1980 the governments of Manitoba, Quebec, and Newfoundland had submitted references to their respective courts of appeal concerning the
constitutionality of the federal government's patriation initiative. The
Manitoba and Quebec courts eventually upheld the federal position,
with minorities dissenting in both cases, while the Newfoundland
court unanimously rejected it. All the decisions were then appealed to
the Supreme Court of Canada, which deliberated for several months
and handed down its decision on 28 September 1981. The court
upheld the legality of unilateral patriation with only two justices (both
appointed by the Diefenbaker government) dissenting. However, a different although overlapping majority, with Chief Justice Bora Laskin
among the dissenters, ruled that there was also a convention requiring
provincial consent to major constitutional changes, and that the government's proposals were therefore "unconstitutional" in the British
sense of the term.[22]

The argument that a convention requiring provincial consent to
major amendments had grown up during the twentieth century was
probably correct, but it involved a non-legal question that the
Supreme Court could very properly have refused to answer. Regret-

ably, this dubious venture into the realms of history and political science overshadowed the Court's clear decision on the question that was within its competence, namely the legality of a unilateral request by the Canadian Parliament for constitutional amendments, and the legality of the amendments themselves when made by the Parliament of the United Kingdom. The "gang of eight" claimed that the discovery of a convention vindicated their position, and the NDP reversed itself by suggesting a further round of federal-provincial negotiations before Parliament proceeeded with the resolution. The impact of the second half of the Supreme Court's decision seemed certain to be even greater at Westminster. Because the United Kingdom has no entrenched written constitution, constitutional conventions are considered to be of fundamental importance in that country, and British parliamentarians would be reluctant to participate in violating a Canadian convention discovered by Canada's highest court. Probably for this reason, Prime Minister Trudeau agreed to meet the provinces again in early November.

On 5 November 1981, three days after the conference met, a totally unexpected outcome was announced. The federal government agreed to an amending formula based on the so-called "Vancouver consensus," with only the provision for fiscal compensation removed. It also agreed to remove from its proposals the guarantee of aboriginal rights; to modify the provision for mobility rights so that provinces with unemployment rates above the national average could still discriminate in favour of their own residents; and to include in the Charter a "notwithstanding" clause allowing Parliament or any provincial legislature to override the fundamental freedoms, legal rights, and equality rights enumerated in the document. In return for these concessions, which eliminated virtually all the innovative or significantly progressive features of the federal government's proposals, every provincial government except Quebec agreed to support the constitutional package.

Several accounts of these last-minute negotiations have been published, and all suggest that Ontario and Saskatchewan played decisive parts in arriving at a compromise. On the federal side the more pragmatic and right-wing Minister of Justice, Jean Chrétien, rather than Prime Minister Trudeau, assumed the major responsibility for negotiating with the provinces. Chrétien seems to have been lukewarm about some of the more innovative features of the federal proposals, particularly the provision for constitutional referenda. The governments of Ontario and New Brunswick shared these misgivings to an even greater degree, and both were too Tory in their outlook to have any real enthusiasm for the charter of rights and freedoms. These attitudes reflected the ambiguity and fragility of the coalition of forces that supported both the patriation initiative and the federal state itself. The Business Council on National Issues, representing interests to

which both Jean Chrétien and Premier Bill Davis of Ontario were
highly sensitive, had given very qualified support to the original Trudeau proposals. Their brief to the Special Joint Committee of Parliament in early 1981 had supported a charter of rights and freedoms but
had demanded entrenchment of property rights, a committment to
economic growth as well as equalization, and a proviso that rights
would apply to corporations as well as individuals. The brief also
opposed patriation without provincial consent and opposed the use of
constitutional referenda.[23] Trudeau himself never quite decided
whether he wanted the support of the people more than the support of
economic and political elites, a fact which explains why he was not
fully trusted by either. In the end the limited and ambiguous character
of Canadian liberalism was revealed by the fact that compromise with
the representatives of western Canadian resource capital was deemed
more important than preserving a sensible amending formula or the
substance of the charter.

Since Quebec's lonely dissent threatened to undermine the legitimacy of the revised constitution, further modifications were made in
an effort to attract Quebec's support before the resolution was presented to Parliament. The provision for financial compensation for
provinces that opted out of amendments was restored, although it
would operate only if the amendment transferred powers over education or culture. In addition Quebec was exempted, until it chose to
declare otherwise, from the provision that would have forced it to offer
English language education to the children of Canadian citizens of
English mother tongue educated outside of Canada. It would, however, be required to offer English language education to the children of
Canadian citizens who had received an English education anywhere
in Canada. This compromise coincided with the policy of the Liberal
opposition in the National Assembly, but did not satisfy the Parti
Québécois.

Organizations representing the native peoples, the most obvious
losers from the agreement among the first ministers, lobbied stre-
nuously for the restoration of the clause affirming their aboriginal and
treaty rights. Feminist groups expressed concern about the notwithstanding clause allowing legislatures to override Section 28 of the
charter, which stated that rights in the charter applied both to men and
women. (For some reason they appeared less concerned about the
possibility of overriding the far more significant Section 15, which
prohibited discrimination on grounds of sex.) The natives and women
were noisily supported by both the opposition parties in the House of
Commons: a singularly hypocritical performance since both had
insisted on the further negotiations with the provinces that led to the
changes being made in the first place. By 23 November 1981, however,
all provinces except Quebec had accepted a modified native rights
clause, which in deference to the wishes of Alberta specified that only

"existing" native rights were protected by the constitution. The provinces also agreed that Section 28 would not be subject to the notwithstanding clause. The way was thus cleared for the passage of the resolution through Parliament, although a few members voted against it for various reasons. In March 1982 the British Parliament adopted the revised constitutional package, now known as the Constitution Act of 1982, and a month later the Queen visited Ottawa to sign the document. Henceforth Westminster would have no jurisdiction over Canada's constitution, and the British North America Acts of 1867 and subsequent years were retroactively renamed the Constitution Acts.

In the immediate aftermath of all the sound and fury, few observers appeared capable of an objective appraisal of what had happened. Quebec nationalists predictably complained that there had been a massive transfer of powers to the federal government, and cited the acquiescence of nine provinces in the final compromise as evidence of anglophone Canada's determination to oppress Quebec. The lingering effect of the anti-patriation campaign by the "gang of eight," and the failure to appreciate the fundamental differences between Trudeau's original proposals and the final compromise, apparently convinced even some anglophone Canadians that the changes of 1982 had left the constitution more centralized than before. Trudeau himself seemed to give credence to this view with his campaign against the Meech Lake accord five years later.

The reality was quite different from the perception. The Constitution Act of 1982 did not give the government or Parliament of Canada any new powers, while it expanded the powers of provinces to legislate regarding their natural resources, including the export of natural resources to other parts of Canada. The amending formula made it easier than before to transfer Parliament's powers to the provinces, since neither Ontario nor the Senate could block an amendment to this effect. On the other hand, the bizarre opting out provision, without parallel in the constitution of any other federation, meant that Parliament could only increase its powers, or regain powers previously transferred to the provinces, with the unanimous consent of every province, unless it were willing to exercise powers in some parts of the country and not in others. Symbolically, this amending formula suggested that the provinces were sovereign states whose powers could not be taken from them without their consent, a notion that is incompatible with the true meaning of federalism.[24] Even the ill-fated Southern Confederacy, during the American Civil War, adopted a constitution allowing two-thirds of the states to impose constitutional amendments on the others.

The Charter of Rights and Freedoms might have been potentially centralizing in one sense, insofar as it would impose common standards on the legislation of the ten provinces and allow a federally-appointed court to interpret the standards. However, its effect was largely negated by the "notwithstanding" clause, which allows provincial legislatures to override most provisions of the Charter. The three Prairie premiers, all vehement opponents of the Charter in its original form, insisted on this provision as the price of their consent. Quebec used the notwithstanding clause repeatedly until the Parti Québécois was defeated in 1985. Saskatchewan used it to restrict the collective bargaining rights of its public employees in 1986.

The sections of the Charter to which the notwithstanding clause did not apply, and which therefore genuinely reduced the power of provincial legislatures, were the provisions for democratic rights, mobility rights, and language rights. The first merely required the provinces to hold elections every five years and annual legislative sessions. The second was qualified, at Newfoundland's insistence, to provide that provinces with high levels of unemployment could still discriminate against non-residents. The provisions regarding language, which in Trudeau's view were the most essential part of the Charter, merely obliged Quebec to provide education in English, and the other provinces to provide it in French, "where numbers warrant." The categories of persons who could take advantage of these provisions were defined in a very restrictive manner, particularly in Quebec (see Appendix 2).

All in all, it was not much in the way of centralization or constitutional progress. Canada proved unable to achieve either a democratic and sensible amending formula (as in Australia), or an ironclad bill of rights (as in the United States), or a constitution that would truly express its collective will as a nation. Even more than the original model of 1867, the "new" Canadian constitution was an untidy collection of miscellaneous provisions reflecting sordid and undignified compromises with a variety of provincial interests, and with no basis of legitimacy other than the bargains of politicians. In the last analysis the compact theory, that malignant legacy of Canadian history, triumphed over democracy, freedom, and national unity. If people get the constitutions they deserve, Canadians have no cause to congratulate themselves on the events of 1981–82.

SECURING QUEBEC'S ASSENT

Although it had no legal significance, the fact that Quebec was the only province whose government did not accept the Constitution Act of 1982 was widely regretted. The movement to reform the constitution had grown out of Quebec's Quiet Revolution in the 1960s, and until 1980 many people in Quebec and elsewhere had assumed that no major constitutional changes would ever be made unless the government of Quebec agreed to them. Even the decision to amend the constitution unilaterally in 1980 did not isolate Quebec, and in fact brought about an alliance between the Quebec government and its counterparts in seven other provinces. The compromise of November 1981, on the other hand, humiliated Quebec because Quebec was the only government excluded from the deal. Justice Minister Jean Chrétien, who understood this, even hoped that Manitoba would refuse its assent at the last moment so that Quebec would not appear isolated.[25]

Defenders of the November compromise argued that a Parti Québécois government could never have been persuaded to accept the Charter of Rights and Freedoms. The Quebec government itself cited mobility rights, minority language educational rights, and the amending formula as the most objectionable features of the compromise. Its objection to the amending formula was not the absence of a Quebec veto but the fact that fiscal compensation to provinces opting out of amendments transferring powers to Parliament would be restricted to cases in which the amendment pertained to education or culture.

Prime Minister Trudeau retired in 1984, and the federal Liberals were defeated at the polls a few months later. The new Prime Minister, Brian Mulroney, was a Quebec anglophone who promised efforts to bring his native province into the constitutional accord "with honour and enthusiasm."[26] The chances of achieving this goal were improved dramatically in December 1985 when the Parti Québécois lost office and Robert Bourassa formed a new Liberal government in Quebec. Although the provincial Liberal Party had opposed the imposition of constitutional changes on Quebec by the federal Liberals, their constitutional views could be more easily incorporated within a new compromise than those of the Parti Québécois. Bourassa and Mulroney also had a personal acquaintance dating back at least to 1975, when Bourassa appointed the future Prime Minister to a Royal Commission on labour problems in Quebec's construction industry.

The views of Bourassa's government on the constitution had already been foreshadowed in a Quebec Liberal Party document entitled *Mastering our Future*, which was released while the party was still in opposition.[27] In May 1986 these views were formally stated in a speech to an academic conference by the new Minister of Intergovernmental Affairs, Gil Remillard. Remillard set out five conditions for Quebec's acceptance of the revised constitution: explicit recognition of Quebec as a distinct society, increased powers for Quebec over immigration, limitation of the federal spending power, changes in the amending formula, and participation in the appointment of judges to the Supreme Court of Canada.[28] The revised amending formula would have to give Quebec a veto over changes to federal institutions, and would also have to extend fiscal compensation to the province if it opted out of any amendment diminishing provincial powers, whether or not the amendment pertained to education or culture. The important implicit message in the speech, and in *Mastering our Future*, was that the Charter of Rights and Freedoms, including the provisions for minority language education rights, could be left intact. This sharply distinguished the Bourassa government's position from that of its predecessor and was politically important because the charter had become almost universally popular by 1986. Any federal government proposing to tamper with it, or to curtail its application to any province, would have run serious political risks.

Nonetheless, there were still the other nine provincial governments to be considered. According to the amending formula in effect since 1982, the consent of all of them would be necessary for any change in the amending formula itself or in the "composition" (whatever that may mean) of the Supreme Court of Canada. The consent of at least six of them, in addition to Quebec, would be needed to restrict the spending power, to transfer powers over immigration, or to recognize Quebec explicitly as a distinct society. If Quebec's five conditions were treated as an indivisible package (which proved in fact to be the case), all provinces would have to accept the five conditions before Quebec could sign the constitution. The conditions regarding the amending formula and the recognition of Quebec as a distinct society were likely to be controversial. In return for accepting them, some provinces might demand acceptance of additional concessions to their specific interests, thus opening a new round of the divisive and seemingly interminable constitutional controversies that Canada had endured between 1968 and 1982.

To its credit, the federal government decided to take the risk. Senator Lowell Murray was appointed to the cabinet as Minister of State for Federal-Provincial Relations and placed in charge of the constitutional agenda. Discreet soundings of the opinion of various provincial governments began almost immediately. Less than a year after the Remillard speech, the Prime Minister and the premiers met at Meech Lake, near Ottawa, and agreed on a statement of principles that embodied all five of Quebec's conditions.[29] However, the wording of the clauses referring to the spending power and to the recognition of Quebec as a distinct society was not fully accepted by all of the premiers and caused some anxiety among anglophone Canadians when the terms of the accord were publicly announced.

At a further meeting in Ottawa about a month later, the first ministers were able to agree on the precise text of a lengthy amendment to the constitution, after Premier Bourassa accepted some slight changes in the original accord.[30] The Constitution Act of 1867 would be amended to state "that Quebec constitutes within Canada a distinct society" and that the constitution should be interpreted accordingly. This is balanced, however, by an explicit reminder that French-speaking Canadians are "present elsewhere in Canada" and that English-speaking Canadians are "present in Quebec," a reminder that is given equal weight with the distinct society clause as a guide to interpretation of the constitution. It is therefore not correct to argue, as some have done, that the distinct society clause endorses the notion of a unilingual Quebec.

The proposed amendment also included Section 16, which states that the recognition of Quebec as a distinct society, and the recognition of English-speaking and French-speaking Canadians, do not affect the sections of the existing constitution that recognize aboriginal rights and multiculturalism. This section was inserted at the insistence of the premiers of Ontario and Manitoba, two of the most culturally diverse provinces. It provides an important reassurance that neither the sociological reality of Quebec nor that of Canada is being defined in an invidious or ethnically exclusive manner. Regrettably, and with a complete absence of logic and common sense, feminist groups in the predominantly anglophone provinces demanded that Section 16 include a reference to women's rights as well. This demand was absurd because it raised an issue completely irrelevant to the delicate balancing of ethnic and cultural interests that Section 16 represents. While an excessive preoccupation with bilingualism or Quebec's distinctiveness might be detrimental to multiculturalism (or vice versa), there is no conceivable way in which it would be detrimental to sexual equality, which involves a completely different dimension of human diversity. Quebec feminists, unlike their anglophone sisters, indicated clearly that they understood this. Unfortunately the issue lingered on as a source of unnecessary discord and confusion, much as the issue of "property rights" had played a similar role in the constitutional discussions of 1980–81.

Quebec's request for more power over immigration, a field that was already one of shared jurisdiction between Parliament and the provincial legislatures, was met by a part of the amendment stating that the government of Canada and the government of any province can, at the request of that province, negotiate agreements on immigration having the force of law. In addition to the constitutional amendment, the constitutional accord included a committment by the governments of Canada and Quebec to negotiate such an agreement, specifically so as to provide that Quebec will receive its fair share of all the immigrants admitted to Canada and that Quebec rather than Canada will be responsible for the "reception and integration" of all foreign nationals desiring to settle in Quebec. It should be noted that federal-provincial collaboration on immigration matters took place in the days of John A. Macdonald and that a Quebec-Canada agreement on the subject was signed in March 1979, when Pierre Trudeau was Prime Minister.

The section of the amendment dealing with the federal spending power states that the Government of Canada shall provide "reasonable compensation" to a province that chooses not to participate in a shared–cost program. This requirement is subject to three important restrictions: it applies only to programs established after the amendment comes into effect; the program must be in an area of exclusive provincial jurisdiction; and the province must establish a program of its own that is "compatible with the national objectives." The second restriction presumably means that the shared–cost program must be in the field of education or one of the subsections of Section 92 of the Constitution Act of 1867. As noted in Chapter 7 of this book, the idea of opting out of shared–cost programs and receiving compensation can be traced back at least to the Pearson era. The Trudeau government proposed entrenching the practice in the constitution in April 1969, almost two decades before the Meech Lake accord.[31] The 1987 accord wisely omits the other half of the 1969 proposal, namely the requirement that the two central provinces and at least four of the others give their assent before any program is established at all.

The Meech Lake amendment included two significant changes in the amending formula. Provinces that opted out of amendments transferring their powers to Parliament would now receive "reasonable compensation," even if the amendment did not pertain to education or culture. Secondly, the types of amendments requiring the unanimous consent of the provinces were extended to include any amendment relating to the Supreme Court (and not merely to its "composition") amendments concerning the powers, composition, and selection of the Senate, amendments to the principle of proportionate representation in the House of Commons, and amendments creating new provinces or extending the boundaries of existing provinces into the territories.

As stated above and elsewhere, the writer of this book regards the principle of provinces opting out of constitutional amendments as totally objectionable, with or without a requirement for compensation. The Meech Lake amendment would make a thoroughly bad provision slightly worse, if that is possible, but the essential damage was done in 1981, not in 1987. The subject of compensation has for some reason received more attention, from both supporters and opponents of the 1982 version, than the fundamental principle of opting out itself. In part this is because the amendments of 1940 (unemployment insurance) and 1951 (pensions) had important implications for public expenditure. It should be noted, however, that future amendments transferring legislative powers are more likely to involve regulatory powers that can be exercised at relatively little expense to the government concerned. The implications of "reasonable compensation" in such a case are unclear.

The extension of the unanimity principle to additional categories of amendments entrenches the existing structures and institutions of the federation more rigidly. Given the quality of some of the alternatives that have been proposed, this is probably just as well. The requirement of unanimity for the creation of new provinces, while unusual in a federal constitution, does not fundamentally offend the federal principle. Neither of the northern territories is likely to merit provincial status in the foreseeable future, and the concern that has been expressed on their behalf over this feature of the amendment appears misguided. The Yukon's economic base consists of little more than federal transfer payments and the tourist industry, while its population is largely transient and barely numerous enough to comprise a respectable attendance at a baseball game. The Northwest Territories are a diverse collection of small communities scattered over an area as large as Western Europe and with no common focus of identity. The climate probably ensures that their total population will never be much larger than at present.

Quebec's fifth condition, participation in the selection of justices of the Supreme Court, was also included in the Meech Lake amendment, but the details have been discussed in Chapter 3 of this book. Whatever the merits of the procedure suggested, the entrenchment of the Court itself in the constitution is a desirable consequence. The effect of the new appointing procedure on the Court's operation remains to be seen, but it is not likely to be very significant.

Three other features of the Meech Lake amendment indicate the price that the other provinces demanded for their acquiescence in Quebec's five conditions. The price is perhaps not as high as might have been anticipated, but is still not negligible. Firstly, senatorial vacancies will be filled by persons who have been nominated by the government of the province to which the vacancy pertains, until such time as a new method of selecting senators can be agreed upon by the eleven governments and entrenched in the constitution. Secondly, the annual first ministers' conference on "the economy," one of the most regrettable innovations of the 1970s, will now be entrenched in the constitution. Thirdly, the constitution will be amended to require an annual constitutional conference of the first ministers, beginning in 1988, with a requirement that Senate reform and jurisdiction over fisheries be placed on the agenda, along with "such other matters as are agreed upon." The reference to fisheries was presumably included at the insistence of Newfoundland and Nova Scotia, which have been seeking some jurisdiction over that subject since 1978.

Provincial nomination of senators has precedents elsewhere. The members of India's upper house are elected by the state legislatures, as were United States senators until 1913. Some Swiss cantons choose their representatives to the Council of States in the same manner, although most have now opted for direct election by the people. Since the Meech Lake procedure is to be used only as vacancies arise, it may take fifteen or twenty years for provincial nominees to become a majority in the Senate. Whether an entirely new approach to constituting the Senate will have been agreed upon by that time remains to be seen; a cynic might suggest that provincial governments will lose their interest in Senate reform (such as it is) once they become accustomed to making the nominations. On the other hand, vacancies will arise infrequently so that the benefits of senatorial patronage to the provincial governments will not be particularly great. Since they need not stand for renomination and will have no further responsibility to the governments that nominated them, provincially-nominated senators are unlikely to behave much differently from those appointed in the traditional way.

The entrenchment of further first ministers' conferences, on the other hand, is an unfortunate development. With at least two such conferences each year, one on the economy and one on the constitution, the first ministers will have less time to devote to running their own jurisdictions. As noted in Chapter 8, the conferences on the economy serve no useful purpose, provide premiers with a platform for irresponsible and partisan criticism of the federal government's policies, and negate the principle that each government is responsible for its own fields of jurisdiction. Constitutional conferences may be essential from time to time, given the amending formula now entrenched in the constitution, but the requirement that there be one every year is excessive. One every five years, the same length of time that elapses between revisions of federal-provincial fiscal arrangements, would certainly suffice for any legitimate purpose. A constitution that is constantly amended creates uncertainty and can hardly inspire much respect. If one regards the first ten amendments to the constitution of the United States as a single package, that constitution has been amended on the average every twelve years, which would seem to be a reasonable frequency. An additional objection is that by requiring the conferences to begin in 1988, the amendment appears to entrench the misguided procedure which the Pearson government followed twenty years previously. Beginning the process of constitutional change with a conference guaranteed years of sterile controversy. By contrast the Meech Lake conference itself was fruitful because it followed a four-year period of reflection and a year of informal soundings and bilateral discussions between the various governments involved.

All three national party leaders supported the Meech Lake accord, although Mr. Trudeau's public opposition to it contributed to the considerable dissent that emerged within the Liberal Party.[32] Quebec nationalists predictably complained that Quebec had not received enough, but their numbers were fewer and their voices more muted than in the past. By the end of January 1988 the constitutional amendments contained in the accord had been accepted by the National Assembly of Quebec, the Legislative Assemblies of Saskatchewan and Alberta, and by the House of Commons. There was some uncertainty about New Brunswick, where a new Liberal premier had replaced the durable Richard Hatfield following an October election, and about the Senate, since a number of Liberal senators were determined to delay passage of the amendments as long as possible. Under the constitutional amending formula, however, the Senate can only delay passage of an amendment for 180 days, provided the House of Commons adopts the amendment for a second time after that interval has passed. It thus seemed probable, although not certain, that the amendments would be incorporated in Canada's constitution by 1989.

NOTES

1. Frank R. Scott, *Essays on the Constitution: Aspects of Canadian Law and Politics* ix. c University of Toronto Press, 1977.

2. Joseph Pope, *Correspondence of Sir John Macdonald* (Toronto: Oxford University Press, 1921) 379.

3. "The Special Nature of Canadian Federalism," in *Essays on the Constitution*, F.R. Scott, 189.

4. Alexander Brady, *Democracy in the Dominions*, 3rd ed. (Toronto: University of Toronto Press, 1958) 59–60.

5. Canada, House of Commons Debates, 1940, pp. 1116–1118. The portion quoted in both the majority and minority opinions is the last 12 lines of p. 1117.

6. Quoted in Arthur Berriedale Keith, ed., *Speeches and Documents on the British Dominions: 1918–1931* (London: Oxford University Press 1961) 161.

7. The early history of constitutional amendment is outlined in Paul Gerin-Lajoie, *Constitutional Amendment in Canada* (Toronto: University of Toronto Press, 1950), and more briefly in Guy Favreau, *The Amendment of the Constitution of Canada* (Ottawa: Queen's Printer, 1965). The latter includes both the Fulton and the Fulton-Favreau amending formulas.

8. Daniel Johnson, *Egalité ou Indépendance* (Montreal: les editions de l'homme, 1965).

9. The Constitutional Committee of the Quebec Liberal Party, *A New Canadian Federation* (Montreal, 1980).

10. Marcel Faribault and Robert M. Fowler, *Ten to One: The Confederation Wager* (Toronto: McClelland and Stewart, 1965).

11. Special Joint Committee of the Senate and the House of Commons on the Constitution of Canada, *Final Report* (Ottawa: Queen's Printer, 1972); Task Force on National Unity, *A Future Together* (Ottawa: Supply and Services, 1979).

12. "Canada and Quebec: A Proposal for a New Constitution," *Canadian Forum*, LVII, no. 672, 4–5.

13. Pierre Elliott Trudeau, *Federalism and the French Canadians* (Toronto: Macmillan, 1968).

14. Lester B. Pearson, *Federalism for the Future* (Ottawa: Queen's Printer, 1968).

15. The text of the Victoria Charter may be found in the Special Joint Com-

mittee of the Senate and the House of Commons on the Constitution of Canada, *Final Report* (Ottawa: Queen's Printer, 1972) 106–09.

16. *Reference re. Legislative Authority of Parliament to Alter or Replace the Senate* [1980] 1 S.C.R. 54.

17. The federal position on this issue was expressed in Jean Chrétien, *Securing the Canadian Economic Union in the Constitution* (Ottawa: Supply and Services, 1980).

18. Jean Chrétien, *Straight from the Heart* (Toronto: Key Porter Books, 1985) 177.

19. This phenomenon is explored more fully in Larry Pratt and Garth Stevenson, *Western Separatism: The Myths, Realities, and Dangers* (Edmonton: Hurtig, 1981).

20. Edward McWhinney, *Canada and the Constitution 1979–1982* (Toronto: University of Toronto Press, 1982) 92.

21. The writer was informed of this by a public servant who was lobbying in London at the time on behalf of one of the western provinces.

22. *A.G. Manitoba et al. vs. A.G. Canada et al.* 1 S.C.R. (1981) 753.

23. See their testimony in the Minutes of Proceedings and Evidence of the Special Joint Committee of the Senate and of the House of Commons on the Constitution of Canada, Issue No. 33 (7 January 1981), 133–54.

24. For a fuller discussion see Garth Stevenson, "Constitutional Amendment: A Democratic Perspective," *Socialist Studies* II (1984) 269–84.

25. Chrétien, *Straight from the Heart*, 186.

26. The phrase is from a speech at Sept Iles, Quebec, on 6 August 1984.

27. The relevant parts of the document are reproduced in Peter M. Leslie, *Canada: The State of the Federation 1985* (Kingston: Institute of Intergovernmental Relations, 1986) 75–81.

28. An official translation of the speech appears in Peter M. Leslie, *Rebuilding the Relationship* (Kingston: Institute of Intergovernmental Relations, 1987) 39–47.

29. The spelling "Meech" was used in the communiqué of 30 April 1987 and in all subsequent documents relating to the accord. The correct spelling is actually "Meach," according to several maps in the writer's possession.

30. The text of the amendments appears in *A Guide to the Meech Lake Constitutional Accord* (Ottawa: Government of Canada, August 1987).

31. Pierre Elliott Trudeau, *Federal-Provincial Grants and the Spending Power of Parliament* (Ottawa: Queen's Printer, 1969) 34–36.

32. For the text of Trudeau's statement on the accord see "Nothing left but tears for Trudeau," *The Globe and Mail* 28 May 1987.

11 Epilogue: Continental Free Trade and Canadian Federalism

Whether the four blocks of territory constituting the Dominion can forever be kept by political agencies united among themselves and separate from their Continent, of which geographically, economically, and with the exception of Quebec ethnologically, they are parts, is the Canadian question.

GOLDWIN SMITH[1]

At the beginning of October 1987, just four months after reaching a constitutional accord with the provinces, the Mulroney government announced a successful conclusion to another, and even more complicated, series of negotiations. After one and a half years of discussions, representatives of the Canadian and United States federal governments had reached an agreement which, if implemented, would abolish tariff barriers between Canada and the United States. Ever since May 1985, when the Royal Commission on the Economic Union and Development Prospects for Canada recommended such an agreement in its report, the issue of "free trade" had figured largely in political debate and in the Canadian media. Both supporters and opponents of the idea had mobilized their arguments, some of which could be traced back to previous debates on the same subject in 1878, 1891, and 1911. The dramatic outcome was nonetheless unexpected, since only a few weeks earlier the Canadian negotiating team had publicly announced that negotiations were at an impasse. Whether one welcomed or deplored the unexpected course of events, it seemed probable that Canada would soon enter a new era in its history, and that its future would be significantly different from its past. This impression was reinforced, for better or for worse, by the cumulative effect of the agreements on the constitution and on free trade, both within a space of only a few months.

A book about federal-provincial relations is not the place for an exhaustive treatment of the issue of free trade, or for the presentation of the arguments either for or against such an agreement. Nonetheless, as Goldwin Smith and others have suggested over the course of a century, federal-provincial relations and Canadian-American relations may have some impact on one another. The parliamentary debates on the

Quebec resolutions in 1865 indicate that the politicians of those days perceived such a relationship.[2] Much more recently, Donald Smiley has referred to Canadian-American relations as one of the "three axes of Canadian federalism."[3] It seems fitting, therefore, to conclude this book with some observations on the relationship between Canadian-American free trade and Canadian federalism.

An optimistic scenario regarding that relationship was presented in the report of the Royal Commission on the Economic Union and Development Prospects for Canada, where it formed a part of that Royal Commission's argument in favour of continental free trade.[4] According to this view the protective tariff, the perceived benefits of which are mainly concentrated in Ontario and Quebec, has been a major source of discontent in Canada's peripheral regions. By reinforcing the regional specialization of the economy, it has made the economic interests of the different provinces more diverse. At the same time its apparently discriminatory effect has undermined the legitimacy of the federal state in the regions that are perceived to suffer from it. Thus on balance the tariff has not only failed to integrate the nation, but has had a contrary effect. Free trade with the United States will eliminate an important source of discord among the regions, will enable the hinterlands to flourish, and will reinforce the unity of Canada and the legitimacy of the Canadian state.

This optimistic scenario is not, however, very persuasive. Firstly, free trade with the United States will not eliminate the tariff barriers against other countries, so that the manufacturing industries of central Canada will continue to be protected against what are becoming their most serious competitors: Japan, Taiwan, South Korea, and so forth. Secondly, the tariff has never been the only, and is no longer the principal, focus of regional discontent. The western separatists who flourished briefly in 1980–82 scarcely bothered to mention the tariff among their litany of grievances. Finally, an ostensibly economic grievance may survive as a powerful symbol long after its substance has become insignificant. Those seeking to mobilize regional discontent will make use of any argument that presents itself, whether valid or otherwise. Howard Darling has demonstrated that freight rates survived as an emotional issue in the western and maritime provinces for decades after the substance of the issue had been overtaken by events.[5] It seems naive therefore to anticipate that continental free trade would usher in a new era of good feelings among Canada's provinces.

Far from promoting a consensus among the provinces, or between them and the federal government, continental free trade contributed to discord among them even while the negotiations were in progress. It also revived one of the most durable controversies regarding Canadian federalism, namely the proper role for the provinces, if any, in international relations. Ever since 1937, when the Judicial Committee of the

Privy Council rejected the argument that Parliament could legislate regarding minimum wages and labour conditions because in doing so it was carrying out Canada's obligations under an international treaty, the power to implement treaties has apparently been divided between Parliament and the provincial legislatures, depending on whether the subject matter of the treaty falls under federal or provincial jurisdiction. During the Quiet Revolution Quebec began to argue that the executive power to make treaties was similarly divided, a view that was regrettably given some credence by Lord Watson's doctrine that prerogative powers in Canada's monarchical federalism are shared between the two levels of government. Quebec's pretensions to international status were encouraged by France and achieved some success, despite the strong opposition of the Canadian federal government.[6] Other provinces also began to open foreign offices, to attend international conferences, and to establish permanent missions in foreign countries. In 1978 the government of Alberta recommended that the constitution should "include provisions that confirm the established legitimate role of the provinces in certain areas of international relations," a suggestion that understandably received no sympathy from the federal government.[7]

The free trade negotiations with the United States again brought this issue to the forefront. It seemed likely that some of Canada's obligations under a free trade agreement would relate to matters of provincial jurisdiction and policy, and thereby require provincial acquiescence to implement the agreement. In particular, certain discriminatory provincial practices, such as preferences given to local suppliers of goods and services, might be viewed by the United States as "non-tariff barriers" so that their elimination would be demanded as part of any free trade agreement. The Canadian government would be unable to promise the elimination of such practices unless it had secured the agreement of the provinces beforehand.

Partly for this reason, and partly because the provincial governments themselves insisted on being involved, the question of provincial participation in the actual negotiations soon arose. It was even suggested at one point that the Canadian negotiating team should take its instructions from the First Ministers' Conference rather than from the federal government, a proposal that has grotesque overtones of the Holy Roman Empire or the Continental Congress rather than a modern federal state. Attorney-general Ian Scott of Ontario argued for provincial participation in the free trade negotiations by drawing the analogy between the Mulroney government's negotiation of free trade and the Trudeau government's effort to patriate the constitution by agreement with the United Kingdom and without provincial consent.[8] (Scott neglected to remind his audience that Ontario had supported the patriation initiative.) While the more extreme claims for provincial involvement were rejected, the Mulroney government did agree to brief the provincial premiers periodically during the free trade negotiations, and presumably to listen to their suggestions.

Behind these procedural wrangles, of course, lay a variety of perspectives on the substance of the issue. The issue of free trade, like most other major issues, divided Canadians along lines of sector and class as well as along the more conspicuous lines of region and province. In 1911 "reciprocity" was supported by most Liberals and most farmers, but opposed by Tories, big business, and the urban working class. In 1987 continental free trade was supported by Tories, big business, and some farmers, particularly the producers of beef and pork. It was opposed by Liberals, New Democrats, organized labour, many farmers, and a handful of dissidents within the business community. In 1911 the provincial governments took sides on the basis of their party affiliations. In 1987 they were influenced in part by partisanship but also by sensitivity to the functional and sectorial interests at stake. On both occasions Ontario was governed by the party that constituted the official opposition at the federal level, and on both occasions the government of Ontario was a strong opponent of the federal government's trade policy. On neither occasion, however, did the positions taken by provincial governments lend support to the view that the issue was essentially a conflict between central Canada and the hinterlands.

The revival of the free trade issue in the 1980s coincided with changes of government in several provinces. In May 1985, when the Macdonald Royal Commission presented its report, Ontario still had a Progressive Conservative government which supported free trade, as did the Parti Québécois government in Quebec. Both provinces elected Liberal governments in the course of the year, and Ontario's new government, led by David Peterson, quickly restored the province to its traditional position as the defender of economic nationalism. Quebec's Robert Bourassa seemed to oppose free trade with the United States when he took office in 1985, but by 1987 he had become one of the strongest supporters. The Parti Québécois, once it was in opposition, also reversed its position and became an opponent of the free trade agreement.

Divisions were also apparent between, and within, the smaller provinces. British Columbia, a firm opponent of reciprocity in 1911, was an equally firm supporter of free trade seventy-five years later. Alberta and Saskatchewan predictably supported Mulroney's free trade initiative, since partisan affiliation, tradition, and economic self-interest all pulled them in the same direction. Manitoba's NDP government was unenthusiastic about free trade in 1985 and strongly opposed by 1987. The four Atlantic provinces adopted the traditional anti-tariff position of their region in 1985, but by the time the agreement was actually achieved their enthusiasm had diminished, apart from Richard Hatfield of New Brunswick who suffered electoral defeat a few days later. Liberal Premier Joseph Ghiz of Prince Edward Island, who had been elected to office in 1986, was an adamant opponent of the free trade agreement.

On balance it made little sense to view the free trade agreement as a "regional" issue. Public opinion polls in October 1987 showed that westerners and Québécois tended to support it while Ontarians and Atlantic Canadians were more sceptical, but the differences were not particularly pronounced between provinces and no province could be said to have a real consensus on one side or the other. In reality the issue revolved around different perspectives on the market economy and the role of the state. Supporters of economic laissez-faire supported the free trade agreement because it would prohibit some interventionist policies and would tie Canada more closely to a country where faith in the free market is far more powerful, and more clearly reflected in public policy, than it is in Canada. Supporters of the interventionist state, just as logically, were suspicious and fearful of any closer association with a country where laissez-faire is a secular religion, and where even hospitals are owned by private investors and expected to make a profit. Opponents of the free trade agreement suspected that the "level playing field" demanded by American trade negotiators was a euphemism for the largely unregulated market economy of the United States, and that important elements of the Canadian bourgeoisie supported free trade for precisely that reason.

Supporters and opponents of continental free trade seem to agree that it would diminish the opportunities for intervention in the Canadian economy by the state. That still leaves open the important question of whether the "state" in this context means primarily the federal or the provincial level of government. Presumably both levels would be affected, but in what proportions? Insofar as the question can be answered, the answer would depend in part on an estimate of the degree, kind, and importance of intervention currently practised by Canadian governments at both levels, and in part on the explicit provisions and anticipated longer-term consequences of the agreement. Although there is no obvious way to quantify for comparative purposes the interventionism of various governments, particularly when their formal powers differ as is true between levels of government in a federation, most observers would agree that Quebec and the western provinces have been more interventionist in the second half of the twentieth century than Ontario and the Atlantic provinces. In terms of committment to an interventionist philosophy the federal government, most of the time, seems to fall somewhere between the two groups of provinces, although the range of policy instruments at its disposal is, of course, very different from that of a province.

It is interesting to note that both governments and public opinion in the more interventionist provinces tend to support free trade with the

United States, while both governments and public opinion in the less interventionist provinces tend to oppose it, or at least to be sceptical of its benefits. Since this is the reverse of what one would expect given the relationship between free trade and laissez-faire discussed above, it suggests that the lesser scope for interventionism as a result of the free trade agreement would mainly affect the federal level of government. Since interventionism at the provincial level is partly, although not exclusively, the result of dissatisfaction with federal policies that are viewed as either ineffective or harmful to the interests of the province concerned, it would then be logical and consistent for anti-centralist westerners and Québécois to support both continental free trade and the relatively interventionist policies of their own provincial governments.

While the free trade negotiations were in progress it was widely assumed, for better or for worse, that the outcome might have a strong effect on the policy instruments available to the provincial governments. Given the divided power of treaty implementation under Canada's constitution, and given the fact that Ontario opposed the very principle of continental free trade, the Mulroney government had a strong incentive to keep matters of provincial jurisdiction off the agenda. Judging by the terms of the agreement it largely succeeded, although the Americans predictably insisted on a provision that would prohibit the discriminatory pricing policies of the provincial liquor boards. In announcing the agreement, the Prime Minister insisted that it could be implemented with or without the approval of the provinces. The Ontario government, although strongly opposed to the agreement, subsequently conceded that this was the case.

The agreement of October 1987, while leaving provincial powers largely intact, would considerably diminish the scope for interventionist policies of the Canadian federal government.[9] The imposition of tariffs or other restrictions on imports from the United States would, of course, be prohibited, by definition, in any free trade agreement. The agreement would also prohibit any restrictions on exports, "including quantitative restrictions, taxes, minimum import or export price requirements or any other equivalent measure, subject to very limited exceptions." Both import and export restrictions, of course, fall under exclusive federal jurisdiction, so the provincial governments would lose nothing by this provision. Canada also agreed to eliminate its export-based duty remission program for the automobile industry, an important instrument of the federal government's industrial strategy. In addition, the agreement promised "non-discriminatory access for the United States to Canadian energy supplies," a provision which seemed to rule out any return to the interventionist energy policies of the Trudeau era.

These provisions related to trade and commerce were by no means all the powers that the government of Canada signed away in the agreement. It also promised "to make permanent its recent policy of not screening new business investments, to end the screening of indirect acquisitions and to reduce the screening of direct acquisitions of Canadian enterprises by American investors." The agreement "achieved major progress in ending the imposition of performance requirements on U.S. investors" and ensured that Canada could not restrict the transfer of profits and other remittances to the United States, another area of exclusive federal jurisdiction. Other areas of exclusive federal jurisdiction in which Canada agreed to restrict its freedom of action included broadcasting policy and patents and copyrights. Canada also agreed to eliminate discrimination against American firms in the financial sector of the economy, most of which is regulated at the federal level.

Under continental free trade the Canadian federal government would, of course, retain substantial powers. Canada would still have its own flag, its own criminal code, and a publicly owned railway system, as does New York State for that matter. Yet the original purpose of the federal state, which was to unite a number of scattered settlements into an economy and society distinct from that of the United States, would to some extent be undermined. Some Canadians might even argue that a federal government with few powers to influence the economy was an unnecessary expense, so long as the provinces continued to control education, natural resources, and social services. Could federal politicians still argue successfully, as they did during the Quebec referendum campaign of 1980, that a Canadian government was needed to guarantee Quebec's energy supplies and its access to markets? Unlike traditional nation-states and the present-day superpowers, the Canadian state must find its *raison d'être* in matters of this kind, for it has no real power, and very little influence, over the fundamental issues of war and peace.

Supporters of continental free trade often try to reassure their opponents by referring to small European countries that participate in free trade arrangements or even common markets involving larger partners.[10] Most of the countries in question, however, have a compact territory, a homogeneous population, a distinctive language, a unitary form of government, and a corporatist tradition of close collaboration between business, labour, and the state. Canada has none of these assets, and it has powerful provinces, some of which resemble the European model of a nation-state more closely than does Canada itself. Free trade advocates ignore the fact that Scottish and Welsh nationalism in the United Kingdom, Basque, Breton, and Corsican separatism in France, and conflicts between the linguistic communities in Belgium all increased in strength after the countries concerned adhered to the European community.[11] Their assertion that continental free trade would have only benign consequences, or none at all, for Canadian federalism and national unity should therefore be taken with a grain of salt.

Goldwin Smith's "Canadian question" thus remains unanswered almost a century after the publication of his book. In a sense this is reassuring; Smith probably did not expect Canada to last as long as it has. Between 1960 and 1980 many observers, including the present writer, followed Goldwin Smith's example by underestimating the durability of the Canadian state. Relatively few sovereign states have disappeared in the twentieth century as a result of either disintegration or absorption. On the other hand, Canada remains an improbable experiment created and maintained in defiance of both continentalism and ethnic nationalism, two of the most powerful forces of our times. Those committed to the preservation of a Canadian state should not despair, but neither should they be complacent.

NOTES

1. Goldwin Smith, *Canada and the Canadian Question* (Toronto: University of Toronto Press 1971, reprint of 1891 edition) 5.

2. W.L. White et al., *Canadian Confederation: A Decision-Making Analysis* (Toronto: Macmillan of Canada, 1979).

3. Donald V. Smiley, *Canada in Question* 3rd ed. (Toronto: McGraw-Hill Ryerson, 1980) 269–74.

4. Royal Commission on the Economic Union and Development Prospects for Canada, *Report* (Ottawa: Supply and Services, 1985) I, 357.

5. Howard Darling, *The Politics of Freight Rates* (Toronto: McClelland and Stewart, 1980).

6. For the federal position see Paul Martin, *Federalism and International Relations* and Mitchell Sharp, *Federalism and International Conferences on Education* (Ottawa: Queen's Printer, 1968).

7. Government of Alberta, *Harmony in Diversity: A New Federalism for Canada* (Edmonton: October 1978) 7–8.

8. Ian Scott, "The Provinces and Foreign Policy: Form and Substance in Policy-Making Process," in *New North American Horizons*, Elliott J. Feldman and Priscilla Battis (Cambridge, Mass.: University Consortium for Research on North America, 1987) 7–16. This is the text of a speech delivered in the autumn of 1986.

9. References in this paragraph and that which follows are to the "Summary of the Agreement" made public by the U.S. government on 4 October 1987.

10. Royal Commission on the Economic Union and Development Prospects for Canada, *Report*, I, 352.

11. On this subject see Tom Nairn, *The Break-up of Britain* (London: New Left Books, 1977) especially pages 92–125 and 306–28.

Appendix 1

Constitution Act, 1867*
(excerpts)

89. Repealed. (43).

6. — THE FOUR PROVINCES.

Application to Legislatures of Provisions respecting Money Votes, etc.

90. The following Provisions of this Act respecting the Parliament of Canada, namely, — the Provisions relating to Appropriation and Tax Bills, the Recommendation of Money Votes, the Assent to Bills, the Disallowance of Acts, and the Signification of Pleasure on Bills reserved, — shall extend and apply to the Legislatures of the several Provinces as if those Provisions were here re-enacted and made applicable in Terms to the respective Provinces and the Legislatures thereof, with the Substitution of the Lieutenant Governor of the Province for the Governor General, of the Governor General for the Queen and for a Secretary of State, of One Year for Two Years, and of the Province for Canada.

VI.—DISTRIBUTION OF LEGISLATIVE POWERS.

Powers of the Parliament.

Legislative Authority of Parliament of Canada.

91. It shall be lawful for the Queen, by and with the Advice and Consent of the Senate and House of Commons, to make Laws for the Peace, Order, and good Government of Canada, in relation to all Matters not coming within the Classes of Subjects by this Act assigned exclusively to the Legislatures of the Provinces; and for greater Certainty, but not so as to restrict the Generality of the foregoing Terms of this Section, it is hereby declared that (notwithstanding anything in this Act) the exclusive Legislative Authority of the Parliament of Canada extends to all Matters coming within the Classes of Subjects next hereinafter enumerated; that is to say,—

---

(43) Repealed by the *Statute Law Revision Act, 1893*, 56–57 Vict., c. 14 (U.K.). The section read as follows:

5.—Ontario, Quebec, and Nova Scotia.

89. Each of the Lieutenant Governors of Ontario, Quebec and Nova Scotia shall cause Writs to be issued for the First Election of Members of the Legislative Assembly thereof in such Form and by such Person as he thinks fit, and at such Time and addressed to such Returning Officer as the Governor General directs, and so that the First Election of Member of Assembly for any Electoral District or any Subdivision thereof shall be held at the same Time and at the same Places as the Election for a Member to serve in the House of Commons of Canada for the Electoral District.

* Published with permission of the Minister of Supply and Services Canada.

1. Repealed. (44)
1A. The Public Debt and Property. (45)
2. The Regulation of Trade and Commerce.
2A. Unemployment insurance. (46)
3. The raising of Money by any Mode or System of Taxation.
4. The borrowing of Money on the Public Credit.
5. Postal Service.
6. The Census and Statistics.
7. Militia, Military and Naval Service, and Defence.
8. The fixing of and providing for the Salaries and Allowances of Civil and other Officers of the Government of Canada.
9. Beacons, Buoys, Lighthouses, and Sable Island.
10. Navigation and Shipping.
11. Quarantine and the Establishment and Maintenance of Marine Hospitals.
12. Sea Coast and Inland Fisheries.
13. Ferries between a Province and any British or Foreign Country or between Two Provinces.
14. Currency and Coinage.
15. Banking, Incorporation of Banks, and the Issue of Paper Money.
16. Savings Banks.
17. Weights and Measures.
18. Bills of Exchange and Promissory Notes.
19. Interest.

---

(44) Class 1 was added by the *British North America (No. 2) Act, 1949,* 13 Geo. VI, c. 8 (U.K.). That Act and class 1 were repealed by the *Constitution Act, 1982.* The matters referred to in class 1 are provided for in subsection 4(2) and Part V of the *Constitution Act, 1982.* As enacted, class 1 read as follows:

> **1.** The amendment from time to time of the Constitution of Canada, except as regards matters coming within the classes of subjects by this Act assigned exclusively to the Legislatures of the provinces, or as regards rights or privileges by this or any other Constitutional Act granted or secured to the Legislature or the Government of a province, or to any class of persons with respect to schools or as regards the use of the English or the French language or as regards the requirements that there shall be a session of the Parliament of Canada at least once each year, and that no House of Commons shall continue for more than five years from the day of the return of the Writs for choosing the House: provided, however, that a House of Commons may in time of real or apprehended war, invasion or insurrection be continued by the Parliament of Canada if such continuation is not opposed by the votes of more than one-third of the members of such House.

(45) Re-numbered by the *British North America (No. 2) Act, 1949.*

(46) Added by the *Constitution Act, 1940,* 3–4 Geo. VI, c. 36 (U.K.).

20. Legal Tender.
21. Bankruptcy and Insolvency.
22. Patents of Invention and Discovery.
23. Copyrights.
24. Indians, and Lands reserved for the Indians.
25. Naturalization and Aliens.
26. Marriage and Divorce.
27. The Criminal Law, except the Constitution of Courts of Criminal Jurisdiction, but including the Procedure in Criminal Matters.
28. The Establishment, Maintenance, and Management of Penitentiaries.
29. Such Classes of Subjects as are expressly excepted in the Enumeration of the Classes of Subjects by this Act assigned exclusively to the Legislatures of the Provinces.

And any Matter coming within any of the Classes of Subjects enumerated in this Section shall not be deemed to come within the Class of Matters of a local or private Nature comprised in the Enumeration of the Classes of Subjects by this Act assigned exclusively to the Legislatures of the Provinces. (47)

Exclusive Powers of Provincial Legislatures.

Subjects of exclusive Provincial Legislation.

92. In each Province the Legislature may exclusively make Laws in relation to Matters coming within the Classes of Subject next hereinafter enumerated; that is to say,—

---

(47) Legislative authority has been conferred on Parliament by other Acts as follows:

1. The *Constitution Act, 1871*, 34–35 Vict., c. 28 (U.K.).

2. The Parliament of Canada may from time to time establish new Provinces in any territories forming for the time being part of the Dominion of Canada, but not included in any Province thereof, and may, at the time of such establishment, make provision for the constitution and administration of any such Province, and for the passing of laws for the peace, order, and good government of such Province, and for its representation in the said Parliament.

3. The Parliament of Canada may from time to time, with the consent of the Legislature of any province of the said Dominion, increase, diminish, or otherwise alter the limits of such Province, upon such terms and conditions as may be agreed to by the said Legislature, and may, with the like consent, make provision respecting the effect and operation of any such increase or diminution or alteration of territory in relation to any Province affected thereby.

4. The Parliament of Canada may from time to time make provision for the administration, peace, order, and good government of any territory not for the time being included in any Province.

5. The following Acts passed by the said Parliament of Canada, and intituled respectively, — "An Act for the temporary government of Rupert's Land and the North Western Territory when united with Canada"; and "An Act to amend and continue the Act thirty-two and thirty-three Victoria, chapter three, and to establish and provide for the government of "the Province of Manitoba", shall be and be deemed to have been valid and effectual for all purposes whatsoever from the date at which they respectively received the assent, in the Queen's name, of the Governor General of the said Dominion of Canada.

1. Repealed. (48)
2. Direct Taxation within the Province in order to the raising of a Revenue for Provincial Purposes.
3. The borrowing of Money on the sole Credit of the Province.
4. The Establishment and Tenure of Provincial Offices and the Appointment and Payment of Provincial Officers.
5. The Management and Sale of the Public Lands belonging to the Province and of the Timber and Wood thereon.
6. The Establishment, Maintenance, and Management of Public and Reformatory Prisons in and for the Province.
7. The Establishment, Maintenance, and Management of Hospitals, Asylums, Charities, and Eleemosynary Institutions in and for the Province, other than Marine Hospitals.
8. Municipal Institutions in the Province.
9. Shop, Saloon, Tavern, Auctioneer, and other Licences in order to the raising of a Revenue for Provincial, Local, or Municipal Purposes.
10. Local Works and Undertakings other than such as are of the following Classes:—

---

6. Except as provided by the third section of this Act, it shall not be competent for the Parliament of Canada to alter the provisions of the last-mentioned Act of the said Parliament in so far as it relates to the Province of Manitoba, or of any other Act hereafter establishing new Provinces in the said Dominion, subject always to the right of the Legislature of the Province of Manitoba to alter from time to time the provisions of any law respecting the qualification of electors and members of the Legislative Assembly, and to make laws respecting elections in the said Province.

The *Rupert's Land Act, 1868*, 31–32 Vict., c. 105 (U.K.) (repealed by the *Statute Law Revision Act, 1893*, 56–57 Vict., c. 14 (U.K.) had previously conferred similar authority in relation to Rupert's Land and the North Western Territory upon admission of those areas.

2. The *Constitution Act, 1886*, 49–50 Vict., c. 35, (U.K.).

1. The Parliament of Canada may from time to time make provision for the representation in the Senate and House of Commons of Canada, or in either of them, of any territories which for the time being form part of the Dominion of Canada, but are not included in any province thereof.

3. The *Statute of Westminster, 1931*, 22 Geo. V, c. 4 (U.K.).

3. It is hereby declared and enacted that the Parliament of a Dominion has full power to make laws having extra-territorial operation.

4. Section 44 of the *Constitution Act, 1982*, authorizes Parliament to amend the Constitution of Canada in relation to the executive government of Canada or the Senate and House of Commons. Sections 38, 41, 42, and 43 of that Act authorize the Senate and House of Commons to give their approval to certain other constitutional amendments by resolution.

(48) Class 1 was repealed by the *Constitution Act, 1982*. As enacted, it read as follows:

1. The Amendment from Time to Time, notwithstanding anything in this Act, of the Constitution of the province, except as regards the Office of Lieutenant Governor.

(a) Lines of Steam or other Ships, Railways, Canals, Telegraphs, and other Works and Undertakings connecting the Province with any other or others of the Provinces, or extending beyond the Limits of the Province;

(b) Lines of Steam Ships between the Province and any British or Foreign Country;

(c) Such Works as, although wholly situate within the Province, are before or after their Execution declared by the Parliament of Canada to be for the general Advantage of Canada or for the Advantage of Two or more of the Provinces.

11. The Incorporation of Companies with Provincial Objects.

12. The Solemnization of Marriage in the Province.

13. Property and Civil Rights in the Province.

14. The Administration of Justice in the Province, including the Constitution, Maintenance, and Organization of Provincial Courts, both of Civil and of Criminal Jurisdiction, and including Procedure in Civil Matters in those Courts.

15. The Imposition of Punishment by Fine, Penalty, or Imprisonment for enforcing any Law of the Province made in relation to any Matter coming within any of the Classes of Subjects enumerated in this Section.

16. Generally all Matters of a merely local or private Nature in the Province.

Non-Renewable Natural Resources, Forestry Resources and Electrical Energy.

Laws respecting non-renewable natural resources, forestry resources and electrical energy.

92A. (1) In each province, the legislature may exclusively make laws in relation to

(a) exploration for non-renewable natural resources in the province;

(b) development, conservation and management of non-renewable natural resources and forestry resources in the province, including laws in relation to the rate of primary production therefrom; and

(c) development, conservation and management of sites and facilities in the province for the generation and production of electrical energy.

Export from provinces of resources.

(2) In each province, the legislature may make laws in relation to the export from the province to another part of Canada of the primary production from non-renewable natural resources and forestry resources in the province and the production from facilities in the province for the generation of electrical energy, but such laws may not authorize or provide for discrimination in prices or in supplies exported to another part of Canada.

Authority of Parliament.

(3) Nothing in subsection (2) derogates from the authority of Parliament to enact laws in relation to the matters referred to in that subsection and, where such a law of Parliament and a law of a province conflict, the law of Parliament prevails to the extent of the conflict.

Taxation of resources.

(4) In each province, the legislature may make laws in relation to the raising of money by any mode or system of taxation in respect of

> (a) non-renewable natural resources and forestry resources in the province and the primary production therefrom, and

> (b) sites and facilities in the province for the generation of electrical energy and the production therefrom, whether or not such production is exported in whole or in part from the province, but such laws may not authorize or provide for taxation that differentiates between production exported to another part of Canada and production not exported from the province.

"Primary production".

(5) The expression "primary production" has the meaning assigned by the Sixth Schedule.

Existing powers or rights.

(6) Nothing in subsections (1) to (5) derogates from any powers or rights that a legislature or government of a province had immediately before the coming into force of this section. (49)

Education.

Legislation respecting Education.

93. In and for each Province the Legislature may exclusively make Laws in relation to Education, subject and according to the following Provisions:—

> (1) Nothing in any such Law shall prejudicially affect any Right or Privilege with respect to Denominational Schools which any Class of Persons have by Law in the Province at the Union:

> (2) All the Powers, Privileges, and Duties at the Union by Law conferred and imposed in Upper Canada on the Separate Schools and School Trustees of the Queen's Roman Catholic Subjects shall be and the same are hereby extended to the Dissentient Schools of the Queen's Protestant and Roman Catholic Subjects in Quebec:

> (3) Where in any Province a System of Separate or Dissentient Schools exists by Law at the Union or is thereafter established by the Legislature of the Province, an Appeal shall lie to the Governor General in Council from any Act or Decision of any Provincial Authority affecting any Right or Privilege of the Protestant or Roman Catholic Minority of the Queen's Subjects in relation to Education:

Section 45 of the *Constitution Act, 1982*, now authorizes legislatures to make laws amending the constitution of the province. Sections 38, 41, 42, and 43 of that Act authorize legislative assemblies to give their approval by resolution to certain other amendments to the Constitution of Canada.

(49) Added by the *Constitution Act, 1982*.

(4) In case any such Provincial Law as from Time to Time seems to the Governor General in Council requisite for the due Execution of the Provisions of this Section is not made, or in case any Decision of the Governor General in Council on any Appeal under this Section is not duly executed by the proper Provincial Authority in that Behalf, then and in every such Case, and as far only as the Circumstances of each Case require, the Parliament of Canada may make remedial Laws for the due Execution of the Provisions of this Section and of any Decision of the Governor General in Council under this Section.(50)

Uniformity of Laws in Ontario, Nova Scotia and New Brunswick.

Legislation for Uniformity of Laws in Three Provinces.

94. Notwithstanding anything in this Act, the Parliament of Canada may make Provision for the Uniformity of all or any of the Laws relative to Property and Civil Rights in Ontario, Nova Scotia, and New Brunswick, and of the Procedure of

---

(50) Altered for Manitoba by section 22 of the *Manitoba Act, 1870,* 33 Vict., c. 3 (Canada), (confirmed by the *Constitution Act, 1871),* which reads as follows:

22. In and for the Province, the said Legislature may exclusively make Laws in relation to Education, subject and according to the following provisions:—

(1) Nothing in any such Law shall prejudicially affect any right or privilege with respect to Denominational Schools which any class of persons have by Law or practice in the Province at the Union:

(2) An appeal shall lie to the Governor General in Council from any Act or decision of the Legislature of the Province, or of any Provincial Authority, affecting any right or privilege, of the Protestant or Roman Catholic minority of the Queen's subjects in relation to Education:

(3) In case any such Provincial Law, as from time to time seems to the Governor General in Council requisite for the due execution of the provisions of this section, is not made, or in case any decision of the Governor General in Council on any appeal under this section is not duly executed by the proper Provincial Authority in that behalf, then, and in every such case, and as far only as the circumstances of each case require, the Parliament of Canada may make remedial Laws for the due execution of the provisions of this section, and of any decision of the Governor General in Council under this section.

Altered for Alberta by section 17 of the *Alberta Act,* 4–5 Edw. VII, c. 3, 1905 (Canada), which reads as follows:

17. Section 93 of the *Constitution Act, 1867,* shall apply to the said province, with the substitution for paragraph (1) of the said section 93 of the following paragraph:—

(1) Nothing in any such law shall prejudicially affect any right or privilege with respect to separate schools which any class of persons have at the date of the passing of this Act, under the terms of chapters 29 and 30 of the Ordinances of the Northwest Territories, passed in the year 1901, or with respect to religious instruction in any public or separate school as provided for in the said ordinances.

2. In the appropriation by the Legislature or distribution by the Government of the province of any moneys for the support of schools organized and carried on in accordance with the said chapter 29 or any Act passed in amendment thereof, or in substitution therefor, there shall be no discrimination against schools of any class described in the said chapter 29.

all or any of the Courts in Those Three Provinces, and from and after the passing of any Act in that Behalf the Power of the Parliament of Canada to make Laws in relation to any Matter comprised in any such Act shall, notwithstanding anything in this Act, be unrestricted; but any Act of the Parliament of Canada making Provision for such Uniformity shall not have effect in any province unless and until it is adopted and enacted as Law by the Legislature thereof.

3. Where the expression "by law" is employed in paragraph 3 of the said section 93, it shall be held to mean the law as set out in the said chapters 29 and 30, and where the expression "at the Union" is employed, in the said paragraph 3, it shall be held to mean the date at which this Act comes into force.

Altered for Saskatchewan by section 17 of the *Saskatchewan Act*, 4–5 Edw. VII, c. 42, 1905 (Canada), which reads as follows:

17. Section 93 of the *Constitution Act, 1867*, shall apply to the said province, with the substitution for paragraph (1) of the said section 93, of the following paragraph:—

(1) Nothing in any such law shall prejudicially affect any right or privilege with respect to separate schools which any class of persons have at the date of the passing of this Act, under the terms of chapters 29 and 30 of the Ordinances of the Northwest Territories, passed in the year 1901, or with respect to religious instruction in any public or separate school as provided for in the said ordinances.

2. In the appropriation by the Legislature or distribution by the Government of the province of any moneys for the support of schools organized and carried on in accordance with the said chapter 29, or any Act passed in amendment thereof or in substitution therefor, there shall be no discrimination against schools of any class described in the said chapter 29.

3. Where the expression "by law" is employed in paragraph (3) of the said section 93, it shall be held to mean the law as set out in the said chapters 29 and 30; and where the expression "at the Union" is employed in the said paragraph (3), it shall be held to mean the date at which this Act comes into force.

Altered by Term 17 of the Terms of Union of Newfoundland with Canada (confirmed by the *Newfoundland Act*, 12–13 Geo. VI, c. 22 (U.K.)), which reads as follows:

17. In lieu of section ninety-three of the *Constitution Act, 1867*, the following term shall apply in respect of the Province of Newfoundland:

In and for the Province of Newfoundland the Legislature shall have exclusive authority to make laws in relation to education, but the Legislature will not have authority to make laws prejudicially affecting any right or privilege with respect to denominational schools, common (amalgamated) schools, or denominational colleges, that any class or classes of persons have by law in Newfoundland at the date of Union, and out of public funds of the Province of Newfoundland, provided for education,

(a) all such schools shall receive their share of such funds in accordance with scales determined on a non-discriminatory basis from time to time by the Legislature for all schools then being conducted under authority of the Legislature; and

(b) all such colleges shall receive their share of any grant from time to time voted for all colleges then being conducted under authority of the Legislature, such grant being distributed on a non-discriminatory basis.

Old Age Pensions.

Legislation respecting old age pensions and supplementary benefits.

94A. The Parliament of Canada may make laws in relation to old age pensions and supplementary benefits, including survivors, and disability benefits irrespective of age, but no such law shall affect the operation of any law present or future of a provincial legislature in relation to any such matter.(51)

Agriculture and Immigration.

Concurrent Powers of Legislation respecting Agriculture, etc.

95. In each Province the Legislature may make Laws in relation to Agriculture in the Province, and to Immigration into the Province; and it is hereby declared that the Parliament of Canada may from Time to Time make Laws in relation to Agriculture in all or any of the Provinces, and to Immigration into all or any of the Provinces; and any Law of the Legislature of a Province relative to Agriculture or to Immigration shall have effect in and for the Province as long and as far only as it is not repugnant to any Act of the Parliament of Canada.

See also sections 23, 29, and 59 of the *Constitutional Act, 1982*. Section 23 provides for new minority language educational rights and section 59 permits a delay in respect of the coming into force in Quebec of one aspect of those rights. Section 29 provides that nothing in the *Canadian Charter of Rights and Freedoms* abrogates or derogates from any rights or privileges guaranteed by or under the Constitution of Canada in respect of denominational, separate or dissentient schools.

(51) Added by the *Constitution Act, 1964*, 12–13 Eliz. II, c. 73 (U.K.). As originally enacted by the *British North America Act, 1951*, 14–15 Geo. VI, c. 32 (U.K.), which was repealed by the *Constitution Act, 1982*, section 94A read as follows:

> **94A.** It is hereby declared that the Parliament of Canada may from time to time make laws in relation to old age pensions in Canada, but no law made by the Parliament of Canada in relation to old age pensions shall affect the operation of any law present or future of a Provincial Legislature in relation to old age pensions.

Appendix 2

Constitution Act, 1982* (79)

PART I

CANADIAN CHARTER OF RIGHTS AND FREEDOMS

Whereas Canada is founded upon principles that recognize the supremacy of God and the rule of law:

Guarantee of Rights and Freedoms

Rights and freedoms in Canada

1. The *Canadian Charter of Rights and Freedoms* guarantees the rights and freedoms set out in it subject only to such reasonable limits prescribed by law as can be demonstrably justified in a free and democratic society.

Fundamental Freedoms

Fundamental freedoms

2. Everyone has the following fundamental freedoms:

(a) freedom of conscience and religion;

(b) freedom of thought, belief, opinion and expression, including freedom of the press and other media of communication;

(c) freedom of peaceful assembly; and

(d) freedom of association.

---

(79) Enacted as Schedule B to the *Canada Act 1982*, (U.K.) 1982, c. 11, which came into force on April 17, 1982. The *Canada Act 1982*, other than Schedules A and B thereto, reads as follows:

An Act to give effect to a request by the Senate and House of Commons of Canada

Whereas Canada has requested and consented to the enactment of an Act of the Parliament of the United Kingdom to give effect to the provisions hereinafter set forth and the Senate and the House of Commons of Canada in Parliament assembled have submitted an address to Her Majesty requesting that Her Majesty may graciously be pleased to cause a Bill to be laid before the Parliament of the United Kingdom for that purpose.

Be it therefore enacted by the Queen's Most Excellent Majesty, by and with the advice and consent of the Lords Spiritual and Temporal, and Commons, in this present Parliament assembled, and by the authority of the same, as follows:

1. The *Constitution Act, 1982* set out in Schedule B to this Act is hereby enacted for and shall have the force of law in Canada and shall come into force as provided in that Act.

2. No Act of the Parliament of the United Kingdom passed after the *Constitution Act, 1982* comes into force shall extend to Canada as part of its law.

* Published with permission of the Minister of Supply and Services Canada.

Democratic Rights

Democratic rights of citizens

3. Every citizen of Canada has the right to vote in an election of members of the House of Commons or of a legislative assembly and to be qualified for membership therein.

Maximum duration of legislative bodies

4. (1) No House of Commons and no legislative assembly shall continue for longer than five years from the date fixed for the return of the writs of a general election of its members. (80)

Continuation in special circumstances

(2) In time of real or apprehended war, invasion or insurrection, a House of Commons may be continued by Parliament and a legislative assembly may be continued by the legislature beyond five years if such continuation is not opposed by the votes of more than one-third of the members of the House of Commons or the legislative assembly, as the case may be. (81)

Annual sitting of legislative bodies

5. There shall be a sitting of Parliament and of each legislature at least once every twelve months. (82)

Mobility Rights

Mobility of citizens

6. (1) Every citizen of Canada has the right to enter, remain in and leave Canada.

Rights to move and gain livelihood

(2) Every citizen of Canada and every person who has the status of a permanent resident of Canada has the right

(a) to move to and take up residence in any province; and

(b) to pursue the gaining of a livelihood in any province.

Limitation

(3) The rights specified in subsection (2) are subject to

(a) any laws or practices of general application in force in a province other than those that discriminate among persons primarily on the basis of province of present or previous residence; and

(b) any laws providing for reasonable residency requirements as a qualification for the receipt of publicly provided social services.

Affirmative action programs

(4) Subsections (2) and (3) do not preclude any law, program or activity that has as its object the amelioration in a province of conditions of individuals in that province who are socially or economically disadvantaged if the rate of employment in that province is below the rate of employment in Canada.

---

3. So far as it is not contained in Schedule B, the French version of this Act is set out in Schedule A to this Act and has the same authority in Canada as the English version thereof.

4. This Act may be cited as the *Canada Act 1982*.

(80) See section 50 and the footnotes to sections 85 and 88 of the *Constitution Act, 1867*.

(81) Replaces part of Class 1 of section 91 of the *Constitution Act, 1867*, which was repealed as set out in subitem 1(3) of the Schedule to this Act.

(82) See the footnotes to sections 20, 86 and 88 of the *Constitution Act, 1867*.

Legal Rights

Life, liberty and security of person

7. Everyone has the right to life, liberty and security of the person and the right not to be deprived thereof except in accordance with the principles of fundamental justice.

Search or seizure

8. Everyone has the right to be secure against unreasonable search or seizure.

Detention or imprisonment

9. Everyone has the right not to be arbitrarily detained or imprisoned.

Arrest or detention

10. Everyone has the right on arrest or detention

(*a*) to be informed promptly of the reasons therefor;

(*b*) to retain and instruct counsel without delay and to be informed of that right; and

(*c*) to have the validity of the detention determined by way of *habeas corpus* and to be released if the detention is not lawful.

Proceedings in criminal and penal matters

11. Any person charged with an offence has the right

(*a*) to be informed without unreasonable delay of the specific offence;

(*b*) to be tried within a reasonable time;

(*c*) not to be compelled to be a witness in proceedings against that person in respect of the offence;

(*d*) to be presumed innocent until proven guilty according to law in a fair and public hearing by an independent and impartial tribunal;

(*e*) not to be denied reasonable bail without just cause;

(*f*) except in the case of an offence under military law tried before a military tribunal, to the benefit of trial by jury where the maximum punishment for the offence is imprisonment for five years or a more severe punishment;

(*g*) not to be found guilty on account of any act or omission unless, at the time of the act or omission, it constituted an offence under Canadian or international law or was criminal according to the general principles of law recognized by the community of nations;

(*h*) if finally acquitted of the offence, not to be tried for it again and, if finally found guilty and punished for the offence, not to be tried or punished for it again; and

(*i*) if found guilty of the offence and if the punishment for the offence has been varied between the time of commission and the time of sentencing, to the benefit of the lesser punishment.

Treatment or punishment

12. Everyone has the right not to be subjected to any cruel and unusual treatment or punishment.

Self-crimination

13. A witness who testifies in any proceedings has the right not to have any incriminating evidence so given used to incriminate that witness in any other proceedings, except in a prosecution for perjury or for the giving of contradictory evidence.

Interpreter   **14.** A party or witness in any proceedings who does not understand or speak the language in which the proceedings are conducted or who is deaf has the right to the assistance of an interpreter.

Equality Rights

Equality before and under law and equal protection and benefit of law   **15.** (1) Every individual is equal before and under the law and has the right to the equal protection and equal benefit of the law without discrimination and, in particular, without discrimination based on race, national or ethnic origin, colour, religion, sex, age or mental or physical disability.

Affirmative action programs   (2) Subsection (1) does not preclude any law, program or activity that has as its object the amelioration of conditions of disadvantaged individuals or groups including those that are disadvantaged because of race, national or ethnic origin, colour, religion, sex, age or mental or physical disability. (83)

Official Languages of Canada

Official languages of Canada   **16.** (1) English and French are the official languages of Canada and have equality of status and equal rights and privileges as to their use in all institutions of the Parliament and government of Canada.

Official languages of New Brunswick   (2) English and French are the official languages of New Brunswick and have equality of status and equal rights and privileges as to their use in all institutions of the legislature and government of New Brunswick.

Advancement of status and use   (3) Nothing in this Charter limits the authority of Parliament or a legislature to advance the equality of status or use of English and French.

Proceedings of Parliament   **17.** (1) Everyone has the right to use English or French in any debates and other proceedings of Parliament. (84)

Proceedings of New Brunswick legislature   (2) Everyone has the right to use English or French in any debates and other proceedings of the legislature of New Brunswick. (85)

Parliamentary statutes and records   **18.** (1) The statutes, records and journals of Parliament shall be printed and published in English and French and both language versions are equally authoritative. (86)

New Brunswick statutes and records   (2) The statutes, records and journals of the legislature of New Brunswick shall be printed and published in English and French and both language versions are equally authoritative. (87)

---

(83) Subsection 32(2) provides that section 15 shall not have effect until three years after section 32 comes into force.

Section 32 came into force on April 17, 1982; therefore, section 15 had effect on April 17, 1985.

(84) See section 133 of the Constitution Act, 1867, and the footnote thereto.

(85) Id.

(86) Id.

(87) Id.

288   *Unfulfilled Union*

Proceedings in courts established by Parliament

19. (1) Either English or French may be used by any person in, or in any pleading in or process issuing from, any court established by Parliament. (88)

Proceedings in New Brunswick courts

(2) Either English or French may be used by any person in, or in any pleading in or process issuing from, any court of New Brunswick. (89)

Communications by public with federal institutions

20. (1) Any member of the public in Canada has the right to communicate with, and to receive available services from, any head or central office of an institution of the Parliament or government of Canada in English or French, and has the same right with respect to any other office of any such institution where

(a) there is a significant demand for communications with and services from that office in such language; or

(b) due to the nature of the office, it is reasonable that communications with and services from that office be available in both English and French.

Communications by public with New Brunswick institutions

(2) Any member of the public in New Brunswick has the right to communicate with, and to receive available services from, any office of an institution of the legislature or government of New Brunswick in English or French.

Continuation of existing constitutional provisions

21. Nothing in sections 16 to 20 abrogates or derogates from any right, privilege or obligation with respect to the English and French languages, or either of them, that exists or is continued by virtue of any other provision of the Constitution of Canada. (90)

Rights and privileges preserved

22. Nothing in sections 16 to 20 abrogates or derogates from any legal or customary right or privilege acquired or enjoyed either before or after the coming into force of this Charter with respect to any language that is not English or French.

Minority Language Educational Rights

Language of instruction

23. (1) Citizens of Canada

(a) whose first language learned and still understood is that of the English or French linguistic minority population of the province in which they reside, or

(b) who have received their primary school instruction in Canada in English or French and reside in a province where the language in which they received that instruction is the language of the English or French linguistic minority population of the province,

have the right to have their children receive primary and secondary school instruction in that language in that province. (91)

(88) *Id.*

(89) *Id.*

(90) See, for example, section 133 of the *Constitution Act, 1867*, and the reference to the *Manitoba Act, 1870*, in the footnote thereto.

(91) Paragraph 23 (1) (a) is not in force in respect of Quebec. See section 59 *infra*.

Continuity of
language
instruction

(2) Citizens of Canada of whom any child has received or is receiving primary or secondary school instruction in English or French in Canada, have the right to have all their children receive primary and secondary school instruction in the same language.

Application
where num-
bers warrant

(3) The right of citizens of Canada under subsections (1) and (2) to have their children receive primary and secondary school instruction in the language of the English or French linguistic minority population of a province

(a) applies wherever in the province the number of children of citizens who have such a right is sufficient to warrant the provision to them out of public funds of minority language instruction; and

(b) includes, where the number of those children so warrants, the right to have them receive that instruction in minority language educational facilities provided out of public funds.

Enforcement

Enforcement
of guaranteed
rights and
freedoms

24. (1) Anyone whose rights or freedoms, as guaranteed by this Charter, have been infringed or denied may apply to a court of competent jurisdiction to obtain such remedy as the court considers appropriate and just in the circumstances.

Exclusion of
evidence
bringing
adminis-
tration of jus-
tice into
disrepute

(2) Where, in proceedings under subsection (1), a court concludes that evidence was obtained in a manner that infringed or denied any rights or freedoms guaranteed by this Charter, the evidence shall be excluded if it is established that, having regard to all the circumstances, the admission of it in the proceedings would bring the administration of justice into disrepute.

General

Aboriginal
rights and
freedoms not
affected by
Charter

25. The guarantee in this Charter of certain rights and freedoms shall not be construed so as to abrogate or derogate from any aboriginal, treaty or other rights or freedoms that pertain to the aboriginal peoples of Canada including

(a) any rights or freedoms that have been recognized by the Royal Proclamation of October 7, 1763; and

(b) any rights or freedoms that now exist by way of land claims agreements or may be so acquired. (92)

---

(92) Paragraph 25(b) was repealed and re-enacted by the *Constitution Amendment Proclamation, 1983, See* SI/84–102.

Paragraph 25(b) as originally enacted read as follows:

"(b) any rights or freedoms that may be acquired by the aboriginal peoples of Canada by way of land claims settlement."

Other rights and freedoms not affected by Charter

26. The guarantee in this Charter of certain rights and freedoms shall not be construed as denying the existence of any other rights or freedoms that exist in Canada.

Multicultural heritage

27. This Charter shall be interpreted in a manner consistent with the preservation and enhancement of the multicultural heritage of Canadians.

Rights guaranteed equally to both sexes

28. Notwithstanding anything in this Charter, the rights and freedoms referred to in it are guaranteed equally to male and female persons.

Rights respecting certain schools preserved

29. Nothing in this Charter abrogates or derogates from any rights or privileges guaranteed by or under the constitution of Canada in respect of denominational, separate or dissentient schools. (93)

Application to territories and territorial authorities

30. A reference in this Charter to a Province or to the legislative assembly or legislature of a province shall be deemed to include a reference to the Yukon Territory and the Northwest Territories, or to the appropriate legislative authority thereof, as the case may be.

Legislative powers not extended

31. Nothing in this Charter extends the legislative powers of any body or authority.

Application of Charter

Application of Charter

32. (1) This Charter applies

(a) to the Parliament and government of Canada in respect of all matters within the authority of Parliament including all matters relating to the Yukon Territory and Northwest Territories; and

(b) to the legislature and government of each province in respect of all matters within the authority of the legislature of each province.

Exception

(2) Notwithstanding subsection (1), section 15 shall not have effect until three years after this section comes into force.

Exception where express declaration

33. (1) Parliament or the legislature of a province may expressly declare in an Act of Parliament or of the legislature, as the case may be, that the Act or a provision thereof shall operate notwithstanding a provision included in section 2 or sections 7 to 15 of this Charter.

Operation of exception

(2) An Act or a provision of an Act in respect of which a declaration made under this section is in effect shall have such operation as it would have but for the provision of this Charter referred to in the declaration.

---

(93) See section 93 of the *Constitution Act, 1867*, and the footnote thereto.

Five year limitation

(3) A declaration made under subsection (1) shall cease to have effect five years after it comes into force or on such earlier date as may be specified in the declaration.

Re-enactment

(4) Parliament or the legislature of a province may re-enact a declaration made under subsection (1).

Five year limitation

(5) Subsection (3) applies in respect of a re-enactment made under subsection (4).

Citation

Citation

34. This Part may be cited as the *Canadian Charter of Rights and Freedoms*.

PART II
RIGHTS OF THE ABORIGINAL PEOPLES OF CANADA

Recognition of existing aboriginal and treaty rights

35. (1) The existing aboriginal and treaty rights of the aboriginal peoples of Canada are hereby recognized and affirmed.

Definition of "aboriginal peoples of Canada"

(2) In this Act, "aboriginal peoples of Canada" includes the Indian, Inuit and Métis peoples of Canada.

Land claims agreements

(3) For greater certainty, in subsection (1) "treaty rights" includes rights that now exist by way of land claims agreements or may be so acquired.

Aboriginal and treaty rights are guaranteed equally to both sexes

(4) Notwithstanding any other provision of this Act, the aboriginal and treaty rights referred to in subsection (1) are guaranteed equally to male and female persons. (94)

Commitment to participation in constitutional conference

35.1 The government of Canada and the provincial governments are committed to the principal that, before any amendment is made to Class 24 of section 91 of the "*Constitution Act, 1867*", to section 25 of this Act or to this Part,

(a) a constitutional conference that includes in its agenda an item relating to the proposed amendment, composed of the Prime Minister of Canada and the first ministers of the provinces, will be convened by the Prime Minister of Canada; and

(b) the Prime Minister of Canada will invite representatives of the aboriginal peoples of Canada to participate in the discussions on that item. (95)

---

(94) Subsections 35(3) and (4) were added by the *Constitution Amendment Proclamation, 1983*, *See* SI/84–102.

(95) Section 35.1 was added by the *Constitution Amendment Proclamation, 1983*. *See* SI/84–102.

PART III
EQUALIZATION AND REGIONAL DISPARITIES

Commitment to promote equal opportunities

36. (1) Without altering the legislative authority of Parliament or of the provincial legislatures, or the rights of any of them with respect to the exercise of their legislative authority, Parliament and the legislatures, together with the government of Canada and the provincial governments, are committed to

(a) promoting equal opportunities for the well-being of Canadians;

(b) furthering economic development to reduce disparity in opportunities; and

(c) providing essential public services of reasonable quality to all Canadians.

Commitment respecting public services

(2) Parliament and the government of Canada are committed to the principle of making equalization payments to ensure that provincial governments have sufficient revenues to provide reasonably comparable levels of public services at reasonably comparable levels of taxation. (96)

PART IV
CONSTITUTIONAL CONFERENCE

37. (97)

---

(96) See the footnotes to sections 114 and 118 of the *Constitution Act, 1867.*

(97) Section 54 provided for the repeal of Part IV one year after Part VII came into force. Part VII came into force on April 17, 1982 thereby repealing Part IV on April 17, 1983.

Part IV, as originally enacted, read as follows:

Constitutional conference

"**37.** (1) A constitutional conference composed of the Prime Minister of Canada and the first ministers of the provinces shall be convened by the Prime Minister of Canada within one year after this Part comes into force.

Participation of aboriginal peoples

(2) The conference convened under subsection (1) shall have included in its agenda an item respecting constitutional matters that directly affect the aboriginal peoples of Canada, including the identification and definition of the rights of those peoples to be included in the Constitution of Canada, and the Prime Minister of Canada shall invite representatives of those peoples to participate in the discussions on that item.

Participation of territories

(3) The Prime Minister of Canada shall invite elected representatives of the governments of the Yukon Territory and the Northwest Territories to participate in the discussions on any item on the agenda of the conference convened under subsection (1) that, in the opinion of the Prime Minister, directly affects the Yukon Territory and the Northwest Territories."

PART IV.1
CONSTITUTIONAL CONFERENCES

Constitu-
tional confer-
ences

37.1 (1) In addition to the conference convened in March 1983, at least two constitutional conferences composed of the Prime Minister of Canada and the first ministers of the provinces shall be convened by the Prime Minister of Canada, the first within three years after April 17, 1982 and the second within five years after that date.

Participation
of aboriginal
peoples

(2) Each conference convened under subsection (1) shall have included in its agenda constitutional matters that directly affect the aboriginal peoples of Canada, and the Prime Minister of Canada shall invite representatives of those peoples to partici- pate in the discussions on those matters.

Participation
of territories

(3) The Prime Minister of Canada shall invite elected repre- sentatives of the governments of the Yukon Territory and the Northwest Territories to participate in the discussions on any item on the agenda of a conference convened under subsection (1) that, in the opinion of the Prime Minister, directly affects the Yukon Territory and the Northwest Territories.

Subsection
35(1) not
affected

(4) Nothing in this section shall be construed so as to dero- gate from subsection 35(1). (98)

PART V
PROCEDURE FOR AMENDING CONSTITUTION OF CANADA (99)

General
procedure for
amending
Constitution
of Canada

38. (1) An amendment to the Constitution of Canada may be made by proclamation issued by the Governor General under the Great Seal of Canada where so authorized by

(a) resolutions of the Senate and House of Commons; and

(b) resolutions of the legislative assemblies of at least two-thirds of the provinces that have, in the aggregate, according to the then latest general census, at least fifty per cent of the population of all the provinces.

Majority of
members

(2) An amendment made under subsection (1) that deroga- tes from the legislative powers, the proprietary rights or any other rights or privileges of the legislature or government of a province shall require a resolution supported by a majority of the members of each of the Senate, the House of Commons and the legislative assemblies required under subsection (1).

---

(98) Part IV.1 was added by the *Constitution Amendment Proclamation, 1983. See* SI/84–102.

(99) Prior to the enactment of Part V certain provisions of the Constitution of Canada and the provincial constitutions could be amended pursuant to the *Constitu- tion Act, 1867.* See the footnotes to section 91, Class 1 and section 92, Class 1 thereof, *supra.* Other amendments to the Constitution could only be made by enactment of the Parliament of the United Kingdom.

Expression of dissent

(3) An amendment referred to in subsection (2) shall not have effect in a province the legislative assembly of which has expressed its dissent thereto by resolution supported by a majority of its members prior to the issue of the proclamation to which the amendment relates unless that legislative assembly, subsequently, by resolution supported by a majority of its members, revokes its dissent and authorizes the amendment.

Revocation of dissent

(4) A resolution of dissent made for the purposes of subsection (3) may be revoked at any time before or after the issue of the proclamation to which it relates.

Restriction on proclamation

39. (1) A proclamation shall not be issued under subsection 38(1) before the expiration of one year from the adoption of the resolution initiating the amendment procedure thereunder, unless the legislative assembly of each province has previously adopted a resolution of assent or dissent.

Idem

(2) A proclamation shall not be issued under subsection 38(1) after the expiration of three years from the adoption of the resolution initiating the amendment procedure thereunder.

Compensation

40. Where an amendment is made under subsection 38(1) that transfers provincial legislative powers relating to education or other cultural matters from provincial legislatures to Parliament, Canada shall provide reasonable compensation to any province to which the amendment does not apply.

Amendment by unanimous consent

41. An amendment to the Constitution of Canada in relation to the following matters may be made by proclamation issued by the Governor General under the Great Seal of Canada only where authorized by resolutions of the Senate and House of Commons and of the legislative assembly of each province:

> (a) the office of the Queen, the Governor General and the Lieutenant Governor of a province;
>
> (b) the right of a province to a number of members in the House of Commons not less than the number of Senators by which the province is entitled to be represented at the time this Part comes into force;
>
> (c) subject to section 43, the use of the English or the French language;
>
> (d) the composition of the Supreme Court of Canada; and
>
> (e) an amendment to this Part.

Amendment
by general
procedure

42. (1) An amendment to the Constitution of Canada in relation to the following matters may be made only in accordance with subsection 38(1):

(a) the principle of proportionate representation of the provinces in the House of Commons prescribed by the Constitution of Canada;

(b) the powers of the Senate and the method of selecting Senators;

(c) the number of members by which a province is entitled to be represented in the Senate and the residence qualifications of Senators;

(d) subject to paragraph 41(d), the Supreme Court of Canada;

(e) the extension of existing provinces into the territories; and

(f) notwithstanding any other law or practice, the establishment of new provinces.

Exception

(2) Subsection 38(2) to (4) do not apply in respect of amendments in relation to matters referred to in subsection (1).

Amendment
of provisions
relating to
some but not
all provinces

43. An amendment to the Constitution of Canada in relation to any provision that applies to one or more, but not all, provinces, including

(a) any alteration to boundaries between provinces, and

(b) any amendment to any provision that relates to the use of the English or the French language within a province,

may be made by proclamation issued by the Governor General under the Great Seal of Canada only where so authorized by resolutions of the Senate and House of Commons and of the legislative assembly of each province to which the amendment applies.

Amendments
by Parliament

44. Subject to sections 41 and 42, Parliament may exclusively make laws amending the Constitution of Canada in relation to the executive government of Canada or the Senate and House of Commons.

Amendments
by Provincial
legislatures

45. Subject to section 41, the legislature of each province may exclusively make laws amending the constitution of the province.

Initiation of
amendment
procedures

46. (1) The procedures for amendment under sections 38, 41, 42, and 43 may be initiated either by the Senate or the House of Commons or by the legislative assembly of a province.

Revocation of authorization

(2) A resolution of assent made for the purposes of this Part may be revoked at any time before the issue of a proclamation authorized by it.

Amendments without Senate resolution

47. (1) An amendment to the Constitution of Canada made by proclamation under section 38, 41, 42, or 43 may be made without a resolution of the Senate authorizing the issue of the proclamation if, within one hundred and eighty days after the adoption by the House of Commons of a resolution authorizing its issue, the Senate has not adopted such a resolution and if, at any time after the expiration of that period, the House of Commons again adopts the resolution.

Computation of period

(2) Any period when Parliament is prorogued or dissolved shall not be counted in computing the one hundred and eighty day period referred to in subsection (1).

Advice to issue proclamation

48. The Queen's Privy Council for Canada shall advise the Governor General to issue a proclamation under this Part forthwith on the adoption of the resolutions required for an amendment made by proclamation under this Part.

Constitutional conference

49. A constitutional conference composed of the Prime Minister of Canada and the first ministers of the provinces shall be convened by the Prime Minister of Canada within fifteen years after this Part comes into force to review the provisions of this Part.

PART VI
AMENDMENT TO THE CONSTITUTION ACT, 1867

50.(100)

51. (101)

PART VII
GENERAL

Primacy of Constitution of Canada

52. (1) The Constitution of Canada is the supreme law of Canada, and any law that is inconsistent with the provisions of the Constitution is, to the extent of the inconsistency, of no force or effect.

---

(100) The amendment is set out in the Consolidation of the *Constitution Act, 1867*, as section 92A thereof.

(101) The amendment is set out in the Consolidation of the *Constitution Act, 1867*, as the Sixth Schedule thereof.

Constitution of Canada

(2) The Constitution of Canada includes

(a) the *Canada Act 1982*, including this Act;

(b) the Acts and orders referred to in the schedule; and

(c) any amendment to any Act or order referred to in paragraph (a) or (b).

Amendments to Constitution of Canada

(3) Amendments to the Constitution of Canada shall be made only in accordance with the authority contained in the Constitution of Canada.

Repeals and new names

53. (1) The enactments referred to in Column I of the schedule are hereby repealed or amended to the extent indicated in Column II thereof and, unless repealed, shall continue as law in Canada under the names set out in Column III thereof.

Consequential amendments

(2) Every enactment, except the *Canada Act 1982*, that refers to an enactment referred to in the schedule by the name in Column I thereof is hereby amended by substituting for that name the corresponding name in Column III thereof, and any British North America Act not referred to in the schedule may be cited as the *Constitution Act* followed by the year and number, if any, of its enactment.

Repeal and consequential amendments

54. Part IV is repealed on the day that is one year after this Part comes into force and this section may be repealed and this Act renumbered, consequentially upon the repeal of Part IV and this section, by proclamation issued by the Governor General under the Great Seal of Canada. (102)

Repeal of Part IV.1 and this section

54.1 Part IV.1 and this section are repealed on April 18, 1987. (103)

French version of Constitution of Canada

55. A French version of the portions of the Constitution of Canada referred to in the schedule shall be prepared by the Minister of Justice of Canada as expeditiously as possible and, when any portion thereof sufficient to warrant action being taken has been so prepared, it shall be put forward for enactment by proclamation issued by the Governor General under the Great Seal of Canada pursuant to the procedure then applicable to an

---

(102) Part VII came into force on April 17, 1982, *See* SI/82–97.

(103) Section 54.1 was added by the *Constitution Amendment Proclamation, 1983. See* SI/84-102.

amendment of the same provisions of the Constitution of Canada.

English and French versions of certain constitutional texts

56. Where any portion of the Constitution of Canada has been or is enacted in English and French or where a French version of any portion of the Constitution is enacted pursuant to section 55, the English and French versions of that portion of the Constitution are equally authoritative.

English and French versions of this Act

57. The English and French versions of this Act are equally authoritative.

Commencement

58. Subject to section 59, this Act shall come into force on a day to be fixed by proclamation issued by the Queen or the Governor General under the Great Seal of Canada. (104)

Commencement of paragraph 23(1)(a) in respect of Quebec

59. (1) Paragraph 23(1)(a) shall come into force in respect of Quebec on a day to be fixed by proclamation issued by the Queen or the Governor General under the Great Seal of Canada.

Authorization of Quebec

(2) A proclamation under subsection (1) shall be issued only where authorized by the legislative assembly or government of Quebec. (105)

Repeal of this section

(3) This section may be repealed on the day paragraph 23(1)(a) comes into force in respect of Quebec and this Act amended and renumbered, consequentially upon the repeal of this section, by proclamation issued by the Queen or the Governor General under the Great Seal of Canada.

Short title and citations

60. This Act may be cited as the *Constitution Act, 1982*, and the Constitution Acts 1867 to 1975 (No. 2) and this Act may be cited together as the *Constitution Acts, 1867 to 1982*.

References

61. A reference to the "*Constitution Acts, 1867 to 1982*" shall be deemed to include a reference to the "*Constitution Amendment Proclamation, 1983*". (106)

---

(104) The Act, with the exception of paragraph 23(1)(a) in respect of Quebec, came into force on April 17, 1982 by proclamation issued by the Queen. *See* SI/82–97.

(105) No proclamation has been issued under section 59.

(106) Section 61 was added by the *Constitution Amendment Proclamation, 1983*. *See* SI/84–102.

Appendix 3

1987 Constitutional Accord*

WHEREAS first ministers, assembled in Ottawa, have arrived at a unanimous accord on constitutional amendments that would bring about the full and active participation of Quebec in Canada's constitutional evolution, would recognize the principle of equality of all the provinces, would provide new arrangements to foster greater harmony and cooperation between the Government of Canada and the governments of the provinces and would require that annual first ministers' conferences on the state of the Canadian economy and such other matters as may be appropriate be convened and that annual constitutional conferences composed of first ministers be convened commencing not later than December 31, 1988;

AND WHEREAS first ministers have also reached unanimous agreement on certain additional commitments in relation to some of those amendments;

NOW THEREFORE the Prime Minister of Canada and the first ministers of the provinces commit themselves and the governments they represent to the following:

1. The Prime Minister of Canada will lay or cause to be laid before the Senate and House of Commons, and the first ministers of the provinces will lay or cause to be laid before their legislative assemblies, as soon as possible, a resolution, in the form appended hereto, to authorize a proclamation to be issued by the Governor General under the Great Seal of Canada to amend the Constitution of Canada.

2. The Government of Canada will, as soon as possible, conclude an agreement with the Government of Quebec that would

(a) incorporate the principles of the Cullen-Couture agreement on the selection abroad and in Canada of independent immigrants, visitors for medical treatment, students and temporary workers, and on the selection of refugees abroad and economic criteria for family reunification and assisted relatives,

(b) guarantee that Quebec will receive a number of immigrants, including refugees, within the annual total established by the federal government for all of Canada proportionate to its share of the population of Canada, with the right to exceed that figure by five per cent for demographic reasons, and

(c) provide an undertaking by Canada to withdraw services (except citizenship services) for the reception and integration (including linguistic and cultural) of all foreign nationals wishing to settle in Quebec where services are to be provided by Quebec, with such withdrawal to be accompanied by reasonable compensation,

*Published with permission of the Minister of Supply and Services Canada.

and the Government of Canada and the Government of Quebec will take the necessary steps to give the agreement the force of law under the proposed amendment relating to such agreements.

3. Nothing in this Accord should be construed as preventing the negotiation of similar agreements with other provinces relating to immigration and the temporary admission of aliens.

4. Until the proposed amendment relating to appointments to the Senate comes into force, any person summoned to fill a vacancy in the Senate shall be chosen from among persons whose names have been submitted by the government of the province to which the vacancy relates and must be acceptable to the Queen's Privy Council for Canada.

Motion For A Resolution To Authorize An Amendment To The Constitution Of Canada

WHEREAS the *Constitution Act, 1982* came into force on April 17, 1982, following an agreement between Canada and all the provinces except Quebec;

AND WHEREAS the Government of Quebec has established a set of five proposals for constitutional change and has stated that amendments to give effect to those proposals would enable Quebec to resume a full role in the constitutional councils of Canada;

AND WHEREAS the amendment proposed in the schedule hereto sets out the basis on which Quebec's five constitutional proposals may be met;

AND WHEREAS the amendment proposed in the schedule hereto also recognizes the principle of the equality of all the provinces, provides new arrangements to foster greater harmony and cooperation between the Government of Canada and the governments of the provinces and requires that conferences be convened to consider important constitutional, economic and other issues;

AND WHEREAS certain portions of the amendment proposed in the schedule hereto relate to matters referred to in section 41 of the *Constitution Act, 1982*;

AND WHEREAS section 41 of the *Constitution Act, 1982* provides that an amendment to the Constitution of Canada may be made by proclamation issued by the Governor General under the Great Seal of Canada where so authorized by resolutions of the Senate and the House of Commons and of the legislative assembly of each province;

NOW THEREFORE the (Senate) (House of Commons) (legislative assembly) resolves that an amendment to the Constitution of Canada be authorized to be made by proclamation issued by Her Excellency the Governor General under the Great Seal of Canada in accordance with the schedule hereto.

Schedule
Constitution Amendment, 1987

Constitution Act, 1867

1. The *Constitution Act, 1867* is amended by adding thereto, immediately after section 1 thereof, the following section:

Interpretation

"**2.** (1) The Constitution of Canada shall be interpreted in a manner consistent with

(a) the recognition that the existence of French-speaking Canadians, centred in Quebec but also present elsewhere in Canada, and English-speaking Canadians, concentrated outside Quebec but also present in Quebec, constitutes a fundamental characteristic of Canada; and

(b) the recognition that Quebec constitutes within Canada a distinct society.

Role of Parliament
and legislatures

(2) The role of the Parliament of Canada and the provincial legislatures to preserve the fundamental characteristic of Canada referred to in paragraph (1)(a) is affirmed.

Role of legislature
and Government of
Quebec

(3) The role of the legislature and Government of Quebec to preserve and promote the distinct identity of Quebec referred to in paragraph (1)(b) is affirmed.

Rights of legislatures
and governments
preserved

(4) Nothing in this section derogates from the powers, rights or privileges of Parliament of the Government of Canada, or of the legislatures or governments of the provinces, including any powers, rights or privileges relating to language."

2. The said Act is further amended by adding thereto, immediately after section 24 thereof, the following section:

Names to be submit-
ted

"**25.** (1) Where a vacancy occurs in the Senate, the government of the province to which the vacancy relates may, in relation to that vacancy, submit to the Queen's Privy Council for Canada the names of persons who may be summoned to the Senate.

Choice of Senators
from names submit-
ted

(2) Until an amendment to the Constitution of Canada is made in relation to the Senate pursuant to section 41 of the *Constitution Act, 1982*, the person summoned to fill a vacancy in the Senate shall be chosen from among persons whose names have been submitted under subsection (1) by the government of the province to which the vacancy relates and must be acceptable to the Queen's Privy Council for Canada."

3. The said Act is further amended by adding thereto, immediately after section 95 thereof, the following heading and sections:

"Agreements on Immigration and Aliens

Commitment to negotiate

95A. The Government of Canada shall, at the request of the government of any province, negotiate with the government of that province for the purpose of concluding an agreement relating to immigration or the temporary admission of aliens into that province that is appropriate to the needs and circumstances of that province.

Agreements

95B. (1) Any agreement concluded between Canada and a province in relation to immigration or the temporary admission of aliens into that province has the force of law from the time it is declared to do so in accordance with subsection 95C(1) and shall from that time have effect notwithstanding class 25 of section 91 or section 95.

Limitation

(2) An agreement that has the force of law under subsection (1) shall have effect only so long and so far as it is not repugnant to any provision of an Act of the Parliament of Canada that sets national standards and objectives relating to immigration or aliens, including any provision that establishes general classes of immigrants or relates to levels of immigration for Canada or that prescribes classes of individuals who are inadmissible into Canada.

Application of Charter

(3) The *Canadian Charter of Rights and Freedoms* applies in respect of any agreement that has the force of law under subsection (1) and in respect of anything done by the Parliament or Government of Canada, or the legislature or government of a province, pursuant to any such agreement.

Proclamation relating to agreements

95C. (1) A declaration that an agreement referred to in subsection 95B(1) has the force of law may be made by proclamation issued by the Governor General under the Great Seal of Canada only where so authorized by resolutions of the Senate and House of Commons and of the legislative assembly of the province that is a party to the agreement.

Amendment of agreements

(2) An amendment to an agreement referred to in subsection 95B(1) may be made by proclamation issued by the Governor General under the Great Seal of Canada only where so authorized

(a) by resolutions of the Senate and House of Commons and of the legislative assembly of the province that is a party to the agreement; or

(b) in such other manner as is set out in the agreement.

Application of sections 46 to 48 of *Constitution Act, 1982*

95D. Sections 46 to 48 of the *Constitution Act, 1982* apply, with such modifications as the circumstances require, in respect of any declaration made pursuant to subsection 95C(1), any amendment to an agreement made pursuant to subsection 95C(2) or any amendment made pursuant to section 95E.

Amendments to sections 95A to 95 D or this section

95E. An amendment to sections 95A to 95D or this section may be made in accordance with the procedure set out in subsection 38(1) of the *Constitution Act, 1982*, but only if the amendment is authorized by resolutions of the legislative assemblies of all the provinces that are, at the time of the amendment, parties to an agreement that has the force of law under subsection 95B(1)."

4. The said Act is further amended by adding thereto, immediately preceding section 96 thereof, the following heading:

"General"

5. The said Act is further amended by adding thereto, immediately preceding section 101 thereof, the following heading:

"Courts Established by the Parliament of Canada"

6. The said Act is further amended by adding thereto, immediately after section 101 thereof, the following heading and sections:

"Supreme Court of Canada

Supreme Court continued

101A. (1) The court existing under the name of the Supreme Court of Canada is hereby continued as the general court of appeal for Canada, and as an additional court for the better administration of the laws of Canada, and shall continue to be a superior court of record.

Constitution of court

(2) The Supreme Court of Canada shall consist of a chief justice to be called the Chief Justice of Canada and eight other judges, who shall be appointed by the Governor General in Council by letters patent under the Great Seal.

Who may be appointed judges

101B. (1) Any person may be appointed a judge of the Supreme Court of Canada who, after having been admitted to the bar of any province or territory, has, for a total of at least ten years, been a judge of any court in Canada or a member of the bar of any province or territory.

Three judges from Quebec

(2) At least three judges of the Supreme Court of Canada shall be appointed from among persons who, after having been admitted to the bar of Quebec, have,

for a total of at least ten years, been judges of any court of Quebec or of any court established by the Parliament of Canada, or members of the bar of Quebec.

Names may be submitted

101C. (1) Where a vacancy occurs in the Supreme Court of Canada, the government of each province may, in relation to that vacancy, submit to the Minister of Justice of Canada the names of any of the persons who have been admitted to the bar of that province and are qualified under section 101B for appointment to that court.

Appointment from names submitted

(2) Where an appointment is made to the Supreme Court of Canada, the Governor General in Council shall, except where the Chief Justice is appointed from among members of the Court, appoint a person whose name has been submitted under subsection (1) and who is acceptable to the Queen's Privy Council for Canada.

Appointment from Quebec

(3) Where an appointment is made in accordance with subsection (2) of any of the three judges necessary to meet the requirement set out in subsection 101B(2), the Governor General in Council shall appoint a person whose name has been submitted by the Government of Quebec.

Appointment from other provinces

(4) Where an appointment is made in accordance with subsection (2) otherwise than as required under subsection (3), the Governor General in Council shall appoint a person whose name has been submitted by the government of a province other than Quebec.

Tenure, salaries, etc., of judges

101D. Sections 99 and 100 apply in respect of the judges of the Supreme Court of Canada.

Relationship to section 101

101E. (1) Sections 101A to 101D shall not be construed as abrogating or derogating from the powers of the Parliament of Canada to make laws under section 101 except to the extent that such laws are inconsistent with those sections.

References to the Supreme Court of Canada

(2) For greater certainty, section 101A shall not be construed as abrogating or derogating from the powers of the Parliament of Canada to make laws relating to the reference of questions of law or fact, or any other matters, to the Supreme Court of Canada."

7. The said Act is further amended by adding thereto, immediately after section 106 thereof, the following section:

Shared-cost program

"**106A.** (1) The Government of Canada shall provide reasonable compensation to the government of a province that chooses not to participate in a national shared-cost program that is established by the Government of Canada after the coming into force of this section in an area of exclusive provincial jurisdiction, if the province carries on a program or initiative that is compatible with the national objectives.

Legislative power not extended

(2) Nothing in this section extends the legislative powers of the Parliament of Canada or of the legislatures of the provinces."

8. The said Act is further amended by adding thereto the following heading and sections:

"XII—CONFERENCES ON THE ECONOMY AND OTHER MATTERS

Conferences on the economy and other matters

148. A conference composed of the Prime Minister of Canada and the first ministers of the provinces shall be convened by the Prime Minister of Canada at least once each year to discuss the state of the Canadian economy and such other matters as may be appropriate.

XIII—REFERENCES

Reference includes amendments

149. A reference to this Act shall be deemed to include a reference to any amendments thereto."

Constitution Act, 1982

9. Sections 40 to 42 of the *Constitution Act, 1982* are repealed and the following substituted therefor:

Compensation

"**40.** Where an amendment is made under subsection 38(1) that transfers legislative powers from provincial legislatures to Parliament, Canada shall provide reasonable compensation to any province to which the amendment does not apply.

Amendment by unanimous consent

41. An amendment to the Constitution of Canada in relation to the following matters may be made by proclamation issued by the Governor General under the Great Seal of Canada only where authorized by resolutions of the Senate and House of Commons and of the legislative assembly of each province:

(a) the office of the Queen, the Governor General and the Lieutenant Governor of a province;

(b) the powers of the Senate and the method of selecting Senators;

(c) the number of members by which a province is entitled to be represented in the Senate and the residence qualifications of Senators;

(d) the right of a province to a number of members in the House of Commons not less than the number of

Senators by which the province was entitled to be represented on April 17, 1982;

(e) the principle of proportionate representation of the provinces in the House of Commons prescribed by the Constitution of Canada;

(f) subject to section 43, the use of the English or the French language;

(g) the Supreme Court of Canada;

(h) the extension of existing provinces into the territories;

(i) notwithstanding any other law or practice, the establishment of new provinces; and

(j) an amendment to this Part."

10. Section 44 of the said Act is repealed and the following substituted therefor:

Amendments by Parliament

"**44.** Subject to section 41, Parliament may exclusively make laws amending the Constitution of Canada in relation to the executive government of Canada or the Senate and House of Commons."

11. Subsection 46(1) of the said Act is repealed and the following substituted therefor:

Initiation of amendment procedures

"**46.** (1) The procedures for amendment under sections 38, 41 and 43 may be initiated either by the Senate or the House of Commons or by the legislative assembly of a province."

12. Subsection 47(1) of the said Act is repealed and the following substituted therefor:

Amendments without Senate resolution

"**47.** (1) An amendment to the Constitution of Canada made by proclamation under section 38, 41 or 43 may be made without a resolution of the Senate authorizing the issue of the proclamation if, within one hundred and eighty days after the adoption by the House of Commons of a resolution authorizing its issue, the Senate has not adopted such a resolution and if, at any time after the expiration of that period, the House of Commons again adopts the resolution."

13. Part VI of the said Act is repealed and the following substituted therefor:

**"PART VI
CONSTITUTIONAL CONFERENCES**

Constitutional conference

50. (1) A constitutional conference composed of the Prime Minister of Canada and the first ministers of the provinces shall be convened by the Prime Minister of Canada at least once each year, commencing in 1988.

Agenda
(2) The conferences convened under subsection (1) shall have included on their agenda the following matters:

(a) Senate reform, including the role and functions of the Senate, its powers, the method of selecting Senators and representation in the Senate;

(b) roles and responsibilities in relation to fisheries; and

(c) such other matters as are agreed upon."

14. Subsection 52(2) of the said Act is amended by striking out the word "and" at the end of paragraph (b) thereof, by adding the word "and" at the end of paragraph (c) thereof and by adding thereto the following paragraph:

"(d) any other amendment to the Constitution of Canada."

15. Section 61 of the said Act is repealed and the following substituted therefor:

References
"**61.** A reference to the *Constitution Act 1982*, or a reference to the *Constitution Acts 1867 to 1982*, shall be deemed to include a reference to any amendments thereto."

General

Multicultural heritage and aboriginal peoples
16. Nothing in section 2 of the *Constitution Act, 1867* affects section 25 or 27 of the Canadian Charter of Rights and Freedoms, section 35 of the *Constitution Act, 1982* or class 24 of section 91 of the *Constitution Act, 1867*.

Citation

Citation
17. This amendment may be cited as the *Constitution Amendment, 1987*.

Index

Abbott, Douglas 62
Aberhart, William 88, 130
Accumulation function 74, 125, 155–56
Acton, Lord 244
Agriculture 56, 60, 62–63, 78–79, 82, 205–06
Air Canada 202
Air transportation 53–54, 179, 202
Alberta 52, 63, 66, 78–79, 80–81, 82, 86–87, 91, 101, 102, 119, 130, 131, 137, 140, 141, 142, 143, 144, 145, 146, 158, 167, 169, 170, 171, 179, 180, 181, 193, 196–200, 201, 202, 206, 211, 212, 214, 215, 217, 218, 225, 226, 229, 232, 248, 254, 269, 270
Alberta Heritage Savings Trust Fund 179, 197–98, 247
Alberta Resources Railway 201
Alliance Québec 120
Argentina 10, 187
Argus Corporation 206
Armstrong, Christopher 212
Atkin, Lord 55, 56
Australia 10, 13, 17, 88, 132, 151–52, 155, 156, 194, 220, 231, 232–33, 237, 248, 258
Austria 9–10, 11, 20–21

Balewa, Abubaker, quoted: 14
Bank of Canada 186
Banting, Keith 144
Beard, Charles 12
Beige Paper (see Quebec Liberal Party, constitutional proposals)
Belgium 43, 273
Bennett, R.B. 54, 55, 239
Bennett, W.A.C. 144, 195
Bennett New Deal 54–57, 160
Bertrand, Jean-Jacques 108–09
Bilingualism 37, 64, 118, 245, 251, 253
Bismarck, Otto von 13, 20
Black, Edwin 180
Blake, Edward 219
Blakeney, Allan 64

Bonaparte, Napoleon 97, 129
Borden, Robert 84
Bourassa, Henri 245
Bourassa, Robert 68, 109–10, 114, 115, 245, 259, 260, 270
Brady, Alexander 238
Breau, Herb 171
Breton, Albert 181, 187
British Columbia 35, 55, 56, 61, 76, 79–81, 82, 87, 119, 128, 129, 130, 131, 132, 133, 137, 141, 143, 144, 145, 158, 161, 162, 165, 167, 171, 191, 192, 194, 195, 196, 197, 200, 204, 206, 211, 214, 215, 216, 217, 218, 227, 229, 231, 238, 247, 248, 270
British Columbia Railway 200–01
Broadbent, Ed 251
Brown, George 24, 26–27, 173, 196
Browne, G.P. 58
Burns, R.M., quoted: 124
Business Council on National Issues 255–56

Cairns, Alan 58, 180, 230
Caisse de dépôt et de placement 106, 179, 206
Calgary 82, 86
Cameroun 10, 13
Canada, Province of 21–23, 39–40
Canada Assistance Plan 161, 164–65, 169
Canada Health Act 171–72
Canadian Charter of Rights and Freedoms 90, 206–07, 250–58, 259–60
Canadian Manufacturers Association 198
Canadian National Railways 200, 201
Canadian Northern Railway 215
Canadian Pacific Railway (CPR) 78, 90, 192, 206, 215
Canadian Transport Commission (CTC) 202
Careless, J.M.S. 26, 73
Cartier, George Etienne 23, 24, 26, 34, 37, 216
Chrétien, Jean 147, 255, 256, 259

Churchill, Winston S. 211
Churchill Forest Industries 189
Cité Libre 109
Clark, Joe 113–14, 170, 181, 198, 219, 249, 250
Classes and class conflict 24–25, 77–81, 88–89, 212
Clement, Wallace 84
Clift, Dominique 115
Columbia River Treaty 195
Come by Chance 189
Compact theory of Confederation 40–41, 100–01, 107, 239, 258
Conditional Grants 151–74, 222, 261–62
Confederation 6–7, 20–41, 74, 127–28, 177
Conservative Party 100, 216–17 (see also Progressive Conservative Party)
Constitutional Act (1791) 95, 236
Co-operative Commonwealth Federation (CCF) 16, 57, 159, 161, 162, 240, 241
Corry, J.A. 152, 153, 160, 165–66
Criminal Law 31, 52–53, 57, 64–65, 232
Cross, James 109
Crown Zellerbach 188
Czechoslovakia 11

Darling, Howard 268
Davis, Rufus 7
Davis, William 89–91, 185, 256
Debt allowances 127
Declaratory power 31
de Gaulle, Charles 108, 211, 243
Delegation of powers 59–60
Democracy, weakness of, in Canada 38–41, 258
Depression (1929–1939) 81–82, 130–31
Dicey, A.V. 14–15, 43–44
Dickson, Brian 65
Diefenbaker, John 84, 161–62, 164, 183, 194–95, 196, 240, 254
Dikshit, R.D. 13–14, 23
Disallowance 7, 35, 76, 88, 214–15
Dorion, A.A. 6
Douglas, Tommy 135, 183, 218, 240
Drew, George 132–33, 134, 211

Duplessis, Maurice 53, 60–61, 89, 100, 103–05, 133–34, 154, 157, 163, 164, 211, 212, 217, 225, 241, 243
Durham, John Lambton, Earl of 21, 74, 95–97, 108, 156, 252
quoted: 95

Edmonton 86, 196, 201
Edmonton Chamber of Commerce 88
Elazar, Daniel 7
Electricity 83, 181, 193–96
Elgin, Lord 97
Elizabeth II, Queen 250, 257
Equalization payments 134, 140–45, 250, 253
Established Programs Financing 168–73
European Community 4, 13, 112, 273

Family Allowances 159, 169
Federalists (U.S. political party) 6, 21
Federal-provincial conferences 132–40, 162, 164, 185–87, 223–29, 239–41, 245, 247–56, 260–61, 263, 264
Ferns, H.S.
quoted: 210
Financial Post 87
Fisheries 27, 53, 263
France 43, 269, 273
Friedrich, Carl J. 7
Frost, Leslie 135
Fulton-Favreau formula 240–41, 245, 248

Galbraith, John Kenneth 184
Galt, A.T. 26, 32
Gazette (Montreal) 100
Gendron Commission 118–19
General Motors 191
Germany 4, 9–10, 11, 13, 20–21, 66, 231, 232
Ghiz, Joseph 271
Globe and Mail 104, 252
Godbout, Adélard 105
Guindon, Hubert 105

Haldane, Lord 51–53, 60, 159
Halifax 24
Hall, Emmett 162, 170
Hamilton, Alexander 5–6, 28–29

Hatfield, Richard 264, 271
Health Insurance 161–62, 164–67,
   168–73
Hepburn, Mitchell 53, 131, 212, 213
Highway transportation 129, 154,
   202–03
Hitler, Adolf 10
Hogg, Peter 66
Holmes, Oliver Wendell 45
   quoted: 43
Horizontal balance 126–27
Horowitz, Gad
   quoted: 89
Hudson's Bay Company 23, 35
Hydro-Québec 106, 204

Imperial Oil 196
India 10–11, 231
Industrial Estates Limited 188
Inflation 182–87
Innis, Harold A. 199
   quoted: 27, 72, 177, 191
Intercolonial Railway 26, 27, 31
Interprovincial Conference (1887) 101,
   103, 231
Iran 198

Jackson, Andrew 96
Japan 20–21, 268
Jay, John 5
Jefferson, Thomas 233
Jehovah's Witnesses 17, 99
Johnson, A.W. 173
Johnson, Daniel 95, 115, 226, 243, 245
Johnson, Pierre-Marc 115
Judicial Committee of the Privy
   Council 17, 45–58, 66, 72, 153,
   160, 178, 202, 205, 214, 221, 237,
   268–69

Key, V.O.
   quoted: 100
Keynes, John Maynard 182–84, 187
King, William Lyon Mackenzie 54,
   129, 157, 159–60, 192, 193, 211,
   224, 238, 239
Korea 268

Lafontaine, L.H. 96
Lalonde, Marc 195
Language legislation 111, 119–20

Laporte, Pierre 109, 114
Laskin, Bora 61–62, 65, 66, 255
Latin America, federalism in 10
Latouche, Daniel 105
Laurendeau, Andre 244
Laurier, Wilfrid 84, 192, 214, 224, 238,
   252
l'Ecuyer, Gilbert
   quoted: 66
Le Devoir 114
Legitimization function 125, 156–58
Lemelin, Roger
   quoted: 1
Lesage, Jean 105–08, 118, 135, 164,
   211, 225, 226, 241, 242, 245
Lévesque, René 63, 91, 105, 108,
   110–15, 119, 183, 196, 212, 243, 252
Lewis, David 251
Liberal Party 102–03, 109, 161, 166,
   168, 170, 217, 218–19, 230–31, 246,
   248, 270
   in Quebec: 105–08, 109, 134, 243
Lieutenant-governor 30, 36, 50,
   214–15
Lijphart, Arend 117
Liquor, regulation of 48–50, 129,
   204–05, 228
Livingston, W.S. 7
Lloyd George, David 211
London (Ontario) 212
Loranger, T.J.J. 100–01
   quoted: 100
Lougheed, Peter 87, 89, 186, 211, 212
Luther, Martin 99
Lyon, Sterling 252

Macdonald, Donald S. 90, 207
Macdonald, John, A. 6, 10, 17, 23, 24,
   28, 29–30, 31, 33–36, 46, 47, 50,
   72, 76, 84, 174, 180, 181, 192, 193,
   210, 214, 215, 219, 230, 236–37,
   239, 261
   quoted: 34
Macdonald Royal Commission 90,
   173, 207, 267, 270
MacEachen, Allan 143, 171
Mackenzie, Alexander 46, 47, 76, 84,
   230
Macmillan Bloedel 206
Macpherson Royal Commission 203
Madison, James 5

Malaysia 10
Mallory, J.R.
    quoted: 177
Manitoba 35, 64, 78–79, 80–81, 86,
    102, 130, 135, 136, 145, 154, 165,
    191, 194, 195, 196, 197, 200, 201,
    205, 215, 216, 217, 237, 246, 248,
    254, 270
Manitoba Development Corporation
    188
Manufacturing 77–78, 82–83, 84, 85
Marchand, Jean 190
Marketing boards 56, 60, 62–63,
    205–06
Marshall, John 21
Marx, Herbert 117
Marx, Karl 25
McCully, Jonathan 32
McGee, Thomas D'Arcy 24
McGill University 109
McNaughton, A.G.L. 195
McWhinney, Edward
    quoted: 252
Meech Lake Accord 67–68, 232, 257,
    258–65
Merchant capital 24–25
Mercier, Honoré 80, 101–02, 103, 211,
    212, 239
Michelin Tire 188
Mill, John Stuart 38
Montesquieu, Baron de 15–16
Montreal 25–26, 76–77, 78, 81, 82, 85,
    97, 106, 110, 118, 120, 129, 130, 217
Morin, Claude 226
Mouvement souveraineté-association
    108, 109
Mowat, Oliver 76, 80, 101, 174, 210,
    211, 239
Mulroney, Brian 92, 115, 172, 173, 199,
    232, 259, 267, 269, 270, 272
Murray, Lowell 260

National Energy Program 87, 90,
    198–99, 231
National Policy 75–77, 107, 180–81
Nationalism, in Quebec 91, 100–04,
    107–15, 212, 225–26, 242–45, 247,
    252
Native peoples 253, 256
Naylor, R.T. 25
Nelles, H.V. 192, 194, 196
Neumann, Franz 17

New Brunswick 1, 23, 24, 27, 32, 33,
    37, 50, 55, 56, 64, 98, 104, 127,
    128, 154, 160, 170, 192, 194, 200,
    201, 202, 230, 253, 255, 271
New Democratic Party (NDP) 88, 109,
    111, 219, 244, 255, 270
New England Confederation 4–5
Newfoundland 24, 28, 82, 85, 89, 133,
    140, 146, 188, 189, 192, 193, 194,
    195, 200, 207, 221, 226–27, 247,
    254, 258
New Zealand 17, 156
Nigeria 11, 242
Nixon, Richard 169
Nordair 202
Norontair 202
Norquay, John 216–17
Nova Scotia 1, 23, 24, 27, 28, 32, 33,
    36, 59, 98, 104, 128, 160, 179, 188,
    192, 193, 194, 200, 206, 215, 247,
    248

Oates, Wallace 8
O'Connor, James 74
O'Connor, W.F. 57–58
Olson, H.A.
    quoted: 235
Ontario 30, 48, 49, 55, 56, 76–78,
    79–80, 85–86, 87, 89–92, 105, 112,
    119, 127, 128, 129, 130, 131, 132,
    133, 134, 135, 136, 140, 141, 142,
    143, 144, 145, 147, 154, 157, 161,
    162, 165, 167, 168, 170, 172, 173,
    179, 180, 181, 189, 191, 192, 194,
    197, 200, 202, 203, 204, 205, 206,
    211, 212, 215, 217, 218, 227, 232,
    239–41, 245, 246, 248, 249, 250,
    251, 255, 257, 268, 269, 270, 271,
    272
Ontario Hydro 194
Ontario Northland Railway 200
Orban, Edmond 179
Organization of Petroleum Exporting
    Countries (OPEC) 137
Ostry, Bernard
    quoted: 210

Pacific Western Airlines 202
Pakistan 10, 13, 14, 242
Palmerston Lord
    quoted: 75
Parizeau Jacques 183–84

Parti Québecois 4, 88, 91, 108–15, 119, 218, 243, 244, 247, 258, 259, 270

Pearson, Lester 84, 108, 135, 162, 165, 178, 183, 195, 218, 225, 226, 262

Pensions 159–61

Pentland, H.C. 25

Pepin, Jean-Luc 184

Peterson, David 270

Petro-Canada 90, 198, 199, 252

Petroleum 86–87, 90–91, 137–38, 142–43, 181

Pickersgill, J.W. 218

Porter, John 2

Post-secondary education 138, 155, 167–74

Pratt, Larry 87

Prince Edward Island 79, 128, 145, 160, 167, 170, 190, 192, 200, 201, 206, 216, 232, 253, 271

Progressive Conservative Party 109, 113, 169, 172, 219, 230, 244, 252, 270

Progressive Party 192, 217

Property and Civil Rights 29, 48–65

Purchasing, by governments 204

Quebec (province) 14, 28, 29, 30, 37, 55, 59, 63, 64, 66, 68, 79–80, 85, 88–89, 94–120, 127, 128, 129, 131, 133, 134, 135, 136, 144, 145, 147, 148, 154, 157, 158, 160, 163–65, 167, 168, 169, 170, 172, 179, 180, 183, 185, 189, 191, 192, 194, 195, 196, 197, 200, 202, 204, 205, 206, 211, 212, 218, 225–26, 230, 231, 232, 235, 239–41, 242–44, 245, 246, 248, 249, 254, 256, 258–65, 268, 269, 271, 273

Quebec Act (1774) 29, 95

Quebecair 202

Quebec City 97, 130

Quebec Conference (1864) 32, 38–39

Quebec Liberal Party, constitutional proposals 206, 231–32, 243

Quebec Resolutions 31, 33, 34, 39–40

Quiet Revolution 105–09, 110, 117, 118, 225, 242, 269

Railways 31, 179, 200–01

Ralliement National (RN) 108

Rassemblement pour l'indépendance nationale (RIN) 108, 114, 118

Reagan, Michael 7

Reagan, Ronald 199

Reference cases 47–48, 220

Regional disparities 77
 (see also equalization payments)

Remillard, Gil 58, 226, 259–60

Reservation of bills, 35, 214–15

Resources, natural 32–33, 79–80, 83, 192–200
 (see also petroleum)

Rhodesia and Nyasaland 10

Richards, John 87

Riel, Louis 35, 101

Riker, W.H. 7, 13, 17, 23, 216
 quoted: 72

Robarts, John 165, 212, 245

Robichaud, Louis 104

Robin, Martin 211–12

Roblin, Duff 136

Rogers, Norman
 quoted: 73

Roman Catholic Church 31–32, 95, 97, 104, 105, 107, 117, 118, 163

Roosevelt, Franklin D. 16, 55, 160

Rowell, N.W. 131

Rowell–Sirois Commission 130–31, 146, 153, 160, 178, 224, 242

Royal Proclamation (1763) 95

Ryan, Claude 114

Ryerson, Stanley
 quoted: 38

St. Laurent, Louis 55, 134, 140, 157, 172, 183, 216, 218, 222, 240, 241
 quoted: 94

St. Lawrence Seaway 104, 195

St. Leonard 118

Sankey, Lord
 quoted: 54

Saskatchewan 16, 30, 78–79, 80–81, 86, 91, 102, 130, 131, 135, 137, 142, 143, 146, 158, 161, 162, 165, 169, 172, 173, 180, 183, 194, 195, 196, 201, 206, 215, 218, 227, 240, 241, 246, 251, 253, 255, 258, 270

Sawer, Geoffrey 7

Schlesinger, Rudolf 11

Science Council of Canada 191

Scott, F.R. 57, 61, 237
 quoted: 235

Scott, Ian 269

Senate 230, 231–33, 262, 263, 264–65

Sharp, Mitchell 136, 162, 165
Simeon, Richard 227–28
Smallwood, J.R. 85, 188, 195
Smiley, Donald V. 152, 153, 216, 223, 229
  quoted: 151, 268
Smith, Adam 177
Smith, Goldwin 267, 274
  quoted: 99, 187, 267
Social Credit Party 162, 197, 214, 215
Société générale de financement 106
Société St. Jean Baptiste 112, 243
Sovereignty-association 4, 111–14
Spending power 151–74, 222, 259, 261–62
Spillovers 154–55
Stalin, Josef 211
Stanfield, Robert 104
Statute of Westminster 240
Statutory subsidies 33
Sun Life 119–20
Supreme Court of Canada 46, 47, 51, 58–69, 72–73, 120, 202, 205, 215, 220–21, 246, 254–55, 260, 262, 263
Switzerland 7, 9, 13, 44, 231, 248

Taiwan 268
Tariffs 33, 112, 204
Taschereau, L.A. 163
Taschereau, Robert 61
Task Force on Canadian Unity 206, 231, 248
  quoted: 227
Task Force on Federal-Provincial Fiscal Arrangements 171
Taxation 31, 33, 124–48
Thankerton, Lord 55
Thatcher, Ross 218
Tilley, Leonard 31, 39
Toronto 26, 76–77, 82, 106, 118, 120, 129, 217
Trade and Commerce 48–65
Tremblay Commission 103–04, 129, 163–64, 183
Trudeau, Pierre Elliott 3, 16, 58, 61, 89–91, 99, 109, 113, 144, 157, 162, 165, 172, 181, 183, 185, 186, 215, 219, 226, 231, 242, 244–45, 246,

247, 249–50, 252, 255–57, 259, 261, 262, 264, 269, 272
  quoted: 94
Tupper, Charles 27, 29, 32, 39
Turner, John 168

Underhill, Frank
  quoted: 20
Unemployment insurance 56, 238, 262
Union Act (1840) 95, 96, 236
Union Nationale 103–04, 108–09, 112, 217–18
Union of Soviet Socialist Republics 10
United Kingdom 7, 9, 156, 182, 273
  influence on Canada's constitution 29–30, 31, 236–57
United States of America
  federalism in 4–6, 12, 20–21, 23–24, 30, 43–44, 132, 155, 194, 220, 221, 228, 231, 233, 237, 258
  influence on Canada 35, 82–87, 98, 179, 267–74

Van Buren, Martin 96
Vancouver 82, 86, 201
Veilleux, Gerard 222–23, 225
Vertical balance 126–27
Victoria Charter 68, 225, 245, 247, 251

Watson, Lord 49–51, 52, 237, 269
  quoted: 50
Watts, Ronald 229
Weber, Max 153
West Indies Federation 10
Wheare, K.C. 7, 12, 13, 23, 30, 216
Whitaker, Reginald 216, 218
Whitlam, Gough 16
Wilhelm II, Kaiser 252
Wilson, Harold 14
Wilson, Michael 147, 173
Winnipeg 78, 81, 82, 86, 230
Wolfe, David 139
Woodsworth, J.S. 159, 160

Yugoslavia 11
Yukon 263